EVERY DAY SPIRIT

EVERY DAY SPIRIT

A Daybook of
Wisdom, Joy and Peace

MARY DAVIS

Rich River Publishing Company
Florida
2017

RICH RIVER PUBLISHING COMPANY

I Believe in Me: A Book of Affirmations.
Unity Village, MO: Unity Books, © 2014.
Used with permission of Unity Books, www.unity.org.

Quotes from Paramahansa Yogananda
used with permission of Self-Realization Fellowship,
Los Angeles, CA., www.yogananda-srf.org.

Diligent effort was made to determine if previously
published material included in this book required permission
to reprint. Please accept apologies for any errors. Corrections
will be made in subsequent editions.

No parts of this book are intended as medical advice or
prescribed treatment for physical, emotional or medical problems
and the author assumes no liability for your actions.

Printed in the United States of America
on 100% postconsumer-waste recycled paper
Book Design by Mary Davis
Every Day Spirit: www.everydayspirit.net

Paperback ISBN: 978-0-9995046-0-4
eBook ISBN: 978-0-9995046-1-1

For Maya and Mom—

the wind in the sails of my soul.

Introduction: Hunters Road

Between my married years and now, I spent a year-and-a-half in a rented cabin on Hunters Road in Rappahannock County, Virginia. I didn't plan it that way. As life would have it, all of my other options dropped away and this very cabin rose to the fore when I needed to move from the house of my marriage. The place was teaming with wildlife, and although I was more alone than I have ever been in my life, I was enveloped by a newfound sense of belonging—to nature, to the earth, to myself, to spirit. Grace seemed to rise up freely from the rocks, the fields and the evergreens, and point the way to just the wisdom I longed to imbibe. The melding of raw loneliness and spiritual exhilaration made for an inner adventure of a lifetime.

Hunters Road is seated near the rise of the Shenandoah National Forest at the foot of the Blue Ridge Mountains. Not only is it exquisitely beautiful, it is radically isolated. For me, anyway. I love silence and I thrive on creating in quiet, but this was a whole new level of stillness. No cell service, no TV, no news unless I drove into town. I had a dish and just enough gigabytes per month to post to my Every Day Spirit pages and do my monthly updates for the wallpaper app. No clicking on videos or opening pages with spinning ads. No surfing my Facebook feed. Definitely no streaming.

Most days, the only sounds I heard came from nature, the thoughts in my head and the beating of my heart. I meditated and did yoga daily. I walked. I worked on Every Day Spirit. And I wrote.

Each morning, I sat at a wall of windows in the cabin's main room, watching every little movement of nature and listening to my heart. I listened to what the pain and joy were telling me. I listened for spirit and the inner voice of guidance. I made friends with horses, cows, a skunk, a snake, wasps, frogs, bugs and birds. And every day I wrote a story.

I wrote with a connection to you. There was an underlying sense that if I could see my way through the fog of loss and change, disappointment and fragility, all of us could.

I wanted to be able to tell you and my daughter Maya what I had learned. I wanted to report back from the void that gratitude was actually possible in the midst of confusion. I wanted to prove that all was well even when all seemed decidedly not well. I wanted to make an archeological dig into my darkest places and discover what was saving my life. I wanted to be like Thoreau on Walden Pond, on an adventure into the wilderness of raw spirit. I wanted to find beauty in small things when I couldn't find it in big things. And find it, I did.

What you hold now is my survival manual. This is a collection of stories and devotions, musings and lessons, practices and prayers that brought me from brokenness to wellness. This is the ride from barely breathing to confidence. This is the year between surviving and thriving.

I did not worry about what the writings would become. I just knew I needed to write every single day by the wall of windows, gazing out on hallowed ground. I knew this was why I was on Hunters Road.

I'm private by nature. It's outside of my comfort zone to share my personal story, but I do this because after all, you were there with me. We made this journey together—I talked to you the whole time.

And I learned that perhaps Hunters Road is not a place, but a state of the heart. Maybe Hunters Road is where gratitude heals things and where joy grows out of self-love and simple things. Perhaps it's where the peace of our spiritual nature is part of our every thought and action, and where hope rises like the sun.

Daybooks

I have always held a soft spot for the daybook format. Daybooks have been part of my morning spiritual practice for decades. Sarah Ban Breathnach's *Simple Abundance,* Joan Borysenko's *Pocketful of Miracles,* Paramahansa Yogananda's *Spiritual Diary,* Rolf Gates and Katrina Kenison's *Meditations from the Mat,* Sarah Young's *Jesus Calling,* Marianne Williamson's *A Year of Miracles*—they make a tower near my spiritual practice seat. I never tire of bite-sized wisdom in tandem with the longer, deeper books for devoted spiritual seekers. Daybooks speak to my soul and make a prayer of the precious hours of the day that follow.

Chasing this book has been my pastime for years. I began writing it a decade ago, when I set out to find a daybook of spiritual wisdom for my teenaged daughter but couldn't find what I was looking for. Using a few crafty skills, I printed out ten pages, punched holes in one side and bound it with ribbon. I presented the prototype on her pillow for review. It bombed. "I would *never* read that much every day, Mom." Hmm.

Not to be deterred, I boiled the gems down to a mere paragraph each, printed, punched and ribboned once more, adding a few beads in the binding as a bribe to my audience of one. And again, "Still *waaaayyy* too long, Mom."

One morning, as I contemplated my next move, I watched her over breakfast, eyes riveted on her phone, glued with laser focus on the little box in her hand. "*That,*" I thought with a smile, "is where I need to be."

So I distilled the wisdom down even further until there were but a few words left in the pan. With these I created mobile phone wallpapers, and from those, I created the Every Day Spirit Lock Screens app. The side trip took many years and great love, and brought me purpose and positive focus when my marriage was beginning to falter. Each day after Maya left for school and before I taught piano lessons, I focused on creating one thing. Just one beautiful thing.

Today, the road has arrived full circle, back to the daybook I started those many years ago. We flow, like the hours of the day, like the seasons of the year, toward what we are meant to do. One step at a time, making an offering as we go. We ask for direction, listen for signs, follow the trail, act on guidance, and sometimes we arrive, just for a moment, to receive what we were seeking and to give thanks.

And so I kneel in gratitude.

Gratitude

Thank you, dearest Mom, Tiny Guru, wisdom seeker, strong woman, pioneer, teacher, loving spirit. Your unwavering belief in my life as a writer of songs, poetry, prayers and prose grew me wings. Your unconditional love built a safe haven for failure. Your thoughtful edits on this book illuminated the manuscript, opened my heart and gave me courage. Your constant willingness to love, to help, to protect, to advise and to uphold is my greatest earthly gift.

Thank you, Maya, daughter, gentle soul, courageous woman, spiritual seeker, kind friend, gifted goddess. Your presence has brought out a love in me I never knew possible. Your belief in my mission and your daily— sometimes hourly—counsel with the app made me brave and brought me joy. You are my life's most beautiful teacher. You are my beloved, my soulmate, my heavenly blessing.

Thank you to my editor, Nancy Griffin-Bonnaire of Mark My Words, Inc. for applying the brilliance of your virtual pen with tenderness, talent and wisdom. Your enthusiasm and keen eye for detail melded to bring a special grace to these pages. Gratitude from the heart.

Thank you, friends and family who supported me along the way, cheered my successes, cried with me in my doubt and fear, encouraged, gifted me with grace and perspective, brought me day by day through the darkness to the light. I love you all beyond measure.

Thank you to my yoga teacher, Susan Van Nuys, for seeing me fully and imparting an understanding of the vastness and beauty of yoga that nourishes me daily in mind, body and soul. It is the gift of a lifetime.

Thank you, community of souls who have gathered here to walk the path of this year. You are in the heart and soul of every word. Your presence is living proof of the unshakable power of love. I walk with you in every step. There's no place I'd rather be.

Thank you, God, for the pain and the light. Thank you for the challenges and the blessings. I offer them all to you.

About God

There are many words in this book that point to the concept of God. Along with the word *God*, you will find *spirit, the divine, divine love, love, the Creator, source, divine source, higher power* and *the universe*. I'm sure you can add to this list, or perhaps for you there is no special name at all, but simply a feeling, a knowing.

I use these beautiful words with consciousness, and without assumption about your beliefs. We will soon embark on a journey through days of love, light, goodness, peace, gratitude, kindness, calm, joy, faith and positivity—and all are welcome. Woven within, I leave space for you to fill in the blank with what you believe. May you take pieces of these ideas to your primary belief system and let them germinate there, rise in a new way and grow you toward an even deeper love.

My mission for Every Day Spirit, with each phrase, image, poem, prayer and essay, has always been guided by these three tenets: to compassionately awaken the soul, to offer unconditional love and positivity, and to be honest to my experience. Everything I do passes through these gates.

There is nothing new here in the following pages—nothing that does not already exist inside of you. But each day's thought will offer some bit of hope, some guidance for your next step, some way to make the world a more compassionate place, some love that thaws the heart for new life or some wisdom that awakens your soul.

Whether we voice it plainly or not, we are all on a spiritual journey. We are all connected to God and to each other. When we align with that, when we lead our lives from this understanding, we live with love and compassion for ourselves and for all beings. Peace within, peace without. When we lead our lives from our highest selves, we bless all others with our light. We change the world with our love. That is the prayer.

This book is for you, my friend.

Blessings,

Bless this day
with love and light.
Bless this day
with faith and sight.
Bless this day
with grace and ease.
Bless this day
with joy and peace.

January Blessings

Be present. Be here. Today, we can guide our thoughts back to the present moment with gentle focus and live fully right where we are.

Let the day flow with grace. Grace flows through us easily when we are in tune with the subtle voice of intuition. Open and listen for guidance.

Expect joy. Be positive. Imagine a fulfilling day unfolding, in which we accomplish much and experience joy in the process. Welcome the light.

Serve with compassion. Acts of service when performed with love lend immeasurable light to our day. Be watchful for ways to serve.

Speak only kindness. Speak only kind words. Think only kind thoughts. Be kind to yourself and to those who cross your path or your mind.

Impart only love. Send out all thoughts and words on the wings of love so that we may love one another, love ourselves, love the unlovable.

Never forget you're not alone. Let's remind ourselves often today that we are always supported, guided and unconditionally loved as we are.

Give thanks for everything. Gratitude will shift the perspective of the day from one of lack to one of abundance. Give constant thanks.

See goodness in others. Each of us has a soul that is made of beauty and love. Assume the best in others so they may rise to their highest light.

The Spiritual Sun

Extraordinary love springs from ordinary blessings.

Finding yourself on this path as a brand new year begins is no small coincidence. We are destined to take this journey of the heart; an adventure of the soul with lessons drawn from simple things—from birds and horses, trees and plants, joys and sorrows, angels and stardust. Nothing big really happens on Hunters Road, yet everything happens here. Extraordinary love springs from ordinary blessings.

Just as these words were given in the complete solitude of a cabin near the foot of a mountain, you were meant to read them in the complete solitude of your heart at the feet of your own wisdom. It is there that you connect with the guidance, insight and love that has always been within you, and that will fuel your life with a hum of joy for having found sacred things in everyday places.

This journey is one of finding the holy in the small; the unseen behind the seen. It's about recognizing the divine flow that seeks to sweep us into her current and assist us in all things. It's about a personal experience with God, with divinity, with our higher power, with our inner voice.

It's all one thing and it's right here; the flow we seek is here. It's everywhere. It's accessible, helpful and made from love. The universe was designed perfectly, aligned in harmony and created in such beautiful order that our business is only to be completely ourselves on a path to understanding our spiritual nature and creative magnificence.

Today marks the dawn of something totally different. As the sun rises in your heart, it illuminates all of the sleeping wisdom within. You have everything you will ever need to awaken the soul and remember who you really are. Face the light and let the spiritual sun reveal the ordinary blessings in this extraordinary day. They are right here in the room.

In The World:

* Journey through today with an eye for beauty. Notice the ordinary miracles that surround you; the tree, the sky, a deep breath, a kind smile. Allow joy to surface. Be in awe.

In The Heart:

* I open my soul to a new beginning, a journey of love, wisdom and contentment. I have everything I need inside of me now.

Resolve to Release

Live simply. Laugh freely. Give easily. Receive graciously. Think calmly. Grow radically. Pray continuously. Love deeply.

A new year knocks at the door of our hearts and we prepare to receive her. In anticipation of welcoming a beloved house guest, we might make up an extra bed, tidy the tables and assemble a meal. We might pack away decorations, put away presents and clear our schedules. We make room in our home and open our arms. This loving hospitality can be offered to the precious year in wait on the doorstep.

Making space is key to welcoming in the new. Instead of adding to our already overflowing plate of activity this year, perhaps we need to sweep some things away, creating a comfortable and inviting room for a little divine company. Let's make space by letting go of yesterday's artifacts. Let's make a resolution to release what no longer serves us.

It is no wonder that only a fraction of those who set resolutions at the start of the year see them through. It's another duty in our already dutiful lives and is the first to be thrown overboard when we become overwhelmed.

For now, let's simply open the windows. Welcome in the light that might illuminate inspiration, intuition, self-care, joy, gratitude, creativity and the gift of some delightful, unscheduled time for play and adventure.

Then let's answer the door and welcome in the new year with a new language that comes from a deeper place, the voice of the soul. Then we'll be ready for the joy of new blessings and new beginnings.

In The World:

✳ Release old commitments that you have continued out of habit. Release material things in your home by gifting them to those who truly need them. Release addictive or negative behaviors that no longer serve the person you are becoming. Release doubt, fear and negativity. Release any unkindness toward yourself. And make room for beautiful small things.

In The Heart:

✳ I welcome in the light of the coming year, and make room in my heart and home for the transformation of my mind, body and soul.

Light up the Landscape

Joy is finding the holy in the small and the sacred in the everyday.

There's a brilliant yellow goldfinch outside my writing window, hopping from limb to limb on the old oak tree. They are my favorite of birds, so the sight of her is beating my heart with crazy joy. She's just a tiny flash of brightness but she has the power to create a big stir. She has me thinking that when it comes to spirituality, a little goldfinch and matters of spirit have a bit in common.

For one thing, a goldfinch likes wide open spaces, like the field, where she can maneuver her roller coaster flight of ups and downs with ease. Our spirits, too, love wide open space, even when stolen from the ups and downs of a busy day to check in with our inner wisdom. These silent connections can leave us feeling that we, too, can fly. Even a quiet act of tea can be cause for flight.

Our tiny friend is also uniquely radiant. She stands out like a summer flower and can light up a barren winter landscape. Our spirits are like that when we remember that we are an irreplaceable part of an unlimited whole, with divine guidance always present for the asking. Like the goldfinch, our radiance lights up the landscape. Really, it does.

Best of all, the goldfinch came for a visit today to be a living example of the countless small gifts of beauty that surround us in this very moment. Maybe in noticing her presence—like noticing a smile, or a flower, or a kind word—we are reminded that joy is finding the holy in the small, and the sacred in the everyday.

Joy is here, in this moment, right where we are.

In The World:

✳ Be present to small beauties today. Notice, with amazement and gratitude, the countless blessings that surround you. Find them in the miracle of a breath, as well as in a not-so-miraculous mess. See how an average day can become a brighter one when you notice the gift in all things.

In The Heart:

✳ I embrace this day with new eyes and see the beauty that surrounds me now. In simple things, I find great joy.

Love is the Road

Peace is the answer. Joy is the goal. Thanks is the prayer. Love is the road.

About half of Hunters Road is unpaved, rattling the bones of my CRV—the one that the local mechanic told me is the only vehicle in town without 4-wheel drive. I arrived here limping in spirit, with no experience in isolation, bearing only a few carloads of stuff plus determination, 2-wheel drive and all. The rocky trip down Hunters Road is symbolic of my journey of transformation.

Before I moved here, I had been separated and living in the house of my marriage for a few years, my daughter in college. My heart was broken, my future an abyss, and it seemed that everything I thought I knew for sure had completely unraveled. I poured myself into creative projects out of an intense drive to focus on something good—something tangible that I could find hope in. In those 80-hour weeks I picked up fragments, once again, of who I might become.

The real transition dawned with the first morning sunrise on Hunters Road. I knew I had to write down the lessons. Not for the sake of being read, but as an archeological dig into what had happened. I wanted to know what I believed in, what brought me joy, who I was beneath the exterior of my circumstances. What spiritual practices saved my life? The answers that were uncovered, dusted off and brought to light, were answers meant for all of us. They became the journey of this year.

The road to ourselves is part paved and part unchartered. It's raw and rocky and full of surprises especially after it rains. It's also covered in natural beauty that awaits the joy of discovery. On this road, there are no wrong turns. The purpose of the adventure is not to accomplish or to please others, but to get to the very heart of ourselves—which has always been love. And always will be love. Love is the road.

In The World:

* At any crossroads, you have the power to decide what qualities you want to emerge with from this chapter of life. You can always choose to evolve to a higher and more conscious version of yourself when you let love lead in everything you do.

In The Heart:

* I am never stuck in one place in the journey of my life. Even through challenges, I am becoming a more loving version of myself.

Perfect Abundance

Gratitude makes sweet miracles of small moments.

Slow down a little. Notice more. Breathe it all in. Give thanks. We are rich with gifts, right where we are, when we begin this day with a grateful heart.

Today, let's register the sight of natural beauty and linger over small moments of tea and friendship. Let's pause to soak up the sounds of laughter or a lilting bird song. Let's be amazed that our spirits are embodied here in the world to feel a soft blanket, a soapy dish, a loving hand.

Let's breathe in the joy of the perfect abundance that surrounds us now.

Sunrise, sunset and the spin of the earth in between are nothing short of miracles. Let's be stunned. Let's be awed. Let's be jaw-dropped by the amazingness of life and pierce the jaded boredom of automatic pilot with a sword of gratitude. Let's greet this day mindfully, noticing the small moments of which miracles are made.

Let's offer up our gratitude on the wings of the only prayer we ever need:

Thank you.

In The World:

∗ See the world today through sacred eyes. Notice the abundance of gifts.

∗ Feel the world today with a loving heart. Allow a layer of defense to fall away and for your heart to open just a little bit more. Breathe into it. Feel the gifts.

∗ Be thankful today with a grateful spirit. Give thanks, aloud or in the silence of the heart, for the gifts.

In The Heart:

∗ I am filled with joy and gratitude. I see the beauty in the small moments of today. I open my heart with words of thanksgiving. I am rich with gifts and miracles.

The Only Offering

Be yourself with all your heart.

It takes a little bit of practice to open our hearts and allow the truth to surface, especially if we've gotten good at stowing things away. It seems that to "be yourself" should come pretty naturally, but not when we've been hiding the light of our soul away from the light of day.

When my Hidden Truths and I got to the quiet of Hunters Road, I gave myself permission to be me. Since there was not a soul around, it made the most sense. I allowed myself permission to speak my truth, to write from a place of presence and honesty, to listen and follow my inner wisdom, to not second guess my personal relationship with the divine.

Strangely, most of us need to grant this permission to ourselves, perhaps because this right was stealthily revoked somewhere down the line. Someone implied that our unique version of ourselves was not enough. But we know better.

With permission comes an invitation to allow our personal discoveries to come to the surface to be celebrated. When we accept the birthright of our worth, the doors to a mysterious and eternal grace swing wide. We have invited our truth to the forefront and a force greater than our own hears our call, feels our alignment and swoops in with a flow of support and insight.

Not only are we enough, but we begin to understand that we are playing a sacred role that was created just for us.

And our hearts are the only offering we ever need to make. Today, just bring your authentic gifts to the table. It's all that's required.

In The World:

* You are spirit in human form, filling a role that only you can fill. Today, make a humble offering of who you are—right here, right now—and it will far surpass good enough. Give yourself permission to love yourself. Accept your sacred role in the universe. Be yourself with all your heart.

In The Heart:

* I relax into the knowing that I am a unique and beautiful creation of God.

The Good Kind of Viral

Every act of kindness spreads peace to the world,
love to the heart, light to us all.

Every act of kindness, each loving word, every peaceful thought, changes the energy of those around us. And now there's proof. New research shows that when a person sees someone act in a kind way, they are far more likely to engage in that behavior themselves. When we are kind to another in the presence of others, our kindness is multiplied—perhaps infinitely.

A few years ago, there was a kindness campaign in our area, and my daughter and I heard on the radio that people were picking up the tab of the person behind them at drive-through windows. The next time we found ourselves at a drive-through, we told the cashier that we'd like to pay for the car behind us. "Tell them to have an amazing day!" we said with obvious joy from our small anonymous kindness.

A few months later, Maya was a new driver. One day after school she burst through the door with, "Guess what I just did?" Yep, she had repeated our act of kindness, on her own, with her own money, and with the same feeling of joy.

We heard later that one particular sequence of paying for the next car continued, spontaneously, for over thirty cars.

Our actions speak volumes. When we create a world based on kindness and love, we unsuspectingly model that to others, lifting the consciousness of all—spreading peace, love and light to the world.

In The World:

✳ Keep a watchful eye for opportunities to say or do something kind in the presence of your kids or friends. No need to teach or preach. Your actions say it all.

In The Heart:

✳ Kindness flows from my heart with ease. I see the light of these small acts reverberating around the world.

Expect a Day of Miracles

Anticipate beauty. Believe in miracles. Count on grace.
Decide on joy. Expect peace.

You, my friend, are a magnificent piece of work; a powerful consciousness, driven by boundless love and housed in a miracle of a body. Yes, you. Your cells spin like sparkling stars. Your love rises like a thousand rainbows. Amazing does not begin to describe you.

So today, we start off by owning our awesome truth—that we are spirits endowed with strength and grace, unconditionally loved and hardwired to grow toward the light.

The story of this day has everything to do with how we perceive ourselves when we rise in the morning. When we acknowledge our vastness, all things are possible. What is *impossible* is to manifest our expansive creativity while anchored to the earth in a place of unworthiness. No, today unfolds from the script of who we believe we are. Let's remember:

We are a sun ray of divinity. We are a sparkle in the eye of God's consciousness. We are filled with light and radiating love in every possible direction. We are an extension of divine wisdom, overflowing with joy, knowledge and peace. This is who we are in spite of our earthly challenges—or maybe *because* of them.

Who are we not to believe in miracles? When we align with the truth of who we are, we see miracles as not only possible, but probable. When we expect a day of miracles, we experience a day of miracles.

In The World:

✳ Anticipate a beautiful day ahead. Affirm that you are a miracle and believe that anything is possible. Remember the flow of benevolent grace and count on it to be here when you need it. Know that you are a spirit of joy and peace, then decide on joy and expect peace today.

In The Heart:

✳ I am in the flow of grace, participating in the miracles that surround me. I am aligned with all good and believe in my limitless potential.

The Horse that Jumped for Joy

I have the soul of a free spirit—enthusiastic, radiant and uniquely me.

Of the four horses in the field, Shadow is the free-spirited one, the least predictable, the renegade. I once glimpsed the breathtaking sight of him galloping at full speed around the field in the pouring rain, exhilarated and joyous. After his victory lap, he stopped short and reared up on his hind legs, kicking toward the sky. For the encore, he rolled on his back from side to side until he was caked with mud and thoroughly covered with delight.

Last night, as the sun retired over the mountain and the clouds colored themselves in orange and pink, the horses came up over the ridge to graze. As I cooked dinner, I kept an eye on them, marveling, mesmerized by the gift of beauty. I saw Shadow throw his head back—a sign that he might run—so I left my pot and went to the window in time to see him take off down the hill and out of sight...then gallop back up the hill...*on my side of the fence.* He was free!

Oh, how many days I have balanced on top of the split rail fence, aching to jump over and stand next to Shadow with no barrier between us. Now here was my giant friend, walking proudly up to my house to see me! Before I drove over to tell his owner of the escape, I busted out of the door, barefoot, and ran to meet him. We danced around and laughed on the open field together. Carrots were shared in celebration. It was a delicious, impromptu, juicy moment of spirited freedom.

Perhaps the word *spirited* has gotten a bad rap. After all, it means: enthusiastic, (literally, "God within"), full of energy, determined. I have been in survival mode for so long that I have all but forgotten this passionate feeling of freedom; arms up, face to the sky. Maybe it's time to decide I am going to wake with joy and enthusiasm each morning and treat myself to simple delights that awaken my soul. Maybe it's time to bust out of my field of habit and sail over the split rail fence of new beginnings. Maybe it's time to run in the rain.

In The World:

❋ Joy is a spiritual practice. Carve out a few moments each day for something delightful, joyful, playful. Just for you, just because.

In The Heart:

❋ I have the soul of a free spirit—enthusiastic, radiant and uniquely me. I welcome sweet small moments of unbridled joy today.

The Right Time to Rise

I am strong. I am whole. I am enough.

Sometimes, healing begins in private—like the kind that follows betrayal, or living with someone who has an addiction, or mental health problems, or any number of unspoken issues. Shedding the thick skin of an old life is slow work. Isolated by the private nature of the secret, you stare down the Big Lonely of not telling your truth and hearing in your very own words what your life has become. But you finally admit it to yourself.

It wasn't really a huge leap for me to move to the middle of nowhere—I was already walled off from all of the seemingly sane, happy people. I had been living in an alternate universe for many years, pretending things were fine outwardly, while dealing with the dissolution of my marriage on the inside. A few friends knew parts of the story, but I held on to the heaviest parts, tenderly feeling the need to examine the secrets, and my role in them, alone. But I was never really alone. And you're not either.

Like me, you have a celestial team of guides and angels cheering you on, making like this is the best, most important part of life—this pain. They whisper encouraging words. They make hope visible and grace possible. They keep us in the moment, they ease the pain, they point the way, they remind us there are no mistakes, they tell us that you and I are never a solo act in life's drama.

Through the dense fog of this morning, I could see the outline of only one small, bare tree. The little tree seemed like me, my life covered in a fog of unknowing. Nothing was clear—not the past, not the future.

But right now, the sun is rising and it's burning off the mist, and even the tree knows that the sun was never gone. It was there all along, waiting for the right time to rise.

In The World:

✳ Just recognizing your truth is a giant step. Naming it is the start of your healing. Many have walked a similar path and survived. The sun is there and will rise for you.

In The Heart:

✳ I am strong. I am whole. I am enough. I have faith that my pain is meaningful and will help me grow like nothing else in my life can.

Everything We Need

Every aspect of today is a co-creation with the divine.

No book. no teacher, no religion, no guru or saint can teach us how to have a personal experience of God. They can lead us to the doorstep of heaven. They can tell us what it's like to commune with spirit. They can inspire us with teachings of the ages. Great wisdom from experienced teachers is irreplaceable; but there's something even they can't do for us. They can't be a substitute for our own relationship with our own God.

And for that, we have everything we need. We are so infused with spirit, so saturated in the divine, so deeply loved, so magnificently wired that God is impossible to avoid. There is no place where God is not. There is nothing to search for, nothing to remove or to add, only layers to unveil.

My last house was in a neighborhood where each home was surrounded by acres of centuries-old maples and oaks. One morning I woke to the sound of chainsaws. My neighbor had a team of tree workers preparing to fall some of the tallest sentinels. I ran over, distraught. "Ron! What are you doing?" To which he responded, "I can't see the forest from my deck because the trees are in the way."

Which is similar to saying, "I can't experience God today because there are so many distractions." The distractions are also God. Everything is. And when we look at the world this way, where all things are connected, it's easy to initiate a casual conversation and request guidance from a friendly God. We find that we are led, sign by sign, to the right choice in each moment. We need only to remember to start talking.

It's beautifully simple. We were born for this. The wealth of wisdom and guidance is not something that is available only when we're meditating, praying or in church. It's who we are. We have access to a pure connection from within at all times. We never take a step alone.

In The World:

* Look at the world today through the eyes of your highest self. Consider the possibility of co-creating every aspect of today in relationship to a benevolent God who loves you unconditionally.

In The Heart:

* I believe in myself and in the magnificence of my spirit. I am supported and guided in every step I take and every decision I make.

Bless My Eyes

Bless my eyes to see goodness. Bless my words to speak kindness. Bless my heart to feel compassion. Bless my soul to radiate love.

Bless my eyes to see what is good, loving and kind. Bless them to see what is whole, light and calm. Bless them to see the humble, the quiet and the small. Bless them to see the beauty in nature and in all living things. Catch my gaze when my eyes wander only to that which needs mending. Guard my vision when it strays to that which is dark and discouraging. Restore clear sight when they gravitate to violence. Bless my eyes.

Bless my words to speak only kindness and impart only love. Bless them to be used only to build up and create confidence. Bless them to put light into the world where there was darkness before. Hold my words when they might cause pain. Keep them within when they have the power to tear down and crush. May I never use them as a weapon of power. Bless my words.

Bless my heart to feel compassion for every being. Bless me to understand that the suffering of one of us is the suffering of all of us. Bless me to see a spark of divine light in every face. Bless me to see a piece of me in all others. Keep my heart blind to the faults of others. May I resist a view of the world that creates separation and judgment. Lead me away from comparisons and jealousy for the experience of another. Bless my heart.

Bless my soul to shine love on all who cross my path today. Bless me to express gratitude for small miracles of daily life. Bless me to joy and contentment for the gifts of this precious life. Gently remind me when I slip into lower vibrations of fear. Let me not linger long in the valley of self-pity. Nudge me out of needless worry. Bless my soul.

In The World:

✳ Ask for assistance today in gently turning toward the light, the beautiful and the good in every choice you make.

In The Heart:

✳ Throughout this day, in thought, word and action, I am in perfect alignment with my highest and most loving wisdom.

I Am Not My Breasts

Your inner light is what makes you beautiful.

Decked out in their finest, Mom and Dad were on their way down Route A1A in Florida to an anniversary party at an elegant yacht club. They didn't go to many social events and were excited to celebrate this special evening in the lives of their old friends. Mom chose flowing blue silk and pearls; Dad wore his best suit. The previous summer, Mom had endured a double mastectomy for breast cancer, and this party marked a return to the small joys of life.

Now several towns from their home, cupping her hands to her chest in panic, Mom exclaimed, "Lou! I forgot The Girls!" Her prosthetic breasts, which she carefully slipped into a specially made bra whenever she went out, had become an uncomfortable fact of life. They were heavy and never felt quite right over her newly healed scars. Well tonight, The Girls were home alone.

Dad, sincere and at-the-ready to help with this predicament, gripped the wheel and began to maneuver a U-turn. "Wait." she said. "Let's go without them." As she told me later, she had the time of her life at that party and never wore The Girls again. And then she tossed out a phrase that I'll never forget:

"I am not my breasts." Well, amen, Mom.

Our beauty is the light of our soul, the light of our heart, the light of our love and of our spirit. When something knocks us off our game today, let's remember that the wattage of our inner light can be so mesmerizing that what we thought was a glaring imperfection is insignificant when standing in the light of our love. This inner light is what makes us beautiful.

In The World:

✳   Take a few moments, right now, to imagine the light of love in your heart center. See it as radiant, glowing, compassionate, beautiful. This is the you that is projected to anyone who crosses your path today. This is the feeling they will walk away with. This is who you are.

In The Heart:

✳   Today I radiate the love and beauty of my inner light.

Guardian Angel Friendship

Angels, be with me. Watch over me and guard my every step. Guide me through the endless details of this day. Let's walk together.

They are here for us. Each of us has at least one angel with us right now. We can ask them for absolutely anything, but we do have to ask. The angels that are closest to earth, the guardian angels, are here for the sole purpose of assisting us, but they will never interfere with our free will. They act on our behalf only when they are called upon. So, when we want their assistance, we just need to have a chat.

Life changes completely when we make friends with our angels.

It takes a moment of quiet focus, but connecting with angels is as easy as talking to a dear friend. And what beautiful friends they are. We don't have to endure the difficulties of this day alone. We only need to call on our friends in high places.

In The World:

✳ *Ask often and pay attention.* You can talk with your guardian angel as you would talk to your dearest friend—about anything and everything. You can request assistance in all aspects of the day. Then pay attention to the guidance you will receive in the form of signs, feelings or an intuitive sense of what to do next.

✳ *Ask on behalf of others.* We don't directly communicate with someone else's angel, but we can ask our angel to enlist their angel's help in healing, in sorting out a problem between you, in helping them with their lives or their health today.

✳ *Give thanks.* Show gratitude as if it has come to pass. *Thank you for my complete healing. Thank you for always helping me.*

✳ *Leave room for something better.* This allows us to open to answers beyond our expectations. *May this or something greater happen for the highest good of all.* Or the equally beautiful and eloquent: "Thy will be done."

In The Heart:

✳ My angel is here for me today, lovingly guiding me in every choice I make.

Grace and the Bluebird

Sometimes when we just stand still, the grace finds us.

For hours I heard the heartbreaking flutter of little wings in the pipe of the wood burning stove, with no idea of how to help. A friend advised opening the flue and letting the little guy drop into the stove, then fishing him out from there. *Really? Just catch a bird?* This was all new territory.

When I opened the stove door, I was shocked to be eye-to-eye with a beautiful little bluebird. He was huddled in the back corner, frightened, and in a fleeting moment I was within his tender body looking out. I was stuck in the darkness with no sky. I was born to fly free, but not seeing any good options. I recognized myself in him. Then gently closed the door to ponder my next move.

I retrieved a tea towel from the kitchen and slowly opened the door again. I reached in to cover him and in a flash he flew out past me into the room and along the ceiling to the first available window. Up and down the screen he flew, then to the next window and to the next, where he stopped, out of gas, alone, scared, checking out the room. And still not seeing any good options.

Stunned by his stillness, I stood motionless as well, only a few feet away. *You are beautiful*, was the thought I sent to him. He was sizing me up. *Stay still. Just surrender, little one.* I reached out with the towel in a smooth movement, and he let me pick him up without struggle. Cradled gently, I took him outside on the front step, where I let the cloth fall open and he flew up to a tree branch. We talked for a moment and off he went to new, bluebird-of-happiness adventures.

Sometimes when we are cornered, we surrender to something bigger. Sometimes when we don't see a way out, we breathe and wait patiently. Sometimes when we have no answers, we listen for guidance and open to the unexpected. Sometimes when we just stand still, the grace finds us.

In The World:

* Today when faced with an unsolvable dilemma, be still, ask, allow and receive the gift of grace in the form of higher wisdom.

In The Heart:

* I ask for assistance and receive answers in new and creative ways. I am learning to tolerate stillness and the art of allowing.

Meditations on Meditation

Just breathe.

Meditation is one of many tools that can lead us toward a calmer, more joyful day. By resting the habitual thoughts of Me The Thinker and giving space to Me The Soul, we see how much calamity our thoughts and emotions can whip up, and how calm the space is that lies just beneath that calamity. We understand that this ocean of peace is always available when we turn down the volume of our thoughts. It's not a cure-all for our issues, but we become less attached to them, knowing that thoughts are transient while the soul is eternal. Divine wisdom, guidance and intuition rise to the surface when we take the time to quiet the mind.

In the first few breaths of a seated meditation, you realize how rowdy your mind really is and it can leave you feeling as if you are not doing it right or that meditation is not for you. No worries. Me The Thinker is just doing her job and trying to run the show. Gradually, the mind takes a back seat, and increasingly more time is spent in a restful state of calm. You return to the day feeling refreshed, clear, calm, mindful, aware, kind.

The benefits trickle down to all other parts of your life, including your health, your relationships, your connection with your higher wisdom and your ability to show compassion to yourself and all beings. All that when you just breathe.

In The World:

∗ Sit cross-legged or in a chair with your feet on the floor. Your hands rest on your thighs, palms up or down. Your spine is straight. Relax your face. Set a timer for five minutes to start, working slowly up to ten minutes twice a day.

∗ Simply bring your awareness to your breath as it goes in and out. It's a soft, gentle yet vigilant awareness. You're present with the breath as it goes in, and present with the breath as it goes out. Breathe in. Breathe out.

∗ When thoughts take over and you find yourself in the frozen food aisle of Trader Joe's buying mahi-mahi, smile and label it "thinking," and go back to observing your breath. Repeat until your timer rings, then sit for a moment.

In The Heart:

∗ I meditate with joy and reap the rewards with gratitude.

The Gift of Mahi-Mahi

I'm totally trying to meditate but my mind has other plans.

So let's get back to the mahi-mahi from yesterday. We all live with an incessant talker in our heads. According to scientists, our minds generate an average of 70,000 thoughts a day—that's about 49 per minute. No wonder we're all tired. Me The Thinker spews thoughts that jump from topic to topic in rapid-fire conversation with themselves. Then there's Me The Soul, the witness behind the chatter, observing it all.

Most people who have not thought about consciousness and have never attempted meditation go through life unaware that this distracted "monkey mind," as Buddha described it, is not who we are. Who we are is the peaceful Self or Soul or Atman, the eternal consciousness beneath the drama of our thoughts, that will live on after we leave our bodies. So it makes a lot of sense to get to know her better now, right?

Imagine you are meditating and you catch your mind wandering. And you will. The practice is to label the thinking as "thinking." I actually go a step further: I tap the thought on its little head with a wand. Really. I lightly hit it with the star end of a virtual wand and see the word "thinking" rise up. Then I smile and go back home to my breath awareness.

If you spend your entire meditation going back and forth between tapping your thoughts and coming back into focused awareness, you have had an extremely helpful practice.

Because at some point, your mind will slow down and absolutely everything in life will seem less dire and troubling. You will know who You are, and You will be at peace. So sit. Stay. You've got this.

In The World:

∗ Persist with your meditation practice. Make it a priority each morning. Just five minutes daily to start. You can do it!

In The Heart:

∗ I am a calm oasis of loving consciousness connected to the divine and to all beings.

Calm in the Storm

Bless me with a calm center in the storms of my life.

Storms are scary, but inevitable. All things are in constant motion and at one point or another, we are in their path and will endure suffering. But don't retreat to the storm cellar just yet.

Although we can't avoid the storms of life, it's comforting to know that calm wisdom and infinite support are within reach at any time through the gifts of our spiritual practice. These are beautiful daily practices that become especially valuable *within* the storms of life.

Our spiritual practice does not add something extra to our lives as much as it lifts the veil that hides our natural state of grace. We are, in essence, souls of love, joy and peace. It is from this calm center that we have access to our own powerful inner wisdom, which is part of the endless wisdom of divine love. The calm and safety of the storm cellar door is right here within us. It's always here and it's always open for business.

There are countless practices that foster this deep sense of peace. Practices that help us on ordinary days as well as in our darkest hours. Throughout the year, we will integrate your favorites into a morning routine and find that the journey to peace is one of life's most amazing adventures. Be patient. Be persistent. The rewards await.

In The World:

✳ Begin each day with gratitude. *Thank you for this day.* Write it on a note and place it on your nightstand so you remember. Then follow that with a favorite verse or a beautiful quote that inspires your heart. Add a short reading from an inspirational book, a conversation with your angels about the day ahead and a five-minute meditation. You have just started a morning practice.

✳ Get a notebook that will serve as a spiritual journal in which to capture insights that feed your soul. As the year goes on, we will explore many spiritual practices, and you can keep the ones that resonate with you close at hand, cultivating your own oasis of inspiration.

In The Heart:

✳ I am peaceful. I am calm. I am centered in the storms of my life.

Silent Sunrise Offering

In a silent morning moment, with a silent voice I pray, to lift a silent sunrise offering, on silent wings of grace.

Whatever we offer up in the silence of the morning is magnified throughout the day. Those first thoughts create the joyous momentum for all that follows. When we open to receive our highest wisdom, we continue to access assistance and clarity in the form of intuition, knowledge and guidance as the day unfolds. What a glorious invitation we send out when we empower the dawn of the day with focused attention on practices that reward us with the gifts of joy, inner peace and divine connection.

Our morning spiritual practice is not homework, but an investment in every aspect of our lives. A few minutes a day assists us in making the transformation from our smaller selves to our higher selves. It's as if our perception is shifted from monochromatic black and white, to full, blooming, brilliant HD color.

It doesn't have to be involved or overly planned, just authentic. It doesn't have to be long, but our focus has to be all in. It doesn't have to please anyone else; it is for your soul alone.

As the gift of this day lays out before us, we begin by practicing peace, joy, strength, gratitude and oneness with all things. With a morning moment like that, everything that follows flows with a little more ease and grace.

In The World:

✳ Commit to a few short spiritual practices each morning if possible. After a few days, you will find your ideal time and place.

✳ Consider any combination of prayer, meditation, sacred reading, walking, journaling, gratitude practice, daybook lessons, visualizing, angel cards, yoga or pranayama. Collect ideas and inspirations in your journal.

In The Heart:

✳ I create time with ease and grace for contemplative practice each morning. My day is inspired when it starts from a place of spiritual connection with all wisdom, light and love.

A Winter Night

Beneath the drift of earthly sound, strong silent soul unbound. Unique as a snowflake, soft as her flight, still as the ground beneath the quiet winter's night.

It happened years ago in the midst of a mid-winter blizzard near the end of the evening. The fireplace in the dimly lit barroom cast a golden glow over the dark paneled room as candles danced alone on empty tables. Behind the bar, Larry was cleaning up, anticipating an early closing time. Behind the keys on the grand piano, I nodded safe travels to the last couple to leave.

As if out of nowhere, a man stood at the door, leaning, arms crossed, listening as I sang what I thought would be my closing number. Before I finished, he was seated by the fireplace, watching me intently. I smiled at him and welcomed him in from the storm. Larry got him a drink as I played a few more songs, guessing by his weathered face and his age what he might like. I wish I could remember what I played. When I finished, I went straight from the piano bench to his table, introducing myself and asking if there was a special song he'd like to hear. No, he said, but could I sit down for a moment?

Then his story spilled out. After a long marriage and years of fighting, his wife had recently left him. The kids didn't come around anymore, and soon he would retire from his job. He had nothing to live for. Calmly, he left his house about an hour ago, intending to drive his car into a tree in the snowstorm. It would look like an accident. As he came around the corner on River Road, he suddenly felt drawn to come into the bar and have a drink. One last drink. Then he heard the music. And in the lyrics, he heard hope. And in the hope, he decided he was not going to take his life that night after all. I knew in that moment, that if I never did another thing in my life, that I was meant to be in just that place for a stranger at the crossroads.

In The World:

* Perhaps our purpose is not a grand accomplishment, but a small kindness that we don't think much of, that changes the life of another. You are here for a reason and someone needs your light today.

In The Heart:

* Every action and interaction in my life has meaning. I journey through this day mindfully, humbly and kindly.

JANUARY 22

Be Present with Peace

Look back with joy. Look forward with hope. Be present with peace.

James Doty is a Stanford neuroscientist who conducts studies in the field of neuroplasticity—the ability of our habitual thoughts to change the brain—in the context of compassion and kindness. Dr. Doty says that some 80% of our thoughts are regrets of the past or worries of the future. Eighty percent! But the only place we can be compassionate and connect with others is in the present moment. We are missing the best hours of our lives while we entertain regret and worry.

Although we all have regrets about the past, certainly there are many moments of joy we might rather remember on a regular basis. Dr. Doty reminds us that it's easier to think the thoughts we are accustomed to thinking instead of learning new ones. But isn't it worth learning new thought patterns when the old ones are bringing us down? Instead of dredging up the same painful memories, doesn't it make sense to remember some beautiful ones?

As for our future thoughts, many of us have become expert worriers, a sport we need to retire from, as our worry magnifies the negative scene that we are worrying about! We don't want to imagine the worst case scenario over and over, giving energy to an undesirable outcome. In addition, worrying adds to our stress levels, leading to a cascade of physical and emotional challenges. Let's be mindful about our thoughts and shed some positive light on this precious day. We can all learn to be present with peace.

In The World:

✳ Today, begin to create some new pathways in your brain using mindfulness. Continue to draw your thoughts gently back to the present moment over and over again. Notice details, colors, sounds. Walk and eat more slowly. Stay present with what you are doing.

✳ Release habitual thoughts of the past and conjure a more beautiful memory. Replace worries about the future with a visualization of a perfect, joyous outcome to the challenge. Shoot off a prayer or affirmation surrounding the end result.

In The Heart:

✳ I look back with joy. I look forward with hope. I am present with peace.

Virtual Hibernation

I am in balance with the wisdom of nature.

From this big window in my tiny corner of the Northern Hemisphere, it's abundantly clear that it's time to hibernate. The trees are bare, the ground is frozen, and come to think of it, so am I. I can't seem to get warm in the cabin without a blanket around my shoulders, which I drag like an Ice Queen's train from room to room. The sky is grey with clouds that sail on a chilly wind. It's a perfect time to go back to bed—at noon.

My buddies are sleepy too. The horses are moving slower, the bears are fast asleep in their dens, the squirrels are tucked into their nests. Two friends texted me today that they are at their best under duvets, willing themselves out of bed in the morning, as drowsy as I am when the rooster crows.

Could it be that people, too, feel the need to hibernate in the winter?

Like our friend the lemur in Madagascar, some of us would love to sit zombie-like in a tree hole and wait it out. It seems perfectly normal that the shorter days would signal a slowdown of metabolism, when we eat and sleep more to conserve energy for the winter chill. If you are feeling this way, it's real, and the best thing to do is to quiet the voice of self-judgment, relax and lean into something soft.

Noticing our natural rhythms as they respond to the seasons is all part of self-care. When our bodies ask for virtual hibernation, chances are that our minds and souls are requesting down time as well. Accept it for what it is, trusting in the wisdom of your body. It's okay to be slow, Ice Queen.

In The World:

✳ Listen to your inner wisdom as it speaks to the changes of the seasons. In winter, give in to the natural rhythm of slowing down, allowing more space for relaxing, snuggling, reading, sleeping and eating comfort food. Trust that your mind, body and soul know what you need.

In The Heart:

✳ I listen to my inner wisdom and am in balance with the wisdom of nature. I allow myself to slow down and enjoy stillness.

Raise the Vibration

Today may I judge less and love more.

Our thoughts and words have the power to build up and to tear down. They can sow joy or spread suffering. They can be a reminder of our oneness or a weapon of our separation. These choices are ours to make every day.

It's natural to think that our way is the right way. We have opinions of how things should be done and are passionate about certain issues. We may have an education that leads us to certain conclusions. Each of us has an individual view of the world as it is and as we would like it to be. But it's important to keep in mind that everyone else believes in their own vision as well.

When we judge another's choices, we immediately build a wall of division and separation. Judgment and love can't live in the same thought or the same sentence. When we put our focus on loving more, the habit of judging others falls away.

To accept the choices of others with compassion doesn't mean we have to agree. Their behavior is not a reflection on our lives, but our negative reaction to their behavior is. No good ever comes from criticizing another.

Using our thoughts and words mindfully empowers us with the ability to spread joy and kindness, and to raise the vibration of those around us. Today, may we judge less and love more.

In The World:

* Refrain from thinking judgmental thoughts or using words that in any way cause suffering or separation.

* Consider the Golden Rule: Treat others as you wish to be treated.

* Channel activism and plant seeds of change in constructive ways.

In The Heart:

* I refrain from judgment and am generous with compassionate thoughts and words toward others.

A Ripple in the Water

Prayer. There's always something we can do to change the world.

After listening to the news, I used to have the overwhelming feeling that there was nothing that I could do to make a difference. I am one small voice, one single heart, one tiny grain of sand, one of a million little shining stars. How could I make any impact on the fear, the division, the defeat, the devastation?

Then I received a beautiful image of a stone dropping into a huge, still, brilliant blue body of water. It created a ripple in the water starting near one shore and traveling far across to the other. The circles grew wider and wider, and their impact arrived in places I could not see or even imagine.

We change the world one by one; one positive thought, action or prayer at a time, rippling endlessly. We change the world by our passionate will. We change the world by clearly imagining it as whole and healed. We change the world by peaceful, compassionate action. We change the world by sending forth fervent blessings over and over again. Our souls need not be deterred by the constant repetition of negative thoughts and images. The unseen is vastly more power than that which we see.

When we feel helpless to make a difference in the world, or in times of challenge and suffering, there's always something we can do. We can call upon the power of prayer, blessings, love, visualization and compassionate action. We always have a weapon. Shed some light. Light always wins.

In The World:

* Listen less often to the news. Don't leave it on in the background. Keep your thoughts focused on constructive change.

* Allow news of tragedy to evoke compassion. Then use this connection with those who are suffering to send them a blessing or a prayer. Imagine a moment of peace for the people involved.

* Pray for our world and for all beings. Be a ripple in the water.

In The Heart:

* I am a warrior of light. I spread thoughts of love and light all over the planet.

Be Yourself Bravely

Beauty is born and blooms from within.

Someone's opinion of us is just that, an opinion. It never defines us, and it's not required that we shop in the costume closet of another's expectations. Lasting happiness never ensues as a result of living up to external ideals. And the real dichotomy here is that the pressures of society pale into black and white next to the truth of our own brilliant color pallet. Period. There is no point in walking onto the stage of our lives if we are not playing the colorful part of ourselves.

To be ourselves bravely, we must know ourselves. When we look within, we encounter our essence as the incredible expression of divine love that we are. Trust this. Believe this. And be positively, relentlessly on your own side.

Call on courage as a companion on this journey as it requires vulnerability and honesty to expose our truth. We've been trained to ask ourselves, *Am I good enough?* when the real question might be, *Am I me enough?* Bravery clears the path to the other side of self-doubt. And waiting there confidently to walk through this day with you is your magnificent, authentic, beautiful self.

Beauty, like confidence, radiance, self-love and joy, is born and blooms from within. Nothing in the external world ever changes our essence. Be an original. Be quirky. Be yourself bravely.

My friend Michelle's husband puts a point on it when he says with a laugh as he reaches for the leash, "It takes a confident man to walk a poodle."

In The World:

✳ Today, begin with just one kind compliment directed toward yourself and repeat it often.

✳ Be kind in your expression of your true self. It's possible to be both honest and kind.

In The Heart:

✳ I honor my divinity by sharing my authentic self and unique gifts with others.

Last Day on Earth

Say "I love you" out loud and often.

My neighbor Gene died yesterday. I loved Gene. When he wasn't at his restaurant, you could find him in his garden. Hundreds of tulips and daffodils would sing out joy each spring; topiaries were lovingly trimmed into whimsical shapes; maple trees and rhododendrons looked like they would rather live in his dirt than anywhere else on earth. Everything he planted grew brilliantly.

After my husband moved from the old house, Gene had my back. When he knew I was alone and busy, he would leaf blow so my piano students could find the driveway. He shared vegetables in the spring and plowed me out when it snowed. He was relentlessly thoughtful, kind and generous. Two days ago Gene was in his garden. Yesterday morning, he woke with an aortic aneurysm. Today the garden is gently still. I wish I told him how much he meant to me.

In Gene's honor, I imagine that today is my last day on earth. What will I do differently? The first thing that comes to mind is to do what I didn't do with Gene: Tell my loved ones that I love them. Out loud. And tell them what I love about them. And how they make me feel. And what a gift they are in my life. And how beautiful they are. Rumi's words drift through my heart as if part of Gene's garden, "With life as short as a half taken breath, don't plant anything but love."

My sister-in-law Julie has lived out her entire adult life with a rare, life-threatening disease. She is a mom of four. I once asked her how she copes with knowing that her life is so fragile and that tomorrow is not a given. She said, "It's an amazing gift! If only everyone knew what it was like to live every day like it is your last." So I'm starting today. And I want to tell you that I love you.

In The World:

* Take a moment to imagine the scenario of today as your last day. What would you do differently? What words need to be said? What situation resolved? What brings you joy? Say "I love you" out loud to your beloveds today.

In The Heart:

* I am thankful for my precious life and live today with every ounce of my being. I am generous in my expression of love.

Three Grace Notes

Open your soul to grace.

It's comforting to know that grace is always here. Every day, no matter what challenge presents itself, we have ready support and wisdom that far surpasses our mind's ability to see our way clear of earthly dilemmas. Generously bestowed upon us from the divine, grace is always present, always free and always ours. Here are three grace notes for a stress-free day:

1. First, we remember that we are not alone and that the gift of grace is already here for us. Stress will begin to melt away as we soften, aligning with the current of ease, allowing an opening to divine wisdom. So, remembering that grace is available is the first step to receiving her gifts.

2. Next, we ask. *Divine Grace, I step into your flow and know that I will receive the perfect guidance. Thank you for assisting me in each decision of this day.* We can be specific, knowing that grace immediately flows toward perfect resolutions. With open arms, we ask and we trust.

3. The third step in opening to grace is noticing and following the guidance that will be clearly given. Through signs large and small, answers will be provided and we will know what to do from one moment to the next. What we get done in the flow of grace happens easily and effortlessly. What does not get done today is meant for another day.

Relax. Breathe. Our minds can remain free of worry as long as our souls are open to grace.

In The World:

✴ If it resonates with your heart, make a note in your journal to open to grace. Write down the three grace notes. Let them be a reminder to make the request for a lovely helping of grace each morning.

In The Heart:

✴ I am open to the grace that is here for me at all times, assisting, guiding and supporting my day.

The Inner Voice

Ask, listen, trust and receive.

It can arrive as a feeling or as a sense of which way to go. It reveals itself as a vivid dream, as synchronicity or in just plain words. It can be as subtle as a soft nudge. Our inner voice or divine guidance provides direction and assistance from the source of all universal wisdom, and therefore is always positive and light-filled. It will never lead us to do anything that is negative or destructive as our soul's wisdom only operates on a plane of light.

Perhaps you wonder, as I do, if the inner voice is *my* voice or that of a guide, an angel, a deity or God. It is my belief that it can be any or all of these possibilities. If our pure consciousness, or soul, is connected to all things, then we can access loving information from a wide variety of sources. Each of us must ask for guidance from a deeply personal place in alignment with our most precious beliefs. There is no one right way, only the right way for you.

It's important not only to listen to the inner voice in order to receive the message, but also to listen to what you are being guided to do and act upon it. The more we act on our guidance, the more we are able to hear it. We hear best when we trust in ourselves and in the benevolence of the universe. Ask, listen, trust and receive.

In The World:

* Listen for your inner voice in every decision today. Your meditation practice will calm your mind and enhance your ability to hear and to feel on a higher vibrational plane.

* Ask your more important life questions during your spiritual practice when your mind is calm. Remain open for answers and clues that may come in unusual ways. Trust and act on the guidance received.

* Use your journal to collect stories about guidance requested and insights received. They will become uplifting and powerful reminders to look back upon.

In The Heart:

* I trust that I will receive clear guidance and I will follow the promptings of my heart.

Anticipating Abundance

I am thankful for the blessings of this day.

As we now know, the first thoughts that we impress on our subconscious mind in the morning can powerfully direct the course of our path throughout the day. Affirmations ("I am..." statements) are especially effective and can be used as a mantra, or repeated phrase, keeping our intention on track as the day unfolds. Below are a few examples. Affirmations work best when they are personal. If any part of a written affirmation doesn't resonate seamlessly in your heart, you have the creative license to rewrite it until it represents your energy.

I am clear, focused and efficient in my work today.

I am peaceful, joyful and patient with my kids and friends.

I flow through the day with ease and grace.

I have all the time I need for all I need to do.

I listen for guidance and follow my inner voice.

The power of affirmations comes from imagining ourselves as our best selves and believing in the best possible outcomes. We don't need to detail how things will happen. The universe will find ways of manifesting our hopes in ways beyond our wildest dreams.

Be thankful for the blessings of this day and countless blessings will be on their way.

In The World:

✴ In your journal, create a few affirmations that fit your day or use some of the ones above. Close your eyes and sit for a few moments with relaxed breathing, repeating the affirmation, feeling gratitude as if the gifts have already been received.

✴ For more ideas, every **In The Heart** section is an affirmation.

In The Heart:

✴ I am thankful for the blessings of this day. Joy and gratitude radiate from me as I anticipate the abundant gifts of today.

JANUARY 31

Flight Preparations

*As I walk to the edge of the darkness and take one step over the side, I
believe I'll land on my feet, or I will learn to fly.*

It can take a lot of precious time to make big changes in our lives. It can
take many years and thousands of steps to get to the precipice of
transformation. Our next destination and the spiritual truths that are
required on the journey will unfold at a pace that is right for each of us.
But one thing is for sure: When you decide the time is right, it only takes
one step over the side to become airborne. And surely you will soar.

Sometimes change is not our choice, and we find ourselves facing
inevitable and unforeseen turmoil in our lives. Sometimes it is our
choice—we feel stuck and choose to initiate a transition. Should you be
facing great change or challenge, know that you are the pilot and ground
crew of this bird, and your timing, no matter how long it takes, will be
perfect for you. You will fly, sweet bird, with the wings of faith on the
wind of grace.

It never hurts to have a short list of flight preparations for when the time
comes to spread your wings and take to the skies of your new journey.
Know that you are infinitely loved and divinely guided. Have patience
with your heart and with your timing. Turn grace into your compass, and
take some flying lessons for the soul.

In The World: Flying 101

* Sharpen your vision by clearly imagining scenes of future
  contentment.

* Strengthen your wings by making gradual changes.

* Be present and grateful for the moment you are in.

* Focus your ability to hear your inner voice by meditating daily.

* Rewrite fear thoughts with encouraging affirmations. You can do this.

* Assemble a navigational team of the finest guides in the heavens.

In The Heart:

* I spread my wings with courage, grace and divine assistance. I am
  prepared for things to work out even better than my wildest dreams.

February
Be present.
Let the day flow with grace.
Expect joy. Be positive.
Serve with compassion.
Speak only kindness.
Impart only love.
Never forget you're not alone.
Give thanks for everything.
See goodness in others. mary davis

EVERY DAY SPIRIT
.NET

February Blessings

Be present. Be here. Today, we can guide our thoughts back to the present moment with gentle focus and live fully right where we are.

Let the day flow with grace. Grace flows through us easily when we are in tune with the subtle voice of intuition. Open and listen for guidance.

Expect joy. Be positive. Imagine a fulfilling day unfolding, in which we accomplish much and experience joy in the process. Welcome the light.

Serve with compassion. Acts of service when performed with love lend immeasurable light to our day. Be watchful for ways to serve.

Speak only kindness. Speak only kind words. Think only kind thoughts. Be kind to yourself and to those who cross your path or your mind.

Impart only love. Send out all thoughts and words on the wings of love so that we may love one another, love ourselves, love the unlovable.

Never forget you're not alone. Let's remind ourselves often today that we are always supported, guided and unconditionally loved as we are.

Give thanks for everything. Gratitude will shift the perspective of the day from one of lack to one of abundance. Give constant thanks.

See goodness in others. Each of us has a soul that is made of beauty and love. Assume the best in others so they may rise to their highest light.

~·\/~

The Making of Miracles

Miracles don't happen to you. They happen through you.

Miracles happen through small moments and great beauty; through small prayers and great faith; through small rays of hope and great love. Through us.

The humble lotus plant grows through the dark, muddy water to finally expand into layers of petals and open her blossom to the light. It may seem that the miracle is the brilliant lotus blossom that floats on the surface of the lake. But the incremental journey through the dark to the light is the real miracle. And like the lotus plant, the incremental journey of our lives, day by day through the dark to the light, is the real miracle.

Nothing really happens *to* us. The co-creation of our lives ultimately unfolds through the thoughts we think, the prayers we pray, the intentions we set, the guidance we invoke. We shape this day by the deliberate choice to act in ways that bring us closer to the light, and to allow the light to act *through* us.

Small actions can align us with powerful change and shape this day by transforming us into instruments through which miracles are made. It's all about small things—with great love.

In The World: The miracle of today lies in:

✳ planting positive morning thoughts of love;

✳ acts of kindness for ourselves and for others;

✳ gratitude and awe that awaken the spirit to the beauty around us;

✳ pain or joy that brings newfound depth of compassion and understanding;

✳ the awareness of signs, symbols, divine guidance and insight;

✳ choosing small actions, over and over again, that bring us closer to the love and to the light.

In The Heart:

✳ Today, I am a channel for miracles and a vehicle for positive transformation for myself and others.

Filled to Overflowing

Today I give thanks for all of the things in my life that don't need fixing.

A sweet friend of mine is the dedicated full-time caretaker of a child and a spouse, both of whom suffer from debilitating diseases. She holds down a demanding job while coordinating all of the shopping, cooking and cleaning. She creates time to schedule and take everyone to their medical appointments and to get their medications before the bottles and homeopathic remedies run out. She falls into bed exhausted every night and gets up after a few hours of sleep to do it all again, with great love.

When I ask her how she is, I am always amazed and inspired by her response. After a deep breath, she will let out a long exhale and say, "Well...pretty good! Yes...we're doing *good* over here!" It sounds a bit like a pep talk for herself, but I noticed as the years passed that she never complains. Not one word. Ever. She cries sometimes from exhaustion or frustration, but she never wishes her challenges away or looks at her life as the movement from one disaster to another as any rational person might.

Continuing to answer my question, she always counts the blessings that she does have. Someone had a good day yesterday. A symptom may have improved slightly with new meds. There was a snow delay and she got an extra hour of sleep. Noticing the victories first, she always cheers the smallest step forward and celebrates any inkling of the positive.

The simple act of noticing what's going right opens us to the abundance that lies in and around us all the time.

Today, may we give thanks for all of the things in our lives that don't need fixing, and fill our glass to overflowing.

In The World:

✳ Notice the tendency to complain. Replace complaint today with the awareness of all that is going well, of all that is beautiful, of the hundred precious things that deserve our gratitude.

In The Heart:

✳ Today I give thanks for all of the things in my life that don't need fixing.

Keeping a Sabbath

Sabbath: a day to feed the soul and remember
who we are without electronics.

Just think. There can be a day when we can linger longer in our morning meditation. A day when we can stretch, breathe and align without a phone chirping on the corner of the yoga mat. There can be a day when our gratitude practice is not confined to a time of day, but a joyful lingering with the Creator of all gifts. A day to read, to contemplate, to welcome and to allow.

The word Sabbath originates in the word *sabat,* meaning to stop or to rest. It honors God's rest following six magnificent days of creation. We, too, need rest after six long days of creation. We need the space to remember the tender truth that most real creation doesn't take place on the phone. It happens in the heart. The heart deserves uninterrupted time to integrate the lessons of the magnificent co-creation of the past six days.

The Sabbath is a day to honor the sacred spirit, remembering that our wisdom and clarity originate in moments of stillness and listening. After all of our *doing* this week, it is a retreat for the soul to step off the train of 24/7 connectivity to bask in uninterrupted *being.* Consider unplugging each week to recharge your heart, create with your hands, nourish your soul and answer the call of spirit.

In The World:

* Plan for a day or part of a day when you refrain from social media and email. Check your accounts a few times during the day if you need to, but don't feel compelled to answer what can be answered tomorrow. Your friends and colleagues will get used to it.

* Your time can be completely unscheduled, or you can have at the ready a good book, your journal, some cooking or hobby supplies, your kayak, your walking shoes—whatever supports your favorite contemplative activities.

* Do something with your family or a friend without electronics. Discover each other in a new way.

In The Heart:

* I joyfully allow myself a day of rest and renewal, of lingering and listening, of being and allowing.

Befriending the Dark

Darkness is the fertile soil of the soul.

The first time I came home to the Hunters Road cabin after dark and shut off my lights at the end of the long gravel driveway, I sat in dread. This was a huge mistake. There was no way I was going to walk from the car down the tiered steps through the tunnel of trees to the front door. Nope. It was pitch black, coal black, not-a-drop-of-light black. Perhaps the universe was sending me down a little joke, handing me a reflection of my life at that time. I sat for long minutes in my humorless terror before a heart-pounding race to the door.

So why does darkness provoke fear and light provide safety? Why in spirituality do we equate dark with evil and light with goodness? Why do we dread the dark and race for the light? Isn't it possible that this dark night of my life was the most fertile ground I had ever walked upon?

During this year, I allowed myself not only to tolerate, but to befriend my darkest stories. I allowed myself to sit at the table with them. I allowed myself to look into the eyes of losses and see how they took me apart, how they washed me out, how they grew me back again, how they colored me in. And I found that God was in the dark too, shining a light that can only be seen from within it, a lighthouse to the ship. It's a precious place, really, if we can bear to anchor there for a while.

Late last night, I rolled down the driveway and shut off my lights. I got out of the car, walked to the middle of the clearing and looked up. The coal black served as a backdrop for a glorious rendering of sparkling constellations. There, under the North Star, I knew, for the first time in my life, that I was not afraid of the dark and that within my darkness was also the face of love and courage, the face of beauty and faith. In my darkness was also the face of God.

In The World:

✳ When the dark is asking for your attention, follow her to the table and see what secrets she imparts. Love her as part of you. Learn from her and treasure her wisdom. Thank her, and allow her to leave when she's ready.

In The Heart:

✳ I accept and love every part of myself, the light and the dark. I learn from the dark as I learn from the light.

Life is a Gift

Through the eyes of gratitude, everything is a miracle.

What if, instead of our habitual mind chatter, the background of our consciousness was the rhythm of a constant, soft *thank you?*

This is not merely positive thinking or glass-half-full mentality. This is our soul in conversation with an abundant universe, expressing gratitude for the infinite miracles that surround us now and that will be arriving soon.

It's like floating in a sea of awe. It's like lying on your back under a sky of thanksgiving. It's like seeing everything through the eyes of gratitude.

It is not a stretch by any means to recognize our lives as being made up of an unending series of gifts. From sunrise to sundown we are being given countless blessings that expand us, grow us, delight us and show us who we are. Even times of pain and suffering come with moments of the radiant awareness of divinity.

It depends on which eyes we use to see.

Gratitude acknowledges the magnitude of our lives as embodied spirit and the real truth of our short time here: Life is a gift.

In The World:

* Gratitude Awareness Practice: Beginning today, write down in your journal twenty things you are grateful for each day for three days. It sounds like a lot, and it's meant to be a lot. It will ask you to be aware of all of the tiny gifts and precious moments that might otherwise go unnoticed.

* In three days of Gratitude Awareness, you will have trained yourself to be in the habit of noticing the countless precious gifts that surround us.

* Continue the practice after the first three days, writing three gratitudes morning and evening. Begin and end your day through the eyes of thanksgiving and abundance. It's a small practice that will change your life.

In The Heart:

* I see the world through the eyes of gratitude. I am aware of the constant miracles that surround me now.

❧

The Greater Plan

Be patient with yourself. There may be a greater plan that you cannot see.

Sometimes the timeline in our mind is not at all what's going on in our lives. We set ourselves up against noble goals with deadlines that come and go without the results we are expecting. Let's be patient with ourselves. There is a lot more happening behind the scenes than we can see from here.

When I was looking for a rental house in the country to begin this new chapter in my life, I found the perfect cabin on a mountaintop. The views were incredible and I could imagine myself writing there. I even knew where I would put each piece of thrift-store furniture that I didn't have yet. At the last minute, someone swooped in and bought my dream cabin. I had no place to live with only weeks before I needed to be out of my old house. I was devastated and adrift.

A few days later, two acquaintances who knew I was looking for a cabin wrote to me at almost the exact same time to tell me they just heard of a pretty place that would be coming up for rent the next day. It turned out that they were both telling me about the same cabin, where I now sit, bursting with gratitude that I'm here and not on the mountaintop. This is exactly where I need to be.

Prayers, desires and requests are always answered. There are ways of praying and tools of manifestation that we can use to better align with our goals and lay a path to their fruition.

But if we do our best praying and aligning, and still don't meet our goal, it's not a failure. A greater plan is at work. Have patience knowing that everything happens in its perfect time.

In The World:

✳ Know that you are always taken care of for your highest good and be open to the possibility that your greatest disappointments may reveal themselves as blessings at some point down the road.

In The Heart:

✳ I am patient with myself and have faith that the perfect plan is unfolding for me now.

I Am Moving Tomorrow

Simplify.

Although I don't have big pack rat tendencies, with a move on the horizon I was stunned by the sheer volume of my possessions. My ship was anchored in place with a load of heavy goods onboard. Relocation would not be easy under these conditions. There was always the option to leave it for others to manage, you know, after I've gone on to the next life—which does sound like an appealing plan for my inner procrastinator—but really?

Well in advance of the move, I started chipping away at one drawer, one closet at a time. I did it thoughtfully and slipped it in here and there between students. As the move drew closer, I had to get more ruthless. I was not going to drag boxes of I-don't-know-what from the house to the cabin after they had already taken up space, unused for 16 years. So I took a page from Marie Kondo's *Life-Changing Magic of Tidying Up* playbook and asked of each item, *Does this bring me joy?* And honestly, the answer was usually a resounding, *No!*

Even if you're not moving, there is no time like the present. My mom leaves an index card out in her laundry room that says, "I am moving tomorrow." She wants to keep the mentality of living lightly for when the time comes for an inevitable move.

One of my favorite Mary Oliver poems is called "Storage." In it, she tells of how she filled a rented storage space and left it to sit for years without any longing for its contents. One day she was inspired to call someone to come and haul everything away. She felt free as a bird when it was empty!

We, too, can know the feeling of freedom when we lighten our load. And the space we create when we simplify our lives makes more room for what we truly love.

In The World:

✻ Do your heart and your loved ones a favor and consider simplifying. Start small with one drawer, one closet, one corner at a time. Make more room in your heart for love.

In The Heart:

✻ I simplify my life, creating space for the expansion of my soul.

FEBRUARY 9

You're Driving Me Nuts

Today may I be patient and kind to those who drive me a little nuts.

Patience is in the pause. It's in the heat of that small space right before we react when someone is making us crazy. Yes, I know, when we reach the boiling point, it's very hard to hold back the avalanche of frustration and anger. But that one little saving-grace pause can allow us to respond thoughtfully instead of reacting randomly.

It's easy to be kind to kind people. Not so much with those who seem, by their very nature, to drive us to the brink of insanity. There are times when we all have the right to be angry and express it, but mostly it just fuels the fire. Anger is multiplied in the presence of anger. Anger is divided in the presence of love.

As the Dalai Lama famously tells us, it's always possible to be kind. And it's usually possible to fend off anger with a little patience and perspective.

Maybe we owe a debt of gratitude to those who test our patience and leave us exhausted and emotionally waving a white flag. They are our best teachers. Just think, they give us endless practice at patience, kindness, compassion, setting limits, and speaking our truth.

Every experience in life can be used as a lesson if we are willing students. And come to class with a little good humor.

In The World:

* *Patience.* Take a breath before reacting.

* *Kindness.* Formulate the kindest response possible.

* *Compassion.* Be open to understanding why they act the way they do.

* *Setting limits.* Respectfully find a way to set boundaries.

* *Truth.* It's possible to be honest and kind at the same time.

In The Heart:

* Today I will be patient and kind to those who drive me a little nuts.

We Invite You, Angels

Where your fears are, put angels there.

Let's begin today with a collective exhale, releasing the companion of anxiety. Take a shorter inhale of clear light, and a longer exhale of all that is troubling. Repeat. Shorter inhale of light, longer exhale of all the worries. Be present in this moment where all is manageable.

We invite you, Angels, into this space of uncertainty. We invite you into our fear and rapid heart rates. We invite you into our lack of time and lack of contentment. We invite you into the home of our heart where the weight of the world has taken up residence. We invite you into our messiness and chaos.

We invite you, Angels, into children's innocent minds, where their fears reside. We invite you to be with us during the influx of bad news and too much information. We invite you here when we feel alone or lacking direction.

We invite you, Angels, into every step where help and healing is needed and welcomed. We invite you, Angels, into this day.

In The World:

Special invitations for the Archangels:

✳ Archangel Michael, defend me, protect me and guide me. Fill me with strength, peace and wisdom.

✳ Archangel Raphael, heal me in mind, body and soul. Fill me with clarity, creativity and health.

✳ Archangel Uriel, light the fires of illumination. Fill me with the energy of transformation and rebirth.

✳ Archangel Gabriel, help me to overcome fear. Communicate messages of clear guidance. Fill me with strength of spirit, love and grace.

✳ Archangel Metatron, shine your light, dazzling like the sun, in my darkest corners. Fill me with a clear connection with the divine.

In The Heart:

✳ I am always guided and guarded by the divine presence of angels. They help me to release my fears to the power of love.

The Relief of Impermanence

I flow with ease and grace through the constant change in my life.

After talking about death with hospice patients, I often entertain thoughts of my own transition. It may seem heavy on the surface, but actually, it's a relief to be reminded that everything is impermanent. Life will go on after we have gone, and knowing this while we're still here can really lighten our burden.

Last week during my hospice volunteer time, I had a patient confess that she felt as if nothing would be changed by her death. Yes, a few friends and family members would miss her, but the world would keep spinning pretty much as usual. I assured her that her energy had already changed the world and would be part of it forever. There, there, dear.

But wait! She brings up an essential perspective. If we're not in charge of anything truly permanent, why are we pulling our hair out over all these details? *Because our minds are in control.* Shouldn't we put our focus on enjoying the precious moments of this life while we're here? *Absolutely.* Shouldn't we be stressing less and loving more? *You got it.*

That takes a lot of rocks out of the backpack. Feeling lighter. So today we delight in a few affirmations, noting the joys of impermanence.

In The World:

* Instead of resisting change, I flow with the blessings and notice the gifts.

* Instead of controlling, I unclench my fists and let go of the outcome.

* Instead of being in charge, I surrender to the divine wisdom of ease and grace.

* Instead of losing my balance, I maintain a spiritual practice to stay centered in the challenges of my life.

* Instead of being angry or regretful, I am compassionate and forgiving.

* Instead of holding on to the darkness, I release it and open to all that is loving and light.

In The Heart:

* I flow with ease and grace through the constant change in my life. I relax, ask for guidance, listen for direction and respond from a place of love.

~¥~

Lovey and Dovey

You are loved, valuable, blessed, beautiful, enough and worthy—
every day of the year.

Once mourning doves fall in love, they vow to stay together for life. When Maya was small, upon learning this, she named a pair of mourning doves Lovey and Dovey. Well, this morning, a new Lovey and Dovey are visiting outside the window, reminding me of what I'd rather forget—that Valentine's Day is coming.

For twosomes across the land, Valentine's Day is a chance to express love for each other through greeting card sentiments, flowers, chocolates, a special dinner and time set aside for Just We Two. The Loveys and Doveys pair off and enter their own world of love, sweet love.

So what happens to Lovey on Valentine's Day when Dovey is off in another field?

I'll tell you what happens. Come to think of it, she's totally fine. In fact, better than fine. She is perfectly capable of buying her own chocolates and flowers, and she absolutely loves the idea of making it a special night of self-care. Right. That's what Lovey is going to do. She's going to make it a night to remember the love that she's made of every single day of the year. Lovey does not need a holiday to know just how loved—and how lovable—she is.

Lovey knows her worth and she honors her unique gifts by taking care of herself, mind, body and soul. She does this so that the love within her can flow freely from source energy to the world. It's a pretty big job.

Lovey wishes Dovey a lifetime of peace and love in the other field—then thinks no more about it. Lovey is busy radiating love to fields all over the planet.

In The World:

* If you find yourself solo on Valentine's Day, make it a special day for you. Ask yourself what you need and respond to your inner knowing. Treat yourself to something special and lavish abiding love on the beautiful soul that you are.

In The Heart:

* I am loved, valuable, blessed, beautiful, enough and worthy—every day of the year.

Happy Sailing

Love is the wind in the sails of the soul.

You, my friend, are a boat, and not just any boat. You are a beautiful sailboat with sails up, ready to catch the wind. The boat is your body, offering protection from the water and containing you as you make your way through the ocean of this day. The sails are your soul, moving you in the right direction, propelling you on the path to your most adventurous life lessons.

You might be facing clear, open waters, or maybe choppy seas or a full-blown storm. Yikes. But no matter what your beautiful sailboat faces today, it can be an amazing day when your sails are filled with the wind of love. And yours already are.

It's easy to drift off course when we fill up on too much daily news and social media where the images and stories paint a seascape of fear. We see the ocean differently though the eyes of love, which is the most important thing we will do today. It's what we're here for. Love is the endless power behind all creation and the gentle essence of our radiant spirit.

Love is the wind in the sails of the soul.

It is not where we are going or how fast we get there that gives this day worth. It is how much we are able to radiate love to everyone who crosses our path, no matter who they are or what we are trying to get done. Love is what a successful day is built upon.

If we could lift up above our lives and see as the angels see, we would see that love is all that shines through the haze of humanity. The love of our soul is all we really leave behind. Happy sailing!

In The World:

* Just for today, speak only loving words and think only loving thoughts, taking a break from negativity, complaint and constant media.

* Refrain from judgment, offering compassion to all beings.

In The Heart:

* Today, all of my thoughts and words are empowered by love. I leave behind the light of love in all of my travels.

Love Letter to St. Valentine

Love is always the answer.

Dear St. Valentine: You, my dear, have captured my heart with your steadfast faith, limitless love and unfortunate beheading. Now we live in a brighter world where today, in honor of you, true loves will be showered with flowers and chocolates. It seems we got the better deal.

Although your life remains quite the mystery, some stories tell us that you were a priest or bishop who met your gruesome end in Rome on this very day back in the third century. You found yourself imprisoned by following your heart and illegally marrying lovers in the church.

Then there is the tale of you restoring sight to the blind daughter of your jailer. It seems you had an unwavering belief in doing what we must in the name of love, regardless of the consequences. When it comes to love, you didn't hold back and you didn't back down. And you paid the ultimate price. What appears to be an airy-fairy holiday in your name down here on earth may have more depth beneath the surface than it first seems.

I like to imagine that you believed in the magic of love. I like to imagine that you knew there were no conditions to love's generosity. I like to imagine that you elevated love as the most beautiful and the sweetest gift ever given. Maybe the flowers and chocolates aren't such lightweight symbols after all; the beautiful and the sweet gifts of love.

The big ideals that you contemplated before you gave your life are only beginning to dawn on me, dear Valentine. That it's imperative we follow the heart. That it's honorable to value our beliefs as sacred. That we can actually love our enemies and their families. That amidst all her contradictions and complications, no matter what the question is, love is always the answer.

Thanks for showing us what is means to be someone's Valentine.

With all my love. <3

In The World:

✳ Today, celebrate the beautiful and sweet blessings of love.

In The Heart:

✳ I believe in the magic of love and the unconditional gifts of love's generosity.

FEBRUARY 15

Compassion in the Ambulance

We are one family, made of love.

I had been sick for weeks with relentless internal bleeding from a uterine fibroid. My scheduled surgery was still a week off, and I was trying to power through my days, anemic and determined. I looked like the walking dead. Then I fainted and actually looked like the dead dead.

In the ambulance I left my body.

I was hovering outside myself, over the young EMT's shoulder, watching her as she tried to set up an IV in my left arm. She was panicking. "I can't get a vein! I can't find anything! We're losing her!"

In the clarity of pure consciousness, I had an overwhelming flood of compassion for her. I could feel her distress as if it were mine and was filled with empathy. I was overflowing with an incredible love and wanted to console her, to tell her everything would be alright. Years later, I can still feel my compassion for her.

Isn't it interesting that in spirit form, our thoughts are not of ourselves first but of others? I wasn't thinking, *Hurry up, you fool! I'm dying here!* Instead, I wanted it to work out so it would be well for her also. She and I were one. I was filled with the greatest love imaginable.

This experience confirmed my belief that our essence is made of light, beauty, kindness, love, generosity. In order to love one another, we need only to sweep off the dust of our everyday lives and look under the veil.

We are one family, made of love.

In The World:

* Move through the world as a being of unconditional love. Be reminded of the light that you are made of, and you will shine your love in all of the dark places—and on all of the people—that need your light today.

In The Heart:

* I am made of light and love, and share uplifting energy with all who cross my path and my mind today.

Winter Faith

Everything is unfolding in its perfect time.

If you are waking within, feeling the stir of a new beginning but not yet at the actualization of the dream, today is a good day to have Winter Faith. New beginnings stir in the mind, body and soul before they ever break ground in our outer lives.

They start with faith in possibilities. They start with small steps and big dreams. They start with a knowing that you *can* do this. They start with a belief in yourself and in the seeds you have been planting and nurturing with love through the dark days of winter.

Sometimes we ration kindness toward ourselves, basking in the rewards of contentment only when we feel we have accomplished something tangible. It is during these times, when no rewards are visible, that we need our kindness and inner support most of all.

Last week, after two isolated winter months in the cabin, I wrote myself a note. Higher self to earth self. It addressed me as a kind friend: "Be patient. You have all the time you need. Your work is meaningful, and you are being guided by a powerful connection with the divine. Enjoy the journey and the questions. There is no race or struggle. This is only a path of love." I read it every morning.

Today, let's look at our dreams and our creativity in a new way. Let's believe in the germinating of ideas. Let's be patient as we create space for growth. Let's get comfortable not having all of the answers yet. Let's reach for an understanding that allows us to be grateful even during the time of no tangible results. Let's open to Winter Faith and see the void, too, as sacred time.

In The World:

✳ Hold strong to an unshakable belief in your dreams and be gentle with yourself in their time of gestation. Believe that everything happens in its perfect time and that you are where you are meant to be.

✳ Write yourself a note, higher self to earth self. Tell yourself in kind, loving words what you most need to know.

In The Heart:

✳ I have the heart of patience and the soul of faith. I believe that everything is unfolding for me in its perfect time.

꧁

Forgiveness

Free the soul. Open the heart. Release the body. Give the gift.
Invoke the grace. Validate the good. Embrace the peace.

Over the years I have created a lot of memes on the art of forgiveness in the process of trying to figure it out myself. During the entire birthing of Every Day Spirit—the app, as well as the daily social media posts and the website—I have been making my way through the landmines of marital separation and have only recently arrived in a little home of my own. It's been a road—oh yes it has.

The actions that brought me here changed my world as I knew it and gave me a golden opportunity to look at forgiveness from every angle. I found myself wondering if there was a way around it, an option to do it part way and still get to hold a little grudge, because after all, I was the victim, right?

Nope. By holding on to my hurt, pain and anger, I was doing more harm to myself than anything that had happened in the marriage. By not fully forgiving, I was interfering with my own growth and interrupting my own healing. Shards of hate, anger, fear and retribution remained in my heart and their presence within was making me into someone that I did not want to be.

I came to realize that forgiveness was not an action I had to take, but an attitude I wanted to adopt. I didn't have to do it; it was the next best step to healing. Not only did the change of attitude free my soul from the negative storyline, but my heart seemed to open to even more compassion, love and peace than I ever dreamed possible. Forgiveness was an amazing gift—to me.

In The World:

✳ Make the effort to understand the art of forgiveness, discovering articles and books that resonate with your beliefs. Take gentle steps toward forgiveness and freedom from past drama as you are ready.

✳ Replace anger thoughts of past transgressions with calming affirmations. *I am strong and safe. I will be guided to the right actions at the right time. All will be well.*

In The Heart:

✳ I have the power to choose to forgive and release myself from the pain of the past. I have the strength to forgive freely and fully.

~ ¥ ~

Ahimsa

From the deepest valley to the sky above, let's cover the world with love.

The other day at a busy eye doctor's office, a woman ahead of me at the reception desk said in broken English that she needed help understanding her bill. In the most compassionate way, the receptionist took her aside and explained everything slowly, respectfully and clearly. Although the line was growing, there was not a note of impatience in her voice.

As I was leaving, in front of me was the same receptionist walking an elderly man all the way to his car. Chatting joyfully with him, she exuded pure love. I waited for her to gently close his car door and I told her what a beautiful person she was and how she changed several lives today by her kindness. She smiled shyly and said quietly, "That's just who I am."

I was reminded of an ancient little Sanskrit word that takes on the depth of the receptionist's love. *Ahimsa* translates to "non-injury," and it is a key virtue based on the belief that we are all sparks of divine love so to harm any living thing would be to harm all living things. When we take away all violence, what we find is the essence of abiding love. Gandhi describes it this way: "True *ahimsa* should mean a complete freedom from ill-will and anger and hate, and an overflowing love for all." Yes, on the soul level, that's just who we are.

The purest love flows up from the endless well that resides in all of us. By walking gently on the earth, taking care to harm as few of God's creatures as possible, we discover the great love that cannot possibly refrain from spreading lovingkindness to all who cross our path.

In The World:

∗ Walk through today with a gentle step, spreading pure love while doing no harm.

∗ The yogic sage Patanjali described an eightfold path to enlightenment of which the *Yamas,* ethical codes of conduct, are the first step. *Ahimsa* is the first *Yama.* If you are drawn to yoga, you might be enriched by learning these guidelines to a peaceful, loving and enlightened life.

In The Heart:

∗ By a spark of divine love, I am connected to all other beings. With a kind and loving heart, I take care not to harm any living thing.

Be at Peace

A calm connection is just a moment away.

Be at peace, and let go of all attachments to outcomes.

Be at peace, and know that love always lives right here, right now.

Be at peace, you are doing the best you can in this moment.

Be at peace, and let the world spin without you.

Be at peace, and breathe, just breathe.

Be at peace, releasing stress, anxiety and worry.

Be at peace, allowing each moment to enter without resistance.

Be at peace, shoulders soft, heart open, spine aligned with heaven.

Be at peace, knowing you are never alone.

Be at peace, and call on angelic assistance for any task.

Be at peace, and listen for guidance.

Be at peace, imagining the highest good for all.

Be at peace, and make an offering of your day.

Be at peace, and feel how infinitely loved you are.

In The World:

✻ When you have reached the bottom of the well and there is no more for you to give, or when stress has robbed you of your composure, remember that a calm connection is just a moment away. Stop. Breathe. Be at peace.

✻ Step back for a moment of perspective, bringing serenity to your mind and body, welcoming your soul wisdom. You've got this. Peace. Love. Joy.

In The Heart:

✻ I am peaceful. I am calm. I am eternal. Today, divine grace protects me, strengthens me and leads me on my way.

Date Night with the Soul

May I quiet my words and listen. May I calm my thoughts and be. May I soften my heart and open. May I still my soul and receive.

When I sit down to meditate, the noise of the world can be insanely jarring. My ears are ringing, my thoughts are galloping, my body is buzzing. I can be so filled with motion that I require a transition, a place of in-between in which I gently put on the brakes and roll to a stop. To that end, I sit for a few minutes, breathing in deeply, and exhaling longer than my inhale to remind my body that it's okay to slow down, and to announce to my mind that she is going to be offline for a bit. I feel my mind resisting—*Can't you see I'm busy here?*—so I must tell her that she can have my plans and concerns back just as soon as I'm finished meditating. She usually behaves after that.

Yes, there is Her and there is Me. There is the Little i, and the Big I. There is the Thinker and the Observer. There is the judgmental, controlling Ego Mind, and the limitless, unbound Soul. Meditation is when the Soul plugs into the source energy and recharges so it can intuitively lead the Mind.

When I don't give time to Me, my Mind takes control of everything and powers through in a Blitz of Doing. I become too serious and sometimes, seriously off track. There is infinitely more fun and flow under the insightful direction of the Soul.

So now that we've decided who's boss, I just watch my breath flow in...and out...gently floating a mantra or phrase over the top. I breathe in. I breathe out. In. Out. It feels like a very cool mini-retreat.

When my Mind gets unruly and tries to jump in, I tap her on her little head with the wand, call it what it is—*thinking*—and go back to the wide open Soul space. This little tapping game is like gymnastics for the Mind, training her to chill while the Soul gets a date night. After I'm finished, we say goodbye at the Door of Noisy Thoughts, and I know that I bring a greater piece of Me, and of love, into the world.

In The World:

✳ Keep up your daily meditation dates with your Soul. You will fall in love again and again.

In The Heart:

✳ I make time for the sweet pleasure of finding peace within.

Unfailing Strength

Live with gratitude for the gift of time.

Last week, my friend Olga sent me a beautiful essay that was written by one of her former students, Gabriela, who was diagnosed with cancer. As a 38-year-old mother of six, she broke down under the weight of her thoughts; imagining her husband and children living on without her. The future was inconceivable and her anxiety going forward was unbearable.

A friend of Gabriela's shared with her the following passage from St. Francis de Sales: "Do not look forward to what might happen tomorrow; the same Everlasting Father who cares for you today, will take care of you tomorrow and every day. He will either shield you from suffering or He will give you unfailing strength to bear it. Be at peace, then, and put aside all anxious thoughts and imaginings."

She pinned it on her fridge and read it every morning. As she meditated on the words, she asked that her fears about the future be lifted and to have faith in what she could not understand with her rational mind.

Eventually, peace came over her. She found ways to stay in the moment and to appreciate, with gratitude, the blessing of each day. Gabriela reordered her priorities to spend more time with her family at home. In her words: "Most importantly, I also learned to live day by day. I learned to savor each moment, not to dwell on the past, not to grow anxious about the future, but to appreciate the simple, small moments of my daily life and to trust that with God, there can be peace amidst distress."

When we are faced with a frightening diagnosis, we are also given the chance to change the way we think about our lives. It offers a precious chance to surrender in faith to the divine and to live with gratitude for the gift of time.

This lesson is ours, right here and now, even without the diagnosis.

In The World:

✳ As an extension of our call to peace from yesterday, offer your greatest trials and fears to the divine. Have faith that you will find peace within your challenges. Savor each moment with gentle gratitude and courageous trust.

In The Heart:

✳ Today I surrender my challenges to the divine and live with gratitude for the gift of time.

The Garden of the Future

Every act of kindness plants a seed.

Thoughts are energy, and as we learned in physics class, energy stays around forever: It is neither created nor destroyed. What they didn't tell us was that our thoughts have great power, germinating into new buds that grow endlessly into the future. We all change the world whether we intend to or not. And we always change the world for the better when we plant the seeds of kind thoughts and words.

As our spiritual awareness grows, we pay more deliberate attention to our thoughts and actions because we are aligning more and more with our shared humanity. In connection with all beings, compassion is our most natural state of consciousness. We come from one love, so to lift up one of us is to lift up all of us.

It begins with the smallest offering of a smile or an encouraging word. A seed is planted and paid forward, perhaps from hand to hand as the result of a single kindness shared. Our everyday actions of love propagate and spread infinitely.

Today each of us contributes to the garden of the future. Even if we don't see the results of our actions, no kindness, no act of love, is ever wasted.

We leave the world a more beautiful, a more colorful and a more loving place when we sow kindness generously and freely.

Because every act of kindness plants a seed.

In The World:

* Sow kindness liberally today. Keep your heart open for opportunities to share a kind word or action, no matter how small.

* Include yourself in your acts of kindness.

* Look for nothing in return. Give with an open hand and share with an open heart.

In The Heart:

* Through generous acts of kindness and love, I sow never-ending seeds in the garden of a loving future.

Lessons from a Fire-Breathing Bull

Be in awe of creatures great and small.

I crossed the one-lane bridge and caught site of the enormous black bull who lives in the bucolic field next to a lake on Hunters Road. Walking up the hill, I wonder, *What is your name, Big Bull?* In rhythm with my steps, I roll over possible names for him. He needs a regal name. A big name for a big guy. A name for the ages. *Abraham. That's your name.*

Standing at the split rail fence I call him bravely but sweetly. "Abraham! Abraham! Come here, honey! Come on, boy!" He stares at me, then slowly and thoughtfully the ginormous bull lumbers my way, male parts sashaying with each thunderous step. I stand my ground, holding on to the fence until Abraham is standing directly in front of me within arm's reach. I can see his beautiful brown eyes with hundreds of eyelashes over each one. His body is over three feet wide, his head towers over mine. Surely this is the biggest animal I've ever been this close to.

I'm not sure at what point I lose my senses, but I am overtaken by the sudden desire to reach out and pet Abraham on the head. He has a little tuft of curls where his third eye would be, and I think, *Oh! I must touch that!* (So much for inner wisdom.) I reach out my hand to give him a little pet, and he instantly inhales and exhales with such hurricane force that—like a dragon—a cloud of steam comes from his gigantic nostrils! Straight out of Harry Potter. I scream and jump back (I have no wand), rolling backwards down the hill. *Oh, Abraham.*

You might be thinking that the moral of the story is: Do not try to touch a bull on the third eye. Good one. I'm also trying a few others on for size: 1. Our uniqueness is what makes life an adventure of discovery and open-mindedness. 2. Don't assume. Because one thinks they are offering love does not mean it will be received as such. 3. Respect all living things and be humble in their presence. 4. Always carry a wand. Since that time, whenever I pass Abraham, I send him a blessing and continue on up the street, marveling at my insanity—and his incredible beauty.

In The World:

✳ All creatures, from the bulls to the bees, need our support, love and protection to thrive and survive. Assist in ways that resonate with your heart to respect their uniqueness and protect their habitats.

In The Heart:

✳ I honor the miraculous design of every living inhabitant of the earth.

꜀ ꜀

The Art of an Apology

An apology is an act of grace, a soul truth, a beautiful thing.

I vividly remember making my first real apology as an adult. I was in the car with a friend and as he was talking, I was working on how to phrase my wrongdoing. His sentences were like double Dutch jump ropes—I couldn't find a way in. I couldn't blurt something out into dead air or thread it into a light-hearted conversation. As we crossed the 14th Street Bridge into D.C., I was losing my breath and my nerve.

Then, a light bulb. I needed a "bridge" line to introduce my apology. It's funny that I can't remember what I was apologizing for, but I remember the way I figured out how I was going to do it. These bridge lines are an essential part of my communication toolbox to this day.

An apology is an act of grace, a soul truth, a beautiful thing. Hard, but beautiful. It asks us to get humble, and (oh, no) vulnerable. It asks us to accept our imperfections and the inevitable screw ups that come with being human. It asks us to put someone before us. It asks us to lay down our pride and confess honestly. It asks us to take responsibility for the way our actions feel to others. If it is sincere, an apology is a non-negotiable part of our spiritual integrity and a bonding thread of light between one soul and another.

Being forgiven is not the goal of an apology. We apologize because we can see with new and more compassionate eyes that what we have done has caused harm and we are truly sorry. If the art of an apology does not come easily to you, join the party and start practicing. It's one of the most beautiful actions on earth.

In The World:

✳ Try out a few possible bridge lines to introduce your apology: "I'd like to tell you something important. Is this an okay time?" "I've done something I don't feel great about and I want to tell you about it." "I feel badly about what I said yesterday."

✳ Then without excuses and with heartfelt love, jump right in with the naked words: "I am so sorry I..."

In The Heart:

✳ I apologize from the heart and embody an openness that is honest, freeing and healing for all.

The Same Sky

The darker the night, the brighter the stars.

I was forty weeks pregnant and a few hours this side of my due date. My doctor's office in Vienna, Austria was humming with the polite buzz of German and my long, flowered dress made an irreverent statement in the sea of fitted black and brown. Funny the things we remember.

After I was called in, a flurry of worried hands took turns on the Doppler. Then the world stopped. Time. Stood. Still. I could see my doctor shaking her head. "I'm sorry..." I heard only clanging in my head.

The next many years saw me drowning in an ocean of crushing grief. And strangely, some unexpected moments of hope. First came the relentless search for God. If my child was *there*, I wanted to know exactly where *there* was. I searched until I found her through the veil, within me, in all things beautiful. Next came compassion. I was now in fiery solidarity with all loss—great, small, different—these were my new people. I understood more about the precious nature of humanity and was united with all suffering beings.

Small talk and surface living burned away along with my old self. The depth of my grief was the darkest of nights, yet my capacity for joy seemed to reach the same distance in the other direction, to the stars. Life was an ocean of feelings that words could not touch. One step at a time in what was an eternity, I inched toward trusting life again.

There are dark nights of loss and dark nights of the soul. Dark nights of betrayal and dark nights of fear. And in that night, the stars will beam their light and with it, the grace of an insight, an illumination with a prompt to feel, to grow, to change, to be in awe, that would not be felt or seen were it not for the darkness. Look up toward the stars. We are all there looking up at the same sky, shoulder-to-shoulder, never alone.

In The World:

* We all have our own path through grief. This holy road is not linear but one of blinding darkness and flashes of stars. Be patient with your heart.

In The Heart:

* I am the guardian of my own unique grief process. I am patient as I come to understand who I am becoming. I feel everything with an open heart and know that I am never alone.

Faith is Winning

May my faith be stronger than my fear.

I have lots of faith. I also have lots of fear. The fears tug at me relentlessly. Real ones like the illness of a family member and finances, and not-so-real ones like slipping hopelessly behind in some imaginary race to get through the piles on my desk.

But on most days, faith is winning.

Not by default, but because each morning I roll out of bed at dawn to lock in practices that I can pull out of my back pocket when fear strikes.

Each day I remind myself to watch for the sacred woven through the small moments. Each evening I give thanks for the divine order and its perfect timing. Every hour in between, I remind myself that I am not alone in this. These things seem to shore up my faith stockpiles and straighten up my shoulders a bit.

Faith is not really an underdog when we realize that we have a pretty strong faith practice already. Most of us don't have much fear about waking up or breathing, right? We have faith that we will be here to open our eyes in the morning. We have faith that air will fill our lungs without too much conscious effort. We take for granted this daily testament of trust in the universe.

Faith doesn't have to wrestle fear to the ground or banish it from the kingdom. It just needs to have the upper hand. And we have everything we need to make faith the victor.

Use your spiritual practice as a candle of faith in the dark room of fear, and voila! Fear is illuminated into obsolescence.

In The World:

✳ When worries threaten to rob your peace of mind today, call on the faith tools of your spiritual practice. Enlist prayer, affirmations and patience. Activate thoughts of trust and light; surrender to a higher plan, and they will gradually illuminate the situation. Stay with the practice until you feel the shift. Fake it 'til you make it if need be. Fear doesn't know the difference.

In The Heart:

✳ I focus my energy on positive outcomes for the highest good of all. My faith is stronger than my fear.

Just Play Monopoly

Find joy in small things.

In 2010, a historic snowstorm dumped more than two feet of snow on the D.C. area, and we became frozen in time. I rejoiced in what seemed to be a windfall of freedom. Maya found Nirvana in a series of cancelled school days and in the prospect of not having to work so hard for so many hours a day. It was like an impromptu vacation in our own home.

Oh, the gift of unscheduled time.

As several days went by with still no school opening in sight, I began to see projects in the house that I "needed" to do. It seemed that the house was suddenly begging for a serious facelift. I wanted to scrub the kitchen floor, wipe down the cabinets, clean baths, set up the basement for recording projects. My list gathered more steam to include painting the baseboards, organizing files and practicing piano. I found myself feeling quite busy in our formerly relaxed vacation house in the snow.

On the third Snowmageddon afternoon, Maya made a proposition. "Mom, let's play a game of Monopoly." Without missing a beat, I said, "Okay, honey, but I have to get some things done first. I need to put some laundry in, vacuum upstairs and..."

She interrupted me with an annoyed expression and said, "You know, Mom, no one would care if you didn't 'get things done.' None of the things you think you have to do really need to be done *now*."

Don't you hate it when your kid nails you? I had made a list and given priority to crossing things off. And it dawned on me in that moment that she probably wouldn't ask me to play Monopoly many more times. It was fun for her today, on a snow day, with none of her friends around. Suddenly it became clear that there was nothing more important in the world.

We should just play Monopoly. And find joy in small things.

In The World:

* Be where you are today. That's where the joy is.

In The Heart:

* I am flexible with my plans, following love's lead. With lightness in my heart, I am present for joy in the small moments of this day.

The Computer Coma

I surrender my small plans to divine order.

When we call on the divine for ease and grace in all circumstances, we are met with support. Trouble for me is, I lose consciousness and forget to ask.

My daughter tells me that when I'm at the computer, I'm in a coma. I'm staring so rabidly at the screen and my focus is so white hot that fire comes out of the top of my head. Not really, but she can stand at the door and ask me a question, and I don't hear, don't move and don't even flinch.

Then comes the exasperated, "Blink twice if you can hear me talking."

When I get up after hours of making art, updating the app or even answering email, I feel disoriented. *Where was I?* The more disturbing thought is, *Why did I try to muscle out all that work without constantly calling on the divine for assistance as I went along?*

So here's what I do now. I set my phone alarm for every hour as I work. When the alarm rings, I bring myself to the present moment and surrender my work to the divine.

My prayer usually starts with a surprised, *Hey there!* As in, *Wow, God, are you still here?* I get my bearings and continue, *I know you are assisting me in all my work and bringing light through my hands, my eyes and my thoughts. With your help, everything happens with ease and grace. Please send extra angels for... Thank you!* And bam. I'm back to work.

What I surrender is my small self, the one that thinks she's in control and has all the answers. It doesn't feel like I'm giving up power but instead releasing control and allowing the power of a much greater force to step in and take the lead.

The results of teamwork are remarkable.

In The World:

✳ Set your phone alarm for every hour while you work. Take a minute each hour to ask for companionship on your daily round.

In The Heart:

✳ Wisdom and grace from my higher power guides all my actions today.

Leap Day Prayer

May this day be especially blessed.

May this day be especially blessed.

May this day be grounded in the radiant energy of love.

May this day use my gifts for the work of the divine.

May this day be the best day of the rest of my life.

May this day bring the opportunity to lift someone up with kindness.

May this day remind me that I am unique, worthy and irreplaceable.

May this day flow with ease and grace through every activity.

May this day be one of peace and patience.

May this day be a constant prayer of gratitude, no matter what I am given.

May this day bring moments of hope, joy and laughter.

May this day give me the chance to let someone know they are loved.

May this day reflect my faith in the perfect imperfection of all events.

May this day find me humble in my thoughts and words.

May this day be especially blessed. Amen.

In The World:

✳ What you pour into this precious and unique Leap Day, you will receive back in a cup of beauty. Pour in your most magnificent self.

In The Heart:

✳ I step out into this day knowing that infinite love is mine in every moment, and that I am especially blessed in all things.

March
Be present.
Let the day flow with grace.
Expect joy. Be positive.
Serve with compassion.
Speak only kindness.
Impart only love.
Never forget you're not alone.
Give thanks for everything.
See goodness in others. mary davis

EVERY DAY SPIRIT .NET

March Blessings

Be present. Be here. Today, we can guide our thoughts back to the present moment with gentle focus and live fully right where we are.

Let the day flow with grace. Grace flows through us easily when we are in tune with the subtle voice of intuition. Open and listen for guidance.

Expect joy. Be positive. Imagine a fulfilling day unfolding, in which we accomplish much and experience joy in the process. Welcome the light.

Serve with compassion. Acts of service when performed with love lend immeasurable light to our day. Be watchful for ways to serve.

Speak only kindness. Speak only kind words. Think only kind thoughts. Be kind to yourself and to those who cross your path or your mind.

Impart only love. Send out all thoughts and words on the wings of love so that we may love one another, love ourselves, love the unlovable.

Never forget you're not alone. Let's remind ourselves often today that we are always supported, guided and unconditionally loved as we are.

Give thanks for everything. Gratitude will shift the perspective of the day from one of lack to one of abundance. Give constant thanks.

See goodness in others. Each of us has a soul that is made of beauty and love. Assume the best in others so they may rise to their highest light.

Presence

May your path be clear before you. May you be at peace with yesterday. May you be present in the moment for the blessings of this day.

For just a moment, let's set down the burden of the future. Let's take that box, with all of its concerns and dreams, close the lid and set it down. Now imagine a clear path before you, illuminated in brilliant white light, where the perfect experiences manifest for your future.

And for just a moment, let's set down the weight of the past. Take that box, with all of its regret and sadness, close the lid and set it down. Now looking back, bless your experiences, surround them in brilliant white light and allow yourself to be at peace with yesterday.

Here we are, present in the moment for the blessings of this day.

In *The Power of Now*, Eckhart Tolle explains, "Unease, anxiety, tension, stress, worry—all forms of fear—are caused by too much future, and not enough presence. Guilt, regret, resentment, grievances, sadness, bitterness, and all forms of non-forgiveness are caused by too much past, and not enough presence."

In other words: It's not possible to be completely present and worried about the future. It's not possible to be completely present and regretful about the past.

Today, let's leave those boxes alone and be here now. Let's stay in the present as it unfolds and experience the wonder and the gift of each moment.

In The World:

✳ Practice presence by taking any routine activity and giving it your fullest attention. When washing the dishes, driving your car or making coffee, notice your actions with all of your senses.

✳ Notice how your inner peace grows along with your ability to be present.

In The Heart:

✳ My path is clear before me. I am at peace with yesterday. I am present in the moment for the blessings of this day.

The Circle of Love

Lift up someone else and you will lift yourself.

We can be the kindness that reminds someone that the world is a loving place. Today, we can be a ray of sun in someone's darkness. Into this day we can weave a simple kindness that can gently ease the pain of another while bringing a lightness to our own hearts as well.

Through small offerings and acts of kindness, we activate the flow of love from ourselves, into the heart of another and back to our hearts in a circle of divine love without end. Today we can show unconditional love to others that will fill our hearts with love in return.

In The World:

* Lift up others by preparing yourself in the morning for a positive day. Your spiritual practice sets the tone by bringing you home to your highest self.

* Be aware of the energy you bring with you as you leave the house.

* Be generous with compliments to family, co-workers and strangers alike. It only takes a genuine kind word to awaken someone's inner joy.

* Listen well when someone is talking. Consider waiting a little longer today before adding your thoughts. Ask a question that shows your interest.

* Assume everyone comes from a place of love, even when it seems otherwise. When you are present without judgment, you bring out the best in others. Wayne Dyer put it beautifully when he said, "See the light in others and treat them as if that is all you see."

* Smile easily. A smile almost always evokes a return smile and raises the energy of the room.

* Be encouraging to those who are struggling. If you know someone is going through a challenging time, ask about it. Offer some words of support.

In The Heart:

* Today I have the power to lift the spirits of anyone who crosses my path or crosses my mind. I find it easy to spread love and feel the flow of love back into my heart.

Horse Whispering at Dawn

Sometimes silence says it all.

On a frosty morning I woke in near darkness to see that the sun, pregnant with light, was just under the ridge. I heard a silent message that there was something going on in the field, so I wrapped in a blanket and moved to the window. I gasped in awe at the scene.

Three horses were standing in perfect formation on a hill near the house, heads bowed, facing in the direction where the sun would soon rise, totally still. I felt I had been transported to an important ceremony, one of reverence, wisdom and grace. I watched, barely breathing, then in a note of solidarity I sat as near to them as I could—at the kitchen table— and parked my consciousness on the fence next to them. We meditated together. It was as if I was right there. Sounds crazy—I know.

I peeked at the brightening sky, and the moment the first ray of sun broke over the mountain, the horses began to gently stir. Without another thought, I pulled on my rain boots with the blanket still wrapped tightly around me and walked, ever so slowly toward the field. One foot crunched on the frozen leaves. Then I stopped. Then another step, slowly, mindfully, head down, in reverence for the silence of the dawn. I continued my slow march as all three horses stood still watching my approach, grooms on the altar.

I arrived at the fence and looked up. They were walking slowly toward me. Shadow put his head down on the fence, and with arms still enclosed in the blanket, I bowed and put my third eye on his, and stayed, connected like that, joined and still. Ever so slowly, the two other horses put their heads on either side of Shadow. I lifted my hands to the heads of the outer horses and we all four stayed bonded in a silent group hug for minutes. I looked up with grateful tears. No words necessary.

In The World:

* Follow your instincts. Use the gift of silence gained from your meditation practice to allow stillness at times when words seem small.

* Notice something beautiful and receive the beauty in silence.

In The Heart:

* I open my heart to moments of listening, noticing and allowing. I calm my thoughts, still my soul and receive.

Becoming Something Beautiful

Even in the dark soil a seed is becoming something beautiful.

Sometimes we need to be underground before we can bloom. Maybe our life as we know it has unraveled and we are in a dark place, uncertain of our next move, frozen in time, dormant.

When we are in a place of darkness, we put pressure on ourselves—with the help of our loved ones—to be fixed, to snap out of it, to bring our old selves back to life.

The most healing thing we can do in troubled times is to be patient and compassionate with ourselves. Our time in the dormant underground is essential to the bloom. It is not that the darkness has to be fixed, *but it's the darkness that is fixing us.* We just need a little more time in her presence.

Depending upon when a seed is exposed to water, sunlight and warmth, some will germinate very quickly and some will remain dormant for long periods of time. Some seeds, like common vegetable seeds, are immediately ready to germinate. Then there are seeds from a unique lotus plant that are thought to be over two thousand years old and will still germinate—transforming into incredibly beautiful and unique flowers—under the right conditions.

Even in our darkest challenges, before a tiny ray of light shines in, we are already transforming, bursting with the possibility of becoming something brand new. Something authentic. Something bigger. Something lighter. Something unique.

Even in the dark soil a seed is becoming something beautiful.

In The World:

✳ Have patience with yourself today. If you feel stuck—not seeing any outward growth—know that you are growing within and will break ground into the light any day now.

In The Heart:

✳ I am a unique expression of love, and I am patient with myself as I grow at my own pace and in my own time.

~ 〰 ~

The Power of Prayer

Our prayers are always answered. But not always in the ways we expect.

We are always heard—every request, every plea, every note of gratitude, every song of joy. Each and every prayer propels energy toward our intentions in rays of healing light and grace. Our prayers set off an immediate response that conspires to assist. Every prayer arrives safely at its destination. There are no exceptions.

With our endless needs for healing, comfort, love, guidance and protection, it may seem that prayer has limited power. We don't see results as fast as we would like. Plans do not unfold in the ways we expect. We want the kind of miracle that we ourselves imagine.

After a passionate prayer has left our heart, it is powerful beyond our imagining. Energy shifts, grace is unleashed, divine order conspires to assist. It is not given to us to see the plan that is set in motion. Prayers are always answered, but often in ways that we can't fully understand. There may be a higher good at work that does not include perfect healing, ease and calm, or our version of the end result. Our challenges, too, can be part of the plan.

Prayer requires from us a twofold faith: It asks that we wholeheartedly believe that the prayer is heard and answered; and that no matter what answer we receive, the path that follows is for our absolute highest good.

So we send off our intentions and let go, knowing that the prayer we impart has been received and is already manifesting some powerful light in our lives.

In The World:

✳ Always pray with complete focus. A beautiful time for prayer is immediately after meditation when the mind is calm.

✳ Release the idea of a certain result, praying instead for the best possible outcome.

✳ Add the powerful thought that your prayer is *for the highest good of all* or place faith in divine hands with, "Thy will be done."

In The Heart:

✳ My prayers are powerful messengers of light, hope and healing. They are heard and answered in perfect time for the highest good of all.

Road Rage Resolution

Give peace a chance.

There has not been peace on earth in my lifetime, but I'm still holding out hope. Like John Lennon, I'm a dreamer and I believe that one day the world will be as one. Meanwhile, there are concrete ways we can practice peace in our daily lives to bring us closer to the global peace we dream of.

When I was in nursing school, we had classes on communication centered on interviewing sick people under stressful circumstances. That's when I learned the beauty of "I" statements. Used to convey a feeling or belief, it's an easy way to let someone know how they are impacting you or the situation, without placing blame.

For example, you are in the car and your partner explodes into road rage, cursing out another driver. If you say, "You are such an angry driver!" it will feel like an attack and fuel the fire. When you say, "I feel really unsafe when you yell at people while you're driving," you are stating the fact of your feelings. Your partner can't argue with your feelings—they are yours.

Marshall Rosenberg takes it a few steps further in his important teachings on non-violent communication. These steps can be applied in our relationships or in the workplace, and they can lead to conflict resolution even in the most protracted arguments. It won't hurt to try. Give peace a chance.

In The World:

* Non-violent communication has four parts: (1) observations, (2) feelings, (3) needs and (4) requests.

* Using the example above, it might sound something like: (1) *We've been fighting almost every time we take a car ride together. When I hear you yelling at other drivers, I get anxious and angry.* (2) *I feel sad that our time in the car isn't more relaxing.* (3) *I value my peace and have a need for more kindness.* (4) *Would you be willing to stop cursing out other drivers while I'm in the car?*

In The Heart:

* I am contributing to peace on the planet by taking meaningful steps to bring peace into my daily life.

Infinitely Grateful

God, help me to be infinitely grateful for how lucky I am, how much good there is in the world, and how much love I can create. —Maya Davis

Maya wrote this prayer after her high school choir raised up tender hearts of song at a memorial service for the brother of one of their members. Ryan lived on earth for only twenty-two years. He was a unique and beloved soul. His presence lives on through his great love, his beautiful smile and the unspoken reminder that our time here is temporary. We must live our lives in a way that takes nothing for granted.

Ryan's life and Maya's prayer remind us that from a place of infinite gratitude, we can honor this precious day by appreciating all we have been given. We can honor this day by training our eyes on goodness in the world. We can honor this day by giving and receiving love freely and unconditionally.

By living each moment in appreciation and awe, we honor those who have gone before us.

Ryan and so many of our loved ones can't be here today to live out their lives, but we can. They can't offer gratitude for the gift of life, but we can. They can't admire beauty or seek goodness, but we can. They can't give and receive love, but we can.

Let's allow our losses to remind us to live deeply and fully, treating each moment as the precious gift that it is.

In The World:

* Begin the day in the deep, rich soil of appreciation. *Thank you for this most amazing day.*

* Seek out joy, beauty and goodness by noticing it in the simple things that are near you in nature, art, music or a kind face.

* Express your love generously. Say "I love you" often. Shoot off a loving text or email to someone who might need to hear it. Work toward repairing a relationship or patching an argument. Live and love deeply.

In The Heart:

* I am infinitely grateful for the blessings of this precious day. I am generous with my expression of love.

Beautiful Soul

You are not what you have done. You are what you have become.

We are all in the process of coming into alignment with the beautiful perfection of our souls.

We are all in the process of discovering that none of us has a better, purer or bigger soul than another. When we meet up in the afterlife, we will greet each other as divine, radiant, unique reflections of God, perfect as we are.

We are all in the process of remembering who we really are and sweeping off the dust that covers the brilliance, wisdom and joy of the spirit.

We are all in the process of working though lessons that we need to learn for our soul development—lessons learned through joy and pain, dedication and devotion, friendship and love, being and doing.

We are all in the process of becoming. We are always in the midst of change, evolving slowly into greater versions of ourselves, expanding and growing toward an understanding of our essence, which is love.

We are all in the process of realizing who we are at the deepest level and finding joy right here, right now.

So forgive yourself for any past transgressions and turn your thoughts to what you have become.

And have a beautiful day, Beautiful Soul.

In The World:

∗   Release the burdens of past mistakes and seek a constant presence in the moment of now.

∗   Make a plan for moving one aspect of your life into greater alignment with love. Become a higher version of yourself one step at a time.

In The Heart:

∗   I am a beautiful, radiant, unique reflection of divine love.

The Intention of Love

Bless this day with the best of you.

After I had my first daughter, I asked my mother how she did it with four children under the age of six. Her answer surprised me. She said that when you have one child, you give your all to that child—one hundred percent. And when you have four, you still only have one hundred percent, so you give that. And here's the key: You give the best of you and the power of the *intention* of love does the rest.

Imagine a speaker in a large auditorium or a band in a stadium. Everyone, even those standing in the back, receives the impact of the energy coming off the stage. Every person in the place has access to the same intensity of the message because of the intention of the giver.

Even on those days when we feel fractured by the juggling act of work, school, child care, spiritual practice, shopping, cooking, cleaning and keeping up with friends, we have incredible untapped power within. Power that is easy to access.

Our clearest intentions are unleashed in the simplest way—by a mere pause during which our energy is centered and refocused. Even five breaths will open the heart to empower everything that comes after.

We just need to pause, connect with our calm center, then direct it to the next event. When we continue to check in with the source of our love, the intention of love finds its way to the places where we can't always be. It makes up for those moments when we feel that there just isn't enough of us to go around.

Bring the best of your love to this day and know that it is more than enough.

In The World:

* Between activities today, take a short pause to center yourself, open your heart and ask for guidance for the next event. It's not one more thing to do. It's what will make everything else go more smoothly and gracefully.

In The Heart:

* I am peacefully centered and bring the best of myself to this day. The intention of my love goes exactly where it is needed most.

Life Is Fun

May I approach all work in the spirit of joy and creativity.

Whenever we put our attention on what we are doing in the present moment, we are living our lives fully. Conversely, when we are wishing we were somewhere else, we are letting our lives slip by while our minds are off in another place. Right here, right now, in simple things, is where the joy is.

Buddhist nun Pema Chodron encourages us with this practical advice: "Constantly apply cheerfulness, if for no other reason than because you are on this spiritual path. Have a sense of gratitude to everything, even difficult emotions, because of their potential to wake you up." (Those in the midst of acute grief and pain get to take a pass here.)

Applying cheerfulness is merely a matter of showing up to all of our tasks with love and a lightness of spirit. We don't have to do a Sound of Music twirl through the horse field or living room, although that might be helpful. Put on music that you love. Be a domestic goddess and clean the house as if for an honored guest. Slow down as you do the yard work with an eye for the miracles of nature. Bring a positive attitude and a smile to the office.

We are all weighed down by our lists and duties, homework and yard work, housekeeping and bookkeeping. "When you discard arrogance and complexity...sooner or later you will discover that simple, childlike, and mysterious secret known to those of the Uncarved Block: Life is Fun," offers Benjamin Hoff in his classic book, *The Tao of Pooh*.

Life is fun. Really? It's all in the way we think about it.

It's about applying cheerfulness, being present and being grateful. It's about doing small things with great love. All else becomes lighter. On the journey of today, let's find creative ways to remember that our souls are joyous and that life is fun.

In The World:

* Today, bring yourself back to the present moment and to your spiritual path by applying cheerfulness and gratitude.

* Smile inside and out. Create fun ways of thinking about your work.

In The Heart:

* I approach all work in the spirit of joy and creativity.

The Soul Remains Whole

May God bless my brokenness.

To add to the joy conversation from yesterday: it's okay not to be okay. We live in a culture that puts a priority on happiness, and if we are not happy, something must be wrong that needs to be made right to return us to the correct state of happiness.

But joy and sorrow don't live in separate worlds.

Some wounds run deep and can't be healed with any fast and efficient therapy. They take untethered time and an open heart; patience and self-love. Sometimes there is no closure in the healing process, yet joy and sorrow find a way to mingle, co-existing within us in a deep, rich mix of humanity.

During times of grief or challenge, in our anger, vulnerability and humility, we might feel that God is ever so near—or completely absent. Crisis might drive us to rely heavily on spirituality, or to feel abandoned by it. In those dark nights of the soul, remember this:

The spirit is never broken.

While seasons of pain may leave us feeling as if we are shattered into a thousand tiny pieces that will never be put back together again, the soul always remains whole. We may become a new version of ourselves, but on the soul level, we are always complete and made of love.

In The World:

❋ Keep facing the light. Even when it is a long way off, know it is there.

❋ Take small steps toward integrating your pain into your new life. Have patience with yourself and be exceptionally kind to yourself.

❋ Be an advocate for what you need from family and friends. It is yours to experience in whatever way you choose. There's no right way. Just your way.

In The Heart:

❋ I have all the grace I need for whatever life asks of me. I face the light and take steps in the direction of healing as I am able.

Universe at Work

One breath. One hour. One day. One miracle at a time.

My friend Lyndy is leaving in three weeks on a cross-country spiritual journey. She called last night, worried and wondering how she was going to manage to get ready with all that was going on in her life. In addition to the trip planning, she is also selling a property, sifting through the remnants of a divorce, making a financial retirement plan and working as a caretaker.

Sounds familiar, right? At some point or another, most of us are immobilized by the daunting weight of daily demands.

This time, however, the answer she needed was right in the house. Last year when I visited Lyndy, she gave me some Abraham-Hicks CDs to listen to in the car on the long drive home. So I reminded her of an inspiring story that Esther Hicks relates about a day when she was out of sorts with a long to-do list. She was strongly prompted by her wise guides to make two lists.

On one side, she was to list only what absolutely had to get done that day. On the other side, she would list everything else. She would be in charge of the "today" side, and the universe (God) would be in charge of the other side. Off she went to accomplish her side of the list.

Esther did this each day, revising the lists as she accomplished things, until she realized that by the time she turned her attention to the items on the universe side, they had resolved themselves or had very simple, ease-and-grace solutions.

After dividing up her lists last night, Lyndy saw that the trip planning was robbing her peace, and if she could concentrate on that for a few days on the "today" side, she would have more focus for her other duties before the trip. And surely the universe is already working out miracles and creating resolutions for their side of the list.

In The World:

✳   Break it down. Make your lists. Your part on the left, God's part on the right. Do your work and allow the universe to work miracles in perfect time.

In The Heart:

✳   I handle one breath, one hour and one day, one miracle at a time. I am in the constant flow of spiritual assistance.

Stand Like a Mountain

I align with the divine.

There's a small thing we can do right in this moment that will make a big difference in our health, our confidence, our open-heartedness and our spiritual energy: Sit up straight.

Even if it's a little uncomfortable at first, be mindful of your posture today. Your muscles and bones will thank you, your heart will open wide and your healing energy will flow freely.

It's a fact of life that many cell phone users who look down for hours a day at their devices are creating rounded spines. "Computer slouch" is not only a problem for the youngest among us. We should all be paying attention.

There is a pose that is usually taught from the beginning in yoga classes called *Tadasana,* or Mountain Pose, which is a beautiful example of the art of healthy posture. It emphasizes our built-in harmonic balance when we stand as our bodies were created to stand. And when we stand tall, our bones and internal organs are positioned for optimal support, blood supply and alertness.

The spiritual bonus of being in our best possible posture is that an amazing amount of our life energy is held within the spinal column. That's why we meditate with a straight spine. Our chakras, or energy centers, are meant to stack up, one atop the other, for the maximum flow of wisdom and healing energy. We can align with the divine by straightening our spine.

In The World:

∗ For increased joy and energy today, practice Mountain Pose every chance you get. Here are the basics: Your feet are parallel, legs straight and strong without locking the knees; your hips are over your feet, spine lengthens long from sacrum to crown of the head; shoulders slightly back with shoulder blades flat on the back. Relax your face. Ahh.

∗ And at your desk, be mindful to sit tall or consider a standing desk.

In The Heart:

∗ My body is in perfect health, my bones and muscles are strong, my spine is straight and strong, my cells spin with joy and radiant energy.

Free to Sing

Today is a symphony of miracles and we are the instruments.

There was a long period of time when I could not sing. A few reedy notes would come out, then my throat would close completely and I would feel like I was choking. It mystified me, embarrassed me even when I was alone. I sang for a living for 20 years. Where did my voice go?

I traced it back in my mind and realized that when the illusion of my marriage was becoming clear, I was not speaking up. There were years when I tiptoed around the deck of the truth, trying not to rock the boat and incur a storm of change. I knew there were circumstances that I could not live with, but I was stuck, immobilized by the status quo and a child who needed stability. Everyone else came first. I closed off the voice of my intuition because I didn't want to hear what she was telling me.

Speak your truth, she would say.

Coming to live alone on Hunters Road changed that. I met Paul and Cheryl, and whenever we got together, they wanted to sing. I was resistant at first. "I don't sing anymore," I would say. But coaxed further, I would find that I was no longer constricted. I was living my truth and exposing my heart to the ultimate sadness of my story, and my knot untied. I was free to sing—and to speak.

We are here as expressions of our truth.

Although it seems that going into our pain will break us into a hundred pieces, instead, when we walk right into the bones of our honesty, we get a hundred miracles. Go figure. So whenever we are ready, we can open the door of the heart and face the pain that we have kept at bay. We will find our truth there.

We can take a small step toward living in alignment with our new selves and discover that today is a symphony of miracles. And we are the instruments, free to sing.

In The World:

✳   Today, find at least one small way to speak up for yourself. Begin the process of listening to your intuition.

In The Heart:

✳   I am free to speak my truth and know I will be guided as I navigate my way with honesty through life's changes and challenges.

I Believe in Me

I am not just enough. I am magnificent.

When Maya was four years old, my friend Pauline gave her a book for Christmas, *I Believe in Me: A Book of Affirmations*. Written and illustrated by the whimsical and talented artist Connie Bowen, it became one of our all-time favorite children's books to read together.

On one side of the page is a captivating colored pencil drawing and on the other, a simple affirmation. *I am wonderfully creative. I give with joy. I have a place of stillness within me.* Slowly, we would examine the sweet detail of each picture and soak up the good feeling.

I follow my heart. I am thankful. I share my love and watch it grow. We would feel better and better as we read on, expanding, laughing, remembering.

I am filled with greatness. I am whole and perfect just the way I am. I am one with all life. Yes!

The book reminded us, over and over with every read, of who we are.

In our daily life, we have all become familiar with the phrase, *I am enough.* And yes, you are. But that's not all.

You are magnificent. You are the enormous spirit behind the worldly one—watching, knowing, being love in all things—and shining your light on all who cross your path.

You are not just enough. You are magnificent. Remember that always.

In The World:

✳ Today is the day to remind yourself of your beauty and your magnificence.

✳ Revisit your affirmations or copy some of the ones here to your journal and use them throughout the day.

✳ From a place of love and radiant power, allow joy to flow.

✳ Beam that joy on all who stand in the light of your sun.

In The Heart:

✳ I am a magnificent reflection of divine love.

Irish Blessings

May the road rise to meet you. May the wind be always at your back. May the sun shine warm upon your face; the rains fall soft upon your field. And until we meet again, may God hold you in the palm of His hand.

Today in celebration of Saint Patrick's Day, we welcome some traditional Irish blessings. May these gentle prayers settle into your soul like a sweet, soft mantra of comfort and serenity.

> May love and laughter light your days
> and warm your heart and home.
> May good and faithful friends be yours
> wherever you may roam.
> May peace and plenty bless your world
> with joy that long endures
> May all life's passing seasons
> bring the best to you and yours.
>
> When the first light of sun, bless you.
> When the warm day is done, bless you.
> In your smiles and your tears, bless you.
> Through each day of your years, bless you.
>
> Calm me Lord, as you calmed the storm.
> Still me Lord, keep me from harm.
> Let all tumult within me cease.
> Enfold me Lord, in your peace.
>
> May your joys be as deep as the oceans,
> Your troubles as light as its foam.
> And may you find, sweet peace of mind
> Wherever you may roam.

In The World:

✳ The little we know of St. Patrick's life is marked with courage and faith. And so can yours be. Press on with your convictions today with a loving heart. And may you be blessed, wherever you may roam.

In The Heart:

✳ I am strong. I have faith. I am guided. I am blessed.

Divine Timing

May I be a little more patient today than I was yesterday.

I used to be a little hard on myself. Really a lot hard on myself. I set my expectations high and was impatient when I didn't meet my goals. I know. We've talked about patience. But I continued to forget that my timing is not the only timing to consider.

So I decided to boycott the pressure I place on myself and apply a bit of divine timing to my daily routine. A reprogramming of the internal GPS was in order.

The result of my little experiment is the happy discovery that I'm getting more done and having more fun when I exercise a healthy dose of patience and faith. I suspend judgment and trust that all is well. Even when it doesn't look so well from here. I'll share my road map below.

Opening the door to patience changes the philosophy from *making something happen,* my mantra before, to *allowing it to unfold in its perfect time,* my mantra now.

For today, may we relax a little in our expectations for ourselves and others and invite divine timing to settle into our souls. Tomorrow is another day.

In The World:

*   In the morning, write down the three most important goals for the day.

*   Shoot up a prayer requesting assistance. It could look something like, *I know there is a beautiful plan for today and that you will help it unfold with ease and grace. Thank you for showing me the way.*

*   Flow toward the path that seems most open first. When you come up for air, pause, center and repeat the process of a prayer followed by action toward the clearest path.

*   If you hit a wall or end the day without meeting all the goals, release it with the pure knowing that today was not the perfect time for it.

In The Heart:

*   I flow in union with divine timing and am patient in allowing all good to unfold with ease and grace.

~✧~

Bless My Mind

Bless my mind with calm and sight. Bless my heart with love and light. Bless my day with grace and ease. Bless my world with hope and peace.

No matter what kind of day stretches out before us, we could all use a little inspiration to stay on track. It's easy getting lost in the jungle, right? The mind loop can spin false tales of fear and cast us in a charade where we face an uphill battle alone.

On the path of spirit there is a simpler way. We gently awaken to our unlimited nature and practice the ultimate expression of self-love—we ask for blessings for ourselves. It's easy to forget who we are, but it's equally easy to awaken over and over again and ask for the blessings we need.

Shining the light of a beautiful blessing on ourselves wipes out our temporary amnesia. It enlists divine support in connecting with our highest selves so we can view all aspects of the day through the most loving light. It allows us to let go of the idea that we have to control all of this on our own.

We are a team now. We can create something beautiful together. Shine the light of blessings on yourself so you may shine your light on others.

In The World:

Here is a short blessing for you today. After a few calming breaths, repeat silently:

∗ *Bless my mind with calm and sight.* Imagine having clear, focused, calm thoughts sourced from your highest wisdom.

∗ *Bless my heart with love and light.* Imagine your heart center opening, filling with the light of love on the inhale and freely giving love out on the exhale.

∗ *Bless my day with grace and ease.* Imagine the day flowing with easy flexibility when challenges arise.

∗ *Bless my world with hope and peace.* Imagine the world surrounded with light and in perfect peace.

In The Heart:

∗ Today, may I be blessed with all that I need for the best possible day— for myself and for all those who cross my path or my mind.

A Thousand Miracles

To walk in nature is to witness a thousand miracles.

Spring is in the air and Nature invites us to notice her.

The patient brown and grey of bare trees. The lime green tint of tiny new buds. The carpet of last fall's leaves. The hawk circling on the wind current. The dense forest that lives in harmony. The soft path of pine needles under a splash of turquoise sky.

The call of birds and the answer of bird friends. Sunlight making God-light through the trees. The spicy, healing scent of pine. Grass. Rolling hills. Mountains. The clear creek water flowing over stones to create baby waterfalls. The color of any flower. The persistence of vines. The singing of tree frogs. Cardinals and finches. Herons and eagles. Berries, acorns and cones.

The sound of leaves dancing in the breeze. Ferns on the forest floor. The view from the mountain top. The hills of the hollow. Foxes and deer. Moss on tree bark. Wind on skin.

Nature's welcoming arms are always open. They allow our spirits to expand outward from our hearts into her safety, holding space for our wildest dreams and our most intense emotions. She accepts them all and gives them back to us in an awed exhale of peace.

When we need a fresh perspective or a jump start for our creativity, Nature waves flags of infinite beauty. When emotions loom large and problems seem daunting, Nature invites us to walk with her in peace. For spiritual connection, wellness, strength, wonder and focus—Nature donates her gifts. With infinite divine kindness, Nature offers us beauty, health, respite, meditation and solace from our worldly demands. There is no better medicine.

Along with the birth of spring, open to receive, in gratitude, a thousand miracles.

In The World:

* As part of your spiritual practice, walk in nature with a keen eye for beauty. Notice the miracles. Give thanks.

In The Heart:

* I am one with the beauty of all natural things and allow nature's peace to flow through me.

The Worry Tree

I let my worries go so I can be here for the beauty that surrounds me now.

When my daughter was small and wracked with the anxiety of a struggling CEO, we created a guided meditation called The Worry Tree. In her mind's eye, she would walk down a beautiful path, surrounded by colorful flowers, to a grassy spot where the gentle and compassionate Worry Tree always stood in wait. Then she would name her fears, one at a time, and ask Worry Tree if he would mind holding them for her until she might want them back. She never did.

Through this meditation, Maya was able to release her worries and come back to the present moment feeling a little more peaceful. She was able to fall asleep imagining beauty instead of her fears.

Energy flows to where the mind goes. Train her well. When we generate more beautiful thoughts, we create more beautiful outcomes. Ours is a benevolent universe that responds to where we put our attention.

To banish worries, we don't *turn them off* as much as we *turn our head* gently back home to the present moment. As we free ourselves over and over from negative imaginings, we find ourselves doing one thing at a time with love, presence and gratitude.

May we release our worries so we can be here for the precious gifts that surround us right now.

In The World:

✳ If you are a worrier, look into guided meditations to reduce stress and relinquish worries. Or create your own version of The Worry Tree meditation and practice it nightly before bed.

✳ An affirmative prayer in lieu of worrying might be: *I am thankful for the divine plan that is in action for _____. Her health and healing are happening now and all of her needs are being met for the highest good of all.*

In The Heart:

✳ I release my fears and worries with ease, knowing that all is well and in divine order. I gently bring myself to the beauty and the blessings of the present moment.

Where God Is

Right where you are is where God is.

There's nowhere to go. Nothing to search for. No teacher to find. No separation. There's no train that will leave us behind. No platform where we will ever stand alone. There's no place and no situation where God is not.

God is in the details, in the deadlines, in the deaths.

God is in the moments, in the mothering, in our smallest steps.

God is in the wind through the trees and the crashing of the seas.

God speaks through our love and creates through our hands.

God walks through our journey and guides all our plans.

We are a ray of the sun of divine creation and we have, shining within us, divine love. We naturally reflect the love we are made of. We can't escape it or hide from it. We can't lose it or run from it.

We can forget it, but still, it is here. We can ignore it, but still, it remains.

Listen and know. Right where we are, broken and messy, joyous and celebrating, God is here.

Of all the earthly promises broken and disappointments carried, we can trust this one constant. We do nothing alone. We are surrounded and supported right here, right now, just as we are.

In The World:

✳   Be still. In moments of silence we feel our connection with all things.

✳   Be in awe. In beauty we find the signature of God.

✳   Be patient. In all that is challenging we find divine order leading us to new growth.

✳   Be loving. In acts of love we are the hands and feet of divine creation.

In The Heart:

✳   I see the imprint of the divine in all things great and small, right where I am.

～✼～

The Peaceful Warrior

The world is in need of our peace today.

Where I live in the country I have no cable or data connectivity. I have just enough Wi-Fi to make it through my social media postings for the month, but not enough to read articles and watch videos. Once a week on Tuesdays, I get my news driving to and from town to volunteer with hospice patients, and each week the dying people lift my spirits and the news leaves me in despair. The heartbreaking sadness, low-minded controversies, violence and scary weather reports can render us worried and hopeless. This can't be good.

So how do we become a warrior for peace? There are countless ways we can contribute to the cause of spreading peace on our planet. It begins with making peace within ourselves and from this place of light, we can spread the energy of our love consciously in meditation and through our every action in the world.

On my way home, the news turns to static, the static is replaced by a frog chorus and the world rights itself once more. Today, let's listen less to the spin and allow the peaceful warrior within to get to work in a world that needs our peace. We have the power to lift the vibration of the planet.

In The World:

∗ Peaceful Thoughts: Notice negative thinking about yourself and others and gently guide your thoughts to what is loving, kind, encouraging, calm and life-affirming. Imagine our world emanating loving light.

∗ Peaceful Words: Our words, like our thoughts, have the power to shape our experience and guide the universe to manifestation. May all of our words today carry the power of love and peace.

∗ Peaceful Actions: Move through today with a gentle footprint, exuding calm energy to all who cross your path. Led by the wisdom of the heart, take peaceful action for beliefs that you are passionate about.

In The Heart:

∗ I bless the world today with my peaceful light and powerful healing energy. I keep my focus on that which is of the light.

My Manager and the God Box

From challenges grow miracles.

My mother, whom we affectionately call "Tiny Guru" for her small stature and great spirit, takes pride in being my manager. There's nothing much to manage as I am a hermit writer living in the country, and that suits us both nicely. On a daily basis she gives me the priceless gift of her enthusiastic support. No matter the project, she is all in.

She also does a particularly vital task for me: She xeroxes my Facebook posts and sends me hard copies of them. Receiving those papers every few months allows me to organize my stories. I can lay them out on the floor, reorder them and take notes on them. They are invaluable, thus making her an extra great manager.

Facebook occasionally changes things up and recently they restructured the Photos section. Mom's usual procedure of printing out one post at a time was not working. She was deeply troubled and spent hours trying new settings and printing out "that damn frog" over and over. The pages were a mess of ads.

Then came a lightning bolt. "I'll put it in a God Box," she mused. The fact that she didn't have a God Box did not deter her. She searched the house and found a container deemed perfect for the job and carefully worded her short message: *Dear Angels of the Computer, Thank you for Mary's printing job. It is lovely. xx Tiny xx* She then left it in the box to percolate for the weekend.

Monday morning, full of faith, Mom fired up the computer, settings as usual, and the print job came out "half-way better." She said softly to the Angels, "If this is the best it can be, it will be alright. But I'd really like it to be perfect for Mary." She printed it out again, and it was perfect—and has been ever since.

In The World:

✱ Make your own God Box. Place your worries inside, shoot up a prayer and forget them. In Tosha Silver's, *Outrageous Openness*, she explains: "During the period of offering, solutions often spontaneously arise. When the mind is no longer grasping for an answer, space opens. The Box gives room for a divine plan, even in impossible messes."

In The Heart:

✱ I trust that the divine has a plan in progress for all of my challenges.

14 Steps to Calm

I unveil the serenity that I am.

A friend called yesterday and shared how she was suffering from daily anxiety and panic attacks. She was the third person to relay a similar story in past weeks. Embodying calm seems like an elusive dream, but have faith. It's not out of reach. Before we accept anxiety as a companion, there are tools that can bring us closer to our always-calm center. These tools will span the next several days.

1. Make exhalations longer. Start by counting 4 on the inhale and 6 on the exhale, with a goal of 4 in and 8 out. Do this for a few minutes and you will feel the difference immediately. The hallmark of "fight or flight" breathing during a panic attack is rapid breathing and heart rate. By increasing the length of the exhalations, you remind your body that there is nothing to fear and that all is well.

2. Use positive affirmations. There's an extensive body of research that supports the theory that what we think, we create. The body will default to pathways it already knows, so it takes a little retraining to create new thought habits. Here is a starter list of affirmations, and you can add your own. Your journal, phone notes or index cards are good places to keep these. Word everything in the positive and smile with your whole body as you think or say them:

I am in perfect health.   *Today will be an amazing day.*
I am calm and serene.   *I am in the flow of love.*
Everything is in divine order.   *I am relaxed and focused.*
I am safe and all is well.   *I am in the flow of grace.*
I am joyful and peaceful.   *I love my life.*

In The World:

*   Take a few moments several times today for a few rounds of the long exhale breathing followed by positive affirmations. Set a timer for frequent reminders to stop what you're doing for this practice. Take two minutes for renewal.

*   In stressful times, your daily spiritual practice, even when shortened to meet time constraints, is especially important.

In The Heart:

*   I am filled with calm joy to the depth of my soul.

꘎

14 Steps to Calm - Part 2

I listen to the voice of my inner wisdom.

3. Ask for help on a soul level. There's unlimited help available in spirit realms for the asking. The prayer might go something like this:

Thank you for putting a perfect plan in motion to relax my mind, body and soul. Assist me in using my inner tools to find deep peace. I trust that a beautiful plan is unfolding in my life today and that I have nothing to fear. Thank you for helping me return to my natural state of calm.

Divine grace is benevolent and conspires to help us out. But we must ask clearly and positively. After asking, know you have been heard and assistance is on the way.

4. Stay connected. Stay connected with your family and closest friends, and share your journey with them. Stress can be isolating, and it's important to keep an open heart. If you had a physical issue, your beloveds would want to help you out. Same goes for stressful times.

5. Be kind to yourself. Anxiety is exhausting so skip the self-criticism. Think only loving thoughts of yourself. You are doing the very best you can. You are not alone in this.

6. Exercise. Yoga, walking, kayaking, dancing, Tai Chi—pick something relaxing that you can do outside or facing a window. Calm your body and soak up the beauties of nature while you release endorphins.

7. Drink lots of water and less caffeine. Flush toxins and hydrate your cells with plenty of fresh water throughout the day. Cut out soda and limit caffeine to two cups a day, max. Your mind, body and soul will thank you.

8. Visualize your wellness. You don't have to figure out *how* to get to where you want to go. Jump right to the result and visualize the joyful, healthy, calm, vibrant you. Just a few minutes of visualization a day is incredibly powerful.

In The World:

✳   Continue the practice from yesterday with long-exhale breathing and affirmations, adding in the practices that resonate with you. Set a timer to implement the practices several times today. Ahh.

In The Heart:

✳   I take positive steps toward inner peace.

14 Steps to Calm - Part 3

I am filled with peace and calm. I approach my day with joy and clarity.

9. Treat yourself. Now is the perfect time to treat yourself to a massage. With the right practitioner you may find that a monthly massage is not a luxury, but a necessity. Another relaxing treat is an Epsom salt bath. Get a box of Epsom salt at the pharmacy, put a handful in a bathtub and detox away. It has a calming effect and draws toxins out of the body.

10. Use good posture. A couple of weeks ago we talked about Mountain Pose and the importance of good posture for optimum health and spiritual connection. Sitting and standing with a straight spine is especially important for stress relief because it allows the lungs to inflate fully. When your lungs are inflating fully, you can take calming breaths.

11. Spend less time on screens, more time in nature. Computers can short circuit our energy and leave us mentally and physically tense. Spend as much time in nature as possible. Implement a daily walk while leaving the phone at home. Notice your surroundings and be present.

12. Practice Yoga Nidra and play music. There are many beautiful recordings of Yoga Nidra or *yogic sleep* that gently guide the body into a deep and healing relaxation. They range in time from about five minutes to one hour. Experiment with a few until you find one that you love. Relaxing music also has proven to have anti-anxiety effects.

13. Get more sleep. You may find that you need extra sleep. Adjust your schedule to make sleep a priority. Yoga Nidra at bedtime is the perfect setup for a peaceful night's sleep.

14. Meditate. This is the single most important practice for overall mental and spiritual health, and it is suitable for nearly everyone. Learn more about it. Take a class, get a book or read a few articles. Keep it simple. Start where you are. Start today.

In The World:

✳ Use your journal to create your own calming practice. Enjoy the adventure of discovering the built-in tools that stock your virtual medicine cabinet with calm. Check out the Resources in the back of the book for a few of my favorites.

In The Heart:

✳ I am filled with peace and calm and I approach my day with joy and clarity. I am healthy, safe and have faith that all is well.

Feeling Small

Sometimes it's good to feel small. —Maya Davis

It was a perfect early spring morning with a crystal clear sky the color of Santa Fe turquoise. Hiking up the fire road, my new friend asked me about my work. How to explain? Should I say that every flat surface of my cabin is exploding with a creative project? There's a reason I don't talk about my life much in new company. I wear a lot of hats and it's complicated.

But I forgot that, and with a touch of confident swagger (must have been the altitude), I began to explain about writing the daybook of inspirations and developing an app of mobile wallpapers. I told her I also do retail, have an Etsy Store and license images. I went on. I'm writing songs again, producing a CD and I...

I turned around and became mute, deferring to the stunning view of the valley and the rising rounded curves of the Blue Ridge Mountains. Hawks circled. The brilliant sun danced in shimmering drops of light on several lakes. So small. I am so small!

What was I thinking? That *I* was doing all that creating myself? Clearly not. I'm a tiny drop of water in the universal ocean of love, and I would not be doing anything of value if not for the infinite flow of grace that aligns me with the creative power of the divine. Little Me. Big God. Little Me suddenly got very quiet.

It can be a mountaintop view, a mighty ocean or a starry sky that reminds us of the impossible power of that which is greater than we are. It reminds us of all we are part of and all that is part of us. From this scenic overview of humility, with the perspective of our place in the greater whole, we enter the flow of this mighty love. Through humility.

Yes, sometimes it's good to feel small.

In The World:

✳   Imagine the great vastness of the universe and allow yourself to contemplate the interconnection of you and the energy of all things.

In The Heart:

✳   I witness and am one with the greater power of the universe. I am grateful for my daily co-creation with the divine.

∿⚬∿

Create Today

May this day be grounded in love, illuminated by light
and graced with blessings.

May this day be guided by divine wisdom, aligned with goodness and filled with joy.

May this day be guarded by angels, softened by patience and raised by kindness.

May this day be lifted by gratitude, deepened by compassion and calmed by inner peace.

May this day be grounded in love, illuminated by light and graced with blessings.

Starting to feel a little better, dear one? Well good. We are off to a beautiful start in creating a most amazing day.

You see, what we dwell on, we create; what we imagine, we attract; what we ponder, we empower. So surely starting the day with a prayer for all good things will set the momentum for more grace, more blessings and more peace.

We create today one thought at a time, so it's never too late to take a U-turn and change directions. The path is yours to draw; the painting yours to paint over.

Start right here, right now, in creating a day where heaven reaches right down and touches your face, or one in which you reach up and touch the face of God.

In The World:

✳ Use the prayer above or create your own to get in the flow of grace first thing in the morning. Take a moment to get back on track at any time you need a divine, energy-boosting break. Create the day of your dreams.

In The Heart:

✳ When I keep my thoughts on the blessings and the good, more blessings and goodness flow into my life.

Fruit of the Spirit

Every day of your life plants a seed in your soul. Grow roses.

Every day we can till the soil in the garden of the spirit with Gratitude. The rich grace of Thanksgiving permeates the day with an expectation of abundance.

Every day we can sow seeds of Love and Joy as we scatter Kindness and Peace. The seeds arrive in gardens seen and unseen, traveling on the wind to wherever they are most needed.

Every day we can water the soil with the tears of our Grief and Challenge. The rain of Experience penetrates the soil, breaking open the seeds of Love and Joy into the sprouts of Generosity and Compassion for all humanity.

Every day we can shine the light of the sun to warm and feed the sprouts as they grow into seedlings of Patience, Forgiveness and Faith.

Every day we can weed the garden with Mindfulness and nurture strong, healthy blooms that reflect the beauty and bounty of our gentle Goodness.

Every day brings with it the chance to harvest from our gardens the Fruit of the Spirit.

"The fruit of the spirit is love, joy, peace, kindness, goodness, faithfulness, gentleness and self-control." —*Galatians 5:22-23*

In The World:

∗ Honor this day as the precious gift that it is.

∗ Sow the seeds of love and joy today and grow something incredibly beautiful.

∗ Resolve to make this day a beautiful rose in your garden.

In The Heart:

∗ I bless this day by planting and nurturing seeds of love and joy that travel to where they are most needed.

Friendship

*Friends are like the sun in spring, shining the light
that makes our souls blossom.*

My neighbor's yard awes the senses with a field of miraculous flowers. Hundreds of daffodils and tulips pop up with brilliant color in a joyful display of natural beauty. Each one is unique and irreplaceable, arriving just in time after a long winter, radiating love to remind us that life is precious and beautiful. Much like our dear friends do.

In his famous poem, *On Friendship*, Kahlil Gibran tells us, "Your friend is your needs answered. He is your field which you sow with love and reap with thanksgiving." The unconditional love of a friend is one of life's most generous gifts. In their presence we find safety from the judgment of the world. In their company is the freedom to be ourselves. They support, confirm, protect and encourage in the safety of their love. They are willing participants in our joys and laughter, challenges and pain. They are our needs answered.

"For you come to him with your hunger, and you seek him for peace," he continues. Through our best friendships, we learn to know another—and ourselves—with a deep and enduring love. True friends reflect our inner light back to us, allowing our hearts to be seen, bringing to awareness the magnificence of our inner truth.

Gibran finishes the poem with, "And in the sweetness of friendship, let there be laughter and sharing of pleasures. For in the dew of little things, the heart finds its morning and is refreshed."

To those precious friends who make this day beautiful, bearable, meaningful, joyful and new—thank you, dear ones, thank you. My heart finds its morning and is refreshed.

In The World:

✳ Tell a friend how much you treasure their presence in your life.

✳ Share the truth of your most important joys and sorrows with a friend. Honesty is a healing gift for both souls.

In The Heart:

✳ I am completely free to be honest and uncensored with my dearest friends. I can be vulnerable knowing my heart is safe in her hands.

April Blessings

Be present. Be here. Today, we can guide our thoughts back to the present moment with gentle focus and live fully right where we are.

Let the day flow with grace. Grace flows through us easily when we are in tune with the subtle voice of intuition. Open and listen for guidance.

Expect joy. Be positive. Imagine a fulfilling day unfolding, in which we accomplish much and experience joy in the process. Welcome the light.

Serve with compassion. Acts of service when performed with love lend immeasurable light to our day. Be watchful for ways to serve.

Speak only kindness. Speak only kind words. Think only kind thoughts. Be kind to yourself and to those who cross your path or your mind.

Impart only love. Send out all thoughts and words on the wings of love so that we may love one another, love ourselves, love the unlovable.

Never forget you're not alone. Let's remind ourselves often today that we are always supported, guided and unconditionally loved as we are.

Give thanks for everything. Gratitude will shift the perspective of the day from one of lack to one of abundance. Give constant thanks.

See goodness in others. Each of us has a soul that is made of beauty and love. Assume the best in others so they may rise to their highest light.

Dear Guardian Angel

My guardian angel works overtime.

Dear Guardian Angel,

I'm not trying to overwork you, really I'm not. I'm closing down earlier in the evenings. I'm not answering messages after dinner. I'm not looking at social media more than a few times per day. But still, I know, you must be having fits over me. There are not enough hours in the day, and I'm constantly testing the limits of my strength.

All around me, I see faces with dimming eyes. So many of us seem to be overwhelmed by the demands of connectivity; coffers running dry from so much output with so little self-care and connection with spirit. I long for more serenity, more joy, more peace. And I know I can find what I seek with the help of your loving assistance, a slower pace and some self-love.

Oh sweet Angel, guide me on a path of wellness today. I seek balance between doing and allowing, between effort and surrender. This means that with your help, I'm going to have to implement some realistic limits. There's only one of me, and there's always more work to be done. Please help!

Love, Me

In The World: Guardian Angel Requests for Support:

* Help me to honor my limits and listen for signs of burnout. Help me to slow down before I wear thin. Remind me to enjoy relaxation.

* Help me to trust that if I can't get through my list today, you will help me accomplish things easily and in their perfect time.

* Help me to know that this journey is meant to be fun and that joy is a spiritual practice. Remind me to take myself lightly.

* Help me to always lead from spirit, nourishing my soul so I may be able to share with others from a place of abundance.

* Help me to wake up every morning knowing that I am supported and guided, and that when I listen, I will always know the way.

In The Heart:

* My Guardian Angel guides me, protects me and answers every call for assistance with loving attention and joy.

Ease and Grace

When there is an endless stream of to-do's, there is no time to simply be.
Seek silence to nourish the spirit.

Today is a good day to rethink our to-do lists. Or better yet, let's put them aside. Perfect harmony and balance will be revealed to us moment by moment when we listen to the guidance of our inner wisdom and divine support. The right things will happen in just the right time provided that we surrender to the flow of grace and ask for what we need.

As we have seen, when we start the day in the silence of a short spiritual practice, work unfolds smoothly because we are connected to our highest wisdom. Taking a few moments throughout the day for quiet breaths and an invocation for assistance can keep us on track, bringing us instantly to our natural state of joy and light. With spirit in the lead, all else unfolds with ease and grace.

The transition prayer or request might look something like this:

Thank you for pointing me to the best ways to use my energy right now.
Show me what to do next, and help me to accomplish everything with ease
and grace in its perfect time.

Although on the outside it might seem that we don't have time to stop and connect, we soon discover that we accomplish twice as much in half the time when we are in the flow. This process of circling back again and again to our divine assistance and intuition works like a charm.

So today, relax into the river of grace. Ride the flow of the current and you'll never want to swim upstream again.

In The World:

✳ Do a test run. For today, put the lists aside and set your phone timer for every hour or two. When the alarm rings, take a few centering breaths and say the above prayer or any prayer for assistance, adding in any specific details you choose.

✳ If it's feeling good, continue the test run for the entire work week. You may never want to stop.

In The Heart:

✳ Everything unfolds hour by hour in perfect divine timing. I have all the time I need for all I need to do.

~✧~

Joy and the Coffee Cake

Celebrate small moments and find joy in small things.

As I sit in the morning sun considering ways to celebrate joy in small moments, I imagine a colorful tube reaching from the sky to me. Through this open, joy-transmitting tunnel, I feel beams of sheer bliss coming right into the top of my head and landing with laughter in my heart. My joy channel is getting a strong signal, but strangely, it repeatedly sends down but one thing through my tunnel. Coffee cake. Yes, indeed. I'm channeling almond coffee cake.

Since taking all things gluten out of my life some years ago, I dream of my former favorite breakfasts, which all happen to be coffee cake related in some sweet happy way: cheese Danish, scones, banana bread, and the queen of all breakfasts, almond coffee cake. The mere thought of them makes me feel the presence of a happy divine goddess within.

The great news for humanity is that seeing as we are all threads in the same tapestry of oneness, my joy is also your joy. Your joy is mine. We celebrate life's small moments and lift the energy of everything around us in a vibrational fireworks show.

As I drive up the winding mountain road not far from my cabin, I pass a sandwich board sign near a small house that says, BAKERY - GLUTEN FREE. Last week I stopped in to find an adorable room with ten tables adorned with fresh flowers and happy customers. I walk up to the counter laden with gorgeous baked goodies and say, "SO, where is the gluten-free section?" I think I'm dreaming when I hear, "All of it is gluten-free." *All of it?*

I lift my arms overhead as if I had just seen a vision of Mother Mary in Medjugorje. Recovering my voice, I sing out, "Have I told you how much I LOVE you?"

In the distant background, I can hear the Table People cracking up. But me, I'm busy ordering almond coffee cake and lifting up the planet with some big joy fireworks.

In The World:

∗ Be on the lookout for small moments of joy today. Give us all a lift by celebrating what makes you smile.

In The Heart:

∗ I celebrate small moments and find joy in small things.

Plant Seeds

We can't change people but we can plant seeds
that may one day bloom in them.

Although many of us have been warned that "we can't fix people," it's hard to resist the pull to want to change people for the better. We want to impart our wisdom and see the result of our efforts, especially with our loved ones. It's frustrating when changes don't happen when we think they should. Like immediately.

It helps to remember that the energy of every word we speak, especially those empowered by love, has impact that lasts long after the conversation has ended. Every seed of kindness, love, joy, grace, comfort, wisdom and protection is planted in the heart of another to bloom when the time is right—for them.

A few weeks ago there was no sign of the buds that are now bursting forth from every bush and branch. In the winter hush, these very plants and trees appeared lifeless. Deep within, the buds were a mere possibility of a bloom—creation gestating in the dark.

People are full of possibilities too—creation gestating in the dark. Sometimes they're just not ready to apply the lesson, but the seed of our love and caring lies in wait. Be patient with the seeds you have planted in another. They may one day bloom in them.

In The World:

✳ When there is little you can do to help someone evolve, imagine them as their highest selves. Imagine the traits and qualities you know they could possess. Imagine them being blessed with these qualities.

✳ Remain kind. Use words phrased in the positive. Even when results are not visible, know that you have planted a powerful soul lesson in them.

✳ Planting seeds of change does not mean you need to stay in the presence of intolerable behavior or abusive situations. It's possible to plant transformational seeds—and move on.

In The Heart:

✳ I change the world daily by words and actions of kindness, love and peace that are not dependent on the outcome. I have faith that seeds of change will bloom in others when the time is right for them.

Faith over Anxiety

I choose faith over anxiety, hope over worry, love over fear.

Today we can make choices that align us perfectly with what we know to be true: that spirit speaks in the language of solutions, not problems.

When we make an offering of our challenges with a brave, patient and open heart, we will be led to the answers we seek. With affirmations of faith, hope and love, we can turn this day into something beautiful. Starting now.

Today I choose faith and when I do, my anxiety dissolves and my focus becomes the right outcome for the highest good of all. I believe that all things are possible, and I trust that incredible blessings walk the path right beside impossible pain. I know that I will live through this, thrive through this, become new through this. Today I choose faith.

Today I choose hope and when I do, my worries retreat and my focus becomes a better outcome, one beyond my ability to see. I imagine a future where my concerns are solved with the ever-present support of spirit. I surrender my need to control and I offer my problems, great and small, to divine guidance, knowing I am heard. Today I choose hope.

Today I choose love and when I do, my fears fade and my focus becomes seeing all things through the eyes of love. Every decision I make today comes from a heart of love. Every thought I think today is sent out on the wings of love. I have nothing to fear. I am an eternal being and by the power of love, all things can be solved. Today I choose love.

In The World:

✳ Choices are made only in the moment you are in. Today when you recognize the signs of doubt and fear, stop and affirm: *I have faith that all will be well.* Send light and imagine the highest outcome for all concerned. Then let it go and open your heart to the blessings that are yet to unfold.

In The Heart:

✳ I always have a choice, and today I choose faith, hope and love.

As We Grow Wings

I remain calm, centered and grounded in divine wisdom.

At one point in my yoga studies, it seemed that divorce was a limb on the sage Patanjali's eightfold path of yoga. Marriages around me were dropping like flies, and there was a swirling flow of whispered stories of teachers in various stages of separation. It seemed like a strange prerequisite to enlightenment, but nonetheless, four out of five of my spiritual and/or yoga buds were seriously not going to survive the cocoon-to-butterfly thing with marriage intact. I didn't know what was in the water. Then it dawned on me. It was mud.

As we raise our vibrations and see the world from a higher perspective, our partners who are not on the path can feel heavy—angry and entangled in lower vibrational drama. Our souls are busting loose and our loved ones are not keeping up with our changes. The transformation on the planet now is bringing about rapid growth, and at times we feel like we are expanding out of our old lives.

This is a personal journey. Our partners don't have to *get it*, but it is essential that they *respect it*. They don't have to believe it, but they may not belittle it. Thankfully there are bridges that ease the growing pains. These tools help us to show love, patience and compassion to those in muddy water—as we grow wings.

In The World:

* Surround yourself with a protective aura of white or golden light. See the shield as impermeable to negativity and anger.

* Clear the house of negative energy with sage. Bless each room with the love of the divine, allowing the smoke to rise into all corners.

* It's not possible to fix anyone's behavior. What you can change is your reaction. Seek to be calm and centered in the heat of drama.

* Pray for the person and speak to them with your inner voice, from your soul to theirs. This is a conversation from your Higher Self to their Higher Self. Speak your truth. This is a transformative practice.

In The Heart:

* As I energetically expand, I use my light for the highest good of those I love. I remain calm, centered and grounded in divine wisdom.

Be Still My Soul

The harvest of this day grows from the seeds of sacred silence.

Precious, sacred silence is one of our most essential friends. Our silent time reminds us of who we are and gives us access to infinite wisdom from which we are guided when making our daily decisions. So why is it so difficult to write it in on today's schedule?

Many of us now have a spiritual practice during which we meditate, focus on gratitude, pray for assistance, and inspire the heart. But as we know, the world pulls ferociously at our shirttails, begging us to pay attention, to divide our time, to distract our focus and be busier than is good for the soul. It takes a mindful effort to revisit our priorities often, and make the time to connect with spirit. It's the most important thing we will do in the day. And when we do it first, the rest of the day is driven by the ongoing intuition gained from mindfully connecting with the source of all love.

This is not a duty or an effort. We don't work to be more spiritually connected; *it is who we are.* We merely set aside time to check in and to let the noise drop away for long enough to reveal the beauty and calm that resides within. And if we can just hover there...open...for a moment without jumping in with a thought, within that stillness, we activate our soul's wisdom.

Our lives can be driven by our schedules or by spirit. They can be driven by the constant chatter of our minds or by a place of calm. They can be driven by impulse or by wisdom.

May we quiet our words, calm our thoughts, soften our hearts and still our souls daily, so that we may listen, open and receive. And let spirit lead.

In The World:

* Meditation can be your most life-changing daily practice. The rewards will reach across all aspects of your being. Every day is a good day to begin learning or to recharge your practice. One morning at a time. As health guru Kris Carr says, "Progress over perfection!"

In The Heart:

* I have a calm center from which all wisdom arises. I still my soul and receive.

In Giving We Receive

It is always the right time to ask the question: How can I be of service?

When we fill out the volunteer form at a homeless shelter or nursing home, we often go in thinking that we will use our time and talent to help someone else. We are strong, loving, able and have a gift to give or a skill to share. But there is another important truth of service: the gifts of volunteering are really gifts to the soul of the giver. We are fulfilled through our generosity.

The very people we think need our help become our most radiant teachers. Facing poverty, illness, unfathomable loss or impending death can bring God so near that we can find ourselves at the intersection of heaven and earth.

We are here to love one another and to serve those in need with a compassionate heart. We can do this in small ways every day through an act of kindness and the simple art of being helpful. There are countless ways to experience the gift of service.

Gandhi put it beautifully: "The best way to find yourself is to lose yourself in the service of others." Giving is inherent in our nature. And today, someone needs what you have to give.

In The World:

* Consider first what hours you can commit to volunteer work and ease in gently offering one day a month or one day every two weeks to start.

* When donating clothing and household goods, everything should be clean and in good working order. Treat your donations as gifts to a precious friend.

* Contact local organizations and find out what they most need. When you act locally, you make a greater impact.

* Self-care is an important part of serving. This is not selfish, but essential. You can only give of yourself when you are in balance.

In The Heart:

* I am generous, loving and able to be helpful. I give of myself in small ways throughout the day and seek ways to use my gifts in service to others.

Grace Is Present

Lift up my worries and rain down peace.

Did you ever wish that it would rain down exactly the element of grace you need in this very moment? No, money doesn't count. Imagine asking for an extra portion of strength or patience—and it pours down and infuses you with everything you need to move forward. That's the thought from which this arose:

> Lift up my fears and rain down love.
>
> Lift up my tears and rain down joy.

> Lift up my blindness and rain down sight.
>
> Lift up my darkness and rain down light.

> Lift up my doubt and rain down faith.
>
> Lift up my grief and rain down grace.

> Lift up my challenge and rain down ease.
>
> Lift up my worries and rain down peace.

And I do believe that's how this grace thing works. We ask—or beg as the case may be—knowing it's there, knowing it's coming—standing out in the middle of the field looking up at the clouds.

In the instant that we ask, it begins. And when it rains, it pours.

In The World:

✳ Ask for what you need today, then soak in every ounce of it. You don't have to deserve it or earn it. It is grace with your name on it.

In The Heart:

✳ Grace is present for me in my moment of need. I ask for what I need. I receive it with an open heart. I give thanks.

A Rainbow in the Dark

Everything is in divine order.

Adam is one of my dearest friends and has been in my life for as long as I can remember. He is like a brother to me. He is also a recovering alcoholic—meaning ongoing. It's an incredibly helpless feeling to watch someone that you love harm themselves, and it's especially hard if you love them with a mother's love.

My mom, Tiny Guru that she is, can be a worrier. She's totally plugged into the divine, with one foot in both worlds and a deep understanding of all things spiritual, yet when it comes to her loved ones, the Great Mother in her rises strong and she worries about her lambs.

Yesterday in the mail I received the latest pages from her spiritual journal, written during her most recent Silent Week. Just as I sat down at the table to read, an incredibly strong storm blew in. The sky turned black, thunder cracked, lightning danced, wind whipped through tall trees, torrents of rain fell. I latched all the windows and lit candles, expecting to lose power.

I sat back down. And there I read, and wept. Mom's sadness about the state of Adam's life tore at the tapestry of my heart. There she was, confiding in her divine guides about her most intimate sorrow, confessing her fears. She even invoked the help of St. Monica, mother of St. Augustine, who himself was a bit wayward until he saw the light through the grace of his mother's prayers. "Please show me how I can help," Mom implored. She *was* the storm outside.

But then, in the last entry, she surrenders. She decides to trust in divine order and put all things in God's hands. She releases the remnants of resistance and ends with: "Again the words of St. John fill my heart. I leave my cares forgotten among the lilies." At that moment, I turned to look out the window, and there, within the dark rainstorm, at 8:45 in the evening, was an incredible, glowing rainbow.

In The World:

✳ Even in impossible situations, have faith that a higher plan is at work and that your requests for assistance have been heard.

In The Heart:

✳ I have faith that all things are unfolding in perfect divine order. My prayers are heard and answered for the highest good of all.

The Holy in the Small

Joy is finding the holy in the small and the sacred in the everyday.

When we want to find something, we begin by seeking what was hiding or lost for some period of time. *Finding* is the adventure of looking and experiencing the joy of being reunited with the lost thing.

So how do we *find* sacredness in the small moments of everyday life? Fortunately, this is one adventure that allows us to pack lightly, as what we seek is right here with us. All we need is our full attention plus a little resolve to find some amazing beauty today.

We see what we *want* to see—and we create what we concentrate on the most. So if we want love, miracles and blessings, we first decide to notice them. When we turn our attention to finding the beauty and the good, beauty and goodness appear everywhere.

It's hard to fathom that God would even want to be present in the mundane moments of our mosaic lives. But what if God is already in them? What if all of those tiny tiles are made up of some sort of divine clay and paint?

With a little mindfulness, the tiles of the mosaic catch our eye, fill our hearts, show us beauty and lead our way to joy. The morning light, the bird on a limb, the thought of a loving friend, the kindness of a stranger. The bite of food, the soft shirt, the trusty car, the needed rain. The smile of a child, the spoon in the pot, the broom on the floor, the tear over loss.

The common miracle here is love—which always wants to be found. So look. Really look for what you want to find. And you will experience the joy of being reunited with the lost thing—the holy in the small and the sacred in the everyday. Which were there all along.

In The World:

* Decide that beauty surrounds you today. Will yourself to see goodness and light. Watch carefully for beautiful happenings. Stay where the love is.

In The Heart:

* I notice the sacred in each small moment and find joy in everyday miracles. My life is a brilliant mosaic of divine love.

The Water Is Wide

Life can bring mighty challenges but you came here with a mighty soul.

Yes, there are moments when wings would be good. There are nightmares that we wish we could wake from. There are days when the wall of water is so high that the only way to travel is by taking a leap of faith into the next wave. And when you do that, remember something.

You are not alone, and you have all the strength you need to get through this. Ask for guidance through the storm. Believe in the power of the divine to do all things and in yourself as a piece of that divinity. Invoke the assistance of some powerful angels to guide your way to the other side. Persevere by holding on to hope and the crystal clear image of the best possible result.

When faced with a challenge, something important is demanding your attention. So instead of looking the other way or looking for a way out, face it straight on. Ask for guidance and listen to your intuition. Stay alert and watch for signs. Be patient with your progress. There are some valuable lessons to be learned that will serve you in meaningful ways in the future.

And most of all, believe in yourself. Everything in your life so far has prepared you for this moment. All of the wisdom and strength you need is within.

Life can bring mighty challenges, but you came here with a mighty soul. Consider the possibility that there are many more blessings to come as a result of this journey through the deep water. And that you have everything you need to make it to the other side.

In The World:

* Form your own personal positive affirmations for the challenges that you face. Write them in your spiritual journal. Say them often today.

* Enlist divine support and be open to all possible forms of guidance.

In The Heart:

* I have everything I need for the challenges I will face today. I have a constant stream of support and love that is always available to me.

Perfect Harmony

Mind, body and soul are one.

My friend Lyndy started the weekend focused on sorting out her finances, and specifically on finishing her taxes. She had taken an extension which was now a looming deadline, and it hung around her neck like a fifty-pound bag of rocks. No wonder she pulled a back muscle leaning down to pick up a box that was not very heavy.

As she sat to do her taxes, she now had the added worry of back pain, which clung to her all weekend. But as she made her way through the task, as distasteful as taxes can be, she started to feel a lightness of being. When the forms were completed, her back pain miraculously disappeared also.

Medical intuitive Carolyn Myss teaches us that financial stress often takes up residence in our stomach or back. In fact, all of our emotions and traumas, concerns and dramas are not only housed in our thoughts, but also in our bodies. No disease happens in isolation. Our mental, emotional and spiritual health resonates through all aspects of our being.

Learning to associate physical pain with our emotional attachments is a valuable spiritual tool that can serve us for a lifetime—as well as during tax time.

In The World:

✳ For long-term or recurring illnesses, we can augment medical science by aligning mind and soul with the body. Enlist meditation and the healing power of positive affirmations.

✳ Consider a wide range of alternative healing practices in addition to traditional medicine, including acupuncture, homeopathic medicine, Reiki, massage and other body work from experienced practitioners.

✳ Look into nutritional changes as well as vitamins and herbs.

✳ Research the chakra system. Some classic titles are *Anatomy of a Spirit* by Carolyn Myss, and *Eastern Body, Western Mind*, by Anodea Judith.

✳ Consider learning integrative movement like yoga, Tai chi or Qi gong.

In The Heart:

✳ My mind, body and soul are in alignment and in perfect harmony. I am happy, healthy and whole.

Amazing Grace Please

Grace is freely given and assistance is always here.

One of my hospice patients says she can talk to God. And He answers her right back. She slipped this little gem into a conversation as if it was an everyday occurrence. I leaned in close.

"I always start with *please* and end with *thank you*," she whispered. I pelted her with questions. "What exactly do you say? How often does this happen? How does He answer?"

"I say to God, 'Please take this pain away from me now. Thank you.'"

That's it?

"And then something changes," she says with a gleam in her eye. "Right away, something changes. It's hard to explain, but it is immediate. Everything feels better. Everything feels different. Everything is lighter. And that's the answer. He changes things."

He changes things.

We go on to talk about how that *thank you* at the end does not depend on the answer. It is a *thank you* in advance, because she knows that He will answer her. She assumes that she is heard and if she surrenders and asks, it will be given.

The grace that enables this exchange is available to all of us, at any time. The more we open to it and align with it, the more access we have to *feeling* the answers.

It is not that God is here sometimes and not others. God is always here, and it is up to us to align with the ever-present gift of amazing grace.

In The World:

* Have a running conversation with spirit today. Remember to use the very powerful *please* and *thank you*.

* Surrender, be vulnerable, and ask. Suspend judgment and notice how you feel after.

In The Heart:

* Today I open and align to a power far greater than myself, knowing that grace is a gift freely given and assistance is always here.

Joy in a Puddle of Mud

*Joy is the sound of love, the color of gratitude and the song
of your favorite things.*

I'm beginning to think that joy is a slow simmer, slightly under the radar of life's noise, popping up into our consciousness as a sweet sound, color or song that awakens us with a smile—like the Little Guy on the driveway.

I heard his happy announcement as I was walking to the car for my daily trip to the post office. He was so small that at first I didn't recognize him as a bird. Tiny as a butterfly, he was chirping mightily as he hopped in a circle around a mud-puddle gift from yesterday's rain. A combination of surprise, elation and a shout-out to his friends, this was one joyful Little Guy.

Joy is the sound of love.

With the arrival of spring rain for greening this week, it's possible that a newly minted bird was finding his first bathtub. *Could I be so lucky?* he might be thinking as he danced the blue stone perimeter. His grey wings fluttered as a dry run on land of what might happen in the water. *This is too good to be true.*

Joy is the color of gratitude.

A great light of courage rose up from Little Guy. With me, a giant human standing not five feet away, he took the leap of faith. Stunned at first, he stood still in the puddle. Then with a flourish, he dipped his head in and shimmied the water between all of his feathers. Again and again, he delighted in the practice, tasting the freedom of trying something new for the first time and getting the hang of it.

Joy is the song of your favorite things.

In The World:

✴ Today, be an excavator of joy. Let your eyes be vigilant to delights of the soul. Let your heart be open to signs and symbols of love, gratitude and hope. Try something new for the joy of it.

In The Heart:

✴ Joy is not dependent on my circumstances, but arises through sweet, simple moments of love, gratitude and hope. When I seek joy, I find joy.

Prayer Is Light

Prayer always matters. Prayer always bears light. Prayer always changes things. Prayer always changes us.

Imagine this: Prayer is a brilliant light that grows in proportion to our focus on the intention. The more we focus, the bigger and brighter it gets. This light has amazing power to heal and manifest positive change. This light can support and guide, bring calm and peace, and can only be used for good.

It matters not if our prayer is in our own words, from a sacred text, a lovingkindness meditation or a blessing. What brings the real power to our prayer is when the energy of our love and intention is empowered by divine energy. By enlisting divine assistance in prayer, our ray of light becomes a brilliant sun shining on our intention. Our souls can radiate a lot of light. Add divine light—and anything is possible.

Prayer always changes things.

From where we sit, we don't see the whole story of life's challenges. We don't understand the purpose in suffering, so we often don't know what the end result of our prayers should be. As we do in all of our spiritual conversations, we add, *May this prayer be for the highest good of all* or "Thy will be done." By doing this, we accept that our prayer might be answered in ways we don't expect. It invites surrender, faith and acceptance to the outcome.

Prayer always matters. Prayer always bears light. Prayer always changes things. Prayer always changes us.

In The World:

* Everything you do today can become a prayer. Allow divine light to work through you and use you for the highest good of all.

* When praying for a specific intention, focus your light on the outcome of perfect healing for the highest good, no matter what form that might take.

In The Heart:

* My prayers are working to spread light, love and healing. My prayers hold the power to manifest positive change in the world.

APRIL 18

The Engine

Be kind to your beautiful self.

This goddess of all spiritual lessons was a little late coming to me. After all, I was busy giving of myself in service to others, creating, learning, living, being and doing. Self-care always seemed to be the last car on my train. The caboose. A cute addition to my spiritual track, but nowhere near engine status.

Oh, how wrong I was.

I now see self-care as the foundation of all spiritual practices. If we don't honor ourselves, we can't possibly honor our oneness with all creation. If we don't care for ourselves, we are unable to serve others from the empty well. If we don't see that we are a magnificent reflection of God, we can't be God's magnificent reflection in the world.

We can only become what we accept ourselves as being. So let's accept our magnificence.

In The World:

* Be kind in the way that you think of yourself. Edit out any negative or unkind thoughts.

* Be kind to your body in all ways, fueling it with healthy foods, exercise and plenty of joyful activity.

* Be kind to yourself by imagining yourself on the soul level to be a radiant, powerful expression of God's love.

* Be kind to yourself by taking downtime when your mind, body and soul request it from you. You will know when you feel resistance— that feeling of dragging yourself from one event to the other. Stop, check in with yourself, get present, and treat yourself as a beloved. All else will be accomplished with greater ease.

In The Heart:

* I lovingly care for myself, knowing I am a child of God, radiant, powerful and beautiful. When I am clear and healthy, I enjoy life more deeply and I love others more fully.

Confessions of an Insomniac

May we be at peace in our hearts. May we be at peace in our homes.
May we be at peace with each other. May we imagine peace in our world.

It was hard to feel peaceful when I wasn't getting any sleep. I could fall asleep unaided, but would wake at 2:00 a.m. and be up for torturous hours. Worries swirled madly in my mind, proliferating mid-air, whipping up a Kansas-sized tornado of worst-case scenarios right there over the bed.

Sometimes, I'm embarrassed to say, I'd take copious, messy notes in the dark, about problems, solutions, things to say, things to do. After tossing around my fears and turning around in bed, I'd finally fall asleep and awaken to a pile of crazy fear notes.

In the light of day, nearly everything seemed manageable. I'd toss out the notes and question my sanity. And do it again the next night. Until I found a calmer solution. The Rosary.

I'd never been a big Rosary person. Although I grew up in a Catholic family and was named for Mother Mary, I left my Catholic roots behind in college and embarked on a spiritual journey that took me around the world of faith traditions, only to land me back in love with Mother Mary. I even offered her a seat on the board of Every Day Spirit. (I really did.) So the Rosary is a sort of salary.

Mostly, though, it is her gift to me. As soon as I awaken, every night now for years, I reach over, eyes closed, and get the Rosary from my night table. Before any worry thoughts possess me, I silently pray: *Thank you for divinely solving all problems in the highest possible way.* Then, bam, I start.

In my Dad's little leather Rosary book, it says that every prayer can be like a rose gently placed at Mary's feet. So I offer them with that kind of love—until I fall asleep that is—in which case I finish in the morning when I awaken without a single fear note and with major peace inside and out.

In The World:

✳ Any repetitive prayer or mantra can be used on any kind of beads. When you awaken, hold thoughts at bay and begin your prayer.

In The Heart:

✳ When I have peace within, I contribute to peace in the world.

~ ⁊ ~

Darkness to Flight

Just as she thought this was the hardest day of her life,
she turned into a butterfly.

In the twenty years since the stillbirth of our second daughter, Angela, I have been blessed with an important lesson: Healing has the power to transform us when we bring our suffering to the light of day.

Through my infant loss support group, I have learned that healing begins when we weave our truths into the tapestry of our lives. This means telling our story, unedited, to a compassionate listener. In the process of telling it, we own it as an essential part of who we are. Instead of being walled off in a dark cocoon, our sorrow lives as part of a whole—where grief and love can eventually co-exist—and where there is hope of great pain living alongside a fulfilling life.

Major loss and traumatic events are some of the most important things that will ever happen to us. They change us irrevocably and force us to come to peace (or not) with our lack of control over our lives. They also offer us the opportunity for soul growth and transformation when we compassionately share our experiences with others.

By writing into the pages of our lives our greatest sorrow, and by gently accepting her constant presence here, we weave these events into our souls—made ever deeper and more expansive by each and every experience we endure.

Given the chance to see the light, to feel the sun, to expose the soul to transformation, there is no doubt that from the darkness will rise an amazing, powerful, strong, precious set of wings. Yours and mine.

Let's allow the pain to grow us and color us in. Let's emerge from the dark, look up toward the light—and fly.

In The World:

✳   Seek a compassionate soul with whom you can share your true story and bring the whole of you into the light of day.

In The Heart:

✳   Each day I take small steps toward opening my heart to the truth of my experiences. I accept my sorrow as an essential part of life and I weave it into the tapestry of my soul.

More Gratitude, Less Worry

Keep your eyes on beauty, your body in the breath,
and your soul in gratitude.

Soon after I moved to Hunters Road, I noticed something of grave concern: There were wasp nests under many of the eaves of the cabin. Most were fairly small starter homes, but nonetheless, they were there, and I was not going to peacefully coexist with them. Peter, the supremely helpful owner, offered, "You can knock them down with a broom, but they'll just come back. They're pretty benign."

Benign? Are you kidding me? In my mind, they were dive-bombing the plate at mealtime, chasing me down the hill as I gardened, and keeping me from entering the front door altogether. Before I caught sight of their scary little legs dangling down in hot pursuit, I got online and spent hours researching my options, dutifully reading blog threads, and finally settling on a batch of earth-friendly fake paper wasp nests. I dragged out the ladder with a determined air about me, and hung them around the doors to discourage any new wasp activity in places where I needed to tread. That'll teach 'em.

As winter thawed, I watched, fascinated, as the wasps built nests again under the eave of my writing window. They stayed on point and focused on building, floating just above head level, their long legs making them look less like scary creatures and more like dancing ladies. They didn't dive-bomb, they didn't chase, they didn't block the door.

It was I who had dive-bombed worry. I spent a precious day of my life accusing, dreaming up worst-case scenarios and implementing solutions where no problems materialized. I could have chosen to be present for life's beauty and invitations. I could have been grateful for a hundred small, precious things.

But no, I was busy being chased by scary legs in my mind. Next time, I will come home to the moment I am in. I will reside in the only place where gratitude is possible. Right now.

In The World:

✳ Until it's truly time to take meaningful action, consciously release worries as they arise. Choose to be right here where the blessings are.

In The Heart:

✳ I release my worries and bring myself back to the present moment. I release my fears and trust that I will be guided in perfect time.

❦

Tattoo the Earth

May your footsteps be gentle and your imprint be love.

With each step we take, we change things. Our presence on the planet impacts our surroundings and leaves a permanent imprint—a tattoo—that lives on after we are gone.

Each of us is connected to all other beings and to all of creation as reflected in this traditional Navajo prayer: "As I walk, as I walk, the universe is walking with me. In beauty it walks before me. In beauty it walks behind me. In beauty it walks below me. In beauty it walks above me. Beauty is on every side. As I walk, I walk with Beauty." As guests on the earth, we honor her hospitality by walking in her beauty and leaving behind for our children an earth that is healthy and vital.

The natural beauty that surrounds us is our most treasured resource. Every living creature can be cause for admiration and each glorious scene appreciated as an awe-inspiring gift.

Our natural world is one of the greatest sources of joy to our souls, rising with the sun every single day to remind us of her miracles.

As we celebrate Earth Day today, may we commit to respecting our beautiful home. May we leave behind the imprint of our awe and gratitude. May our presence impact our surroundings in a positive way. May our footprints be gentle. May we tattoo the earth with love.

In The World:

* Be a steward of the earth. Leave her as you find her—or better.

* Be frugal in your use of natural resources.

* Be diligent about recycling and use of plastics.

* Be mindful of the energy you use each day at home and for travel.

* Be involved in protecting the environment.

In The Heart:

* Today, I notice and offer appreciation for the magnificent gifts of nature. I treat the earth with love and respect, and tread with a light footprint.

Effort and Surrender

The very act of surrender makes us stronger.

The theme of effort and surrender plays out in many aspects of life. A good example is on the yoga mat. Before a pose, our breath creates space—a surrender and an opening to grace. Then we use effort to achieve the physical form of the pose. Once in the pose, we surrender, opening the heart once again, allowing the pose to soften while breathing in this new, expanded energy. We again assume effort to go a little deeper—to expand a little further.

This cycle of effort and surrender can continue as long as we hold the pose. The alternating balance of effort and surrender creates a circle of ever-widening exhilaration and strength.

The same thing can happen in our spiritual lives. We are surprised to find that, much like in the yoga example, when we surrender and soften—the very actions we associate with weakness—we find deeper stores of strength and energy. The moment we let go and open to something greater than ourselves, we tap into the source of infinite peace, strength and renewal.

Most of us are willing to make the effort it takes to achieve our goals. We live in a world that favors precision, perfection, striving, attaining and grasping. But using effort alone can block that which we seek.

Through the act of surrender, we find our strength. It is by releasing and opening that we are filled beyond all expectation.

In The World:

✳ When we surrender perfection, we open to vulnerability, the key to unleashing our gifts and talents.

✳ When we surrender the outcome of our efforts, we work for the joy of working and give for the joy of giving.

✳ When we surrender control, we open to the perfect plan of the divine, having faith that we will have all the strength we need for all we need to do.

In The Heart:

✳ In the moment of surrender, I feel a strength that is greater than my own. I release control and put my life in the hands of divine guidance. I open to possibilities beyond my wildest dreams.

꙳

The Truth of Who We Are

Shine your beautiful light.

Sometimes it's hard to believe that we are beautiful, shining lights, that our souls are glorious, that our essence is brilliant love. I know, sometimes it's quite a stretch. If this is one of those times, listen up. We all need to be reminded about the truth of who we really are.

You are here to shine your unique rays of light and share your magnificent gifts. No one can replace you. No one has your fingerprint. No one reflects love the way you do. No one expresses divine radiance like you.

Truly believing in our magnificence is not an easy practice. We are trained to be self-critical and to seek beauty in external ways. But if we want to share our gifts with the world, it's essential that we recognize the truth and beauty of who we are.

When we understand the magnitude of our light and the value of our unique talents, we are free to reach out and share our gifts for the good of all who cross our paths. When we accept the greatness of our love, we can offer great love to others.

Acknowledging our amazingness also enables us to make the powerful connection with divine wisdom. It is from this place of self-love and soul truth that we plug into all of the assistance we will ever need.

You are a magnificent, glorious, beautiful reflection of divine love. You are an irreplaceable part of the whole. No one shines like you do—and someone needs your light today.

In The World:

✳ Take a moment to imagine yourself as a channel of radiant light. Everyone you come in contact with today feels your inner beauty, and you lift their vibration by your very presence.

In The Heart:

✳ The brilliant light of my soul is unique and raises the frequency of the energy of all those who cross my path today.

It's Safe to Be Happy

Keep an open heart for joy, beauty and the gift of small things.

My friend Maria called me the other day with a phrase that had been going around in her heart all day—*It's safe to be happy.* So many of her yoga students came to class feeling tender and worried, weighed down by the stresses of their lives and a barrage of negative news stories. Maria's phrase offered a kind of permission slip to allow joy into the mix. She told them that it is okay to exhale and create guilt-free moments for the simple pleasures of life.

Bringing out the joy in our day isn't a function of the things that happen to us, but in the way we treat ourselves along the way. Joy is already present within us as an integral part of our spirit. When we treat ourselves as the precious beings that we are, we align with the joy within.

Self-love is the key.

The people of Denmark, a country often listed as one of the happiest countries in the world, have a word for cherishing yourself by making your surroundings as comfortable as possible. *Hygge* (pronounced "hue-gah") is the feeling that comes from nourishing the soul in an unhurried atmosphere. It's visiting with friends, enjoying good food by candlelight. It's the contentment that arises when we bask in small delights like a savored coffee or a cozy quilt with a good book. It's relaxation, togetherness, presence, enjoyment, appreciation. We might all do well to channel our inner *hygge.*

Honor your right to the pursuit of happiness and allow yourself the pleasure of the things you love. Sometimes it takes a little letting go to realize how tightly we hold on to our worries.

Remember, it's safe to be happy.

In The World:

* Treat yourself lovingly today. Take an extra moment to enjoy a sweet, simple indulgence. Soak up the feelings of deep satisfaction, contentment and joy.

In The Heart:

* I cherish myself and show myself love by making time for the simple pleasures of life that bring me joy.

~\/~

Improve a Life

*Speaking a few kind words might be the most important thing
you will do today.*

When we think about our purpose in life, we would all like to be able to list lofty goals and accomplishments. We want to know we are here for a reason and that we will make an impact on the world. Discovering the cure for cancer, joining the Peace Corps or giving helpful workshops are the path and purpose for a select few. But what of the rest of us with less definable ways of making an impact?

It's not too much to ask to want to change the world. It's important that our lives have meaning and that the echo of our love will remain when we are gone. As creatures of connection, we are wired to want to lift others up and be of assistance on a daily basis.

And we can.

Perhaps we underestimate the power of our kind words. Just this morning, I had a challenging situation that threw me off. I was moping and wandering, stuck trying to work out an unexpected problem, until I got a lovely note of encouragement that became the wind in my sails. It shifted the energy, helping me to relax enough to see the resolution and get back on track. A few kind words changed my day.

Every day, each of us has the power to improve the life of someone else. That's an important ministry. We have the ability, through our kind words, to change the perspective of another. As the poet Rumi so beautifully reminds us, "Be a lamp, a lifeboat or a ladder. Help someone's soul heal. Walk out of your house like a shepherd."

Let's endeavor to improve a life—to change the world for someone today. Let's help someone's soul heal. That's the real-life definition of purpose.

In The World:

✷ Give the gift of kind words today. Speak them. Text them. Call them in. Email them. Write them in a handwritten note. Be the change.

In The Heart:

✷ Speaking a few kind words might be the most important thing I will do today. I lift others with thoughts and words of kindness.

The Circle of Abundance

Abundance grows from the seed of every thank you.

Giving Thanks. When we keep company with a constant inner *thank you* for the blessings of this day, we are appreciating the gifts of our lives exactly as they are. We do this when we notice the joy in a child's smile, the needed rain falling on thirsty plants, the favorite song on the radio. Every whisper of thanks and appreciation for the smile, the rain and the song brings to light the extraordinary riches in the ordinary moments of today. Our sense of lack is replaced by our focus on abundance.

The seeds of abundance are planted.

Giving Credit. Built in to every *thank you* is alignment with the divine. After all, who are we thanking, anyway? As we offer our thanksgiving in small moments throughout the day, we are humbly acknowledging the God in all things and the reality that we are always being showered with gifts in the form of support, beauty, love, joy and guidance.

Abundance grows toward the light and blooms within.

Opening to Grace. After we give thanks and recognize our co-creation with the source of all abundance, we surrender our grasp over circumstances and control over outcomes. Things go a little smoother when we open to the flow of grace and let gifts that far surpass our individual efforts to conjure them up to move toward us. Now we've opened our souls to the possibility of even more to give thanks for.

The roots of abundance are spreading and new seeds of gratitude are germinating.

In The World:

* Today, give thanks for this precious and amazing day, planting the seeds of abundance.

* Give credit by recognizing your co-creation with the divine.

* Surrender control over outcomes, so that the grace of abundance can unfold in ways that are beyond your wildest dreams.

In The Heart:

* I am blessed in countless ways by gifts from the divine. I give thanks as I notice the beauty and see the good that surrounds me now.

❧

Bless Them

When someone crosses your mind, bless them.

Blessings are a powerful, transformative gift that we can offer to others—anytime, anywhere. When given generously from a heart of love, they shine the light of comfort upon the receiver. In his inspiring book, *The Gentle Art of Blessing*, Pierre Pradervand tells us that, "To bless means to wish, unconditionally and from the deepest chamber of your heart, unrestricted good for others and events." To bless is to uplift.

Whenever anyone crosses our path or our mind, we can get in the habit of offering them a quick blessing. It takes only a little mindfulness to recognize the countless opportunities we have in a day to lift up others in ways that are beyond the scope of our material world.

Pradervand puts it beautifully when he tells us, "To bless all without distinction is the ultimate form of giving, because those you bless will never know from whence came the sudden ray that burst through the clouds of their skies..."

Blessing others gives us a positive alternative to aggravation and complaint, helplessness and fear. There is always something we can do to change the world for the better, and in the process, become an instrument of healing.

In The World:

We might offer silent blessings to others in these ways today:

✳ War or Disharmony: *Bless you to a moment of inner peace.*

✳ Grief: *Bless you with the comfort of a compassionate friend.*

✳ Financial Trouble: *Bless you with faith and abundance.*

✳ Anxiety: *Bless you with a sense of calm security and peace of mind.*

✳ Sadness: *Bless you to see your beauty and goodness.*

✳ Anytime: *Bless you, my friend.*

In The Heart:

✳ Today, as people cross my path or cross my mind, I bless them, imagining for them their highest good and happiness.

The Gift of Saying No

Say yes to what inspires you. Say no to what depletes you.
Your dreams are listening.

Recently my mother sent me a short article on speaking "the language of no." She often tells me that I can't be "all things to all people," and this short piece was in keeping with her advice. I reassure her often that I am not overextended, but in truth, I am always feeling behind and groaning under the weight of the long list of tasks on my to-do list.

Many of us have the lovely tendency to put others first. While this show of love brings with it countless rewards, I'm coming to see that if we give of ourselves to the point of exhaustion and leave little time to recharge our own batteries, our giving energy is short-lived and our divine purpose shortchanged.

I know what fills my well and charges my spirit batteries. I'm sure that you do too. Be it music or meditation, yoga or praying, reading or walking with a friend, we must honor this as our soul food—for these are the very activities that nourish who we are and support our road to self-discovery and purpose. When we follow our curiosity and joy, we are always coming home to our inner beauty. This is the place from which all creation springs forth. If we don't nourish it, our lights become dim.

Saying no is not selfish, but spiritual self-care. When we have more energy, we can share our light in ways that best use our gifts.

So, let's say yes to what inspires us and say no to what depletes us. Our dreams are listening.

In The World:

✳ What we study, what we think, what we say, what we do, what we watch—we align with. When we say no to what is not in alignment with our authentic selves, we honor our deepest truth. Today, let's begin to tip the scales in favor of who we are and what we love. Enjoy having more energy for friends and family, and for experiencing the beauty and joy of this precious day.

In The Heart:

✳ I let go of all that does not feed my soul. I see clearly what should remain in my life and what can be released.

The Offering

The measure of your love is in the gift of your offering.

I may have painted a rosy picture of meditation, neglecting to mention that on some days, it might feel like a complete disaster. You sit and the dog sits on you. You sit and your mind just won't quit. You sit and you remember you forgot to do that thing for your boss. You sit and your leg cramps or you fall asleep or you cry.

But there's one thing that saves the day and makes it all worthwhile. You are making an offering of your effort and the offering is received. No matter how humble, no matter how messy, no matter how sleepy, you showed up and you offered your love. This is what we do every day. We show up. We ask for guidance. We surrender our small selves and make an offering of love to something greater. We offer everything we do. *Take it,* we say within. *Use it for good.*

Great power lies in a humble offering. It's the key to unlocking the doors of spiritual support. That's what holocaust survivor and psychologist Viktor Frankl meant when he said that success and happiness cannot be *pursued* but must *ensue* as the result of our surrender to something greater than ourselves. Grace flows when we make an offering.

We don't own our success or failure—we give it back. Botanist and inventor George Washington Carver was born into slavery and rose to become one of America's most influential voices of agriculture in the South. Every day, he woke and asked God for a plan. He was a prolific inventor who offered every invention and every day of his life back to God. And the grace kept coming.

We do what we can, moment by moment, hour by hour, day by day, to make the world better because we have lived. What is undone or partly done or disastrously done, we offer. It's okay. Because the strength to show up the next day will be provided. The grace is unleashed. The flow is open. Tomorrow will come and we will sit once more in meditation practice and make another beautiful gift of our love.

In The World:

✳ Offer your practice and offer the day. *This is yours. What would you have me do with it?* Receive your plan. *Show me. Use me.*

In The Heart:

✳ The measure of my love is in the gift of my offering.

May Blessings

Be present. Be here. Today, we can guide our thoughts back to the present moment with gentle focus and live fully right where we are.

Let the day flow with grace. Grace flows through us easily when we are in tune with the subtle voice of intuition. Open and listen for guidance.

Expect joy. Be positive. Imagine a fulfilling day unfolding, in which we accomplish much and experience joy in the process. Welcome the light.

Serve with compassion. Acts of service when performed with love lend immeasurable light to our day. Be watchful for ways to serve.

Speak only kindness. Speak only kind words. Think only kind thoughts. Be kind to yourself and to those who cross your path or your mind.

Impart only love. Send out all thoughts and words on the wings of love so that we may love one another, love ourselves, love the unlovable.

Never forget you're not alone. Let's remind ourselves often today that we are always supported, guided and unconditionally loved as we are.

Give thanks for everything. Gratitude will shift the perspective of the day from one of lack to one of abundance. Give constant thanks.

See goodness in others. Each of us has a soul that is made of beauty and love. Assume the best in others so they may rise to their highest light.

From Lack to Abundance

When you're feeling stressed, count the ways you're blessed.

It's comforting to know that when we turn our attention toward all that is going right, we disarm the beasts of stress, lack and discontent pretty quickly. It just takes a little focus, a lot of trust and the revving up of our spiritual practice of gratitude.

It's essential to remember during stressful times that what we focus on will grow. What we worry about stays present. What we dwell on, multiplies. When we complain, we whip up more of what we complain about. And when we focus on the gifts, that's exactly what we find—more gifts.

When life gives us something unexpected today, we've got all the tools we need to handle it. Really we do. We are all infinitely blessed. Let's receive this day with a grateful heart and welcome an immediate shift. Let's put our blessings in the forefront where they belong.

In The World:

* *Take a breath.* Take a deep breath with a long exhale to center and to mark the start of your new outlook.

* *Count your blessings.* Release your focus on fears and mentally name some of the ways you are blessed. Look around you and notice them. Feel the joy of having these blessings in your life. Inwardly smile and count them; the soft shirt, the hot tea, the quiet moment. In less than a minute, you have connected with your infinitely wise center and empowered the feelings of calm, abundance and joy.

* *Return home.* When anxiety or lack creeps back in to your consciousness, gently stop the thought loop with a breath and a return to noticing a few beautiful things around you and all that is going right.

* *Train your eye on beauty.* Unless you are actively working on a solution to the stressful problem, train your mind to return again and again to all that is well with your world today. Vibrate high and you will attract the highest vibrations.

In The Heart:

* I shift my experience today by changing my focus from lack to abundance. I am infinitely blessed and more blessings are on their way.

The Art of Listening

To listen with compassion is to give a precious gift.

Speaking our truth is one of the best ways to get to know ourselves. Many a heart can be healed by the simple act of uncensored expression in the presence of quiet compassion. While it may seem passive to be on the listening end of a conversation, you are giving a precious gift.

I'm not sure when my self-conscious veneer started to crack, but I must admit I talk to horses a lot these days. They don't interrupt me when I'm talking; they nod between bites of grass; they have compassionate eyes. They can handle a wide range of emotions without getting squirrelly and their silent kindness reminds me of the gift given by a good listener.

Yesterday I had a long chat with Floyd. After much thinking, I had come to the conclusion that self-love is the foundation of spiritual practice. When we acknowledge the beauty and divinity within, we open to beauty and divinity in all things. I was working through this, wondering how I had missed the obvious for so many years.

It started pretty innocently. "Hi Floyd. You're SO beautiful...*and so am I!*" And with that I started to cry. Why? Because I haven't thought of myself as beautiful in a long time, and saying the words had played a tender chord in my heart. I went on to tell him how we have radiant light that shines out from within that does not stop with this skin or these bones, or that fence or this field; that our radiance connects with divine light and becomes infinitely vast. And off I went, going all cosmic on him. He stood there listening, then walked closer and laid down by the fence near me. I talked on until I felt my heart crack open and integrate the lesson. What a blessing to be able to speak it. Great listener, that horse.

We can all take a cue from Floyd and listen patiently while someone sorts something out, or vents, or cries, or rambles on. Sometimes we just need to speak the fears out of our minds to disarm them. Sometimes we just need to speak the dreams out of our hearts to empower them. With a small act of words and a big gift of listening, the healing begins.

In The World:

* Active listening is easy. Relax, listen, nod between bites of grass and convey understanding. Your loving presence is all it takes.

In The Heart:

* I give love to others by the gift of compassionate listening.

Friends Are Diamonds

Friends are those who grace us with unconditional love and solidarity.

Friends are diamonds who reflect the light of our spirit. They illuminate our souls and recognize our beauty, goodness and love.

Friends are those who listen compassionately and hold our stories with a tender heart. They reflect back to us what we need to know.

Friends are those with whom we can be completely ourselves and totally uncensored. Nothing we confide will ever be used against us.

Friends are those who guide us when we lose our way and offer perspective when we are blind to our path.

Friends are those who allow us to have our fears, but remind us that they are transient and all that truly matters in life is love.

Friends are those with whom we share the hilarity of our messy days and the humor in our drama. They have a smile for us when we need to be lifted up and are the keepers of joyous memories.

Friends are those who are present for us in times of suffering. They comfort us with compassionate companionship through grief.

Friends are those who grace us with unconditional love and solidarity, keeping company with us on earth until we keep company in all other realms.

In The World:

✳   Find a small but meaningful way to let your friends know how much they mean to you and how grateful you are for their presence in your life.

In The Heart:

✳   I am grateful for the beautiful friends who lift me up and remind me who I am, and who I am meant to be.

The Spiritual A-Team

The loving assistance of our guardians will lift us up in all aspects of today.

It takes a village to raise a child, and it takes saints and sages to raise a soul. My dear ones have been assisting me all my life and I could not manage without them. I'm honored to introduce my Spiritual A-Team:

CEO: Stepping into the position left vacant by his Mother, Jesus has been an amazing leader this year. He singlehandedly dragged me through a complicated app update, teaching me about faith in divine timing and love in all things. I allow him to work through my thoughts, words and hands each day. Alongside him, I am looking forward to the best year yet.

CPO: Mother Mary took on the post of Prayer Officer after breaking the glass ceiling last year as the CEO of my first year in business. Her radiant light and healing power resonates in all aspects of the most important job of prayer. She leads nightly Rosaries and daily prayer breaks for countless intentions. The beautiful Mother is unstoppable.

CMO: After many years as a dedicated student of Paramahansa Yogananda, I am honored to have him here in the role of Chief Meditation Officer, connecting me with God in the silence of my heart. A master at teaching Eastern traditions in the West, he shares techniques to clear my channel to divine wisdom, inner peace and blissful joy.

CLO - Mother Meera is my Chief Lighting Officer and has been my daily assistant since the inception of the company. In charge of the Details of the Day, she backs me up in every project. Her purpose on earth is to bring down the light of God, and she is generous with her talents.

CAO - The Angel Officers are everywhere—guiding, guarding, nudging me in the right direction, patiently waiting for me to ask. With their light-hearted sense of humor, they have a way of translating the power of divine love into gentle guidance and endless support. Love you guys.

In The World:

✳ Today, forge a personal relationship with your honored ones, thinking of them as friends and co-workers. Keep a running conversation and enjoy the blessings of a Spiritual A-Team. Use a page in your journal to assign indispensable positions of importance to your team.

In The Heart:

✳ I open my heart to the loving assistance of my guardians and guides.

꙳

Listen to the Heart

Listen to the heart. It always knows.

I rose from bed this morning expecting to do my usual spiritual practice followed by a full day working on the app. As I have been on the path of ease and grace these days, I took note when I felt resistance to my usual morning routine of yoga, spiritual reading and gratitude practices, meditation and writing. I felt off—encumbered by the organized plan I had been following for some months. Busy day or not, it was time to listen to my heart, and she was telling me to streamline my work space.

I pulled out all of my supplies from the yoga area, the meditation area and the writing area. I tucked away everything that I was intuitively done with. I put some photos away and pulled others out. I got rid of all lists and extra notes designed to tell me what to do next. *I will know what to do and what to write,* I told myself. I even made a different kind of tea and did a sage ritual to energize and bless the cabin. Change is in the air.

It's after noon and I'm just getting to the end of my morning routine, but I'm feeling clear and new. Tomorrow I will start fresh with a simplified morning practice that will lead to more connected and efficient work.

When we relax and lean into the flow, knowing we are unconditionally loved and clearly guided, we access that place in the heart that always directs us toward our highest alignment. We know because we are, in our essence, connected to the source of all wisdom, always flowing toward a higher vibration and greater authenticity.

Pay attention to how you feel. Notice the sense of ease or resistance. Listen to your heart and respond. You will not be led astray.

In The World:

✶ Take at least a few minutes for silent meditation and relaxation. Then ask a question or ask for guidance, and trust that the answer will come clearly. And it will! Stay vigilant for signs and guideposts.

In The Heart:

✶ In all situations, I listen to my heart and believe that my intuition is valid. I trust in the wisdom received.

A Froggy Hallelujah

I flow with what life offers me today.

My tinnitus came on gradually as a result of a long music career standing next to a guitar amp and in front of a drum kit. The first few times my right ear made a shrill scream, I was not alarmed. I thought it might be my angel daughter communicating from heaven. No worries, just a hallelujah.

When it came on full force and full time, with both ears emitting many wavy, high-pitched siren sounds in tandem, I was sure a spaceship had taken up residence in my head. It was so loud that nothing in the world was louder than my ears. Not a rock concert, not an airplane, not the ocean, not fireworks. My ears could always be heard over the sounds of the world.

Until, that is, I moved out to the country and witnessed the frog choir coming from the small pond outside the back door.

I do not exaggerate when I tell you it is deafening. After a rain, it only takes one frog to start singing, then a friend joins in, and within minutes, the place goes haywire. They fill the night with non-stop, ear-splitting, mighty joy. Yep.

I use the same technique to manage the Frog Choir in my yard as I use to manage the spaceship in my head. I pretend it's a hallelujah. Instead of folding under the anxiety of my loud ears, I imagine it's a choir of angels singing of love to me and to God. And instead of waking up at night rustling for ear plugs with a sleepy complaint, I imagine a mighty hallelujah rising from the pond.

And roll over and give thanks that the frogs can out-sing my angels.

In The World:

✳   Put a fresh spin on your greatest aggravations. Make light of what sends you over the edge. Welcome the noise instead of steeling for battle. Have the serenity to accept the things you cannot change.

In The Heart:

✳   I am calm and filled with inner peace. Instead of resisting, I flow with what life offers me today.

❧

Everything Is Possible

Have faith. Dream big. Lead with your heart. Follow your bliss.

To all the new graduates and brave adventurers who are setting off on a new journey in life: Change brings with it the opportunity to begin again and move one step closer to who you are and what you love. Face your transformation with enthusiasm, courage, reverence and an open heart.

And know that everything is possible.

In The World:

* *Have faith.* Those of great faith, who are able to imagine the impossible, are those with the foundation of the essential twin beliefs: Belief in yourself, and belief in a benevolent universe that conspires to support and assist. Aspire to great faith. Believe with your whole heart in your magnificence and in the highest, most unlimited version of yourself. Know beyond all doubt that grace is always lifting up your plans and dreams.

* *Dream big.* If you can dream it, you can be it. If you can imagine it, you can build it. In one of my favorite passages from Paramahansa Yogananda, he says, "Tune yourself with the creative power of spirit. You will be in contact with the infinite Intelligence that is able to guide you and to solve all problems. Power from the dynamic Source of your being will flow uninterruptedly so that you will be able to perform creatively in any sphere of activity."

* *Lead with your heart.* Develop the ability to silence your thoughts so you might recognize the voice of your heart through your intuition and higher guidance. Then listen to the promptings and follow them. When the heart leads, you will always have a North Star and a moral compass.

* *Follow your bliss.* When Joseph Campbell came up with this phrase in *The Power of Myth*, a generation of seekers resonated with its truth. Joy is the most important signpost affirming that we are on the right path. The future goal is not your life. The path is your life. Create a life that makes you happy now.

In The Heart:

* I face transition with excitement and an open heart. I know I am always supported and guided toward my highest dreams.

You Will Know

The door that closed was not your door. Your door will invite you in.

"What do you want to be when you grow up?" We have all been rehearsing answers to that question since we were small, and still our high school and college grads are torturing themselves with it, thinking the answer should be clear. Oh, the pressure.

Our outward measure of success is hitchhiking on the back of our degrees and making the future look mighty heavy. From a spirit point of view, finding a job in our field when we graduate does not define who we are. *Because what we want to be when we grow up is happy, compassionate, loving, kind, peaceful and authentic.* At any age, this is alignment, and is the place from which to start.

After I graduated from nursing school, I began playing in bars as a full-time musician—and twenty years went by. It might have seemed like a financial failure to some, but it's exactly where my heart was pulling me. I've never regretted a moment of it. Every day was a celebration.

We are not our titles, our jobs or our salaries. We are so much more than that. We are infinite possibility. When we follow the authentic yearnings of the heart, we can't miss. When doors close, it means others were meant to open.

Believe, pray, pay attention, be the absolute best version of yourself, and life will unfold as it should. Really it will. "Be patient toward all that is unsolved in your heart and try to love the questions themselves..." Rainier Maria Rilke advises.

Love the questions themselves. Start where your heart leads you and allow life to be a joyous adventure.

In The World:

✳ Be patient with yourself and believe that you will know what to do. You will be led by what unfolds with ease and grace. You will be led by what feels joyful. You will be led by following your inner wisdom. Ask your angels and guides for direction, and open to gratefully receive. You will hear the call. You will know.

In The Heart:

✳ I am unlimited possibility. I follow the authentic yearnings of my heart, and I am led to the perfect experiences in their perfect time.

A Degree in Reinvention

You hold within all of the strength and grace you need for
all you were born to do.

Not only can we support the transition from education to real world with patient excitement, we can also open to the infinite possibilities that await as life unfolds in the jungle out there. You see, it's possible that just when you think you've found your calling, a change will occur that sends you careening on another vine. And where your heart goes, you will go, even if it takes a lifetime. My neighbor, Thelma, went to art school at the age of 69 and graduated first in her class. My mom published her first book at 85. There are no limits to what you can pursue.

Some of us manage to find our purpose early on and stay with it, but the vast majority of us grow and evolve in ways that make it impossible to stay planted in one place. So we find ourselves with *another* Fine Art degree in Reinvention. I, for one, can speak from experience after a menagerie of careers that have left me with something of a Ph.D. in Reinvention. And why not? We have but one precious life and so many amazing choices.

Don't ever put a ceiling on your dreams; you are always *becoming* and will transform many times. Life is a garden of chances in which we are planted, germinate, grow, bloom, release seeds of wisdom, and plant ourselves again. There are many shades and varieties of you.

And your gifts will color the world in incredibly beautiful ways.

In The World:

∗   If you are feeling stuck, go to the library and hang out in the biography or memoir section. Thumb through the lives of some inspiring, limitless souls. The choices are endless.

∗   Try something new, even as a volunteer, that you have been passionate about. Begin the path to reinvention, each small step leading to the next. Allow yourself to be inspired.

In The Heart:

∗   Today I open to all the possibilities my life has to offer. I believe in myself and in the power of my dreams. I am unbound.

Life's Most Important Secrets

Inhale: Love in. Exhale: Love out.

Life is out of control. It doesn't take many years of living as an adult out in the world to glean one of life's most important secrets: We have little control over most of the events in our lives.

We could talk for weeks about karma, the purpose of suffering, and manifestation, but the bottom line is that sometimes things appear to be random and unfair. And in response to this seeming reality, I have come up with a secret of my own:

I always hold within my control what kind of energy I'm going to put into this day.

Simple as that. Am I going to radiate love and her family, or fear and hers?

This is a huge thing to be in control of. If my constant question is: *How can I react to this with love?*, then all day long I am vibrating love. The question itself opens the heart and exposes the deep wells of unending, unconditional love.

Two things happen when we deliberately act with love. We instantly make contact with the divine, the infinite source of all love. Secondly, our capacity to love *ourselves* magnifies as we align with our magnificence as beings of love. Magnify our magnificence. Love does that. It connects us with our divine source, and renders us feeling pretty great.

When we bring the energy of love, and not fear, to this day, we become the energy of love to everyone who crosses our path and crosses our mind. We become a catalyst for infinite love, waking it up in others and lifting the vibration of the planet. Maybe life's not so out of control after all.

In The World:

✳ Throughout the day, breathe love as a beautiful mantra for yourself and others. Inhale: *Love in.* Exhale: *Love out.*

In The Heart:

✳ I breathe in love to the center of my heart, magnify it, and send it out into my world today.

The Gift of Life

Enjoy life. It's a gift. Unwrap it with gratitude and love. —*Tiny Guru*

Last night I had a talk with an old friend who is a recovering alcoholic. She sounded clear and bubbling over with life. The purpose of her call, probably a Step 9 mission, was to voice an eloquent apology for any hurt she may have caused me. I'm guessing we both flashed back to some messy times, but the present moment was so energetically beautiful that I was quick to assure her that whatever happened in the past was long over, and that I always knew anything hurtful did not come from her true self anyway.

She went on to tell me that life had become joyful. After a decade of self-destruction and darkness, she was now, after a year of sobriety, able to look back and see herself on the precipice of losing everything—her family, her health, her home and her life. Yes, she almost lost the precious life she had been given and nearly everything in it.

The shock of that vision completely reordered her priorities. Problems became bumps in the road instead of constant drama. Her family became all the more treasured. Waking up seemed to be cause for celebration. Love was literally pouring out of her.

We are not our mistakes. We are beautiful souls who have come here to experience this precious gift of life together. We are who we have always been: Eternal beings of love. It's never too late for a transformation and another chance to unwrap the gift of life with gratitude and love.

In the words of Emerson, "Write it on your heart that every day is the best day in the year."

In The World:

✳ May we be reminded, no matter what today might hold, to be grateful for the gift of life and to use it to reflect to ourselves and others the joy of who we really are.

In The Heart:

✳ I am infinitely grateful to be alive. Each breath reminds me of the sacred gift of life.

Forever Love on Mother's Day

God's most beautiful work of art is a mother's love.

Dear Angela, Mother's Day is a tumultuous day for mamas who have lost children. Because I had only nine months of carrying you while you were growing inside me does not make me less of a mother to you. You live on daily in my thoughts and in my heart. I am your forever mom, and you, my sweet child. Although many bereaved moms would rather avoid Mother's Day entirely (and I respect the individual nature of grief), I have always taken the day to celebrate your time here as my daughter.

Your loss had already taken so much from me: my joy for so many years; my faith in future plans; my connection with those who couldn't understand; my hope, really. I was not willing to let this day, too, be rooted in pain and loss. Every other day might hold an element of your absence, but not this one. No, I'm claiming this day to remember the radiant love that comes with the honor of being your mom. I want to allow your loss to *find* something new in me.

Twenty years ago, my forty weeks with you were an intense and beautiful adventure. We meditated each morning. We walked on the cobblestone streets of the pretty Austrian town and talked about every little thing. We imagined and we made big plans. We sang, we danced and we read together side by side. And most brilliantly, you brought out a love in me that is unlike any love I have known. A love I would trade my life for. Yes, little one, I would have. I think we got this whole thing backwards. My love for you is one I didn't even know I was capable of, coming in waves of grace and waterfalls of joy. You expanded me.

So on Mother's Day, I celebrate being your mom. I've got some flowers here, and a card—this one I'm writing to you. And that's enough. The gift of the love you brought out in me is worth celebrating because it's a love that won't ever die. I've got it tucked safely right here in my heart—and within every cell of my being—as one of the most precious gifts I have ever received in my life. With Forever Love, Mom

In The World:

*   If your mom or your child has left the earth before you, write them a letter or write your thoughts about Mother's Day in your journal.

In The Heart:

*   On Mother's Day (and Father's Day), I allow the best of my memories to come to the surface and keep safe company with my love.

Gratitude in Advance

I am thankful for the miracles that are yet to unfold.

From the moment we utter those sunrise words, *Thank you for the blessings of this day,* we change the energy of the morning to one of prosperity. Our heartfelt *Thank you,* rising up through the sleepy dawn of today, is a deep and transformative acknowledgement that we are not alone in the creation of our experience, and that this day will bear countless gifts.

Through the lens of thanksgiving, small moments become precious, simple things become sacred and life itself becomes a gift.

In the midst of the pain and uncertainty of my separation, I started a Gratitude in Advance practice. In a spiral notebook, I listed all the blessings I wished for my future life, as if they had already happened. I felt the joy of their fruition as I wrote the same list out every day on a new page. To my complete amazement, everything on the list came to pass.

The more grateful we are, the more we have to be grateful for. Waking with a heart of gratitude and giving thanks *in advance* for the gifts of the day is one of the most powerful habits we can practice. Fasten your seat belt and keep an eye out for miracles!

In The World:

✳ Dedicate a new spiral notebook to a Gratitude in Advance practice. Really get one. This is worth it!

✳ After today's date on the first line, write, *Thank you for the blessings of this day!* Then make a list of future blessings that you are thankful for. For example, *I am in radiant health. Maya got into the perfect grad school. The house sale flows with ease and grace. I have all the money I need for all I need to do. The app sells millions worldwide.* (Still working on that one.) *I write my book with divine guidance.* You get the idea.

✳ Make daily entries, each on a new page with the day's date, as part of your morning spiritual practice. The items are exactly the same from day to day until it comes true and another item takes its place.

In The Heart:

✳ I am thankful for the blessings of this day and for the miracles that are yet to unfold.

Celebrating the Sunrise

There is grace in the sunrise, in the light of a new day.

This morning I wrap in a blanket and pad out to be with the sunrise. The early birds begin with tentative melodies, and the answers arrive with joyful enthusiasm. They seem to know something I don't know. They sing, *Are you awake?* Friends join in until it becomes a symphony of bird songs with the rooster and the ravens throwing in their loud solos. They are insistent. *Are you awake?*

The wind in the trees sounds like a distant waterfall as it blows through the towering sentinels. All of the leaves on Hunters Road clap for the sun. Each blade of grass shimmers wet across the horse field. There is a faint *Om* coming up from the very earth.

This is what I think the birds know: Everything is starting over. Just like me. It is the dawn of a new beginning. New life. Every morning we get another chance—and they sing about it. There are two sunrises; one over the field and one in the soul. The birds have somehow figured this out.

Wispy pink clouds gather expectantly around the place where the sun will come up over the ridge, receiving her, beholding her. The Beatles, *Here Comes the Sun*, sings in my heart with the first beam of light. "It's alright," the lyric tells me. *Really?* Yes. Right now, everything is alright.

There is grace in the sunrise, in the light of a new day. There is space now, while worries wait, for hope to rise. There's a chance now to create beautiful things from the ashes of night. There is faith now, that anything is possible in this brand new world. There is peace now. *Am I awake?* I am awake to the possibilities.

The sun breaks free like confetti of gold shining between the branches of the big tree in the field, and the earth stands still for the tiniest of moments, in awe of this precious day. *We are awake.* And here is our chance to begin again. Because every morning the birds sing, and grace pours in with the light.

In The World:

* If it has been a while since your last time, make a date to experience a sunrise outside. Bask in the sights, the sounds, the colors, the grace.

In The Heart:

* I rise each morning grateful for a new beginning. I believe in the infinite possibilities of this day.

The Currency of Love

May the blessings of this day radiate through your smile,
be helpful through your hands and shine through your heart.

We are infinitely blessed—alive, awake and empowered with the ability to give and receive love. May we freely allow the gifts of this day to pour through us like waterfalls of grace, accepting them with a grateful heart and passing them on to wherever they are needed most.

We are not created as containers to catch, collect and carry our riches. We are created to transform energy by opening to the gifts of life, then allowing them to freely flow through us. Rich with a deep well of love, we receive these blessings and give them back to our world in an endless circle of beauty, transforming our blessings into service for others.

In order to facilitate this exchange of love we don't need to possess any extraordinary talents. Martin Luther King, Jr. once said, "Everybody can be great, because anybody can serve. You only need a heart full of grace. A soul generated by love."

We already have a soul generated by love.

When we are open to being of service, opportunities organically appear. We are given the chance to include or compliment someone, to listen in a way that makes another feel important, or to share our time, talents and resources.

We are made for this, to give and to receive. The currency is only and always love.

In The World:

* My blessings radiate through my smile, giving joy to everyone I encounter today, lifting spirits with light and love.

* My blessings are helpful through my hands, serving where I am needed, lifting spirits with skill and generosity.

* My blessings are shining through my heart, raising the vibration of the world, lifting spirits with energy and grace.

In The Heart:

* With gratitude for the blessings I have received, I serve freely and joyfully, creating a circle of abundance for the highest good of all.

Gratitude That Blesses

Kindness changes the world one heart at a time.

Today, someone took time out of his busy life to write me four short lines letting me know that I had a positive impact on him during a hard time. Those words of kindness were a gift to me in that moment, filling my heart and lifting my spirits. This simple, loving act brought immense joy to my work today, knowing that I had helped one person.

We all go through the day putting out love in the best way we know how, but we rarely know how our actions affect the lives of others unless they tell us. And what an unexpected surprise that is. We are delighted to learn that something we did made an impact. We mattered. Someone's heart changed because of us, and the other person took the time to pause and share it.

We have all been changed for the better by the kindness of others. It might be a teacher, or a counselor, a contractor, or the checker at the grocery store. It could be a doctor or a friend, a bus driver or a care giver. It may be a parent or a mentor, a neighbor or someone at a support group.

When we acknowledge their impact in our lives, we become part of the ripple effect of kindness, changing someone's day while we change the world. One heart at a time.

In The World:

* Take a moment out of your day to write a short note to someone who has made a difference in your life. Let them know how they changed you. Tell them how special they are.

* Encourage your children or students to do the same, helping them to identify how someone has changed their lives for the better, how they might express that in a few simple lines and how it might feel to receive a note like this.

In The Heart:

* I let others know how I feel, freely and openly, taking the time to express simple kindness through words of gratitude.

A Moment of Peace

Send your light into the darkness and your peace into our world.

May God bless those whose lives are touched by war. Protect them, comfort them and grant them a moment of peace.

May God bless those whose lives are touched by grief. Hold them close, give them the grace of hope and grant them a moment of peace.

May God bless those whose lives are touched by illness. Heal them, surround them in light and grant them a moment of peace.

May God bless those whose lives are touched by abuse. Keep them safe, show them their worth and grant them a moment of peace.

May God bless those whose lives are touched by discrimination. Strengthen them, confirm their beauty and equality, and grant them a moment of peace.

May God bless those whose lives are touched by depression. Lift them up, bring them a ray of hope and grant them a moment of peace.

May God bless those whose lives are touched by poverty. Feed and clothe them, shower them with love and grant them a moment of peace.

May God bless those whose lives are touched by loneliness. Be present to them, bring them a loving touch and grant them a moment of peace. Amen.

In The World:

✳ Our light and prayers are a powerful tool for healing and peace. Send your light into the darkness and your peace into our world. It will be felt.

✳ Add your own personal intention to the prayer.

In The Heart:

✳ In communion with divine love, I send my prayers and intentions of peace around the world today.

Phone Down, Chi Up

Peaceful energy is just a breath away.

In Chinese traditional philosophy, *Chi (qi)* is our life force, the vital energy of our being. Similar to the concept of *Prana* in Indian culture, it translates literally as "breath" and metaphysically as the creative flow of our energy in the world. It is inherent in all of us, but the strength of our life force may vary depending on how clear and healthy our channel is on any given day.

On days when I'm using screens a lot, I feel a drain on my *Chi*. Sometimes I can literally feel my lights dimming. I might be accomplishing a lot of work but at great cost to my spiritual energy.

We can balance the effects of technology by taking breaks often during the day to still the mind and connect with spirit. We remember the truth of who we are through meditation, quick prayers, or a phone-free walk in nature.

For many years now I have powered down all electronics on Sundays. It was a little stressful at first, but I quickly got used to keeping company with the real me and with real people. I have no doubt that Sundays alone magnify my clarity and replenish my energy for the entire week ahead.

Disconnect to reconnect. Unplug to get centered. Step away to come closer. Peaceful energy is just a breath away.

In The World:

✳ Balance the effects of technology by taking short breaks today for a few deep breaths and a connection with spirit.

✳ During your spiritual practice, put your phone in airplane mode so you won't hear the vibration calling you. This is your sacred time.

✳ Consider a Tech Sabbath one day a week. It's the best gift you can give to your beautiful self.

In The Heart:

✳ I am a radiant soul powered by the creative energy of spirit. I gift myself with undistracted time for peace and spiritual connection.

Calling Your Power Back

Your inner beauty shines.

It doesn't always feel like our inner beauty is so shiny. Sometimes that powerful, inner lighthouse is socked in with fog and our searchlight becomes more like a flashlight. Life events have a way of covering up our shine by insidiously chipping away at our intensity, and we don't realize it until it's almost dark and we are searching for the shoreline in vain. At just these times, we may need to take matters into our own hands.

Which is what my mom did. She has a tool which she refers to as *calling her power back*. The first time she used it, she was rather desperate. After seven months of dragging through the effects of an autoimmune disease, broken bones and sleepless nights, she was sick and tired of being sick and tired.

So she became inspired to change things, and one morning, she lit some candles, and called on her loving spirit guides. She then pronounced, out loud and with great force, "I call my power back NOW!" (Think Gandalf in *Lord of the Rings:* "You shall not pass!" But she didn't fall off the bridge.)

She proceeded to call her power back in no uncertain terms—to heal, to sleep, to dream—repeatedly, until she felt a shift. She then played some sacred music and completed the ceremony by blessing the invocation. And it was the turning point in what had been an exhausting, protracted illness.

Our shining, inner beauty is always there—a radiant, beaming, powerful light. Never worry that you have lost your mojo. You can't lose it. It's who you are. It just gets covered by the weight of the world, and when you're ready, you have the power to reclaim what is rightfully yours. Shine on, beautiful one.

In The World:

✳ When you are in need of a recharge, find a sacred, quiet moment to call your power back. Keep this ceremony in your spiritual tool box, and use it whenever your lights grow dim.

In The Heart:

✳ I reclaim my radiant light as a beautiful child of God.

Moment by Moment Creation

*We create this beautiful day when we speak, when we wish,
when we think, when we give thanks.*

Our thoughts have more power over what happens today than almost anything else; more than our families, more than our schedules, more than the weather. They shape our moods, our feeling of self-worth, our capacity for joy, our sense of abundance. They are constant companions that can be guided to serve us in creating this beautiful day.

Absolutely everything we do is commented on by our ego minds. We are accustomed to this cohort in our heads, defaulting to her usual rhythms and projections. These thoughts color our perception of the day.

With every thought and action, we co-create with the divine, drawing toward us compatible thoughts and actions. We create when we speak, when we think, when we wish, when we give thanks. We create when we have faith, when we feel compassion, when we smile, when we assist. We create when we are silent, when we trust, when we are kind, when we bless.

Our thoughts are the energy of manifestation. The clearer the thought, the more powerful they are. In *The Whole Elephant Revealed*, Marja de Vries explains, "Focused attention strengthens the power of our intention, because focused attention makes the waves we emit more coherent, that is, more unambiguous and therefore more powerful." The more clearly we focus, the more powerful the thought wave.

Focus mightily on all things light and all things love, and you will create a most beautiful day. Treasure every minute of it.

In The World:

✳ Start the day with a grateful heart and a positive prediction for your ideal day. Repeat your affirmation often. Allow negative beliefs to float by, then turn them around to reflect the hope of your desires.

✳ Flow with what arises—surprises and all.

In The Heart:

✳ I co-create this day with every thought. My thoughts today are positive reflections of my most beautiful imaginings.

Thank You, Scuba Man

Behind every online conversation is somebody's soul.

It was my first all-out attack on a Facebook post. I was a newbie on social media, and my post for that day announced, "Every moment is a sacred moment." Dreamland, I know, but it's my truth. And although a sweeping generalization, it never occurred to me that it could be hurtful. My serene little desk chair tipped over by the weight of my jaw dropping to the floor, horror-struck by the angry comment that went something like:

That's utter bullsh-t. I have no clue who wrote this preppy cr-p, but whoever it was needs to take off the rose-colored glasses, throw them on the ground, stomp on them and wake up to the real world. Obviously they've never carried the lifeless body of their friend to a coroner's wagon...Go stick your head in the sand like the rest of the preppy, do-gooder idiots!

Ouch. My first thought: *I am so not preppy.* My second thought: *I had no idea it might feel that way to you.* I clicked on his picture to do a little recognizance and saw he was a scuba diver. *Me too.* This guy can't be all bad.

In the coming days, I thought about Scuba Man a lot. He wasn't just an angry troll; he was a real person. We both felt misunderstood. He felt I was belittling his experience by throwing fairy dust on the most traumatic event of his life, and I felt like he was accusing me of throwing that fairy dust from a naive, pain-free seat of privilege. Neither was true. But we were both sure that the other was out of line.

Email, social media and texts are our main form of communication, yet without our physical presence, intentions can be easily misconstrued. How can we bring more peace into our writing? More thoughts on that tomorrow.

In The World:

✳ Our written words can lift and can wound. We can't predict the way they will land in a heart, but we can be aware of their power as we write today.

In The Heart:

✳ I consciously use the power of my words for peace.

Thank You, Scuba Man - Part 2

Walk a mile in someone else's shoes. Understand more. Judge less.

After deliberating, I apologized to Scuba Man by private message:

I'm the one who wrote the post that you blasted. Sorry that hit a bad spot. I wanted to let you know that I'm far from preppy (more of a hippie), a lifetime scuba diver, (but not nearly as trained as you!), and although I have not carried the lifeless body of a friend (I'm so sorry for your loss), I have held the lifeless body of my child. But I had to make a choice when I realized that there is really only one thing I can control. And that is the energy I put into the world. I've been a student of spirituality all of my life so that's how I process pain. If those are rose-colored glasses, oh well. It's the best I can do. I do believe that even through the tears, holding my daughter in those traumatic moments was sacred. For me. I guess I just wanted to tell you that things aren't always as they seem and we all have a story. I wish you the best.

I shot up a prayer, hit Send, and didn't hear back. When he crossed my mind, I'd think, *Bless you, Scuba Man*, and let it go. Months later, this appeared:

Thank you very much. Your comments and story clear the air. Best wishes!

We were strangers, bonded by similarities. We didn't define our experiences in the same way, but we shared the feelings of loss, emptiness, pain, confusion and grief. Knowing how my words could be felt by a newly grieving person taught me an important lesson. When we imagine what it would feel like to walk in someone else's shoes, the common thread of our shared humanity makes us less likely to assume and to judge.

Thank you, Scuba Man.

In The World:

* Remember the soul behind every unique opinion.

* Choose your battles and consider disagreeing in a private message.

* Be open to unexpected lessons of spirit from the most random places.

In The Heart:

* Today, with an open heart, I love more and judge less.

Unconditional Love

Love and light to all today.

Imagine you are running late for work in rush hour traffic when someone cuts you off and nearly causes an accident. Or the person ahead of you in the express checkout line at the grocery store has about 30 items in their basket instead of the limit of 15. Or you have your blinker on, patiently waiting for a parking space at the mall when someone swoops in from the other direction and slides neatly into your space. We all know them—aggravating behaviors that test the thin limits of our developing patience.

For those who hold a special place in our lives, it's natural to extend our goodwill in support of them and of their intentions. When a friend is sick or a family member is in a challenging situation, we send them light and blessings in hopes of bettering their situation. But what of those who are not in our inner circle? Or those whose behavior is incredibly annoying or extremely rude?

We have no way of knowing the stories behind the absent-minded or even deliberately negative actions of strangers. But if we assume the best of all people, and consider that they may have had an important story behind their behavior, it's evident that they also need our blessings.

There is an endless well of love and light within us that is always ready to be shared. The more we give away, the more we are able to receive. Be generous in doling out blessings. They are so needed and are always received on a soul-to-soul level. Your blessings lift up the hearts of others as a silent but powerful prayer, and as a gift of unconditional love.

In The World:

✳ To anyone who enters your orb today, in a positive or negative way, give them love and light, and bless them on their way.

In The Heart:

✳ I am a being of light and have an infinite amount of love and positive energy to share. I freely bless all those who cross my path today.

Life Is Beautiful

Music unwraps the heart, sings out the prayer,
dances the spirit and opens the soul.

Whenever I feel the urge to wade through the waters of self-pity, I snap out of it when I think of Alice. "Every day, life is beautiful. I am full of joy!" So said Alice Herz-Sommer, the concert pianist, mother, teacher and longest-living holocaust survivor, living to the age of 110. When I heard her speak these words in an interview, tears welled up in my eyes for the sheer beauty and impossibility of her statement. How remarkable that someone who had lost so many of her beloveds and witnessed one of the most traumatic chapters of human history, could exude such love, enthusiasm, delight and gratitude.

Alice credits music with saving her life, and saving it even after the war was over. When the Nazis first occupied her town and took her mother to her death, Alice poured herself into the Chopin Etudes—challenging compositions of the classical piano repertoire.

She practiced sometimes as much as eight hours a day, choosing to see and hear beauty, focusing on the light in an ocean of despair. The hungry and hopeless prisoners who witnessed the more than one hundred performances during her two years in Theresienstadt concentration camp said her music was food for their souls, transporting them to another, more hopeful place. "Music is magic," she explained simply.

So when we wonder if we can bear the unbearable, Alice tells us we can. "The music, the music! It brings us on an island with peace, beauty and love." When we wonder if we can ever know joy again after a loss, Alice shows us it's possible. She expresses little bitterness, choosing instead to turn to beauty and love. "It is up to us whether we look at the good or the bad."

In The World:

✳ In the face of her darkest days, Alice turned to music. Her music could be our pottery, our garden, our cooking, our knitting, our wallpaper app. We, too, can choose to look for the good. Every small step is an offering of love.

In The Heart:

✳ I feel the joy of being alive and allow myself to expand through beautiful works of nature, music and art.

Made from Love

Your mistakes do not define you. Your love does.

If we could lift up off of the earth and see as the angels see, all we would see is the radiant light of our love. And it's a beautiful sight.

No one is free from mistakes and missteps. Some of us even bear the burden of knowing that our actions have hurt other lives. And we need to let all of that go. Without delay. Isn't it possible that those very actions have allowed us to come to a more enlightened place? Berating ourselves on top of the guilt and shame does not assist in our growth; it only serves to exhaust our souls by grounding our flight with a storm of self-doubt.

It's not what we do, or how we do it, that matters in this world. It's how much we love. And every single day, we have a chance to begin again and make it a day in which our thoughts are empowered by love. What lives on until the end of time is the love we share. Our mistakes do not define us. Our love does.

Even in the depths of despair, when we offer a small token of love to another, we begin to heal. Even after a regrettable circumstance, when we ask for forgiveness with love, we begin to heal.

We learn, we love, we heal, we grow, we love more. We can't go wrong. We are made from love.

In The World:

* Disable destructive, self-critical thoughts as soon as you recognize them.

* Replace them with affirmations of kindness and encouragement.

* Make amends for past mistakes. Then let them go.

* Live today from a place of love. Start by reaching out to someone with one loving compliment.

In The Heart:

* I am a being of love. All of my thoughts and actions today are empowered by love.

Contagious Kindness at Walgreens

*Every act of kindness will multiply exponentially
as it spreads from soul to soul.*

Some months ago, when running errands at the nearest city about twenty miles from the cabin, I found myself for the first time at Walgreens when my regular pharmacy did not have my prescription. There were many people in line, and I resigned myself for a long wait at the end of a long day.

But something was very different here. The energy was incredibly...happy. There were four women behind the counter; two taking orders and two filling them. They were constantly checking in with each other—pharmacists assisting cashiers and vice-versa. They were upbeat and friendly with one another, and most wonderfully, they were especially kind to their customers.

They noticed if someone wasn't feeling well and tried to expedite their order. They took care to listen well to each customer and to be patient in answering questions. Next thing I knew, all of us who were waiting in line were in conversations with each other, complimenting an outfit, remarking on the weather. Someone even let someone else go ahead of them in line.

The kindness that the ladies were showing to each other and to us—was contagious.

Yesterday, I had to fill another prescription, and of course I went to the Kind Walgreens. The same four women were there, and once again, they were rockin' the line with kindness and joy. And, no lie, the same thing happened. We who were in line began to chat, with compassion and smiles spreading from one to the next, faster than a virus.

We have learned that people who witness acts of kindness are more likely to show kindness to others, but it was a special gift to see it playing out in a humble line. Who knew? The ladies at the Walgreens are changing the world with contagious kindness.

In The World:

✳ Every act of kindness will be multiplied exponentially as it spreads from soul to soul. Let's change the world with our kindness today.

In The Heart:

✳ Each day, I have the power to change the world for the better.

One Miracle at a Time

One breath. One hour. One day. One miracle at a time.

If the drama of life seems overwhelming today, welcome, dear one, welcome to the party. Sometimes the most important thing we can do, literally, is breathe. And focus on one thing at a time, with love. When we feel ourselves spinning out, we can stop the downward spiral with one...mindful...breath...at a time.

It seems like a small thing, but in truth, our breath is our connection to everything. It has the power to slow our autonomic nervous system, which can ease panic and fear. It has the power to oxygenate our every cell, bringing renewed energy and health to the body. It has the power to focus our racing thoughts on the moment we are in. It has the power to align us with our spiritual selves so we may access the wisdom and grace of our highest love and support.

It's okay to break things down into manageable scenes today. Especially if we are overloaded or in a painful situation. Our bodies and souls are telling us that this moment needs attention. All else will work its way out. This moment needs us now. This moment wants tea and grace. This moment wants us to be open to whatever it asks of us. To be still and present *is* getting something done. Maybe it's the most important thing we will get done today.

We don't have to figure it all out right now. We have all the help we need when we step back and ask for it. Our job is to keep our hearts open and to act from a place of love.

Simply start with one breath. Then one hour. One day. One miracle at a time.

In The World:

✳ Take a centering breath. And another. Then just be fully in this hour. You can do an hour. Pain and all, messiness and all, grief and all, you can stay in it for an hour. Keep your heart open.

In The Heart:

✳ For now, I take it one breath at a time. I stay in the moment while believing that I have all the strength I need for whatever life asks of me today.

May They Feel Our Love

May the infinite light of our prayers shine into the darkness of those who need them today. May they feel our love.

I once read a true story of a near-death experience where a woman had "died" in a car accident. She floated out of her body and her consciousness was above her car. She said she could see, hear and feel the prayers coming from the long line of cars who were now stopped on the congested highway behind the scene of the crash. The prayers looked like lights beaming out of the cars, and the incredible, transcendent love she felt from them convinced her to return to her body, where she recovered and was able to later share her story.

There are countless anecdotal accounts of how prayer has changed the course of circumstances. Some believe these to be true and some don't. But if you choose to pray, there's no halfway. We need not even speak the words without pure passion and love behind them. Having faith that the prayer is indeed working for the highest good of all is where its power and grace comes from. So when you pray, do it all the way, with all the focus you have.

For those in the wake of life's storms and those who have left this world before us, our prayers can make a difference that we will never know about. This is a gift we can give to our families, our friends, to strangers, to our world. They will feel our love.

In The World:

∗   May the infinite light of our prayers shine into the darkness of those who are suffering today. May they feel our love.

∗   May the infinite light of our prayers reach into the hearts of those with special needs today. May they feel our love.

∗   May the infinite light of our prayers reach out to the spirits of those who have gone before us. May they feel our love.

In The Heart:

∗   With compassion for all beings and fueled by divine love, I offer the light of my prayer to all those who might be lifted by them.

Too Good

The story of your life is written with kind words, helpful hands and a loving heart.

If you are out in the dating world, you might want to lean in for this one. No, I don't have tips for profiles or anything like that. But in the increasingly judgmental world of division and separation, there are a few things we might want to keep in mind.

My mom and dad, each from a different political party, cancelled each other out at every major election. On top of that, Dad was deeply Catholic, a lay minister who served Communion at Mass, while Mom fled the church at the beginning of the sex abuse scandal, never to return. She immersed herself in the pursuit of God and developed a deep spirituality of her own making. The Pope and The Buddha I would call them. But they had a happy marriage. Being of differing beliefs did not deter them.

In fact, it's imperative that we maintain respect for various political and spiritual beliefs. We all have to make our own decisions about what we can or can't live with. But know that beautiful souls are present on both sides of the aisle in politics and in church, and our personal partnerships do not have to match if we allow each other the honor of independent thinking. That said, bigotry or hatred of another group on the basis of their appearance or belief system *is* a showstopper, but we know that.

On another note, once Maya described a guy who was interested in her as "too good." I almost crashed the car. *Are you kidding me? There is such a thing as too good?* As you can imagine, I opened the floodgates on that one. "Too good is desirable. Too good is amazing. Too good is what you're looking for, honey! Too good is the deal. You want to be treated like the goddess that you are. Go for too good!" She listened well, and dated Too Good for years. I never once worried when they were out together because I knew he had her back. Politics and religion aside, that's what we want. We want a beautiful soul. One that is Too Good.

In The World:

✳ Be fair and non-judgmental as you navigate the world and your personal life. You want to surround yourself with people who respect you, who treat you with love and compassion, who would never dream of being unkind to you, who protect and cherish you.

In The Heart:

✳ In all things and in all ways, I am worthy of great love and kindness.

◦⌄◦

Today's Grace

I have all the grace I need for all I need to do.

Today's grace is already here and we have been generously provided for. In all we do today, we will have a bountiful *helping* of grace.

Today's grace only asks that we love ourselves enough to open to it. That we soften the angular edges of our plans for today and reimagine the day as a benevolent road with choices and chances.

Today's grace is all that we need to experience beauty and love. It is all we need to mobilize the strength to do the hard things. It is all we need to give thanks for whatever arises and to meet life with an open heart.

Today's grace flows toward ease. Like energy, it will channel us to the path of least resistance, so we may accomplish our tasks with enthusiasm and synchronicity.

Today's grace is all we need for all we *need* to do. Gentle up. Some things might flow smoother tomorrow, or if we had the assistance of someone else.

Today's grace works well with laughter and a light heart. It points the way with flexibility and surrender. It revels in our joy.

Today's grace is already here and there's always enough.

In The World:

✳ Open, allow and welcome the lightness of flowing with grace. Trust that today's grace will lift us in small acts of tea and big acts in the boardroom, in the classroom or with the kids. Remember it's here for us, in every moment.

In The Heart:

✳ I am surrounded and cushioned by the gift of grace. In all I do today, I flow with ease and a light heart.

June Blessings

Be present. Be here. Today, we can guide our thoughts back to the present moment with gentle focus and live fully right where we are.

Let the day flow with grace. Grace flows through us easily when we are in tune with the subtle voice of intuition. Open and listen for guidance.

Expect joy. Be positive. Imagine a fulfilling day unfolding, in which we accomplish much and experience joy in the process. Welcome the light.

Serve with compassion. Acts of service when performed with love lend immeasurable light to our day. Be watchful for ways to serve.

Speak only kindness. Speak only kind words. Think only kind thoughts. Be kind to yourself and to those who cross your path or your mind.

Impart only love. Send out all thoughts and words on the wings of love so that we may love one another, love ourselves, love the unlovable.

Never forget you're not alone. Let's remind ourselves often today that we are always supported, guided and unconditionally loved as we are.

Give thanks for everything. Gratitude will shift the perspective of the day from one of lack to one of abundance. Give constant thanks.

See goodness in others. Each of us has a soul that is made of beauty and love. Assume the best in others so they may rise to their highest light.

Dolphin Dreaming

Pay attention to the valuable gifts that dreams leave for our waking lives.

I have always been a dreamer in more ways than one, entertaining nightly mini-dramas of all kinds. My dreams range from random, to vivid— dreams that seem nearly real in which I remember every detail and color—to lucid dreams, where I realize I am dreaming in the dream and can direct them. I even had a complete song come through me, singing it in the dream and writing it down in its entirety when I woke.

Much about dreams is not well understood but there is agreement that they are an important means of learning about ourselves, that they consolidate our memories, that native peoples throughout time considered them an important source of cultural wisdom, that dreams can lead to creativity and problem solving, and, my new favorite, that sometimes people dream in tandem.

Last week, while visiting my beautiful mother-in-law Kay for her 85th birthday, Maya and I stayed in her basement bedroom. We slept side-by-side in twin beds, heads not three feet apart. In the morning, as a group of us chatted on the porch, I told of my vivid dream the night before.

I was flying over a beautiful landscape when I was drawn to a body of crystal blue water. I looked out over the water to see three dolphins. In my mind, I called them and they swam happily to shore. They lifted their heads, bodies vertical in the water, so I could reach out and pet the head of each one. I looked up and Maya stood jaw-dropped in the doorway. "I had the *exact same dream!*" After comparing notes, we realized that in our dreams we came to the water from different places, but joined there and dreamed the exact same dolphin story in tandem before waking.

At night, just about anything can happen. We rest, we travel, we learn, we are guided and we are refreshed. Pay attention to the signs and the valuable gifts that our dreams leave for our waking lives.

In The World:

✻ To remember your dreams, try using a dream journal. When you awaken, record any images that you remember. Soon full dreams will unfold in your memory upon awakening.

In The Heart:

✻ I dream nightly and absorb wisdom from the gift of my dreams. I allow my sleep time to access my deeper wisdom.

Blue Mind

I am calm. I am content. I am connected. All is well.

Imagine slipping into an easy meditation, where you are awed by the overwhelming beauty of life; feeling calm, relaxed, content and at one with an inexplicable power greater than yourself. This is your brain at the ocean.

Marine biologist Wallace J. Nichols has spent years researching and lecturing about the uplifting effect of water that he calls "Blue Mind." He writes, in his book of the same name, that when we are in or near water, we enter into a mild meditative state that brings us peace, happiness and the sense that all is well. Water provides a precious break from the noise and overstimulation of the world—an antithesis to our time on the tiny blue screens. It mellows our minds with much needed down time, allowing creative solutions to rise to the surface, and for healing to take place on many levels.

We don't have to be on vacation at the beach with our toes in the sand to receive the benefit of water on our souls. All bodies of water have restorative powers. Rivers, waterfalls, lakes and streams have a comforting, calming effect. Pools and mineral springs, even showers, tubs and apps that play the sound of waves crashing on the shore, soothe our inner tension. We are hard-wired to become more peaceful when our senses are resting in a water element.

More than seventy percent of our blue planet is covered with water. It is one of God's greatest gifts to us. Let's dive into the abundant blessings of Blue Mind.

In The World:

✳ Think of exposure to the sight and sound of water as a spiritual practice.

✳ Make an effort to be near water in nature as often as possible. Take a hike by a river or have lunch at the lake in the park.

✳ Notice and appreciate the peaceful and balancing effects of water today.

In The Heart:

✳ Water centers me, calms me, heals me and restores me.

Vacation Packing List

For yourself, patience. For everyone you meet, kindness. For joy, a sense of humor. For the soul, relaxation. For plans, flexibility.
For the journey, gratitude. For all of the above, grace.

Vacations are not always what they seem. While most people look pretty serene in their travel photos, many of us admit to at least a little vacation stress. It can be a lot of work to prepare for the trip with all the laptops, tablets, phones, chargers and cables. When we arrive, we face spotty cell service, no free Wi-Fi connections and slow upload speeds. Okay, just kidding about the tech stuff...but there's some truth here!

Vacations provide a precious opportunity to open the soul to inspiration. One of the beauties of getting away from our daily routine is not being available in the usual ways. So consider traveling light and tech-free in mind, body and soul. With a virtual suitcase that won't cost extra, we can put in a little pre-trip prep that will serve us in all stages of travel and re-entry. Happy trails to you.

In The World: Vacation Packing List:

* Patience - Vacations come with lines, sometimes long ones. Come prepared with a fun way to occupy the time together that doesn't involve a phone. Be creative. Or just talk to each other.

* Kindness - Start by being especially kind to yourself. Show kindness to all those you meet on your journey. Every server, guide and driver was meant to cross your path. Honor them all. Be extra kind to your travel companions.

* Sense of Humor - Choose joy. This can really save the day—yours and others. Be generous with your smiles. Let your heart be light.

* Relaxation - Get a massage. Do yoga. Read. Meditate. Walk. Let go.

* Flexibility - Things change. We can change. Go with the flow and ride the current with ease and grace.

* Gratitude - For everything about this new experience, be thankful.

* Grace - That you might have all of the above.

In The Heart:

* I allow my vacation to be a time of joy and rejuvenation. I am present for new experiences with an open and loving heart.

Bless Someone

*Blessings are silent beams of love that magnify our thoughts
with the light of grace.*

Every time we bless someone, we send them a beam of love. Imagine beautiful light extending from your heart to theirs, lightening their load, lifting up their burdens, providing strength and healing. They feel lifted. You feel lifted.

Blessing others only requires two things of us. First, a focused thought of the other in a state of wellbeing. *Bless Tom in his new house. Bless Becky in her job search. Bless Katie and Ryan's wedding. Bless Bobby in his travels today. Bless Brenda to perfect health. Bless Lisa's concert tonight.* The more clearly and sweetly we feel it, the brighter the light will be.

The only other requirement is to remember to do it. Blessing people and situations can be cultivated into a habit. Having some cues that prompt us to remember is helpful.

For example, whenever someone crosses our mind, we can get in the habit of blessing them. *Bless John and his family.* Whenever you are troubled about a situation or it crops up as a challenge or worry, bless the situation. *Bless Bill in his business presentation today.* Whenever we are prone to anger, we can use a blessing to transform the energy. To the driver that cuts us off, *Bless him to a moment of peace.*

Every single time we send out a blessing, we are also connecting with our own spiritual power, invoking grace from our highest self and a higher source. Each gift of a blessing opens wide the doors of our spiritual locker room and we, in turn, are showered in blessings. A win-win if ever there was one.

In The World:

* Use the art of blessing others as a spiritual practice throughout the day today. Try it in all circumstances, sending blessings to loved ones and strangers alike; in situations of ease and also in ones of challenge.

* Add the practice of blessing others to your spiritual journal.

In The Heart:

* Throughout this day, I bless all who cross my path, generously and in connection with unlimited divine source. Blessing others brings me joy.

Frannie Makes a Comeback

I am ready to succeed, knowing that my effort is a success in itself.

Oh gosh, Frannie, I'm so sorry. That haircut. What can I say? I don't blame you for running away and hiding in the woods at the corner of the field for two days. It was a bit of a disaster. Even for a llama.

I felt like that the other day. I just finished working on a big app update, putting everything I had into it. I was worn down from two months of twelve-hour days. For me, the app is the representation of my best work and it was as good as it was going to get. The testing was done. The early reviews were in. It was time for marketing to begin. It was exhilarating...and terrifying.

All I wanted to do was run into the woods at the corner of the field and lay down. I was asking those "daring greatly" questions. *What if my best work isn't good enough? What if I have created what I call my best work and nothing happens? What if it's embarrassingly horrible? What if it's a terrible bad hair day and I have to face the sheep?*

Today, you are back at your post. You look thin from the sheering but you are proudly guarding your charges. I can see in your eyes that you are confident and alert, no longer self-conscious, ready to rise to greatness should a bear enter the field.

I think I'm ready now too, Frannie. Because the only judgment of my work that really matters is my own and that of my inner circle. I'm ready to come out of the woods and stand tall. I'm ready to walk back to the sheep and to be myself bravely.

In The World:

* Be prepared to fail and to rise up again. But most importantly, be prepared to succeed, knowing that the effort is a success in itself.

In The Heart:

* I let go of all negative thinking and self-judgment that does not serve my highest good. I am a unique expression of divinity and am unchanged by all exterior judgment.

Lovingkindness Meditation - Part 1

May I be well. May I be happy. May I be loved. May I be at peace.

Today is one of those days. We are the camel and the last straw just got added to the pack on the hump. And we know what happens next. The cumulative demands on our body and soul have gotten the better of us. Mama said there'd be days like this.

For starters, this is a *good* day to remember our morning spiritual practice. Just sayin'. Meditation, gratitude journal, inviting in the angels and divine grace—these practices are beckoning now. We know this. Beyond that, there's the rest of the day looming. And Lovingkindness Meditation is here for us.

It's a kind and gentle practice, easy on the heart and mind. It is here to flood our aching places with tender love and kindness, and to wrap our brokenness in wellness and safety. It invites peace and self-compassion.

As with all things love, we must first unleash the joy, love, health and peace within, then we can go outside ourselves with compassion for all beings. First things first. Let's start within.

In The World:

∗ This is a simple version of the traditional Lovingkindness Meditation, which evolved from the ancient *metta* or *maitri* practice of benevolence toward all.

∗ Sit upright and gently relax, releasing preoccupations and distractions. As you repeat these words, allow them to evoke the feeling behind them.

∗ *May I be well. May I be happy. May I be loved. May I be at peace.*

∗ Repeat over and over, allowing the phrases to fill your mind, body and soul. Feel wrapped in lovingkindness. Be easy with this. Float in your goodness. Take a moment for yourself.

∗ Use these phrases as affirmations to accompany you as a soothing balm anytime during the day when you need gentle soul rejuvenation.

In The Heart:

∗ I love, honor and care for myself through the difficult blessings.

Lovingkindness Meditation – Part 2

May you be well. May you be happy. May you be loved. May you be at peace.

Hopefully we have all arrived at today breathing a little deeper, with hearts opened a little wider, and feeling less like a camel. Or a llama. Llamas sometimes have to carry heavy things too. And don't forget donkeys and horses. In any case, if you haven't done so already, take the pack off, dear one.

It's a beautiful day to share some love, and Lovingkindness Meditation is a lovely way to do this. It is a three-part meditation, and traditionally the second and third parts are for others.

Today we look at Part 2 of the practice. Here we direct our thoughts to those closest to us, offering the beautiful blessing of these words to our loved ones.

Then we turn our compassion to those who are, let's say, not so easy to love—those we disagree with and those we might consider to be our enemies. This doesn't hurt a bit, and it just might deepen our well of love.

In The World:

* Like yesterday, start by sitting upright, gently releasing tension and allowing the breath to bring you to quiet. Begin Part 1:

* *May I be well. May I be happy. May I be loved. May I be at peace.*

* Repeat in a continuous, relaxed flow until you feel love and compassion growing like a beautiful light within. Close your eyes and take a moment for yourself here. Then move to Part 2:

* *May you be well. May you be happy. May you be loved. May you be at peace.*

* Repeat for a few minutes directing your thoughts to loved ones, family, friends and those closest to you. Then repeat for a few minutes for those who are harder to love.

In The Heart:

* I am loving and compassionate toward myself. I offer this same love and compassion to others from the infinite well of my heart.

Lovingkindness Meditation - Part 3

May we be well. May we be happy. May we be loved. May we be at peace.

Here we are, in the unfolding of another precious day, with another chance to offer some gifts from our endless well of love. With the addition of Part 3 of Lovingkindness Meditation, we reach out to all beings, including nature and the earth upon which we walk. Look out, World. Big love coming your way.

Combining all three parts, we start by directing compassionate thoughts to ourselves, then to our loved ones and to those who are difficult for us to understand or agree with, then on to include all beings.

If you like the idea of being a light worker and using your love to lift up the vibration of all others, you will love the complete meditation. In doing all three parts of this practice, know that within minutes, you have given a magnificent gift to yourself, to all beings and to the planet.

In The World:

∗ Begin by sitting upright, gently releasing tension and allowing the breath to bring you to quiet. Longer exhales are helpful for grounding. Begin Part 1:

∗ *May I be well. May I be happy. May I be loved. May I be at peace.*

∗ Repeat in a continuous, relaxed flow until you feel love and compassion growing like a beautiful light within. Then move to Part 2, directing your phrases first to loved ones, then to those harder to love:

∗ *May you be well. May you be happy. May you be loved. May you be at peace.*

∗ Repeat for a few minutes for each group. Then move to Part 3, for all beings and all of nature. Imagine your love wrapping around the earth:

∗ *May we be well. May we be happy. May we be loved. May we be at peace.*

In The Heart:

∗ I am a being of limitless love and compassion. I wish for all beings to have the same love and compassion that I wish for myself.

Holy Down Time

How beautiful it is to do nothing and then to rest afterward.
—Spanish Proverb

Maybe it's staying in my PJs and floating from yoga to meditation to a steaming cup of Earl Grey. Perhaps it's the freedom of having no schedule to adhere to. Or it might be that I've shut down the computer for the day. Whatever it is, the mere thought of my Sunday Sabbath makes me light up with pure Mardi Gras joy. After years of practice, the art of allowing and receiving only gets better.

Your body and soul know when you need a break. Listen to that wisdom, and when it raises the red flag, schedule in some holy down time. Without any effort at all, the walls that we have built around us to fend off stress swing wide open to divine wisdom. We receive more focus, clarity and intuitive guidance when we step away and open up the channels once again.

Some of us can't afford the luxury of a whole day without demands of work or family. But it's essential that we carve out an oasis of even a sacred hour once a week where nothing is required of us and we choose what to do or not do during that time.

Within these open moments, our souls speak and our hearts listen. It's not selfish but necessary to enjoy the glorious blessings of resting, being and allowing.

In The World:

✳ Allow yourself guilt-free, do-nothing time at least once a week and as often as needed during demanding times. After unplugging, all that you need to accomplish will happen with greater ease and grace.

In The Heart:

✳ I honor myself enough to stop and rejuvenate when my body and soul are in need of rest. It is an essential part of receiving my highest intuition.

From Survival to Joy

All I have is all I need.

In 1943, Abraham Maslow created a stir when he put forth a paper called, "A Theory of Human Motivation." He wanted to know what made us tick—what impassioned the spirit when there were no external rewards dangling in front of us. Maslow came up with what he called the Hierarchy of Needs, whereby after we attain one level of need, we are able to turn our sights to the next, moving from physical survival to safety, love and belonging, self-esteem, and finally on to self-actualization and self-transcendence. Not everyone goes through all the steps, but in general, we move from survival to joy.

I have friends who make yearly mission trips to a third-world country, and they are always moved by the apparent joyful nature of those with very few possessions. It's not merely happiness because supplies and loving faces have arrived—they feel it lives within them before and after their visits. Perhaps when there is no hope of an abundance of *things*, contentment for what *is* settles in. The focus moves up the ladder to love, belonging, self-esteem and beyond.

When we are in excess of what we *need*, we can get tangled in our *desires*. There's nothing wrong with collecting things, as long as we realize that things are not going to raise us up to higher levels of love and lasting fulfillment.

The first stop in the search for contentment is to simply stay in tune with the spark of divine light within. Then lift our eyes from the inner world to others. From our place of divine connection, we truly love. Through love, we find our connection to all beings, our value, meaning and purpose. The journey to spiritual fulfillment is not about our desires; it's about love and connection. It's never too late to learn that we can be joyful with a bare minimum of possessions.

In The World:

* Ask to be shown what to let go of to create space for spiritual growth. Keep what you love. Hold on to what you need. The rest will fall away.

In The Heart:

* Right here, right now, in this moment, I am complete. I am content. I am joyful as I am. All I have is all I need.

Joy Tenderly Grows

Great love and tender joy can cohabit the space of sadness.

There's a picture I adore of a befuddled guinea pig standing next to red flowers. "I'm totally trying to choose joy," he is saying, and we can almost see his eyes roll and hear his sad thought, *How can I choose joy when I'm sad?* Or a thousand other reasons why choosing joy is hard today. His expression says it all. He's not there yet but he's trying, even staying near to something beautiful and happy. The red flowers are helping.

At our infant loss meetings, we have occasional moments of comic relief. Newcomers are sometimes shocked to see laughter flying in the face of grief. But the truth is, love, joy, sorrow and grief can occupy the same heart. We accept and live with what is honest, real and authentic in each moment. There is no right answer and no one path.

Our circumstances don't dictate our joy or our sorrow; it is our *belief* about our circumstances that holds the power. When we open to all aspects of our grief, we begin to allow her ebb and flow. To consider the thought that great love and tender joy can cohabit the space of sadness and raw grief opens a window.

Sometimes choosing joy is easier said than done. Allow yourself to be where you are and take some guilt-free time to nurture the soul. If, like Alexander, you're having a terrible, horrible, no good, very bad day, just be with it. Know that divine support and unconditional love are always right here in the room with you. And where there is love, joy tenderly grows.

In The World:

✳ When you feel ready, consider leaning toward joy by easing up on resistance, being especially kind to yourself, formulating a hopeful thought, doing something you love or allowing a smile to occupy your face for a moment. Red flowers might also be helpful.

In The Heart:

✳ I open my heart to the possibility of joy and allow myself to connect with the whole of my spirit. I take small steps toward welcoming joy back into my life.

The Army of Love

The most powerful weapon in the universe is love.

It was a perfect day yesterday. A blue sky with crisp air worthy of Santa Fe welcomed in the late spring morning. Joyous and free on my Sunday Tech Sabbath, I was off on a kayak adventure to a nearby lake when I heard the news. The car radio was my harsh messenger of yet another mass shooting. My heart broke. Tears welled. Precious, innocent lives were lost and countless others indelibly changed.

The world—my world—still appeared perfectly beautiful on the outside. But the temperature immediately shifted within. Heat began to rise and energy enveloped me in a huge ball of light. This was not an emotional explosion of rage. This was the rising up of incredible love.

The changes in our world are reflected by great changes in our hearts. It's natural that along with these changes comes a shift—with some of us contracting and some expanding. The continued stream of violence asks us to look within and to stand by our beliefs in this new world. We will choose to empower love or to empower fear. To empower love means we remain relentlessly focused on maintaining our own inner peace and bringing that peace to all who cross our paths in each small moment of this day. To empower love means taking compassionate action in the world as we follow the guidance of the highest wisdom of our hearts.

On some days, no matter how brightly the sun shines, it seems like the world is falling apart. But perhaps it is an opportunity to fall together in an army of love. Everyone is invited. It's a perfect day to change the world. And know, with every ounce of your being, that light always wins.

In The World:

* Allow each step and every breath to be one of lovingkindness. Promote positive change without harming others.

* Be vigilant about not tolerating intolerance of any kind at home and on a global level.

* In a moment of stillness during your spiritual practice, ask how you can best be used to bring light to the world. Every action, great and small, illuminates our way.

In The Heart:

* I have the power to focus on creating more healing light in the world. The way I live my life raises vibrations in all beings.

~⁓⥎⁓~

The Gift of Time

Today is wrapped up in sheer grace. It's an Alleluia.

In the weeks that my father received cancer treatment, my parents stayed at a facility called Hope Lodge, where they bonded deeply with other patients. One day, my parents and a dear friend went on an outing between treatments. They wanted to visit a place called the Angel Gardens but realized there wasn't quite enough time before their friend's radiation appointment. Then came the happy discovery that her treatment had been pushed back 45 minutes and they had time to visit the gardens after all. My mother said, "We have the gift of time." These words became a beloved symbol of the precious nature of life, and the three friends reminded each other often that their time together was a gift.

Along with the diagnosis of a terminal illness often comes the sudden realization of the gift of time. Our future is uncertain, and it becomes more important to live our lives fully, to spend time with those we love, to do what we've always dreamed of doing. When we know our time is limited, we recognize the precious nature of each day.

Even without a terminal diagnosis, the future is uncertain, right? We like to think that tomorrow will proceed as planned, but, hey, my tea leaves aren't talking. And today, right now, we've been given a gift. We can choose to live this day fully, to love well and to be joyful.

We don't know what tomorrow will bring. But today is wrapped up in sheer grace. It's an Alleluia. Today, we have the gift of time.

In The World:

A Gift of Time Prayer:

✴ *Thank you for this precious day. May I use it well. May I have a keen eye for joy and beauty, and the delights of small things. May I spread love and kindness generously, laugh easily, and feel the ever-present peace of your light with every breath and with every step. Amen.*

In The Heart:

✴ I am in love with life and live this precious day deeply and fully, being ever mindful of the gifts and graces that surround me now.

Your Friends Are like Frogs

Lift up someone else and you will lift yourself.

The frogs in my little pond didn't leap into the water today when I approached. They held firm to their rocks, smiles plastered on determined little faces. Maybe it was a dare to see who could remain in place the longest.

It could be that they finally became accustomed to my footsteps on the bridge. Or perhaps it doesn't escape them that I always return their babies back into the pond when I'm cleaning the filter. When the snakes come out to boldly sun on these same rocks, they might notice that I'm the one who chases them off.

I'm pretty sure that frogs don't overthink and what's happening is that they no longer *feel* afraid. I am sending out the message that they are safe and loved, and they receive it and are free to be themselves fully and do whatever good frogs do. Like sing, loudly, all night long. But I digress.

At the risk of comparing your friends to frogs, I believe that we all send out energy that makes others feel safe, or on the other hand, guarded. We vibe the language of love—or fear.

What a gift you give to others when you make them comfortable enough in your presence to be completely themselves. What a gift you give yourself when you give love and create a loving response in return.

In The World:

* Today, look for opportunities to be kind. Be the first to encourage, compliment, help out, cheer for, praise, have faith in, mentor and lift up those in need of your light.

* Notice and offer gratitude for the good feelings that come from offering kindness to others.

In The Heart:

* I put others at ease, offering love, kindness and assistance freely, knowing that what I put into the world returns back into my life.

Calling All Angels

Angel of God, my guardian dear, to whom His love commits me here; ever
this day be at my side, to light, to guard, to rule and guide. Amen
—Guardian Angel Prayer

It's been a morning, oh yes it has. My car has a flat in the driveway. Very hungry caterpillars stripped three trees overnight and are marching on. Adam needs to go to rehab. My friends are on a crushing journey through infertility. My cousin has cancer. One of my oldest friends faces life-threatening heart surgery.

There's more. You too? If we sat down with a legal pad, I'm sure we could fill the page with today's concerns. It's an impossible, unfixable list. When we are alone, that is.

As I stood in the kitchen, my eyes landed on my grandmother's chipped Mother Mary statue, sent to me recently by my godmother, Crissey. Under her base, I have been slipping prayer requests since she arrived. Mary is actually levitating upon the tower of worries. On the black stone counter, I spread out the notes. I blessed and released those that were resolved, and tucked the rest back beneath her mantle.

I implored, *Mary, Queen of Angels, send an army of your angels to those in need today. Big and small, please send them all for the highest good. Thank you, my dear Mary. Amen.*

I can't do this alone, but I can surely organize my mind to *focus* on asking, with all of my strength, for divine assistance. So I asked. And asked. I paced, asked and cried until I was empty—and full of hope, strength and joy.

I am not alone and neither are you. Ever this day, the angels are at your side, awaiting their marching orders. Just ask.

In The World:

＊ When you surrender control of your concerns into the hands of divine grace, all things are possible. Focus is key. Be crystal clear. The more you focus on the offering, the more powerful the request. Be easy about it, exercising your faith. Then release it and you will be shown the next step. Wait not in expectation, but in openness.

In The Heart:

＊ Angels surround me to guide my every step and to support the lives of those I love.

Heart of Divinity

I love and honor myself, knowing that I am valuable, blessed, beautiful, enough and worthy of great love.

I used to have the sense that I was pulling divine light from outside of myself, through my heart, and out to the intention of my prayer. I was like the pipe of an organ. Divine light and love would pass through me, and I was the channeler, not the source, of the music. God existed only outside my being.

Then I began investigating a more personal experience of God. If we truly are a spark of divinity; if we are connected as one to the source of all love; if we are made of the same molecules, then God is not just outside of us, but within, through and around all things. So right here within me is a ray of divine wisdom, power and light. So how can I more deeply experience God within?

By honoring myself. By valuing myself as a beautiful, worthy being. By nurturing my mind, body and soul with loving images, foods and inspiration. By loving myself deeply, cherishing my uniqueness, forgiving my mistakes and continuing to turn back to the joyful work of learning how to move peacefully and passionately through life.

We can only heal ourselves from a place of love. We can only ease the suffering of others from a place of love. We can only find our passion and creative gifts from a place of love. When we love and honor ourselves, nothing external in the world can sway our calm.

We know who we are and that is unchanging. We are a ray of divine sun capable of sowing healing light, and worthy of great love.

In The World:

✳ Honor your beautiful being by talking to yourself as you would your most precious loved one.

✳ Bind your self-worth not to external goals and success, but to your inner light, which cannot be changed or diminished.

In The Heart:

✳ I love and honor myself knowing that I am valuable, blessed, beautiful, enough and worthy of great love, just as I am.

An Instrument of Peace

Unveil the love that is at the heart of you.

One night on The Tonight Show, Johnny Carson had the Dalai Lama as a guest. I'm going back to the archives here, but I have long remembered the essence of this sweet exchange. Toward the end of their conversation, Carson leaned over the desk and said something like, "How did you get it to be so quiet in there?" To which the Dalai Lama crinkled into his beautiful smile and replied, "It *is* quiet in there!"

We don't make ourselves peaceful, inside. We *are* peaceful. So our work in the world is to release the things that are hiding our peace; to pull back the curtain of what is covering our calm; to unveil the love that is at the heart of us all.

Peace Prayer of St. Francis of Assisi

Lord, Make me an instrument of your peace.
Where there is hatred, let me sow love;
where there is injury, pardon;
where there is doubt, faith;
where there is despair, hope;
where there is darkness, light;
where there is sadness, joy.

O, Divine Master, grant that I may not so much
seek to be consoled as to console;
to be understood as to understand;
to be loved as to love;
For it is in giving that we receive;
it is in pardoning that we are pardoned;
it is in dying that we are born to eternal life. Amen

In The World:

✳ Today release one thing that might be interfering with your peace. Pull back the curtain on one thing that might be covering your calm. Unveil the love.

In The Heart:

✳ From the calm place of peace in my soul, I am an instrument of peace in the world.

The Daily Conversation

Ask. Believe. Receive. Give thanks.

Conversations with the divine arise not only in times of trouble but in the small moments and miracles of daily life. Any time is a good time for a chat. Already this morning I have had a few conversations, starting with, *How should I work out this morning? Should I do yoga or weed a garden bed?* I *felt* that I should open the back door. Immediately the smell of the air intoxicated me, and off I went to get my gardening gloves. Not something I usually do at 7:00 a.m. but it was a most beautiful hour outside. I gave thanks.

I also asked for guidance about when to make a sensitive phone call, and soon after, I asked how to direct my prayers and energy for a friend in need. As always, I asked what to write at the desk by the wall of windows today. It's only 11:00 a.m. and I've done a lot of asking.

The power behind the asking is the belief in the right result. That seemingly insignificant and silent surrender to divine will is the key, setting into motion the receiving part: the hints, signs and inner promptings that steer us in the right direction. The feeling before we even get the question out of our hearts is that the perfect answer is already on its way in the perfect time. It's pretty exciting stuff.

Giving thanks is an ongoing process, given at all stages and phases. We can give thanks for helping when the question is asked, thanks for the signs and surprises of received guidance, thanks for answers and the delay of answers because that, too, is a gift.

Ask. Believe. Receive. Give thanks. Enjoy.

In The World:

＊ Carry on a constant conversation with the divine today. In all things, great and small, seek wisdom and guidance, notice answers, allow yourself to flow with grace, and give thanks.

In The Heart:

＊ All things unfold in the perfect way and in their perfect time when I seek divine assistance.

Bad Is Not All Bad

Be patient with yourself. There may be a greater plan that you cannot see.

My friend Thelma was ninety-six years old when she shared what she considered to be one of her greatest life lessons: *Everything that we think is good, has a little bad in it, and everything we think is bad, has a little good in it.* Okay Thelma, let's think about this.

We tend to want to judge our experiences, and label them as either good or bad. If we get into a great grad school, marry the prince, get a publishing deal with Hay House, we consider that a windfall of good fortune. If we don't meet a goal, if a relationship fails, if our dreams don't come true in the way we imagine, we consider that to be a bad chapter in our life.

When we examine what we consider to be our greatest failures and heartbreaks, we can see from the clear vantage point of hindsight that most of them were leading us to a more authentic path. Each twist of fate and synchronistic set of circumstances changed our direction. Not all seemed *good* at the time, but difficult passages grow us and ultimately lay out stepping stones that led to greater courage, compassion, insight and often, contentment.

Patience asks us not to judge things *yet*. Patience wants us to wait until we have a little distance from the experience and can see wisdom at work in our story. Patience begs for faith in a greater plan, a greater God, that has only our highest good in mind.

Patience, and Thelma, remind us that bad is not all bad.

In The World:

* Take a moment and give thanks for the experiences you have endured through what seemed like failure or defeat.

* If you are going through one of those times now, ask to be shown the next step in the greater plan for your life. Ask to be led. Refrain from judgment. Have faith that blessings can emerge from the pain.

In The Heart:

* I trust that my challenges are meaningful. I have faith that a perfect plan is in place for me now. I wait in patient openness for miracles that are yet to unfold.

Summer Spiritual Streamlining

I send my worries out to sea and open my soul to an ocean of peace.

It's summertime and the livin' is easy. The sun is standing still, and so should we. Since December, the days have been growing longer above the equator, culminating in today, the summer solstice, when the sun is at its highest point in the sky. Solstice means *sun stands still*. With the change of season comes the perfect opportunity to pour an iced tea and gain a little perspective. It's an auspicious time to revisit spiritual goals and release what no longer serves us.

Taking stock is a way of spiritual streamlining. The broad questions are: *What worries are occupying my heart? How can I release them? What can I be doing to bring more peace and joy to my days?* If we answer these questions honestly, we can allow ourselves to release some habits that are getting in the way of our peace in mind, and step up a few of the practices that contribute greatly to our sweet connection with our better selves. And all of this can be accomplished from a lounge chair.

Van Morrison brings it home when he sings, "Smell the sea and feel the sky. Let your soul and spirit fly..." This is not big work, so go easy on yourself. It's a small change in course that brings us into alignment with who we really are. It's the reset of the spiritual compass.

In The World:

Answer the following questions, and allow your answers to steer you in the direction of greater peace:

* Is there an activity in my life that I can do without or make more simple?

* Are there spiritual practices I could add or release that might bring more joy and peace to my life?

* Am I spending time with uplifting people?

* Is what I'm reading feeding my soul?

* Am I honoring myself as a spiritual being?

In The Heart:

* With gentle compassion, I guide my life toward greater alignment, authenticity and simplicity.

A Few Morning Moments

Gratitude makes everything grow.

I woke early this morning and took my tea out the back door. The sun had just risen but my thinking mind had not, so I stood there in pure consciousness, soaking in the glorious morning. Everything was wet and waking from the storms last night; birds conversing across the yard saying, "I'm okay! You okay?" Bugs busy at work. Frogs in position on their rocks. Horses circling a hay bale on the field.

Gratitude grew in me like the unfurling of a prayer plant. Slowly, softly, I felt a whole-body thank you, for just the awareness of this one early morning moment. And as my leaves spread out, they reached out to the other plants and the birds, bees, frogs and horses. Under the sky, in the glorious light of the sun, we all offered a unified, *Yes! This is glorious. Thank you!*

Later in the morning, as I sat at my desk, a ray of light landed near my hands and my heart returned to the few minutes outside at the start of the day. The feeling of gratitude rose within me once more.

When we greet the day in gratitude, the silent prayer will take flight and set the day off on the right path. The impact expands for hours as seen in the ray of light across our desks and our hearts. The lingering song of morning gratitude will be magnified all day long.

Gratitude makes everything grow.

In The World:

✳ Plan to get out of bed ten minutes early one day this week and just softly breathe gratitude as the day begins.

✳ Delight in it as a special time for you. Look forward to it as a gift that you give to your spirit. Put on your soul sandals and walk out the back door.

In The Heart:

✳ I awaken today with great joy and gratitude for my very existence and for the chance to live and to love once more.

꙳

Complaint-Free Day

If we could see the power of our thoughts, we would only think loving thoughts.

I once had a roommate who could lead the Olympic complaining team. Her complaints could flawlessly follow a story line from a single person, to a dramatic situation, to a whole country. Nothing was out of bounds. It was woven pretty well into conversations, so at first I didn't notice it. But once I tuned in, it became impossible for me to ignore. It was dark and negative, and most importantly, it had the power to change the energy of the room almost immediately. Complainers thrive on company, and when I began to respond with silence to her complaints, our friendship drifted apart.

As beings of light, we can all be students of our own highest teaching. What is repeated becomes habitual, and it is essential that we become mindful of our tendency to complain and lean instead toward positive, affirmative, light-filled thoughts and words. This is something we can actually control. Step by step we can guide ourselves in the mindfulness and training of our own thoughts.

With every thought, we make a choice about what kind of energy we bring to this day and what we create for our future. A single phrase has the power to encourage, lift and inspire, or to discourage, dampen and block. If we could see the power of our thoughts, we would only think loving thoughts.

In The World:

✳   Today is a complaint-free day. Catch yourself in any complaints and rephrase in the positive. If today works well, continue into tomorrow. After several days the habit of complaining will drop away.

✳   Be vigilant about negative phrasing. Challenge yourself to phrase thoughts and words in the positive. This carries over into prayer and all divine communication—and has the power to create a dramatic shift toward joy.

✳   Let love be the power behind every thought.

In The Heart:

✳   I make a conscious choice to bring only light into the world today.

Bless This Day

Bless this day with love and light. Bless this day with faith and sight.
Bless this day with grace and ease. Bless this day with joy and peace.

On the phone today, Olga lamented that the news was full of viral coverage of people acting cruelly toward each other in the name of defending their beliefs. It was upsetting to witness the lowest vibrations of humanity. From my porch in the country, with no cell service or TV, I assured her that the world was doing just fine, and we laughed. She reminded me that often we do not see the world *as it is*, we see it *as we are*.

Together as light workers, we can pour love into the world through our thoughts, words and actions. We can be powerful activists for change without being negative or destructive and without attacking people personally. We can channel love toward compassionate action and transformation. The world feels better this way, right?

Today, before the phone gets checked and the computer gets turned on, set the day right first thing with silence and a blessing. The way our day starts is often the way our day goes. See today unfolding with grace and hold up to the light all intentions, great and small, to be blessed.

In The World:

* Bless this day with love and light, lifting the vibration of all beings.

* Bless this day with faith and sight, keeping divine perspective, seeing all things through sacred eyes.

* Bless this day with grace and ease, releasing, flowing, opening and surrendering to divine order.

* Bless this day with joy and peace, smiling freely and calming others with serenity.

In The Heart:

* I begin my day in a place of love and light, blessing all of my thoughts, words and actions. I am a radiant channel of divine healing.

JUNE 25

Your Own True Current

Through waves of transition we find the flow of our own true current.

When we least expect it, we find ourselves starting over.

Life's transitions can sweep us out to sea and toss us on the waves, sometimes for long stretches of time. Seasons go by and still we feel unmoored. We might raise a new sail or test out a new port in search of that which resonates with our souls. We seek to dock where the authentic spirit can thrive.

We traverse many oceans in our journey from high school to college, college to independent living; through marriage, divorce, changing jobs, illness, moving to a new city, having a child, losing a child, a friend or a spouse. Stowed away in these times of transition are chances to make some brand new choices based on the promptings of spirit.

When I moved into the cabin on my own when I least expected it, I took with me only the things that truly spoke to my new life. The colors, the books, the clothes, the blankets, the angels—I only brought the treasures that represented what I loved, what brought me joy, and what aligned with my authentic self.

As unsettling as they are, transitions offer us a unique opportunity. They present us with the chance to style our new lives in a way that more deeply reflects our true selves, and to create a life more in keeping with the flow of our own true current.

We have all of the tools we need to navigate from the waves of transition to the peaceful harbor of transformation. One wave at a time.

In The World:

* Write down the traits that you want to embody when you have come to the other side of this transformation. Answer the question: *Who do I get to become as a result of this transition?*

* Write down or imagine what your new life and your new self might look like.

* Add your discoveries as items in your Gratitude in Advance list.

In The Heart:

* Every day I take steps toward becoming my authentic self and aligning with my true voice and my true self.

In Perfect Harmony

My mind, body and soul are in perfect harmony.

At first sight, our visceral response to this affirmation might be along the lines of, *Not in this lifetime.*

Stepping back, it's clear that it doesn't feel like most affirmations, which paint a picture of an ideal world in a way where it is *obvious* that we are stating a goal, and are not actually there already. For example, "I flow with ease and grace through the constant change in my life." Most of us don't do that yet, but it's a good idea and one we want to aim for. It's an affirmation that will bring us closer to the manifestation of that goal.

We are used to talking about the integration of mind and soul in universal language, but bringing in the body can be less comfortable for a lot of us. We'd rather consider our spirituality as separate and leave the body out of it. After all, we are ruthless in the critique of our bodies, drowning in a sea of relentless marketing, pressuring us to look or behave in a certain way. Our negative self-talk reminds us constantly that we can't possibly ever look or feel good enough.

Let's bring this home for a minute and consider something really important: Why can't this affirmation be true for each of us *now?* Having our mind, body and soul in perfect harmony does not mean having a lake-clear, calm mind, a gym rat's healthy body and a soul connected to the divine at some random date in the future when we get it all together.

It means being exactly who we are, right in this moment, loving our body with compassion and gratitude, and with a soul connected to the divine right here and now. This we can do. By welcoming in the harmony that we are right now, we will continue to integrate greater and greater harmony.

In The World:

* Thank your body for housing your soul and for facilitating your creative ideas. Love your body today with compassion and gentle kindness.

In The Heart:

* There is no wrong way to be in my body. Like everyone, I am enough and I am beautiful. My mind, body and soul are in perfect harmony.

Presence as Prayer

To be present in the small moments of daily life is to pray.

Sometimes Sacred stands at the stove; the Divine cheers from the bleachers; Meditation folds the laundry; Holy falls exhausted into bed. Even on the days when we don't say prayers, we are living them. Gunilla Norris reminds us in her lyrical book, *Being Home*, "Sometimes saying prayers keeps us from *being* prayers." So as we face a full schedule, let's *be* prayers.

Life asks much of us in a day, and being present lifts up even the most demanding of them, making an offering of each small moment.

Within the gift of time that today is giving us, let's be fully awake. Let's notice, appreciate and be delighted. Let's be present wholeheartedly, bravely and completely. Let's stay in the moment that we are in without worrying about all that is left undone.

May our presence be our devotion, our love and our prayer. May our presence welcome this day as an honored guest with open arms.

In The World:

∗   Be where you are. Stay in the moment. Let your heart be light. When you notice your mind rushing ahead, call it back to the present.

∗   Keep a running conversation with the divine. Ask for guidance in what to do next and next, allowing yourself to be gently led from moment to moment.

∗   Have faith. Know that you have all the time you need for all you need to do. Feel it in your bones. Assume it. It is here.

In The Heart:

∗   The prayer of my day is in the fabric of each small moment. I rise to greet the day with the flexibility of ease and grace as I flow with inner guidance and mindfulness.

All Events Are Blessings

Everything happens in its perfect time.

We are not asked to exercise our faith muscle when all is well. In joyful chapters of our lives, our inherent awe and gratitude bubble up to the surface unbidden. When there are no emergencies, we are not required to trust that all is right and good with the universe. It just is.

Then there are those times when we put forth our very best effort toward an important goal that never comes to fruition. Or we endure a seemingly random tragedy and it feels like we have been forsaken. We are frustrated and devastated, and we are sure that divine timing has passed us by. Believe me, I know. These are the moments that beg for a deep well of faith.

It's possible that what is meant to come to us will come to us, and what is not meant for us in this lifetime will not. In either scenario, our job is to believe, in all things, that there is a perfection that is stacked in our favor. Our job is to keep our eyes on the light so that more light can flood in. Our job is to accept our defeats so we might open to coming victories. Our job is to open our clenched fists and let go of the pain so exactly what is needed can come fill our hearts.

We are being asked to exercise nothing less than gratitude during the challenging times as well as in the good times. We can choose to accept it all, because in the land of divine order, all experiences are blessings; clear signs of perfect timing and of how infinitely loved we are.

In The World:

✳ Just for today, choose acceptance and gratitude in all situations.

✳ Be flexible when challenges or gifts arise that are not expected.

✳ Assume there is a blessing within all experiences. You have the strength to try this. You are not alone.

In The Heart:

✳ I open my heart to this day with gratitude, knowing that all events are blessings arriving in their perfect time.

❧

Shine Brightly

Shine brightly. See beauty. Speak kindly. Love truly. Give freely.
Create joyfully. Live thankfully.

I wrote the little quote above on a napkin last night. *This is why I'm here,* I thought. I wanted to remind myself of the power of sharing light and love. I wanted to remember when I woke up today that the *way* I live my life was the most important thing I could align with. I wanted to remember beauty, kindness and joy. I wanted to remember love, generosity and gratitude.

My friends and I talk about the hazards of too much *doing* and not enough *being*. Our lives get busy in waves. We get distracted by work and travel, by changing schedules and the needs of others. Our spiritual practices suffer as other things take priority. We are running and spinning, accomplishing and nurturing. It can be exhausting and draining on the inside.

But we can handle all of this if we remain connected to our source energy. It's like plugging into the wall socket. We need it. We have to have it. The Creator of the universe gave us all things. We can squeeze in ten minutes several times a day to sustain our quality of life. *Spirit first* is the non-negotiable priority.

Our *doing* is always informed and empowered by our *being*. Never the other way around. When we are fully our soul selves, there is nothing we can't do. We need to be who we are and be that well. That is why we're here.

In The World:

❋ Shine brightly. See beauty. Speak kindly. Love truly. Give freely. Create joyfully. Live thankfully.

❋ Take a moment to come into balance and connect with your highest energy. Bring the joy with you as you go about your day. Tune up several times today by finding a moment of solitude to put spirit first, to breathe, to meditate, to pray and see life through the stillness of the heart.

In The Heart:

❋ I connect with my spiritual self often today so I may approach all activity from the place of my highest good and with the guidance of my inner wisdom.

To Be Loved and to Love

You are infinitely loved just as you are.

Unimaginable love. Unconditional love. Blinding, expansive, amazing love. It's hard to believe, but we all have this. Every day. Just as we are.

Living proof exists in the growing body of research into near-death experiences. Seekers and searchers unite in the love of these heart-pounding sagas—first-hand experiences of life after death spanning all religions and cultures. Although each story has its individual characteristics, most have one hallmark in common: The amazing love radiating from the conscious source of the universe—God. The "nearly dead" person feels immediately overjoyed, welcomed and instantly healed by unconditional love and the realization that they are, in their essence, part of this love.

Infinite love exists for each of us from the Creator. So who are we not to honor the magnificence of our spirit? May we open to the gift of being truly loved and rise to the humbling honor of being one with God and with all creation.

In The World:

✳ May we allow the infinite light of unconditional love to enter and take up residence in our hearts.

✳ May we be in awe of a magnificent love that is directed at each of us individually.

✳ May we accept the healing power of this love, and may it work through our eyes, hands and hearts.

✳ May we find incredible joy in the knowing that we are always, no matter what, infinitely loved.

In The Heart:

✳ I am tenderly, infinitely and unconditionally loved by God in every moment, just as I am.

July Blessings

Be present. Be here. Today, we can guide our thoughts back to the present moment with gentle focus and live fully right where we are.

Let the day flow with grace. Grace flows through us easily when we are in tune with the subtle voice of intuition. Open and listen for guidance.

Expect joy. Be positive. Imagine a fulfilling day unfolding, in which we accomplish much and experience joy in the process. Welcome the light.

Serve with compassion. Acts of service when performed with love lend immeasurable light to our day. Be watchful for ways to serve.

Speak only kindness. Speak only kind words. Think only kind thoughts. Be kind to yourself and to those who cross your path or your mind.

Impart only love. Send out all thoughts and words on the wings of love so that we may love one another, love ourselves, love the unlovable.

Never forget you're not alone. Let's remind ourselves often today that we are always supported, guided and unconditionally loved as we are.

Give thanks for everything. Gratitude will shift the perspective of the day from one of lack to one of abundance. Give constant thanks.

See goodness in others. Each of us has a soul that is made of beauty and love. Assume the best in others so they may rise to their highest light.

The Real Priority List

Be kind. Be calm. Be joyful. Be humble. Be thankful.

I have always had a wacky ability to raise up over the earth and look down on my life, Google Maps style. Sometimes I go way up and I can see the whole East Coast. (Seriously.) Mostly, I just go a little way up and watch what's happening in my life. It's not always a pretty sight.

This short list came from looking down on what my long list had been for that day, and considering what it *might* have looked like had I been a little more connected to spirit. "Be kind. Be calm. Be joyful. Be humble. Be thankful."

Whenever I lose sight of what's important—and my agenda, instead of love, drives my decisions—I take a look at this list and remember what a real priority list looks like.

In The World:

∗ May I be kind today, seeing the world with a compassionate and gentle heart. May my presence be comforting and helpful to others, especially those who are hurting. May I refrain from negative thoughts and comments about myself and others, and may I embrace myself with the same respect and kindness that I give to all other beings. May love lead my decisions.

∗ May I be calm today, spreading peaceful energy to all who cross my path. May the peace I feel within be a healing light to others and contribute to their joy and wellness.

∗ May I be joyful today, knowing that the light of my smile is contagious and lifts the spirits of others. May I see the positive and the beautiful in this day and remember to take myself lightly.

∗ May I be humble today, recognizing that all souls are radiant in the eyes of the Creator and that all paths are of equal value. May I be an attentive listener and a loving encourager of others.

∗ May I be thankful today, allowing the blessings of this day to grow my heart and render me abundant and grateful.

In The Heart:

∗ My loving actions throughout this day are my gifts to the world.

May I Be Blessed

May I be blessed today with wisdom, patience and strength.

No matter what surprises today might hold, we could all use a little extra assistance. These four small words are packed with intention and make for a powerful start to any request or offering. May I be blessed. This. Let this become our mantra today.

These are words that open doors and windows and let flow waterfalls of grace. They combine a polite request with a dash of surrender and the feel of an affirmation—a sense that the request has already come to pass in real time.

We are born with a direct line to universal wisdom beyond our wildest dreams. We are connected to the source of all that is. But the window to wisdom is opened by the admission of need. The well of patience is filled by the awareness of emptiness. The door to strength is opened by the act of surrender.

When we meditate, we surrender our thoughts and the illusion of control over our lives. Similarly, when we ask to be blessed, we admit that we could use a little divine backup. The gifts of wisdom, patience and strength are granted for the asking.

Whenever we pray these words we get an immediate answer before the prayer has even left our hearts. We can ask for our precious portion of daily gifts and be assured that we will have all that we need. That is what grace is—an endless supply of blessings. May we be blessed.

In The World:

∗ Set up some reminders on your phone, in your journal or on sticky notes to help remember throughout the day to ask for blessings and assistance.

In The Heart:

∗ May I be blessed with wisdom, patience and strength, and with all the gifts I need to flow through this beautiful day with ease and grace.

Pursuit of Happiness

To have peace, be calm. To have love, be loving. To have kindness, be kind.

I haven't even told some of my closest friends the details of the dissolution of my decades-long marriage. I had not been treated in the way that I deserved. Let's leave it at that. Because the exact reasons are not nearly as important as how we dealt with the fallout.

It was the Fourth of July when I told him we were done. Finished. No more tries. How's that for an Independence Day announcement? I had to stop the bleeding, and although I dread speaking my truth when I know it will not be well-received, this had to be the day. Sometimes the truth will tell itself when it can't stand the confines of the dark any longer.

I lived alone in the house during the hardest part of hammering out an agreement. The first lawyer I saw actually rubbed her hands together and laughed, "Well let's see if we can make him miserable for the rest of his life!" I never went back. Why would I want to live with that?

Instead, we did it at the kitchen table. Even though we were both hurting, we didn't take it to the next level of pain by suing each other. We cried, but we didn't get mean. I asked for what I needed but didn't take things for spite. It took months, many meetings and a lot of work. Then we had it notarized and went out to lunch.

I have watched friends go through grueling and expensive divorce battles. It's the most stressful thing on earth because it goes against everything we know within. We use money as a weapon, we grasp and protect, we divide and conquer. Any time we inflict pain on another, we wound ourselves also. Even in despair, we can act from a place of love.

As for us, we have salvaged a loving friendship out of the deal—a real treasure that will last a lifetime. Now that's pursuit of happiness.

In The World:

* If you find yourself here, remember, self-care first. We access our better selves when we eat and sleep. Write out affirmations and carry them with you. Pray like crazy. Journal for sanity. Find one friend, counselor or confidant you can be honest with. Seek out a wise mediator to guide you through the process. Be honest and kind.

In The Heart:

* Calm me, Lord, as you calmed the storm. Still me, Lord, keep me from harm. Let all tumult within me cease. Enfold me, Lord, in your peace.

Actively Calm

Slow down and lighten up.

Once upon a time we said *yes*. We said *yes* to the job, the classes, the children, the dinner, the event. Our calendars are therefore packed with beautiful symbols of the richness of our lives and loves. They reflect our connection with others and the fruits of our labor. Oh so many fruits.

Being a little swamped can be a beautiful thing if we can somehow exempt ourselves from the dreaded feeling that we have way too much to do and not enough time to do it. We have all the time we need. Really, we do.

If we were given a whole bag of gifts at once, we wouldn't want to race through them. We would want to savor the moment, the wrapping and the unwrapping, as well as the friend who gifted it. Today is like that. It asks for presence, not speed. It is an adventure of the spirit, a journey that is meant to bring joy. Paramahansa Yogananda had great advice that makes me relax and breathe a little deeper just thinking about it. "Be calmly active and actively calm."

So today is all about peaceful, lighthearted energy. It's about appreciation without complaint. It's about being in the moment and listening well, inside the heart and outside to those we love. It's about accepting abundance, even if it involves rush hour traffic. It's about fun and peace combined. We can do this when we slow down a little—and let our hearts be light.

In The World:

✱ Appreciate - We can't be truly grateful and be worried at the same time. Express gratitude today in all things, even the mess on the desk. Say *thank you* out loud and often.

✱ Smile - A smile and some laughter can change our biology and lift anxiety.

✱ Exhale - Making the exhale longer than the inhale immediately calms the body and reduces stress. Just breathe. And ask your angels for help.

In The Heart:

✱ I have all the time I need for all I need to do. I am mindful and grateful. I release anxiety and open to the joy that is present in my life today.

Alone but Not Alone

Your spirit is on a human adventure.

As exhilarating as it is to walk a spiritual path, it's not always easy to discuss it with others. It's one of the most personal things we do in our lives. Nothing makes words feel small like trying to explain the vast insights of your journey.

My 86-year-old mother lives independently in an assisted living facility. She has countless wonderful friends who are bursting with life. They go to plays, concerts and movies, and take part in book clubs, art and computer classes. They go to the gym and take walks around the lake. Mom meets a different group of friends most weeknights for dinner in the dining room. But after three years, no one really knows the extent to which she has spent her entire life with one foot on "the other side" as a devoted spiritual seeker.

What a gift to have even one friend who understands our spiritual yearnings. To be able to share signs, symbols, synchronicity, insights, prayers answered, dreams, healings, energy awakenings, angelic assistance and all manner of manifestations of spirit in our lives—is one of the greatest blessings of being a spirit on this human adventure. I wish for you this gift, but if it is not to be, you are not alone. We walk alone with you.

In The World:

✳ Keep an open heart for like-minded souls. Introduce the topic gently to investigate their understanding and interest level. Offer to share a book or movie that resonates with you.

✳ Never judge another's interest or lack of interest in spirituality. There are infinite ways to express ourselves in this lifetime. Spirituality is only one of them.

✳ Your heart knows when you've had a spiritual experience. No one can dispute your personal knowing. Even if you are the only one that knows, it's real. Believe what your heart knows to be true.

In The Heart:

✳ The deep wisdom of my spirit illuminates my earthly path with love and joy. I am never alone in my truth.

Gratitude and Gate 23

I am thankful for this precious life, this precious day, this precious moment.

It started as a simple weather delay on a flight from Orlando to D.C., but as afternoon gave way to evening, the captive audience at Gate 23 began to mill around and chat. I left my seat for the window ledge, where I spied an outlet to charge my phone. A young woman nearby had the same thought and as our tired, hungry souls rested, her story spilled out.

Ayan is the youngest of seventeen children born to Somali parents. The whole clan, which includes scores of nieces and nephews, now live in Dubai. Ayan moved to Washington, D.C. for her college years, and since she was the only unmarried child, her mother moved with her. They both stayed on after Ayan finished her schooling, and they had shared a house in the city for fifteen years.

Missing her family, Ayan planned to spend the entire summer in Dubai. After just a few weeks there, she received the shocking call that her mother was in the hospital, having been diagnosed with a terminal brain tumor. She wasn't expected to live out the week.

When I met Ayan on the window ledge at Gate 23, she was two sleepless days into her journey home. Her mother had slipped into a coma a few hours ago. Her hope now was to see her mother's body before she would be quickly buried in accordance with their Muslim faith.

We finally boarded before midnight and after a harrowing flight, landed at the now gridlocked National Airport. All of the delayed flights had come in together, and as I waited an hour outside for the shuttle to the parking lot, the skies let go another torrent of rain. By the time I found my car, I was soaked to the bone. Yet all I could think about was how *precious* life is. The inconveniences of the trip were insignificant when I thought of my new friend, now on her way to the hospital to say goodbye to her beloved mother. I could not formulate a single complaint. Instead, I counted precious blessings, like streetlights, all the way home.

In The World:

✳ Our challenges today come into perspective when we consider the plight of those who experience greater suffering. Allow your thoughts to go to such a soul, and count your precious blessings all day long.

In The Heart:

✳ Gratitude fills my heart for the gift of this moment in time.

Diving Deep

Do one thing at a time with love.

The spiritual journey is not one that swims on the surface of life. We know there is a deep ocean within, and we are ready to plumb the depths of our power and connection. There are brilliant colors and we want to see them all; the colors of joy, of peace, of healing, of awe and even of pain. In order to do this, we have to transport ourselves to the only place where our life is happening. Right here.

Vietnamese monk and mindfulness master Thich Nhat Hahn defines mindfulness as "the energy to be here and to witness deeply everything that happens in the present moment, aware of what is going on within and without." So the trick is to release our concerns and fears, and gently bring our awareness to where we are. Then we notice how we feel and what is happening. And incredibly, we can always find a moment of peace in the land of presence.

Being mindful means that when we are washing dishes, we are not thinking about getting the car fixed. When we are listening to a friend, we are not thinking of what we are having for dinner. So much for our pride in multi-tasking.

What we gain by not dividing our attention is the gift of peace and joy. When we practice mindfulness, we move from task to task feeling grounded and refreshed. When we practice mindfulness, we offer a beautiful gift of healing to others by our compassionate presence.

Today, let's not swim on the surface of life. Let's dive deeply into one thing at a time with our attention and our love, and discover all of the brilliant colors that we are.

In The World:

✳ With a calming breath, bring your awareness into the present moment over and over today. Notice how you feel and details of your surroundings. Allow a gentle calm to envelop you.

✳ Offer others the precious gift of your undivided attention. Embrace them with your compassionate presence and patient love.

In The Heart:

✳ Today I am deeply present to my experiences. I do one thing at a time with great love.

Ode to a Stink Bug

Walk with a soft step and love with a warm heart.

When I Snapchatted Maya this morning, telling her that Jessie had died after a long illness, she wrote me a sweet condolence with little Emoji angels. Then, confused, the question: *Remind me who Jessie is?*

Jessie is a stink bug in a world where it's not good to be one. They have a terrible reputation for taking over homes and businesses, for dive bombing people while they are reading in bed at night, and for, well, stinking the place up.

But in all my life, I have never had anything but respect for our little armor-clad friends. In the cabin, there are never more than three or four visible at any one time and they are very agreeable about walking onto the paper for transfer to the outdoors. They don't land on me and they don't smell bad if you don't hurt them. And they are wildly unique with their dinosaur style, feathery wings and stripy antennae.

I greet them with, "Hello my fearless leader!" They laugh.

Four days ago, Jessie was happily flying around when, to his grave misfortune, he came in for a landing in the pillar candle on my desk. It had been going for hours and held a deep pool of hot, honeysuckle wax. The second he submerged, I scooped him out with a pencil eraser, but he sat still, his waxy covering now encasing him on the desk with only his antennae free to move. He meditated in his honeysuckle tomb for four days until passing on. The poor little guy. Or perhaps poor little great spirit.

Crazy, I know. For me, it's not part of a particular don't-kill-bugs philosophy. I simply feel their consciousness and can't imagine treating them with anything less than honor and awe. Same goes for birds and fish, trees and plants, and every creature on the planet. We are our brother's keeper. Goodbye, Jess.

In The World:

✳ Today, walk with a soft step and love with a warm heart. Extend the net of your compassion to cover all living things.

In The Heart:

✳ I love and respect all of nature, the creatures great and small.

The Voice of the Heart

Don't let the noise of the world cover the soft voice of the heart.
—Tiny Guru

The voice of the heart is always talking to us. Really. It's there just beneath the action and chaos, the work and play, the full schedules and busy days. Our highest wisdom is ever-present. No matter how busy we remain or how much we ignore it, she will just keep on talking.

We need only to remember that the voice of the heart is a whisper not a shout, leading the way with equal parts humility and grace. She responds to a few long, slow breaths and a simple invitation. She always answers to the song of gratitude and a request for guidance. She awaits our attention, and the very simple and focused:

I'm listening. What do I need to know right now?

When we get used to her gentle way of answering, through signs, symbols, nudges, feelings and intuition, we find we can carry out this entire day in constant communication with a power much greater that ourselves. "Your vision will come clear only when you look into your heart," Carl Jung reminds us. "Who looks outside, dreams; who look inside, awakens." Let's be awake to the language of the heart.

Ask. Believe. Receive. Give thanks.

In The World:

✳   The heart speaks to us when we take a moment to turn down the noise of external sound and open an internal window of quiet.

✳   The heart speaks to us in crisis, in anxiety, in depression, in joy, in gratitude, in peace. She is guiding, lifting and loving us into wholeness. She is there. We are never alone.

✳   The heart speaks to us in the voice of the calm, ever-present companion of intuition and responds to every request.

In The Heart:

✳   My highest wisdom is available to me at all times. I make space to quiet my mind. In the silence of my heart, I tune in, ask and listen.

Please Stay

No matter how dark it seems, remember that you are loved,
that you are never alone and that life is a precious gift.

Some of us appear to be a calm sea on the outside, going about our daily round privately, while volcanoes of suffering explode painfully on the inside. Life becomes dark, ash-covered, achingly lonely, and after days disappear into months, the journey becomes unbearable. No one else seems to notice the devastation. There's hardly enough air under the ash to make life habitable, and you imagine the end of it all.

Last week, I had someone share with me that they were contemplating suicide. Part of me had a hint, aware of a long relationship with depression. The other part of me was blown off the map.

What about your family? What about your meaningful job? What about our dinner next week? *You will be better off without me.*

No, we will not. We will blame ourselves; we will wonder what we could have done to help you for the rest of our lives. We will miss you. We love you. *You do?* You have been a solid provider for your family and you have done work that no one else could do. You are an integral part of a team. *I am?*

And just for the record, you have no idea how much love is blasting down upon you from the heavens. *Really?* Really.

No matter how dark it gets, remember that you are loved, that you are never alone and that life is a precious gift. You need help right now to see that all is not lost and that you are not alone. We are all broken and imperfect, but it's still possible to find meaning. And to love and be loved. Please stay.

In The World:

✳ If you or anyone you know is contemplating suicide, tell someone. Don't wait, get help. You are unique and precious, and we need you here.

In The Heart:

✳ Even in my darkest hours, I know that I am worthy, valuable, courageous and infinitely loved by God.

Team Tranquility

I am constantly, relentlessly blessed.

With a precious day unfolding before us, there's a choice we can make that will send us down the path of divine flow, where we have support and guidance at every turn. All day, in every decision, we get to choose between going with the flow and holding on to control.

Choosing the path of least resistance does sound like the path to a calmer, happier day. But how do we do that? Wayne Dyer tells us, "By practicing thoughts of minimal resistance, you'll train yourself to make this your natural way of reacting, and eventually you'll become the tranquil person you desire to be..."

Tranquil. We want that. Practicing minimal resistance leads us to a calmer place and the feeling of being in the flow of grace. It leads us to tranquility.

We always know in which camp we fall—flow or control—because the heart is like built-in radar for your soul. It will tell us. When we feel peaceful, we are in the flow. When we are worried or trying too hard, we are resistant. Open to receive guidance from your heart. Then choose Team Tranquility.

In The World: Enjoy the gift of affirmations today:

✷ Instead of resisting, I flow with the blessings and notice the gifts.

✷ Instead of controlling, I let go of what was never mine.

✷ Instead of being in charge, I surrender to divine wisdom.

✷ Instead of losing my balance, I maintain a calm center.

✷ Instead of being quick to anger, I am thoughtful and patient.

✷ Instead of holding on to darkness, I release it to make room for light.

✷ Instead of being rigid, I am flexible with my expectations.

✷ Instead of assuming the worst, I expect abundant blessings.

In The Heart:

✷ I believe in a world where I am constantly, relentlessly blessed. It is safe for me to let go of control and ask for guidance. I am listening.

Morning Momentum

I believe in a benevolent universe that conspires for my highest good.

Our first thoughts and actions of the day are like the sunshine that warms the soil for the seeds. They set us up for what's to come. Anything we plant in that soil will have a head start, right?

I have found that starting off the day with a little morning momentum elevates everything that comes after it. There are two parts to this: how we feel and what we do.

The way we *feel* is what sends out the signal that draws abundance to us, so we want to feel good. We want to feel joy. We want to feel passionate and purposeful. We want to feel eager and enthusiastic. Think fist pump and a *woohoo!* That sounds like a lot to do before coffee, I know.

But it's not. The idea is to wake up feeling joyful and get one thing done quickly. It's a good idea to place a "feel-good thought" on the nightstand where it can be seen first thing in the morning. It might simply say *I've got this,* or *This is an amazing morning,* or it might remind us what task we want to start with. Then before or after our morning spiritual practice, we do one thing. It can be a small thing, but we accomplish something on today's list in a joyful way.

Try this for a week to get in the spiritual habit of morning momentum. You will notice that the loving universe conspires to bring back to us even more of the energy we give forth. Prepare for an amazing day.

In The World:

* Choose a short affirmation that will get your day off to a beautiful start.

* Organize your practice and your schedule to accommodate five or ten minutes to accomplish a task first thing in the morning with joy.

* Give it a seven-day test run and see how the morning momentum is working for you. Use a page in your journal to record your results.

In The Heart:

* I believe in a loving universe that conspires to bring me joy and abundance. Today will be an amazing day.

Bless My Soul

Bless my eyes to see goodness. Bless my words to speak kindness.
Bless my heart to feel compassion. Bless my soul to radiate love.

Today we revisit a sweet soul blessing that reminds us to turn our gaze ever so gently in the direction of our highest wisdom.

Bless my eyes to see what is good, loving and kind. Bless them to see what is whole, light and calm. Bless them to see the humble, the quiet and the small. Bless them to see the beauty in nature and in all living things. Catch my gaze when my eyes wander only to that which needs mending. Guard my vision when it strays to that which is dark and discouraging. Restore clear sight when they gravitate to violence. Bless my eyes.

Bless my words to speak only kindness and impart only love. Bless them to be used only to build up and create confidence. Bless them to put light into the world where there was darkness before. Hold my words when they might cause pain. Keep them within when they have the power to tear down and crush. May I never use them as a weapon of power. Bless my words.

Bless my heart to feel compassion for every being. Bless me to understand that the suffering of one of us is the suffering of all of us. Bless me to see a spark of divine light in every face. Bless me to see a piece of me in all others. Keep my heart blind to the faults of others. May I resist a view of the world that creates separation and judgment. Lead me away from comparisons and jealousy for the experience of another. Bless my heart.

Bless my soul to shine love on all who cross my path today. Bless me to express gratitude for small miracles of daily life. Bless me to joy and contentment for the gifts of this precious life. Gently remind me when I slip into lower vibrations of fear. Let me not linger long in the valley of self-pity. Nudge me out of needless worry. Bless my soul.

In The World:

✳ Ask for assistance today in gently turning toward the light, the beautiful and the good in every choice you make.

In The Heart:

✳ Throughout this day, in thought, word and action, I am in perfect alignment with my highest and most loving wisdom.

Hava Nagila

There is only one today. Celebrate the small moments.

Adam is close to my mother and calls her every Sunday afternoon. They catch up on all of the family news, what his kids are up to, where his work has taken him that week. Until recently, their calls were a source of great joy.

Since he has been struggling with drinking again after almost sixteen sober years, it has been a turbulent sea of emotions for all of us. Mom and I compare notes after any contact with him, answering the timid question, "How did he sound?" We rejoice when he is clear. We are devastated when he is slow, slurred and confused. We ride the waves with him in an ocean of silent prayers.

Last Sunday he didn't call. Mom barely slept that night, imagining the worst. On Monday morning she called me with a warning. Something horrible must have happened. Brace yourself.

Monday afternoon, Adam called my mother, apologizing that he had missed his Sunday call. He was clear and playful. He and his wife had gone out to dinner on Sunday to celebrate their anniversary. They had a wonderful time and even saw a beautiful rainbow as they left the restaurant. Another rainbow!

After hanging up with him, Mom was so elated that she jumped up and began thanking the angels. Breaking out into a spontaneous dance, she started singing Hava Nagila at the top of her lungs, prancing alone around the living room. After many enthusiastic choruses she stopped suddenly and thought, *What the heck am I singing? I have no idea what this even means!* So the Catholic Buddha turned to Google for a lovely surprise.

Let us rejoice, let us rejoice, let us rejoice and be happy.
Let us sing, let us sing, let us sing and be happy.
Awake, awake, awake my brothers.
Awake, my brothers, awake, my brothers, with a happy heart.

In The World:

＊ As you ride the waves of joy and challenge today, know that the angels are with you; lifting, supporting and encouraging you. And maybe even singing with you.

In The Heart:

＊ When I rejoice, the angels rejoice with me.

Hiding in Plain Sight

The sunrise is my prayer; the horses are my prayer; the rain in the field
is my prayer for God is in all.

If you are running short on time, don't worry about doing any spiritual excavation today. Fear not if your sneakers have hit the ground running. Don't be anxious if the day dawned with yet another emergency. The searching, the running, and the attending are all in the field of God's love; and every step is the prayer, the yoga, the practice, and the offering. There's nowhere else to look when everything we need is planted within.

Our spiritual practices are important and irreplaceable. They quiet us to open the windows and doors of the soul. They calm our distracting fears and worries. They remind us of our magnificence and beauty. They build faith in the benevolence of a loving universe and an ever-present God. They help us remember the incredible growth and blessings that arise from challenges. They bring abundance and joy through gratitude. And best of all, they help us to remember all of this stuff all day long.

But should we forget, there is not an action in the day that is not of value, that is not precious and sacred. Even when our minds are not being mindful and our presence is not at all present, we are being held in the palm of the greatest love imaginable. At all times we are living out life as a shining ray of divine love, and we are surrounded by the God in all things. Spirit does not have to be persuaded to show up. She's already here. Every thought and action is the prayer.

In The World:

✳ These words from Thomas Merton pried open my busy heart one day: *The sky is my prayer; the birds are my prayer; the wind in the trees is my prayer for God is in all.* So I tried out my own version: *The sunrise is my prayer; the horses are my prayer; the rain in the field is my prayer for God is in all.* What's yours?

In The Heart:

✳ In every step and every breath, I am incredible love in action. I am never alone and never outside the presence of God.

More Room for Love

Forgive everyone.

Holding on to grudges, anger and resentment can take up a lot of valuable real estate in the heart. They swirl around in there even when we are not paying attention to them, growing ever more complicated, painful and dark, blocking the free flow of our wisdom and love.

On the spiritual journey, we want to be as clear of energy blocks as possible and for that, we need to consider enlisting the assistance of forgiveness. When we welcome it in, developing an ongoing friendship of sorts, we give the dark, heavy stuff permission to take a rest, and we make more room in the heart for love.

There are two parts to this:

Forgiving Others. While the circumstances of our scars remain in our soul's history, it's possible to release the cloud of emotions surrounding them. It takes a lot of behind-the-scenes energy to hold anger toward a person or situation, distracting us from the present, and robbing us of our peace and health. When we forgive others, we choose to release our focus on the darkness. That's all. In the act of forgiveness, we make more room for love.

Forgiving Yourself. We are expert critics of our own behavior, holding tightly to regrets for things done and not done, said and unsaid. We think that by punishing ourselves we might somehow right the wrong, but we only succeed in wounding ourselves. And that is not for the highest good of anyone. Forgive yourself and let it go. Make more room for love.

In The World:

✳   Forgiveness is an alternate way of looking at circumstances. It's a powerful choice, a chance, a blessing to your soul. You can approach it slowly, each day taking small steps in the process of releasing. Start by letting go of small transgressions, and move up to the more challenging ones.

In The Heart:

✳   I forgive myself and others with the assistance of divine grace, and open to the freedom of pure love flowing in and out of my heart.

The Harvest of Kindness

*Be kind to yourself. The seeds we plant within are the harvest
we have to give.*

In early spring during my walks around the sheep and llama field, I watched the farmer behind a local inn plant what became a flourishing, organic garden. She tilled the soil and lovingly infused the Virginia clay with rich compost. She padded up the rows, planted precious seeds down the center, gave them a deep drink of well water and covered them with hay. One day when I arrived for a walk in late afternoon, I saw her standing there, caked with dirt after a long day's work, just looking, smiling with arms crossed, admiring her co-creation with nature. *This. This is good. These beautiful, bountiful things.*

By mid-summer, the garden was teeming with every imaginable vegetable. Flowers graced the entrance and cherry tomatoes climbed high on the border fences of the garden. Herbs lined the walkways and painted rock signs marked each row. The harvest was a mirror of the love with which the seeds were planted.

Like the farmer, we can think of every act of kindness toward ourselves as an investment in the harvest of kindness that we have to give to others. *Every act of kindness toward ourselves.* Like the process of preparing the soil, we can be loving to ourselves, even in moments of doubt or failure, when no tangible result of our effort is visible. Like the process of watering and nurturing, we can nurture our spirits when we thirst for encouragement, strength and grace.

Like a farmer at the end of a long day, we can stand back and gift ourselves with gentle kindness. We can admire the strength and courage it took to give what we had to give and love in the best way we knew how. We can forgive our missteps and notice the small victories. *This. This is good. These beautiful moments of today.* Plant seeds within with compassion and tenderness, and grow beautiful, bountiful things.

In The World:

✳ Be kind to yourself today, lifting, encouraging, and loving yourself in thought, word and actions. You are a beautiful, precious spirit deserving of great love. Recognize your magnificence by planting kindness within, and you will have a bountiful harvest to give.

In The Heart:

✳ I am kind and accepting of myself just as I am. I nurture myself daily by being gentle and loving in thoughts and actions.

Unsubscribe

Thoughts are powerful. Think kind ones.

What we think we become, said Buddha. Today he might have added, *What we read or watch, we become.* Everything that enters our consciousness changes us, and so, changes the world around us.

We have countless ways to stay informed. Our news sources have expanded exponentially, with articles and videos showing up in our news feeds, in the margins, popping up in little boxes with dire headlines. To receive essential free tips and tricks from the newest crop of experts and authors, we surrender our email and now our inboxes are exploding with mostly random and unnecessary tidbits and sales pitches. Thankfully, there's an easy fix.

Just because it's there doesn't mean it's worthy of your time or valuable enough to store in the files of your heart. You have the right to be discerning about what your interests are and what will feed your soul. In all things, be ruthless in deleting and avoiding *what you did not choose for yourself.*

Follow your intuition about what you really need to know. You will be kinder for it.

In The World:

* Delete impersonal emails with wild abandon. *Unsubscribe* is good too. Pass over posts if you don't recognize the origin—unless you are super interested. They are merely sending you to the place where the ads live.

* Don't feel the need to read or watch anything that shows up in your feeds. Read or watch what you choose from sources you know and log in to yourself. Avoid negative, violent, divisive content even in the disguise of humor.

* Be mindful to fill your heart with images and stories that feed your soul, grow your life, inspire your path and resonate with your spirit.

In The Heart:

* I am the guardian of my time and energy, and I choose what enriches my mind, body and soul.

God Is in the Leaves

Find joy by walking in gratitude.

One of the most memorable moments of my life occurred when I was in fourth grade. Wearing my first pair of glasses, I was on the way home from the eye doctor in the passenger seat of my mom's Buick. My new eyes caught sight of the most amazing vision. Leaves. What used to be a pretty green backdrop to life was, in reality, millions of dancing, twirling, clapping *leaves*. We broke out in laughter at my incredible discovery.

We are accustomed to walking past the backdrop of life. We are preoccupied with life's drama while we stroll blindly past incredible beauty. It's easy to miss what is unclear. When we slow our step enough to really look, we find the secret at the heart of life: Everything is sacred.

Not in a formal kind of way but in a humble, amazed, everyday kind of way when we allow ourselves to feel the magnitude of the gift of life.

When we really look, love and beauty become the new backdrop of life, impossible to pass by without notice. When we really look, gratitude rises as a way of being, a constant attitude of thanks for the endless blessings. Joy, then, is not found, as much as uncovered. She is a by-product of our thanks. She was there all along. We find joy by walking in gratitude.

All of this can happen in the presence of any life circumstance. We make choices. When we are ready, we can put on our glasses and see things as they really are. Only then will we know that God is in the leaves.

In The World:

✳ Meet today with new eyes, opening wide to grace and beauty as the new backdrop of life.

✳ Be a witness to the sacred in small things.

✳ Be grateful for the gifts and allow joy to inhabit your heart and home.

In The Heart:

✳ I open my eyes and my heart to the sacred in all things.

Grace Is the Wind

Allow grace to settle into the bones of stillness, acceptance and surrender.

I had some big middle-of-the-night worries last night. They swirled around me with thick, ominous energy, and it took me hours and countless prayers to relax enough to sleep again. I forgot that I wasn't in charge of everything. I forgot that I was not alone. I just forgot. Again.

Dawn broke into day with a breathtaking orange sunrise. The plants and trees were glittering proof of morning light; the bees and fireflies were happily working at their flower desks; the frogs took up their posts at their rock stations. Birds chatted good morning, and in a rush of joyous energy—I remembered.

Grace. *Right. Everything is in divine order.*

It was as if the dawn had raised the sails, and the breeze was perfect. I had the momentum of divine support at my back and all that had concerned me felt manageable. I was not in this alone. Grace would carry me through.

Locate the lost compass. Unfold the ripped map. Consult the weather. Wrestle up the sails. Hold tight to the tiller. The sails are the soul. Grace is the wind.

In The World:

* Grace is the light shining in the dark that illuminates our way back to the path.

* Grace is the reminder that even in challenges, there is a divine hand lifting us up.

* Grace is the comfort and support when we feel immobilized by life's demands.

* Grace is the dawn after the dark night of the soul.

* Grace is the sun illuminating our every lesson and decision.

In The Heart:

* The ever-present gift of grace strengthens my heart and lights my way today. There is nothing I cannot do. I allow grace to settle into the bones of stillness, acceptance and surrender.

Presuppose a Spark

*Treat others as if they already are the shining light
they are capable of becoming.*

Every day we are growing, changing, transforming, becoming. Each of us was born with a spark, a potential that we discover by following our passion and using our talents. Some of us nail it early on and some of us search for a lifetime, looking for clues to the meaning of life, matches at the ready. Some of us have given up on feeling the fire.

Then something shifts because someone truly *sees* us.

Sometimes we can see the potential in others before they can see it in themselves. We see their goodness, their talents, their possibilities even when they are blind to them. We encourage our friends by pointing out their strengths when they need them most. We teach our children by gently steering them toward what brings them joy.

Viktor Frankl, psychiatrist, Holocaust survivor and author of the groundbreaking, *Man's Search for Meaning*, says that if we "presuppose a spark" we will contribute to the fulfillment of that spark. In other words, if we assume the best in people, they will rise to the assumption and become their best selves.

What a beautiful kindness we offer to others when we see, before they see, the potential of who they might become. What a wonderful world it would be if we looked only for the possibilities in everyone.

In The World:

✳ Today, with honor and respect for all beings, assume the best in everyone, treating them as the person they are capable of becoming (even when they don't act like it yet).

✳ For those who are struggling with a particularly challenging situation, hold for them a vision of their highest, best self.

In The Heart:

✳ Today I see the potential goodness in all who cross my path. I assume the best of their intentions. I understand that they are doing the best they can do in this moment.

Birthday Meditation Celebration

I am thankful for the miracles that are yet to unfold.

Our birthday is not only a celebration of age but a sacred remembrance of our arrival on earth. On this day we honor our entry into humanity where we experience the embodiment of divine love. From year to year, our birthday is a milestone that marks love given and received, and lessons learned on the path.

It is also a day when our energy is uniquely powerful.

Today is my birthday and also the anniversary of my father's death. Every year, I start the day with a meditation that Maria taught me decades ago. Feel free to take it and make it your own as I have done. If today is not your birthday, you can still give it a whirl and surprise yourself by all the love you have shared this year. It all mattered. Every single act of love.

In The World:

* Take a comfortable seat as you would for meditation: spine straight, cross-legged or feet flat on the floor, palms up or down on your thighs. Take a few deep breaths with longer exhales to relax and become present.

* Begin by seeing clearly your birthday (or this day) last year. Then, slowly take a trip around the sun, month by month, reviewing major events and their impact on your life. Take each month slowly and separately: *In July I...,* allowing yourself to see and feel the experiences. Then move around the sun to August, etc.

* When you arrive again at today, step back and see your year as a circle around the sun. Then give thanks for each and every experience; all of the joy and pain, all of the beauty and challenge, all of the love given and received. Wrap it up in white light and allow it to float up and away.

* Turn to the beautiful space before you, and open to receiving new lessons in love this year. Give thanks for amazing blessings that are on their way.

In The Heart:

* I open my heart to be a channel of divine love on earth. I am thankful for the miracles that are yet to unfold.

Sacred Eyes

May I see this day through sacred eyes, shape this day with helpful hands, end this day with a grateful heart.

There is another level of consciousness going on simultaneously to the material one that we see with our earthly eyes. Under the surface, on a soul level, we *feel* and *know* things—and access our divine connection—in ways that can be of great service to our material lives. Like the phrase, "I want to be *in* the world, but not *of* it," we want to be in the world but with consciousness of our spiritual wisdom.

When we see this day with sacred eyes, we are looking through the lens of our higher self. We recognize the precious nature of the day. We value the holy in the small. We reorganize our priorities to let love take the lead. We ask for guidance, faith and wisdom to get us through. We look for joy, flow and grace to lift us up. We release resistance and fear. We become lighter and clearer.

When we shape this day with helpful hands, we direct the focus of our day from ourselves to others. Energy flowing outward with lovingkindness opens a huge space within for blessings to flow toward us. Small acts of kindness perpetuate the cycle of giving and receiving.

When we end this day with a grateful heart, we see clearly from the overview of our highest self, how many incredible gifts we have been given. We assume that challenges have purpose and meaning. We accept that what is undone will be accomplished in its perfect time. We lay our plans in the arms of the divine and know that all is well and that we are loved. The day is done and we rest with a heart full of gratitude.

In The World:

✳ Endeavor to live the following prayer in the small moments of today. See goodness and beauty, allow love to flow from your heart and give thanks in all things.

In The Heart:

✳ May I see this day through sacred eyes, shape this day with helpful hands and end this day with a grateful heart.

Chakra Love

We can expand into the miracle and power of our unique energy.

There is an elegant, powerful dance of light going on in our bodies at this moment. Seven major energy centers—stacked, spinning wheels of spiritual power called *chakras*—are receiving, transforming and reflecting our unique imprint of embodied spirit. This ancient knowledge is derived from Eastern traditions and is used in wellness and healing practices like yoga, hands-on-healing and Ayurveda.

Although we often refer to seven chakras, there are considered to be many other smaller energy centers in and around the body.

The seven major chakras are lined up from the base of the spine to the top of the head in rainbow colors of progressively lighter energy, forming a bridge between earth and heaven. The Root Chakra grounds us to the earth and to our generational tribe and sense of belonging. Then the chakras proceed upward through higher and lighter vibrations to the Crown Chakra which connects our energy with all beings and opens a window to divine love.

Each chakra is associated with a color, a developmental stage of life, emotions, gemstones, a body system, and particular organs. Disease and imbalances are related to a blockage in a particular chakra or chakras.

The ideal is to keep our energy centers as clear as possible for optimal health and healing. Working with an experienced energy healer can help us to accomplish this, and it can have enormous impact on our health and well-being. Looking holistically at mind, body and soul, we can expand into the miracle and power of our unique energy. More about the chakras coming tomorrow.

In The World:

* If the concept of chakra energy resonates with you, seek out the wealth of valuable wisdom about working with the chakras in areas of health, healing and spiritual transcendence.

* During meditation, sit with a straight spine so your energy centers are lined up for maximum energy, clarity, health, healing and connection.

In The Heart:

* My mind, body and soul are in perfect harmony. My energy is clear and healthy, powerful and connected with all things.

Chakra Love - Part 2

We are balanced, miraculous creations of love.

Today we take a journey up the spine in this very simple introduction to the major chakras. There is a vast amount of information available to you about each one and their connection to the physical, mental and emotional bodies. Although the lower chakras have denser, more earthly energy, and the higher chakras have lighter, more spiritual energy, each one is essential for health and balance. What miraculous creations we are!

In The World:

✴ The first, or Root Chakra is about family, tribal power, grounding, foundation, belonging, survival, balance, trust, health and stability. It is located at the base of the spine and is physically connected to bones, lower extremities and the immune system.

✴ The second, or Sacral Chakra coincides with our relationships with others, abundance, pleasure, creativity, desires, nurturing ourselves and others. It is located at the level of the lower abdomen and relates physically to reproductive organs and lower back.

✴ The third, or Solar Plexus Chakra is about personality, ego, self-esteem, confidence, playfulness and humor, responsibility, control and spontaneity. It is located at the level of the upper abdomen and relates physically to internal organs, abdomen and mid-spine.

✴ The fourth, or Heart Chakra is related to love of self and others, forgiveness, empathy, compassion, giving and receiving. It is located in the area of the heart and physically relates to heart and lung health.

✴ The fifth, or Throat Chakra is about communication, truth, speech, will, expression and decision making. It is located at the throat level and is physically connected to the mouth, throat and neck vertebra.

✴ The sixth, or Third Eye Chakra coincides with intuition, imagination and emotional intelligence. It is located at the level of the eyebrows and is physically associated with the nervous system and the senses.

✴ The seventh, or Crown Chakra relates to our connection with all beings, our divinity, spirituality and transcendence. It is located at the top of the head and is physically related to the brain.

In The Heart:

✴ I am a balanced and miraculous creation of light and love.

I Accept

I focus on the blessings, and more blessings are on the way.

In order to open our hearts to the abundance of the universe, it's helpful to take a moment to look at what's holding us back. Why do we get stuck in habits and patterns that prevent us from moving toward the joyful life we want to be living? It might be a good time to revisit the concept of resistance.

Resistance comes in many guises, the most common symptoms being worry, fear and the need to maintain control. This mindset keeps us spinning at a low vibration and draws low vibrational drama into our experience. On the other hand, acceptance of the experiences that come our way is reinforced by the practice of gratitude, faith and open-heartedness. When we surrender to what is, we are also sending out fireworks to the universe, eliciting assistance that is far greater than our ability to solve dilemmas or get through challenging times alone.

A few months ago, one of my dear friends was being haunted by an unending series of disasters. One night at dinner I told her maybe she should just raise her arms, look up and say, "I accept! No matter what you send me, I accept!" She was not amused. But soon after she performed this little ritual—on the verge of tears, she experienced a huge shift in her life. The resistance lifted and door of flow reopened.

What we focus on will be drawn to us by the feelings of love—or fear—that our attention creates. Our investment in tomorrow is to acknowledge the blessings of today and to trust that more blessings are on their way.

In The World:

* Today, keep your eyes on the blessings. Find them, great and small, everywhere you turn. You will be amazed by how they will multiply throughout the day.

* Activate spiritual alertness to notice when fear or the need to control slips in. Release resistance by facing challenges with surrender, faith and good spirits. Return the focus back to the positive and back to the blessings.

In The Heart:

* I accept what is. I focus on the blessings, and more blessings are on the way. I focus on the good, and more good is on the way.

❧

Many Angels to You

Angels are present right now, awaiting your request.

We can use all the help we can get, and angels are ever-present messengers from God who assist us in any and every way. They are helpful in the smallest decisions and the most complicated matters of daily life. The angelic realm will not intervene unless asked, but once a request is made, help is on the way.

We can also ask angels to help our friends. Many years ago, after my mother had suffered several fractures, her friend Peg, in wrapping up a phone conversation said, "Many angels to you." Mom, who is intimately connected to her angels, felt an immediate rush of love and support.

We've been calling all angels with this phrase ever since. And you can too. Thanks, Peg. Wishing many angels to someone is to send them the most beautiful assistance.

Another way angels can assist us is with our relationships. We can ask them to work on a challenge from higher realms. I have seen misunderstandings and family fallouts melt away after diligent requests for angelic intercession. In situations when it feels like all is lost, there's always hope because angels are near.

Angels are present right now awaiting your request. Share the assistance with family and friends.

In The World:

❋ For help with your most challenging task today, ask the angels.

❋ For someone who needs extra assistance today, send angels.

❋ For help with a seemingly hopeless situation, ask the angels.

❋ For the disenfranchised of our world, send angels.

In The Heart:

❋ Angels assist me today in all of my challenges. I ask clearly for what I need and open myself fully to all forms of answers and resolutions.

Mind, Body and Soul

My mind is calm. My body is healthy. My soul is joyful.

We offer affirmations today for the unity of all parts of our being—that we may integrate our mind, body and soul into seamless, radiant beauty.

Take a deep inhalation, and on the exhale, say within, *My mind is calm.* Another deep inhalation, and on the exhale, *My body is healthy.* One more deep inhalation, and on the exhale, *My soul is joyful.* Repeat these three breaths and imagine mind, body and soul working together today as an integrated and powerful team, held safe in love by divine spirit.

May the light shine upon you
To illuminate your way
May you stand on a mountaintop
And see a brighter day
May all the separate pieces
Of your world become one whole
May spirit hold you safe in love
Mind, body and soul

May you flow like the river
As we kneel upon your shore
May you bend like the tallest tree
In the winter storm
May you fly on wings of freedom
In peace forevermore
May spirit hold you safe in love
Mind, body and soul

May you always love with everything
And know everything is love
May you never cry for what can't be
In your hand is just enough
May you shine the light that shines on you
And teach us what you know
May spirit hold you safe in love
Mind, body and soul

In The World:

* Return to your three breaths at any time during this beautiful day when in need of energy and connection.

In The Heart:

* Today I am held safe in the arms of unconditional love, and treasured as a precious and whole being—mind, body and soul.

Sacredness in Tears

Tears are the legacy of our love and loss.

Though I am a relentless optimist, I've finally learned a big truth: Happiness is not meant to be a full-time job. We are born with intense feelings and it's essential to allow all of our emotions to be seen, heard and welcomed for as long as we are feeling them.

Emotions are not a personality trait; they are transient visitors, like clouds in the sky. We don't freak out on cloudy days—we know the weather will change and we accept that. We don't judge clouds as good or bad, and we know the sky will remain when the clouds have moved on.

Yet still, tears seem to unglue us and our loved ones. We are encouraged to stop crying and dry our eyes. We are told *it's not so bad*, offered a tissue and a distraction. There's little tolerance in most of our hearts for sitting with sorrow.

Tears are a sign of the courage it takes to dive deep with an emotion and stay present with it. They are the legacy of our love and loss. They are what burns us clean. They are a miraculous, natural release that opens our hearts to healing grace. They are a necessity of transformation.

Instead of resisting the vulnerability of crying, perhaps we can be still with it for a moment. Perhaps we can simply allow what is. Flow with the intensity of the feeling. Listen to it. Give it love. Be broken opened by it. Be cleansed by it and breathe in deeply its sacredness.

In Henry Ward Beecher's words, "Tears are the telescope through which we see far into heaven." May tears bless us with clearer vision, a deeper well of compassion and a glimpse of heaven.

In The World:

✳ Travel through this day with compassion for yourself and all beings, staying with emotions as they demand your attention. A multitude of feelings can co-exist within us on any given day.

In The Heart:

✳ I give myself permission to feel all the feelings of my life. When I allow myself to be present with my pain, I am in the presence of healing grace.

An Eye for Beauty

Search for something beautiful in every day.

Early this morning I opened the back door to look around. I noticed the tree limb that was broken by the bird feeder. Under the overgrown hydrangea, I spied red ants taking up shop in the jade plant. Algae needed to be scooped from the pond's surface. The table begged for washing.

Wandering in, I checked to see that my scheduled 7:00 a.m. post made it to my Facebook page. It said, "Search for something beautiful in every day." In the comments section, this message awaited me:

"It is my daily mission. I live to find beauty and to try to make my surroundings beautiful. It keeps my mind beautiful!"

Tea in hand, I went back outside in search of beauty. A different world awaited me. The shiny, sturdy jade leaves were drinking up the morning sun. Pretty, fuzzy bees were visiting the lavender. There were at least 50 shades of green and the sky was a deep, gorgeous purple-blue. The clucking rooster made me laugh. The smell of sage and thyme were intoxicating.

It made me think of a friend who visited Calcutta and said that so many children asked her for money that her heart closed and she ceased to feel compassion. The sheer enormity of need shut down her ability to hear the cry of poverty. Perhaps it is similar with beauty. We see so much of it that we have stopped letting it into our hearts.

Some circumstances require us to look a little harder than others. Beautiful things are often clothed as the small, everyday moments. But if we search for beauty in today, we will surely find it. And it will keep our minds beautiful.

In The World:

* Walk in the world today with a keen eye for beauty. Notice with all of your senses. Breathe it in. Bask in the beauty that surrounds you.

In The Heart:

* With mindful awareness, I notice beauty in and around me. I allow beautiful things to make me more beautiful.

August
Be present.
Let the day flow with grace.
Expect joy. Be positive.
Serve with compassion.
Speak only kindness.
Impart only love.
Never forget you're not alone.
Give thanks for everything.
See goodness in others. mary davis

EVERY DAY SPIRIT

August Blessings

Be present. Be here. Today, we can guide our thoughts back to the present moment with gentle focus and live fully right where we are.

Let the day flow with grace. Grace flows through us easily when we are in tune with the subtle voice of intuition. Open and listen for guidance.

Expect joy. Be positive. Imagine a fulfilling day unfolding, in which we accomplish much and experience joy in the process. Welcome the light.

Serve with compassion. Acts of service when performed with love lend immeasurable light to our day. Be watchful for ways to serve.

Speak only kindness. Speak only kind words. Think only kind thoughts. Be kind to yourself and to those who cross your path or your mind.

Impart only love. Send out all thoughts and words on the wings of love so that we may love one another, love ourselves, love the unlovable.

Never forget you're not alone. Let's remind ourselves often today that we are always supported, guided and unconditionally loved as we are.

Give thanks for everything. Gratitude will shift the perspective of the day from one of lack to one of abundance. Give constant thanks.

See goodness in others. Each of us has a soul that is made of beauty and love. Assume the best in others so they may rise to their highest light.

꩜

The Gift of Stressful Thoughts

Phone down. Cup of tea. Say a prayer. Just breathe. Have faith.
Bless the day. Ask for grace. I'll be okay.

Sometimes there are not enough hours in the day to wrestle our work to the ground. Or so it seems from here. Our minds are dancing with stressful thoughts, and we're more than a little overwhelmed. When you notice this dissonant symphony descending on your brain, stop and do the most logical next thing. Make a cup of tea and sit. Herein lies the gift.

On the sixth day, God did not create stress. We did. In our minds. It's not even a real thing. It's our perception of some made-up future doom. It's the perception of lack, of fear and of mistrust. And we know better. We know that ours is an abundant universe with infinite support waiting to swing into action. We know the perfect outcome for all of our desires is already manifesting if we can just stop resisting and get out of the way of grace. We also know that peace and contentment are within reach.

But sometimes it takes those tea leaves to explain it to us. In a moment of silence, we might remember how infinitely loved we are and how the world will go on spinning just fine if we duck out for a moment. We might be reminded how when we reboot the attitude and plug into spirit, the energy flows.

It's the difference between climbing a mountain with a heavy backpack and floating down the river in an inner tube with a piña colada in one hand. Where would you rather be?

In The World:

* Stressful thoughts are resistant thoughts. Notice when they infiltrate your mind today. And stop. Change gears. Pour a cup of tea and invite your highest wisdom into the situation. Say a prayer and just breathe for a moment. Have faith and bless the day. Ask for grace, then get back in the game with an army of angels by your side. Float. Flow. Know that all is well.

In The Heart:

* I live in an abundant universe, flowing with ease and grace through this day. I set stressful thoughts aside and find joy in each moment.

Working in Angel Time

I have all the time I need for all I need to do.

In a quest to flow through today with ease and grace, we might have to get a little flexible with our usually rigid concept of time. Ever since my friend Lyndy told me about Angel Time, time has become more fluid and more, well, cooperative.

If I were discussing with Lyndy a certain looming deadline or upcoming trip, she would say, "Remember, Mare, ask to go through the day in Angel Time!" When we ask for Angel Time, somehow, activities we think will take longer steal only a fraction of the time allotted them. Other items seem to magically drop off the list, and my favorite feature of all—you do what you are sure is an hour's work and only 30 minutes have gone by. Oh how I love that.

Lyndy also shared the simple phrase she uses for her request that often produces miraculous results: *May time expand to meet my needs.*

In the philosophical concept of time called Eternalism, all moments, past, present and future, exist simultaneously. In my own philosophical concept, if the amazing dimension of Eternalism is possible, then I can manage to organize my powers to wiggle out a few extra hours in this one day, right?

Spend a little precious time this morning on the most important thing you can do to give yourself some extra time today—connect with your spiritual support team. It's the best investment you will make in having the most productive and joyful day possible.

In The World:

＊ Center yourself by meditating for at least five minutes. Yes, you can find five minutes. Imagine your radiant heart beaming with light, then see your connection with divine light in your mind's eye.

＊ Now ask for the angels to shift time today to allow you all the time you need for all you need to do. *May time expand to meet my needs.* Give thanks in advance that this is so, and smile because you are going to have a really efficient day.

In The Heart:

＊ I'm thankful that I have all the time I need for all I need to do.

Little Breath, Big Changes

Using the power of visualization, we can become a frequency of light that can lift the vibration of everything in its path.

Powerful joy can come in humble packages—like today's meditation using the breath as a guide. Ready? Here we go. As you read, sit comfortably and extend upwards from your seat, lengthening and straightening your spine, setting your shoulders slightly back to open the heart. Inhale deeply through your nose and take a long exhale. Once again, inhale deeply and take a long exhale.

Now imagine your heart center glowing with radiant light and connected to an unending stream of grace that pours in through the top of your head.

• Inhale love and see it filling your heart.

• Exhale love and see it flowing around your loved ones and the earth.

• Inhale joy and smile as it enters your heart.

• Exhale joy and watch it envelop your loved ones and all beings.

• Inhale peace and allow it to fill your heart to overflowing.

• Exhale peace and see it wrap around the planet.

• Back to the first step, and repeat with dedicated, blissful focus.

Isn't it amazing that something as small as a breath can make big changes in our mind, body and soul? Using the power of visualization, we can become a frequency of light that can lift the vibration of everything in its path. The light of our love not only changes us on a cellular level, but changes the world as well.

In The World:

✳ Take 5-10 minutes this morning or evening to practice the meditation with focus and dedication. It is a gift to yourself and to each and every one of us.

In The Heart:

✳ I use the energy of my light and love to spread love, joy and peace to all beings.

We Need You

You are a blessing to the world.

Your unique beauty, love and talent are gifts that no other being can offer. No one can replace you. No one radiates love with the same energy that you do. No one is an expression of God in the way you are. You are a magnificent, glorious, good, beautiful, whole reflection of divine love. And we, the people on the planet, need your light today.

This light in you is your essence. It is born and it blooms from within. It is your birthright. Nothing in the external world can ever change this.

You are not alone if you have trouble truly believing this. But the only way you can share the depth of your love and be the blessing you are meant to be is to recognize this truth. You must own the story of your power and grace in order to bless us confidently with the gifts that only you can give.

Release whatever might be holding you back from expressing yourself fully. Know that the only voice that can lead you is the voice of the heart, and it will never lead you astray.

Thank you for the way you bless all of us—by being you.

In The World:

✱ Give yourself permission to be less than perfect. Your precious and messy enough-ness is what makes you uniquely you.

✱ Remember that there's no competition ever. You are the only one with your gifts.

✱ Practice self-compassion as much as you practice compassion.

✱ Know you are a sacred being, here with the rest of us, to share your love. You honor all other beings by becoming fully yourself.

In The Heart:

✱ I love and honor myself and all other beings, and courageously interact with the world as I offer the blessing of my gifts today.

Rooted in Gratitude

Keep your soul rooted in gratitude and your branches open to blessings.

In the early 1960s, three young spiritual seekers planted a garden out of necessity on the windy shores of north Scotland in barren, sandy soil. Having lost their employment, Peter and Eileen Caddy, with their three young sons and friend, Dorothy Maclean, found they had the assistance of nature spirits—angels who guided them in the cultivation of the garden. Through their loving care, the plants grew to enormous size, large flowers bloomed in radiant colors, and people traveled long distances to see their famous 40-pound cabbages.

The gardens of Findhorn are still in bloom today with the help of the nature spirits and the practice of gratitude. Maclean explains in her memoir, *To Hear the Angels Sing*, "Human affirmative thought protects and feeds plants, as it does all of life. Our thanks and appreciation unite us with the life of whatever we are thankful for and appreciative of, making a compatible blend of forces to help development on various levels, including the physical." Gratitude makes everything grow.

We know how gratitude helps us to see the abundance in our lives instead of the lack. But do we understand that our gratitude can physically change things? Maclean goes on to say that one of the angels taught her to view even sickly plants as healthy and robust by thinking of them in terms of light. "According to the devas (angels), gratitude and appreciation have enormous effects, making great swelling movements which complete the circle of life."

When we give thanks, we enhance the light around the object of our thanks. When we appreciate something, we change the very energy surrounding it. Now that is a beautiful thing.

In The World:

* Take along with you today an awareness of the power of your appreciation for all living things. Know that you are a being of light and when you admire any living thing, you feed it with healing energy and change it from within.

In The Heart:

* Every day, I co-create my world by showing gratitude and appreciation in all things.

Lessons from a Brown Hawk

It's not selfish, but beautiful to enjoy the blessings of resting,
being and allowing.

The beautiful brown hawk sits erect and silent on the split rail fence at the near side of the horse field. Only his head turns ever so slightly, taking in every movement in the trees and the grass. He alights and circles the cabin and lifts high to get a wider view before coming in for a landing on a hay bale in the field's center. Vigilant, he watches, listens, trusts and waits with patience.

Mr. Hawk, I want more of your silence. I can only know what God would have me do if I listen quietly in the field of my heart. If only I can hold my noisy needs and wants at bay, muzzle them at the sidelines of my humanity, so my spirit can be directed by divine will. My will too, really. I don't want to fly alone. I want to absorb the wisdom that directs my every action.

Mr. Hawk, I can learn from your patience. You wait to make your move, unlike me, in constant motion, searching for direction, one challenge at a time. If only I can hold my waterfall of thoughts back and be more faithful in the waiting, knowing that the perfect plan will unfold for me if I allow it. I want to slow down in my incessant doing, in favor of being the loving spirit that I am.

Mr. Hawk, I can learn from your sight. I want to turn my head ever so slightly, taking in each small moment of grace and sacred small happening. I dream of lifting up above the earth and gaining perspective, a holy vision of what really matters in my life today. I want to go forth with the sacred all-seeing eyes of guidance and love. Then I will come in for a landing on a seat of the soul, a high place from which I can see where to go, what to do, how to become an instrument of peace.

In The World:

✳ Mindfully take in the blessings of today with renewed and sacred sight. Use the tools of silence, patience and vision to see the beauty in small things and to open patiently to divine direction.

In The Heart:

✳ Today I slow down my thoughts and actions, allowing the day to unfold, one gentle moment at a time, through the soft focus of grace.

Faith and the Comet

Grant me strength when I feel small. Grant me faith when I lose sight.
Grant me hope when all seems lost. Grant me grace in morning's light.

Tiny pieces of the tail of a comet grazed my house last night. Yours too. They may as well have landed on the roof. Fiery, wish-worthy, shooting stars danced in every corner of the sky, lighting up the night and our dreams with ancient stardust. The Perseid meteor shower travels trillions of miles to put on the spectacular, annual fireworks show—and to shake us out of our earthly coma. When we stare at the sky, we can't help but ask the big questions. After, "How could forever be *that far?*" comes the inevitable, "How can I be *this small?*" What kind of powerful God could have concocted this universe? Perseid gives us a pajama-clad chance to see how small we are and how great the universe is.

We are all part of this star stuff, this oneness. We are a tapestry woven from the same elements, made from an omnipotent force of love that envelops every being and entity as far as the eye can see and forever again farther. That's pretty comforting really, when we are brave enough to keep asking for assistance and small enough to lean in silently to receive the answers.

In the words of my daughter, "Sometimes it's good to feel small." Yes, Maya, it is. Because when we pray this prayer, *"Grant me strength when I feel small. Grant me faith when I lose sight. Grant me hope when all seems lost. Grant me grace in morning's light,"* we should have no doubt that the God of all things, the God of solar systems and stars, of comets and planets, of oceans and mountains, of you and me, will have no problem being the God of our pain and loss, of our strength and faith, of our fear and doubt, of our hope and grace, of our morning light. No problem at all. So I keep asking for assistance and leaning in silently for the help that always comes. Thank you, God, for tending to the stardust—and me.

In The World:

* The annual Perseid meteor shower is coming soon. Search the best viewing day and make plans. Sit outside where you can see the sky. You can even sit in the dark by a window. Forfeit sleep to open your mind to the vastness of the universe as you watch her show of beauty.

In The Heart:

* In my time of greatest need, I have perfect faith that when I ask with a humble heart, I will receive everything I need from the hand of God.

#ReedAndSpencer

*Think kind thoughts. Speak kind words. Seek kind friends.
Imagine a kind world.*

Kindness has the power to change things. Even to transform something unimaginably dark and sad into something filled with light. Just ask Jamie Hyman and Matt Huertas.

The saddest day of their lives was August 9, 2013, when their stillborn twins were delivered. Powerful grief took over their formerly happy lives. As the first anniversary approached they got an idea to memorialize their boys. They asked their family and friends to mark the day by an act of kindness. It could be anything—buying coffee for coworkers, bringing toiletries to a homeless shelter, leaving a gift card under a stranger's windshield wiper. Spreading the word on social media, their loved ones used #ReedAndSpencer to share their various acts of kindness with Jamie and Matt.

The personal responses they received were a comforting salve for their deep pain. By the second anniversary in 2015, the idea had gone viral, with kind souls from all over the world taking part. Those silent babies, Reed and Spencer, had been the source of incredible love and unstoppable kindness.

In Jamie's words, "We took something that was unspeakably horrible and turned it into something beautiful. We reclaimed the day."

In The World:

* Today, let's participate in marking this day with a random act of kindness in honor of Reed and Spencer. Search their story to find out more. Post with #ReedAndSpencer to share your kindness.

* Consider making something beautiful of the saddest day of your life. Even if you are the only one that knows, reclaim your day with something special that lifts your heart and lights your path forward.

In The Heart:

* I contribute to the kindness of the world by reaching out with small acts of kindness from where I am today.

Today Is Not a Race

All else will fall into place when we slow down, notice the gifts and give thanks.

"This is a wonderful day. I've never seen this one before." One of my heroes in life, Maya Angelou, not only had a way with words, but a way with gratitude. Her poetry, books and wide variety of other creative offerings drove at the truth with such force as to make us all wonder how we had missed so much depth in our own lives. The beauty of her inspired literature swept us away into her experience and lifted us with the hope of rising through challenges too. No matter how dark things got, Maya found a precious ray of hope to celebrate. She reminded us, over and over again, that today is a gift.

Today is not a race, it is a gift. It is not to be rushed or hurried through, but to be savored and treasured.

Today is not a chore, it is a chance. It is not to be turned away at the door, but to be offered generous hospitality as an honored guest.

Today is not a duty, it is an honor. It is not an obligation that must be fulfilled, but an opportunity to rise into our highest selves.

Today is not a struggle, it is a choice. It is not to be wrestled to the ground and conquered, but loved and cherished and polished into beauty.

Today is not a cloud, it is a light. It is not to be travelled through blindly as a victim, but to be illuminated by the sun of our strength.

Today is not a solo, it is a chorus. It is not to be sung alone but to be orchestrated by a choir of angels and backed by a symphony of all those who love us.

Today is not a race. It is a gift.

In The World:

✳ Accept today as a gift, being mindful of the small miracles, and taking the time to notice the beauty and the good, even in moments of challenge. All else will fall into place when we slow down, notice the gifts and give thanks.

In The Heart:

✳ There is no other day like today. I am thankful to be awake, to be alive, to be here. I walk through this day with a grateful heart.

Lemonade and African Violets

You are never too young or too old to make a difference.

I remember hearing a story of an eight-year-old boy who opened a lemonade stand and raised thousands to feed the homeless. When I searched it to check out the details, up popped seven other examples of kids who did the same thing and that was just on the first page of the search. Way to go, kids! You are changing our world with love.

And way to go, parents. It takes our will and our example to open that window within a child's heart. It is said that kids are naturally compassionate, and I believe that to be true, but they learn quickly that their other choice is looking out for themselves only. When we encourage compassion at a young age, and allow children to feel for themselves the beauty of unconditionally loving others, they will use that gift for the rest of their lives.

A counselor friend once told me of an older woman who suffered from severe depression. She lived alone and rarely left her house except to go to church. When asked what she did with her time, the only thing she mentioned was her love of propagating African Violets. She had made many plants from one plant and loved her collection.

My friend encouraged her to share her plants with those in need. When someone from the church died or was sick, perhaps she could bring a plant to their family or to their room. She did just that, and within a few years she became the African Violet Lady. She would quietly and lovingly bring a beautiful plant and hand written note to the porch of those in her church community who were suffering. And she lifted many lives with her love.

In The World:

* It doesn't have to be a lemonade stand or an African Violet. It can be a prayer or a prayer shawl or the results of your unique talents. You are never too young or too old to make a difference. Dreams, at any age, can change the world.

In The Heart:

* I am an ageless, timeless being of love. I share my gifts freely with those in need and change the world by acts of kindness.

❧

Food for the Soul

If it doesn't feed your soul, have the strength to let it go.

In my twenties, I had a roommate with an aggressive form of cancer. His doctor, at a loss for treatment options, recommended a macrobiotic diet, which is based on whole grains, beans and vegetables. Wanting to help out, I picked up a few cookbooks and learned the basics. Within weeks, some unexpected changes began taking place. I had incredible energy and sense of joyful lightness. I was sleeping better and dreaming beautiful, colorful dreams. My intuition and higher wisdom became like a constant companion, complete with clairvoyance and clairaudience. Who knew that a diet could be so spiritual?

But alas, a diet only works when you stay with it. After a few years, I gradually added a greater variety of foods and the mind-blowing benefits dimmed a bit. I have, however, always returned to this basic form of eating, more recently leaning toward a mostly plant-based diet, complete with morning green drinks.

My challenge is pausing to make healthy meals and snacks during the work day. Woman cannot live on tea and gluten-free ginger snaps alone. That will not feed the soul. So I take steps toward positive nutritional changes each day.

Our bodies are created to be calm, rested, energetic and clear enough to hear the voice of intuition. We are worthy of the finest treatment: healthy, vitamin-packed, organic, real food from Mother Nature. It not only heals the body and prevents disease, but it improves mind function and enables a clearer connection with spirit. Now that's some food for the soul.

In The World:

❋ Identify some simple eating habits that are not serving your mind, body and soul. Choose to make one change today. You have the strength to do this!

❋ Do a little research to get inspiration about healthy eating. Find some new recipes you like and introduce them one at a time.

In The Heart:

❋ I love and honor my beautiful body and choose to nourish it with only the best and healthiest foods.

More Than Teaching Piano

Prayer always matters. Prayer always bears light.
Prayer always changes things. Prayer always changes us.

Between us, I never really was a great piano teacher for at least three reasons. 1. In my crazy love for the kids, I never got on their case for not practicing. I made the lessons fun no matter how unprepared they were. 2. If they wanted to learn the Star Wars theme by ear, I was happy to show them how, breaking the teacher code of keeping their eyes on the sheet music. As you can imagine, that's all they wanted to play from then on because their friends thought it was so cool. (Sorry, Beethoven.) 3. I'm not a great reader, so the kids who *were* good readers passed me in about fourth grade.

But despite my shortcomings, most of them really loved coming for lessons. I always had a full schedule and long waiting list, probably thanks to the kids who were playing the Star Wars theme and making their friends jealous. I knew that even if I wasn't grooming the next Yuja Wang, I was instilling a life-long love of piano. These kids were never going to grumble about their parents making them take lessons. They will remember the fun they had at Miss Mary's house and what an awesome thing it is to make music.

They thought I was just teaching piano. But really, I knew that the most important thing I was doing was blessing them and their families. If somebody had a big test or audition, I would shoot them up a prayer. If a family was splitting up, I'd shower them with blessings. If a kid was struggling at school or being bullied, I'd ask for the angels to help. Everyone who came through my door got blessed, sent good energy and prayed for, and I like to believe it changed things for the better. And in the process, I know I was changed for good.

In The World:

✳ In any line of work, from carpenter to car salesman, from artist to CEO, we can hand out blessings generously and change the world with our love. Make blessing others part of your work day.

In The Heart:

✳ In all of my activities today, I look for chances to offer prayers and blessings where needed. I spread my light freely to all who cross my path.

Give of Yourself

If we don't have it, we can't share it.

In Anita Moorjani's book, *Dying to Be Me*, she tells the story of the terminal cancer that ravaged her body and of her near-death experience that shed incredible light on her soul.

"When I'm *being* love, I don't get drained, and I don't need people to behave a certain way in order to feel cared for or to share my magnificence with them. They're automatically getting my love as a result of me being my true self. And when I am non-judgmental of myself, I feel that way toward others."

Automatically getting my love. This. It happens as a byproduct of loving ourselves. In order to give of ourselves, to another, or to a greater purpose in our lives, we need to be completely ourselves. If we wish to share our unique gifts—our love, our talents, our precious time—then we must come to appreciate ourselves fully and non-judgmentally. There's no way around it. We can't share something that we don't fully embody.

Moorjani goes on to say that it is not our purpose to inspire other people, but to learn what inspires us, then share that inspiration with others. Our joy becomes the gift, automatically. Because that's who we are. It's all love.

In The World:

* We have opportunities to give of ourselves daily by *being love* in each of our encounters. That means being true and non-judgmental of ourselves so we can be less judgmental of others. We can then listen well, show compassion, give a compliment or share an insight without feeling drained. Instead of needing to change others, we are being lovingly present.

* We have opportunities to give of ourselves through service. Consider offering some time each month sharing your unique gifts with others through volunteering in your community.

In The Heart:

* I share the light and love of my spirit freely by honoring myself and by being completely present with others.

Choosing Joy

I trust that the world is a benevolent place that conspires
for my highest good.

When it comes to choosing joy, my heart stands by those who are enduring the most difficult moments that life has to offer. On some days, even the smallest step toward joy is climbing a mountain. The truth is, we can honor a wide range of feelings, in the span of one day, while moving at any pace we choose toward that which is one step lighter.

As we learned earlier, research has shown that although some people are born with a more positive disposition, anyone can reprogram their thoughts to foster more feelings of joy and happiness. Once we become aware of negative repetitive thoughts that keep us distracted and distressed, we turn toward positive affirmations to break the cycle. Over time, these new positive thoughts become habitual.

Choosing joy is a spiritual practice, renewing our connection with the divine as we become lighter, more mindful and more peaceful. When in alignment with spirit, we can relax a little. We are safe. We are home. This is who we are.

In The World:

*   Today, experiment with positive affirmations. Refer to your favorites in your journal. Allow negative thoughts and words to move naturally through you without taking up residence.

*   Love yourself. Compliment yourself. Treasure yourself. Forgive yourself.

*   Eat nutritious foods. Get plenty of sleep. Move your body.

*   Keep company with joyful people.

*   Read uplifting books. Listen to joyful music. Choose inspiring articles, podcasts and movies.

In The Heart:

*   I open my heart to the possibility of joy. I am grateful for the gifts of today. I trust that the world is a benevolent place that conspires for my highest good. I deserve joy in my life.

❧

I Am Always Becoming

Spirit is diligently asking us to joyfully rise.

There have been many days this summer when I have been called out of my cabin on Hunters Road to another arena of life. There was the relocation of boxes and books as Maya moved out of one apartment and into another; there were ten divinely dazed days in Florida helping Mom edit and publish her book; there was the hospice patient on the precipice of life for weeks.

After each outing, I would wonder where my groove had gone, only to discover at this late date that I never really had a groove. Oh drat. As much as we try, life refuses to assemble our days in any linear fashion. So what's the constant? We need some illusion of normalcy down here. Anyone?

Despite our best intentions, spirit doesn't seem to want to approach the co-creation of this day with an agenda or a list. There are only moments in which we are called to be present. Lightbulb! The constant is *becoming*.

Each experience has the potential to grow us. Every daydream and adventure, every call for assistance, every interruption and distraction, stretches us, aligns us, breaks us down and heals us up—and if we allow it—brings us purpose.

It's not all about evolution and accomplishment. It's about being present and being ourselves for the unexpected awakenings that surprise us in an unscheduled moment. No time is wasted. We walk together on the road of perpetual becoming.

And spirit is diligently asking us to joyfully rise.

In The World:

✶   As the day unfolds, be flexible and present, knowing that all experiences, even waiting in line, are precious opportunities to share joy, compassion and kindness.

In The Heart:

✶   I approach the mystery of this day with a lightness of being, knowing that all I need to do is be present and be myself.

When All Seems Lost

*We lift this day with a thought of love, an act of kindness
and a heart of hope.*

Adam is drinking again. After all those sober years, he's sliding backwards down the slope and out of reach. With each passing day, he's disappearing into a shell of the man I used to know and the friend I used to play with. He's almost out of sight.

After denying the truth, along with him, for so many months, I called him yesterday and told him I loved him, no matter what. I told him I knew he wouldn't stop drinking for me if he couldn't stop for his awesome kids and beautiful wife. But there was one thing, I said, only one thing I wanted. To be honest. As messy and messed up as this is, let's just drag it out into the middle of the rug and let it live in the room. "I totally agree," he slurred.

I hung up and hung my head in despair. I can't change this, or fix it, or will it away with all my determined power. No, there is no power here. He's powerless over his drinking, and I am certainly powerless over him. Nothing can be done. I am utterly and completely helpless to assist.

Except...what if I just hold a space...where he's healthy and happy and healed? What if I arrange my thoughts to think only brilliant ones of him, where I envision his highest self, his already perfect soul, his humor and light and radiance? What if I see him only as God sees him? What if I let that be my prayer and my plan?

My Spiritual A-Team, God and I, we're going to hold my friend up to the light knowing that on some level, he is already there.

In The World:

✳ When all seems lost, know that the best and most beautiful version of the person or situation can always be found right here and now. Enlist your Spiritual A-Team in holding your vision up to the light, relentlessly full of hope.

In The Heart:

✳ I lift this day, with hope in my heart, to my highest imagining. I believe that all things are possible.

꠸ⱽꠥ

My Day Is Yours

*Bless me to be the hands of Your work, the steps of Your path
and the rays of Your sun.*

Bless me to be the hands of Your work. In the small moments of today, help me to put my highest self into my every task. Remind me that I don't work alone, but for You and with You. My hands are Yours.

Bless me to see with the sight of Your eyes. In the small moments of today, help me to see You in the pile of notes that ask something of me. Let them be done with You in the fabric of each action and transaction. My work is Yours.

Bless me to be the steps of Your path. In the small moments of today, help me to know what should be done next and next, and how to stay in the flow of grace. Show me where to go, where you would have me be. My steps are Yours.

Bless me to be the song of Your voice. In the small moments of today, help me to remember that it is You who speaks through me, Your kindness that flows from me, Your encouragement that lifts others through me. My voice is Yours.

Bless me to be the rays of Your sun. In the small moments of today, shine Your divine energy through me, so I may raise the vibration of everyone who crosses my path. Help me to be the light of Your radiant love. My love is Yours.

Bless me to be an instrument of Your peace. In the small moments of today, help me to be serene and to share this sense of calm with others. May I be peaceful in my thoughts of others and imagine a world of peace. My peace is Yours.

In The World:

✳ Contribute to peace in the world by asking to be a worthy custodian of your spiritual gifts. In the small moments of today, be grateful for the gift of life. Turn your head to notice the sacred in the small and the holy in simple things. Be joyful and useful. Love your neighbor. Be compassionate. Bring kindness and peace to the part of the world that is within your reach. Offer up your day to be used for love.

In The Heart:

✳ Today, in each step and with every breath, I am an instrument of peace, acting as the hands and the feet of the divine.

❦

Opening Doors

Every line on your face is a thousand sunrises to light my way.

My neighbor Gene was laid to rest today. I had never been to a military funeral in Arlington National Cemetery before. It was an honorable tribute to a man who came from little means and rose to became a well-respected, successful restaurateur. Not an easy path. Gene started his career as one of an early generation of black owner-operators of multiple McDonald's franchises, at one time running the extremely busy stores at both D.C. airports, in addition to stores in five other locations. Gene was also a master gardener, and passersby would slow their cars to marvel at the magnificent gardens he personally nurtured outside his beautiful home.

Gene was a door opener. It is said that we all get to where we are going on the backs of those who came before us. Those who broke down barriers before him opened doors for Gene, and he spent a lifetime opening doors for others.

My parents, both from humble backgrounds, made their way virtually on their own, to educate themselves and put four kids through college. They instilled in us the foundation of integrity, a strong work ethic, an attitude of gratitude and the belief that there was nothing we could not be. Which I took rather literally, following my dreams through nursing school and on to careers as a singer/songwriter, a piano teacher, a yoga instructor, a graphic artist, an app developer, and writer. I did none of this alone. Courageous immigrants and braver women paved my way.

We owe a debt of gratitude to the Genes and the ancestors, the parents, the women, the leaders, the activists and teachers who came before us and opened the doors, or broke them down, then hoisted us up onto their backs and brought us across the threshold.

Now it's our turn to be the opener of doors.

In The World:

* Write, say or think a note of thanks to someone who paved the way for you. Even if only a few words, even if only in your mind, your gratitude will bless the sender and the receiver.

In The Heart:

* I am thankful for all those who came before me who have inspired me, led by example and brought me here to this place in my life.

The Wild, Wild West

Follow your own star.

Yesterday, as I was peacefully writing, four horses stampeded down the hill from the farm next door, just a few yards from the window, trampling the brush and racing into the clearing. One minute I was in a quiet Zen-like Om-worthy cabin, and the next I was in the wild, wild West.

They were totally psyched to be free, pirouetting on their hind legs then taking off toward Hunters Road. Uh-oh—that can't be good. I ran to call Lorraine, the neighborhood horse whisperer. She was my first call when Shadow pulled his escape trick into that same clearing a few months back. I'm sure she wondered what kind of horse vortex I have going on over here.

She told me to drive down to the street and block the horses from going up the road. Sure enough, they were in the middle of Hunters Road, acting wild. When they saw me, they charged off toward yet another farm. I hopped in Lorraine's car and we chased them down to a barn where they had stopped to rest.

How, I asked Lorraine, will we get all these crazy guys back home? It turns out, you only have to reign in the leader, and the rest will follow. She was able to halter the rabble-rouser and sure enough, the others fell in step and walked peacefully, willingly home. Impressive, Lorraine.

It was a powerful image, watching the horses fall in. We, too, tend to follow the lead of those who seem to have more power than we do. But we have choices; we don't have to follow someone into the street.

Listen to your inner voice. March to your own symphony. Forge your own path. Shine your own light. Follow your own star. The world is in need of your unique ray of love today. Shine brightly.

In The World:

✳ Powerful messages from outside sources come at us from all sides. Today, turn down radio, TV, videos, images and people who don't resonate with your highest good and align with your inner voice. Be bravely yourself.

In The Heart:

✳ I am the only one who can direct my path. I have a mind of my own and follow the lead of my highest self.

A Higher Perspective

The soul of you is always, always beautiful.

If you woke up today feeling less than beautiful, remember that, no matter what is going on with you, the soul is always beautiful and radiant beyond imagination. And not only that, it is capable of rising above any challenge you may face today to gain a higher perspective. Like being on an airplane high up over the clouds, the humans on the ground only see a rainy day, while the real you is getting all of the sunshine.

The soul is the immortal essence of your consciousness that is one with all things, but most awesomely, with divine love. That's an enormous thing to grasp if it's still morning. You might want to grab some coffee.

The best part is: Love is at the center of our soul, so it is also at the center of everyone else's soul, and at the center of all of these circumstances and challenges that we pray for. Yes, everything is God, and everything is love, and everything can be viewed and solved from the higher perspective of the soul.

The soul can rise above fear and doubt; it can rise above pain and suffering; it can rise above confusion and uncertainty. There is no judgment or regret. There is no competition or jealousy. Just a really accurate, ethereal GPS system to guide us to experiences that allow us to live deeply, to love ourselves and others unconditionally, and to constantly create with the tools of love and joy.

When it's dark below the clouds, rise to a higher perspective. The soul of you is always, always more beautiful than you could ever imagine.

In The World:

✳ You can handle whatever today gives you. It if feels like too much, rise above it, ask for assistance, listen for signs and you will know what to do. Exercise your right to view today from above the clouds.

In The Heart:

✳ I am an infinite being of love, connected to all other infinite beings of love. Nothing can change the beauty of my soul.

I Have a House by the Sea

What we dwell on, we create. What we think, we become.
What we ponder, we empower.

I bought a house last week, and I wasn't even looking. It happened so speedily and seamlessly that I hardly feel like it happened at all. Olga calls it the power of manifestation. Lyndy calls it a Slice of Heaven. I call it crazy. The universe swooped in and organized the action, leaving me on the sidelines, an excited spectator in the game of awe.

Since leaving the house of my marriage, I knew I would one day land in Florida in closer proximity to my mom in her later years. My parents had lived across the street from the ocean in a sweet villa, and for over twenty years I had been visiting this spot twice a year, falling in love with the mighty ocean, sunsets over the river, the big birds and the live oaks. In my Gratitude in Advance Journal, I wrote the line, "I have a house by the sea," every day for six years.

In July, during my annual birthday pilgrimage to Florida, Mom and I were visiting some dear friends in the old neighborhood. I told them that next summer, I planned to move to Florida. "Well you should look at the place right down the street," Dolores said. "It even looks like you!" The next morning, hours before flying home, I did just that. It was perfect.

Upon arriving home, I lost my mind and my faith for a minute. This was *not* my idea of good timing. It was a year too soon, it was priced out of my league and I had the cabin lease to consider. How could this possibly be right for me? Then I quickly righted my ship and remembered that *I* was not in charge. I put the real estate postcard of the villa under a statue of Mother Mary with a candle and a note. "God, this is your house. If you want me to live there, allow it to happen with ease and grace." And I let go of all worry. Then, with love and respect, I put in a bid below the asking price, but what I could honestly afford. I wrote in my journal today, with tears of gratitude, "I have a house by the sea."

In The World:

❋ Revisit your Gratitude in Advance practice. Update it if necessary or begin one if you haven't already. The practice is described on May 14.

In The Heart:

❋ I believe in the power of my focused thoughts. I release control and leave room for the divine to work her perfect plan.

A Cup of Beauty

Music is the prayer the heart sings.

The language of music has shared chemistry with the language of spirit. Both are like the air in the room—behind, between, within and around everything. Music speaks of us in the beautiful trifecta of words, harmony and feelings, getting to the soul of the unexplainable and the heart of the ineffable. It manages to be both our love story and our suffering, sometimes in one song.

How does it do that? Perhaps music is the cleaner for the window through which we filter our world. When we allow it to do some soulful housekeeping, wiping away the grime and the streaks of the day, maybe we feel a beauty and understanding that was there all along, revealed by this clear, harmonic perspective. "Music washes away the dust of everyday life," explains Bertholt Auerbach.

Or it could be that it's an offering of sorts, as St. Augustine so sweetly put it: "When we sing, we pray twice." Assuming he was talking about sacred music, we have the words of faith or devotion, with their prayerful value doubling when set to music. We can almost see the prayers lifting off the ground and wrapping around their heavenly audience.

My favorite attempt at defining music's magic comes from poet Frederico Garcia Lorca. He believes that the arts are created from the story of humanity, then offered back to the people in a "cup of beauty." When we drink of this cup, (hear the song, see the art), we understand ourselves. And thirst for the beauty.

"The poem, the song, the picture, is only water drawn from the well of the people. And it should be given back to them in a cup of beauty so that they may drink—and in drinking, understand themselves."

In The World:

❋   As you listen to your favorite music today, let your heart be touched by the language of music and spirit.

In The Heart:

❋   I am in perfect harmony with the creative beauty of life. I allow the creative arts to expand me, to teach me and to bring out soul secrets from within.

~✹~

Stand by Love

We can't heal the world today, but we can begin with a voice of compassion, a heart of love, an act of kindness.

Yesterday, while in the checkout line of the grocery store, I noticed that the man in the next aisle was very angry. He began to raise his voice at his partner. My first thought was, *What if he has a gun?*

I was upset by that thought and the ones that followed. *Where would I hide? Would I run or stay and try to help others?* I decided I would stay and help. Crazy line of thinking, right? And I only listen to the news once a week.

Last night, I confessed to my college-aged daughter what had happened. As if it were a fact of life, she said, "Oh, I think that all the time. Especially at school."

This mentality of fear is only as powerful as we allow it to be. Love is the most powerful weapon in our world and we know that. Even if it is not what we *hear* about the most, we must consciously make it what we *feel* the most.

As my friend Gussie so eloquently put it in a post responding to gun violence, "We as a species need to reboot and find a way to embrace and respect our differences, discover that violence is never the answer and learn to respond to the crisis state of our universe with love and compassion."

Love and compassion. Exactly, Gussie. The healing begins today with our voice of compassion, our heart of love, our actions of peace and kindness. We know how to do that. Stay on the high road. Stand by love.

In The World:

✳ Today, be an instrument of peace. Sow seeds of compassion to all mankind. Share the highest vibrations of love.

✳ Resist participating in divisive language through words, videos or posts. Don't pass on images of violence or fear.

In The Heart:

✳ I take off the blinders of fear, and I see the world through the eyes of love. I am a powerful agent of peace in all I do today.

~⚬~

The Gift of Listening

May I give the gift of talking less and listening more.

Each of us possesses the power to lift up others in such simple ways; a compliment, a thoughtful question, an email of love, a hug. An often forgotten way to show kindness to another is by practicing the art of listening. To be present to someone with interest and compassion is a rare kindness, and a healing and transformative blessing.

In conversation, our thoughts often wander off to how we might respond or to another topic completely. We talk over others before they have finished speaking, implying that what we have to say is more important than what they are saying. All of our stories are competing to be heard.

Think about it: we really awaken when someone listens to us. To speak our truth and to be truly heard brings confidence, joy, connection and healing. We come alive when someone validates what we are feeling.

We can be that to someone. Dr. Joanne Cacciatore, an expert in compassionate bereavement and patient listening tells us, "Compassion can be a practice. Holding "space" for another who is hurting is a wisdom of the heart that we can hone."

With a little mindfulness in conversation, listening well becomes a simple practice of patience and compassion—a wisdom of the heart that we can hone.

In The World:

✳ When talking with someone today, make eye contact and give them your full attention. Actively listen by showing understanding and compassion. Resist the urge to interrupt with your own story.

✳ No matter how many notifications come in during a conversation, show respect and avoid looking at the phone while talking with someone. Wait until the conversation is over. Attention to people who are present carries more weight than attention to the screen.

✳ For important conversations, practice running your thoughts through the ancient wisdom of the Four Gates of Speech: *Is it true? Is it kind? Is it necessary? Is this the right time to say it?*

In The Heart:

✳ I give the gift of my full presence in conversation and listen to others with compassion, interest and understanding.

Born to Fly

Friends lift us up on wings of love when we forget we were born to fly.

When we fly, we exercise our inborn strength to move forward in our lives with resilience, over and over again. When we fly, we allow what we love to instinctually carry us toward our purpose. When we fly, we have confidence in our ideas, our self-image, our hopes and dreams. When we fly, we are fully ourselves, divine reflections in the flow of grace.

And wow, is it easy to forget we were born to do these things. In the dark night of the soul, it's hard to be sure of anything. The drama of life can be a heavy mist, socking in our spirits and hiding the sky from our eyes. So that's why God gave us friends. Because friends can see us as we ourselves cannot.

After many years in the process of separating from my long-term marriage and finally moving into this cabin at mountain's edge, I told my friend Liz that I had really lost my confidence. I told her that I wished I was that fearless musician she met all those years ago, who never second guessed herself. I felt vulnerable and lost, nothing like the woman I used to be.

After a moment of silence, she quietly said, "But you *are* that. You have never *not* been that. The same fearlessness I knew in her, I see in you now. You just can't see it yet." Wings of love, Liz, wings of love.

I wish for you a friend who reminds you of the truth: that you are still you. Precious, unique, irreplaceable and born to fly. It's time to lift off and soar.

In The World:

* If you have such a friend, let them know how much they mean to you. Open your heart to opportunities to be that friend to others.

* If you don't have such a friend, be that friend to yourself. Remind yourself of the truth, as many times as it takes to strengthen your budding wings.

In The Heart:

* When I lose my way, I call on my friends for perspective. I am honest in sharing my truth. When I have a friend in need, I remind them of their strength and beauty.

꒰꒱

Synchronicity

*Bless me to be the hands of service, the heart of compassion
and the mind of awareness.*

Ten years ago on a beautiful late afternoon in Acadia National Park in Maine, my husband, daughter and I were driving around the one-way perimeter loop of the park on our way to the exit. We looked forward to returning to our vacation cabin in Booth Bay Harbor after a long day of strenuous hiking. I was at the wheel when suddenly, as if the van had a mind of its own, we pulled over to the curb at an overlook. Ignoring the groan of complaint, and not really understanding it myself, I offered, "I'm just going to take a look. You guys can stay in the car."

The area was quiet except for one family just a few yards in front of me. The father was taking a picture of his wife and two children as they stood at the far side of the path with the valley and beautiful vista behind them. As I watched them, waiting for him to take the picture before I continued past them, the mother took a step...and fell backwards off the cliff.

I ran to the edge with them to see her crumpled body, quiet and bleeding, about thirty feet down on a rock ledge. The children were screaming; the father was holding his head in shock. I raced to the car, grabbed my hiking boots and told my husband and daughter to come quickly. Maya sat with the children, the father paced frantically, paralyzed with fear, my husband stayed on the phone with 911, guiding them to our remote location, and I, without thinking, scrambled and slid down the dirt and rock wall to where the woman lay.

Clearly, spirit organized our vacation and trip out of the park so we would be here, in this very place, for just this moment. (Continued tomorrow.)

In The World:

✳ There are no mistakes. Synchronicity and coincidence are acts of spirit at work in our lives. Listen for their silent call and follow your inner wisdom.

In The Heart:

✳ I am called to the people and circumstances where I can be of help. I listen each day to the wisdom of my inner voice in all things.

❧

Synchronicity - Part 2

Listen to the gentle guidance of spirit.

Nothing in my nursing training prepared me for what I saw. She picked up her head and blood poured out as if from a pitcher. My thought: *No one can lose this much blood and live.* The men threw down their t-shirts, and I made pads, holding them gently to her matted, broken skull. Her only words: "I think I am paralyzed." "No," I said firmly. "You will be well. Breathe. Don't move. Help is coming. The children are fine. Your legs will be perfect." I whispered slow, soft, dream-like comfort until the EMTs finally found us an eternal twenty minutes later.

In the weeks that followed, I prayed for her constantly, all day and all night, blessing her hundreds of times an hour. I had the feeling of being within her body, knitting her spine to perfection, activating new, healthy cells from within. I visualized her glowing and happy, walking with ease.

One morning about three weeks later while I was doing yoga, I felt an urgent pull to call her right then. From news reports, I knew she had been airlifted to a large hospital in Boston, and within moments, she answered the phone in her room. She remembered nothing of that day but she shared the most beautiful news of all: After three surgeries to repair her skull and broken spine, and an initial poor prognosis for walking again, the doctors thought she was making miraculous progress. They expected that in time, she would walk and make a full recovery.

In one step, everything can change. We never know what the next hour will hold. But to be sure, the divine will let us know where we are meant to be.

In The World:

* Every time we send positive light to someone, through prayer, visualization or a loving thought, we co-create with the divine. Today, change the world with the power of your positive thoughts.

* Listen to your inner voice. Follow an urge, a prompt, a pull. Look closely at what attracts your attention. Notice signs and symbols. Keep an open heart for the guidance of spirit.

In The Heart:

* Today I listen for the voice of spirit in my life. I use the power of love to send light where needed.

Things We Are Made Of

I am one with all creation.

Delight. Happiness. Shining. Rays.
Compassion. Wisdom. Radiance. Grace.
Joy. Hope. Kindness. Love.
These are the things we are made of.

Songs. Harmony. Peace. One.
Silence. Power. Will. Sun.
Joy. Hope. Strength. Love.
These are the things we are made of.

Eagle wings. Angel flight.
Soaring. Dancing. Dark. Light.
Joy. Hope. God. Love.
These are the things we are made of.

Light. Stars. Skies. Moons.
Galaxies. Planets. Earth. Ruins.
Joy. Hope. Infinite love.
These are the things we are made of.

Water. Dust. Fire. Flame.
Wind. Rock. Clouds. Rain.
Joy. Hope. Faith. Love.
These are the things we are made of.

Roots. Branches. Blooms. Blades.
Mountains. Rivers. Forests. Lakes.
Joy. Hope. God. Love.
These are the things we are made of.

In The World:

✳ Approach the day from the highest perspective, as one with all creation. No one will know except you that you are seeing the world through sacred eyes. Enjoy the lens of magnificence and unity.

In The Heart:

✳ I am a radiant expression of earth and sky, God and love. I expand the loving energy of my heart to encompass all beings.

An Imperfect World

Forgive daily.

As much as we would like to live a mistake-free life, most of us are a mess of imperfection. We cut people off in traffic. We say hurtful things. We say them at the wrong time. We make choices we regret. We have accidents. We are clumsy. We break things.

What if our peeps held all of our transgressions against us?

We count on forgiveness. Daily. Hourly sometimes. We need to be surrounded by people who don't take our imperfections too seriously, and see the goodness of our intentions. What a wonderful world it would be if we all held up a universal heart of forgiveness for our imperfect state of affairs.

Not quite there yet, I know. But as in all things spiritual, we attempt to do the most loving thing going forward—for ourselves and for others. We can't make others forgive us, but we can clear the air around us by forgiving them, as often and as much as we possibly can.

Our feelings are meant to be temporary visitors, all just passing through, travelers on a journey, each with something to teach us. We don't let them inhabit our personal space. We don't invite them to take up residence in our house. We honor them by allowing them to be felt and heard, then we release them without drama, without grasping. Only then are we really free to be a most loving person in our imperfect world.

Forgive daily.

In The World:

✳ Start with the small stuff. Notice little grudges held against those who are close to you. Sit with it for a bit with a heart of love. Listen for a lesson. And give it permission to leave.

In The Heart:

✳ I freely release all negative feelings arising from the behavior of others and perceived shortcomings in myself. I forgive easily, peacefully and often.

꧁

Meditation Extras

In the silence of my heart, I am one with love.
In the stillness of my soul, I am one with God.

If you have been meditating daily, your practice is getting stronger. You are finding that your 5- to 10-minute morning and evening meditations are a calming oasis that enhance all aspects of your life. As you progress, there are some sweet additions you can make to your existing practice that will magnify your energy, focus and connection with the divine. The benefits can be truly exhilarating. Add what resonates with your heart.

In The World:

✴ *Meditate for longer.* Think about increasing your time, adding five minutes on to your usual morning and evening time, and experimenting with even longer times on the weekends. How does twenty minutes feel? Or thirty? What if there was no timer?

✴ *Add a mantra.* A mantra is a short, sacred, soothing phrase that we float on the breath. Pick one that attracts you. My favorites are "I Am" and "Hong Sau" (pronounced "hong saw"). Both refer to being one with spirit. "I" or "Hong" is mentally said on the inhale, and "Am" or "Sau" is mentally said on the exhale. Your focus remains gently on the breath while also gently on the mantra.

✴ *Eyes gaze upward.* With eyes closed, draw the eyes upwards as if they are looking out between the eyebrows. In time your eye muscles will get used to this and it will accelerate your access to spiritual wisdom.

✴ *Shop around.* Enjoy exploring the world of meditation with some of the many experienced reputable teachers online. It might take a few methods until you find what's right for you. You will know.

✴ *Set up a meditation space.* Arrange a space that is reserved for meditation. It can be a cushion in a corner with a small shelf to hold a candle and some meaningful symbols of your practice, or a chair near a dresser with some special altar items on top.

✴ *Be devoted and dedicated.* Start and end your meditation with a prayer or intention to be in the presence of God and to make an offering of your practice. Make meditation a non-negotiable part of your day.

In The Heart:

✴ In the silence of my heart, I am one with love. In the stillness of my soul, I am one with God.

September

Be present.
Let the day flow with grace.
Expect joy. Be positive.
Serve with compassion.
Speak only kindness.
Impart only love.
Never forget you're not alone.
Give thanks for everything.
See goodness in others. mary davis

EVERY DAY SPIRIT
.NET

September Blessings

Be present. Be here. Today, we can guide our thoughts back to the present moment with gentle focus and live fully right where we are.

Let the day flow with grace. Grace flows through us easily when we are in tune with the subtle voice of intuition. Open and listen for guidance.

Expect joy. Be positive. Imagine a fulfilling day unfolding, in which we accomplish much and experience joy in the process. Welcome the light.

Serve with compassion. Acts of service when performed with love lend immeasurable light to our day. Be watchful for ways to serve.

Speak only kindness. Speak only kind words. Think only kind thoughts. Be kind to yourself and to those who cross your path or your mind.

Impart only love. Send out all thoughts and words on the wings of love so that we may love one another, love ourselves, love the unlovable.

Never forget you're not alone. Let's remind ourselves often today that we are always supported, guided and unconditionally loved as we are.

Give thanks for everything. Gratitude will shift the perspective of the day from one of lack to one of abundance. Give constant thanks.

See goodness in others. Each of us has a soul that is made of beauty and love. Assume the best in others so they may rise to their highest light.

~✧~

Delight Is Gratitude

The more grateful I am, the more beauty I see.

This morning I took my tea out the back door as usual. I wasn't thinking about anything. I wasn't praying. My only agenda was delight.

The sun was just waking up behind the trees in muted rays that gently released the dark. The evergreens donned an ocean blue in the distance and just above their tops lay a sliver of moon lounging on her back.

Inserting themselves into the dawning sky was a skein of geese surely flying South, silent with the effort of transition. A frog sat upright in the crevice of a rock, comical with only his big grin showing. From flower to flower a tiny hummingbird flitted around, spreading her graces with effortless speed.

The rooster's insistent crow for day woke up my hearing with a laugh, and I tuned into a surround-sound chorus of birds singing of morning to each other. My arms felt the cool breeze of early fall as if she could blow from my memory the steamy mornings of late August.

Nature as a work of art, flashing by in mere moments, tea cup in hand, awe. There was nothing missing. Nothing wanting. No formal gratitude required.

God feels it when we notice beauty. He feels it through the rays and the blue, in the geese and the moon, in the frog and the hummingbird, in the rocks and the evergreen. He feels it through the songs of the birds and the voice of the wind. When we notice beauty, we *are* grateful.

Delight is gratitude with a smile on her face.

In The World:

✳   Steal an unscheduled minute to go outside or to sit by a window and simply notice the beauty of creation in a spirit of joy. Allow yourself to be delighted, which is the prayer of gratitude that brings only more joy.

In The Heart:

✳   My heart is full of gratitude and delight as I stand in awe of the beauty that surrounds me now.

Silence

Still the mind. Inhale peace. Let go of worries. Exhale stress.
Notice the breath. Connect to all. Embrace calm.

Spiritual messages can penetrate our awareness in a variety of ways with the divine as the signal source and our hearts as receiver and interpreter of the messages. Tuning into the source, like searching for a radio station frequency, requires finding a place where the signal comes in clearly.

Our practice of meditation and contemplative exercises provides just this kind of clear signal. As we tune in each morning and each evening, we keep our line open for constant wisdom, guidance, support and unconditional love.

Be still and know that all wisdom lies within.

Be still and be vigilant for promptings of the soul.

Be still and remember your magnificence.

Be still and trust in infinite support.

Be still and see the dawn of a new idea.

Be still and sense the next step to take.

Be still and feel the growing courage to follow your dreams.

Be still and believe the perfect plan is unfolding for you.

Be still and ask clearly for your heart's desire.

Be still and make space for the soft voice of the heart to answer.

Be still and offer your services to divine will.

Be still and feel oneness with all things.

In The World:

✳ At least several times today, move away from the static and into a place of pure signal. Patiently still the thoughts and make way for amazingly clear wisdom and guidance. Be a radio station of peace.

In The Heart:

✳ I am an infinite being, connected with the source of all wisdom in the silence of my heart. I listen and receive.

Start in the Middle

Kindness begins at home with yourself.

Whenever my brothers and I got caught in a proverbial tug of war over a particular toy or game, my father would pull out one of his favorite mantras, "Charity begins at home." He would explain that if we could not be kind to each other and learn to share at home, we would not be able to be a charitable person out in the world. I didn't really understand what being charitable meant back then, but I'm starting to get a bigger picture of his message now: Start in the middle and work your way out.

I'm seeing that how we treat ourselves when there is no one looking, be it over the weekend or in our minds, is very telling about how we are able to share our love in the world. If we can't love and honor ourselves, respect our limits and most of all be kind to ourselves in thoughts and actions, we are limited in the ways we can love, honor, respect and offer kindness to others.

We are all in need of love and encouragement. It's up to us to begin the process of filling this need in the home of our own hearts. Even when we feel broken or inadequate, within us is a radiant being worthy of our gentle kindness.

When we love ourselves unconditionally, we are able to pour forth our love without holding back. We can be charitable without a sense of losing anything.

It's a circle. We fill our hearts so we may empty them through gifts of love for all beings, making room to fill the heart again, then to give once more. Kindness begins in the middle. At home. With yourself.

In The World:

❋ This morning I sat staring at a blank page for an hour. Not a single word was typed, not a lone idea sprouted forth. I wrapped up with, "Good job, Mary. You showed up for work today. Way to go." That little spark of kindness encouraged me enough to sit back down later in the day and investigate with words what it means to be kind to myself.

❋ Be kind to yourself today in small ways so your unique gifts might be recharged by tenderness.

In The Heart:

❋ I am a beautiful soul deserving and worthy of my kindness.

SEPTEMBER 5

❧

The Extraordinary Switch

We create more of what we believe is possible.

Is it possible that we can wake up overwhelmed and out of sorts and transform the day into one of the best ever? How do we transition from cranky to joyous? Where is the Extraordinary Switch in an otherwise ordinary day?

If today is a day where you need to "call in sad" and snuggle down with a good movie, there's not a single thing wrong with that. What we need to remember is that there is always a choice. An alternate thought path can lead to a completely different day because the transition, the transformation and The Switch—are in you.

As my mother would say, this change of attitude comes from looking at the world through "sacred eyes." It is a simple, powerful process that changes our reality in an instant. You will be immediately rewarded by the shift, and like any practice, it gets better with time.

We create more of what we believe is possible. We see beauty when we anticipate that it is there. We have an extraordinary day when we expect that is it so.

In The World:

✶ Breathe in deeply and exhale the thoughts that are not serving you. Breathe in light. Breathe out darkness. And again.

✶ Remind yourself: *I am an incredibly powerful spirit and nothing is impossible. This day is a magnificent gift.*

✶ See this moment through the lens of gratitude instead of lack. Look for the gifts. Notice what is going right.

✶ Ask for assistance with a prayer like: *Thank you for making beautiful my path today. I offer it to you, believing that there is a perfect plan that conspires to serve the highest good of all. Support me in each moment as my day unfolds with joy, delight and surprise. I am listening.*

In The Heart:

✶ I believe that everything is possible today. I believe in miracles and expect to be surprised by joy.

Honor the Growth

Love is a balance of holding on and letting go.

As we journey through life, our growth process is not a linear one. There are periods of time when all is well and we feel satisfied with our lives. Then there are times when everything shifts; we experience losses, a change of job or location, or the need for a new sense of purpose. During these times of flux, we are growing rapidly, transforming our lives and raising our spirits to a higher understanding. We have seasons of growth within us that must be honored.

Our relationships, much like the seasons, also have a rhythmic nature. We see this in the growth and development of children. There are times when the rhythm of parent and child is status quo, then periods when the child grows rapidly in the organic need for individuation. This calls for a redefining of roles out of respect for the person they are becoming.

With our partners and friends, we don't often think about this cycle of growth. We want the relationship to remain the same in the easy way it was when we met. But most people will go through dramatic transformation in a lifetime and the greatest gift we can give them is to honor the ways they have changed and who they have become.

When we hold on to a former version of one we love, we are always disappointed. When we open our hand and let go of resistance, love flows with flexibility and grace, making space for the blessings yet to unfold.

In The World:

∗ Think about where in the cycle you are now. Are you holding steady or beginning a season of transformation? Are you in full-blown transition? Set out the intention to allow love and acceptance to flow with the changes in yourself, your children, your parents or your partner.

∗ Be genuinely interested in your loved ones, asking questions and learning about them as they change and grow, not assuming to know all of their secrets. Let go a little and allow the relationship to breathe new life.

In The Heart:

∗ I release all resistance to change and give love unconditionally through life's transitions and transformations.

The Art of the Pause

I'm staying calm no matter what.

Have you ever met someone who pauses after they hear something, taking an extra moment before responding? I love that. It reminds me of another kind of pause—one we witness thousands of times a day.

There's a little space, like a thirty-second note rest in music, after we inhale, appearing again after we exhale. Of the four parts of the breath cycle, we have two that provide silence amidst the activity of breathing life into our bodies: inhale, pause, exhale, pause. The calm is built right in.

In yogic breathing practice, or *pranayama,* this rest, called *kumbhaka,* is the point of perfect stillness. Yoga master, B.K.S. Iyengar, explains that during this pause, speech, hearing and perception are suspended, leaving tiny pools of pure peace to punctuate our hours. Ancient yogic texts tell us that the pause after the inhale is where God is united with the individual soul and the pause after the exhale is when we surrender ourselves totally to God.

As there is an art to the practice of *kumbhaka,* there is an art to the practice of calm. It is the art of the pause. There is always a small window of choice between receiving news and responding to it. In this moment, there is perfect calm when we decide how we will respond.

By extending this pause, we give the heart and mind more space to avoid *reaction* and to organize a useful *action,* keeping us in alignment with the source of all peace. Be calm.

In The World:

* Be mindful today of the moment between receiving information and responding to it. Practice responding with thoughtfulness and compassion rather than with a habitual reaction.

In The Heart:

* My soul is always calm and undisturbed, serene and peaceful. I maintain my serenity in all circumstances.

Thirteen Words

Awaken to your magnificence.

My friend Adam says that the hardest thing he did today was to stand up at an AA meeting and say, "Hi, my name is Adam and I'm an alcoholic. I have five days." Thirteen words.

He cried. He cried for the fifteen years and seven months that he was sober. He cried for the days when he was the leader of the meetings, hanging out at the coffee machine and taking out the trash so he was available for the newcomers. He cried for the days when he was his better self. He cried for the shame he felt saying those thirteen words.

He told me he is nobody now. Today he attended two meetings where he didn't know people and they didn't know him. There were more recovering drug addicts than recovering alcoholics. He doesn't want to tell anyone he blew fifteen years. He only says his thirteen words.

I cry with him. I tell him he's still in there. I tell him he's still that guy. What I'm tasting are the tears. What I'm seeing is his beautiful, magnificent soul. What I'm hearing is the most courageous story I have ever heard. What I'm feeling is proud to be in his life and of his thirteen words.

What I'm touching on but what I don't know how to say is that God doesn't mind about the fifteen years. There is no failure here. The only thing that matters is love. And being bravely true to who you are in this moment. What I say is, *You are loved beyond your wildest imagination no matter what.*

What I meant was, *Today, you said thirteen words. And God felt love.*

In The World:

✳ Remember this: You are worthy no matter what. You are a beautiful child of God and no one and nothing can change that. Walk with your head held high and allow this day to flow forth from the love that you are.

In The Heart:

✳ I awaken to my worthiness, my beauty, my eternal soul of love.

Harmony: A Meditation

Today I choose calm over chaos, serenity over stress, peace over perfection, grace over grit and faith over fear.

With a deep breath in, I welcome this precious day, and gratitude floods my heart with calming joy. With the exhale I allow all that is not for my highest good to leave me. I smile inside and out as I relax and release any overwhelming expectations for the day.

Today I choose calm over chaos. In all work, at home or in the office, my highest wisdom flows through my calm mind and heart. I am present in each moment and I move from one task to another with easy transitions.

Today I choose serenity over stress. With clarity of mind, I accomplish all that needs to be accomplished with ease. I do one thing at a time with love, and I ask for the assistance I need from others and from my divine support team.

Today I choose peace over perfection. I do my best at all times and my best is enough. My priorities are to share love, to act out of kindness, to allow myself to feel joy. All else will get done in its time. I am at peace.

Today I choose grace over grit. In the flow of divine grace, I am relaxed and supported in all I do. I listen for signs, knowing that all that is meant for today will happen with little resistance.

Today I choose faith over fear. I trust that even in challenges, I am right where I need to be. I am present to my pain and aware of my blessings. I know that I am being supported and guided in every step.

With a deep breath, I bless this day and begin with calm, serenity, peace, grace and faith. Harmony surrounds me. All is well.

In The World:

✳ Take a few minutes several times today with this meditation. Choose serenity and harmony over and over.

In The Heart:

✳ In all situations, I am grounded in the center of deep peace.

~✥~

Kindness and the Skunk

*Be the kindness that reminds someone that the world
is a compassionate place.*

A few days ago a rustling caught my eye from the writing window. Heading straight for me was a large, limping skunk with a very puffy tuft of white hair covering her back like a lovely fur coat. As she approached, it occurred to me that no one really prays for skunks, except maybe to say while driving, *Please God, don't let me hit this thing.* No, skunks, like stink bugs have a bad rap with very few finding the good in them. And this girl had two soul-expanding features: she was a skunk *and* she had a disability. A big spirit indeed.

Being nocturnal, or technically crepuscular (they come out at dusk and dawn), we don't see skunks around much. It was special that she came right to the window and looked directly up at me with her near-sighted eyes. Then my new buddy Samantha crossed the frog pond bridge and made her way limping off to visit the horses. I prayed for her front paw.

Yesterday at dawn, she took the same path to the windows but this time taking one labored step at a time, clearly on her last legs. Oh Samantha! She made it to the back patio then fell in a heap on a soft pile of leaves in the flower bed. And lay there for hours. I went out and she lifted her head toward me and put it back down.

I told her it was okay to die now and that all sorts of skunk angels were going to help her cross over. I was doing my "death doula thing" as Olga would say. Hours later I found her. She had moved herself to the compost area away from the house to die. What a thoughtful girl.

As you may have guessed, this morning featured a one-minute skunk funeral. It was a quiet, come-as-you-are affair. In attendance were two doves, four cardinals, a chickadee and a hawk. The horses watched from the field. A rooster crowed along with my hummed verse of Amazing Grace. And Sam went off to new fields in style.

In The World:

✳   We never know. What we perceive as the least among us might just be the greatest. Powerful beings come clothed in humble circumstances. Be kind.

In The Heart:

✳   Today I reserve my judgment and give freely of my kindness.

One with Everything

*We are united by the strength of unity, the power of love
and the vision of peace.*

Today, the United States honors the victims and responders of September 11th, 2001, with a National Day of Service and Remembrance. On this day, we are asked to unite in offering a charitable act of service, coming together again in the spirit of love and peace the way we did at that tragic time.

We are, after all, one family. We are intimately connected as threads of a universal tapestry. Emanating from the same perfect source—God, love, universal mind—we all share the energy of this force. Today, each action we take and each thought we think will affect the whole. When we serve one of us, we serve all of us.

The major religions, sages, saints, mystics, and scientists as well, agree on our interconnection. In her fascinating book on universal laws, *The Whole Elephant Revealed*, Marja de Vries explains: "The essence of all authentic religions, spiritual movements and mystic teachings can be traced back to similar mystical, direct experiences of Becoming-One-With-Everything." At our very essence, we are one. On the anniversary of the events that intended to divide our world, our service becomes a beacon of our shared spirit.

Our small acts of love can begin healing the fabric of our world by overcoming fear with love, anger with kindness, separation with compassion, judgment with acceptance. Our tapestry can be mended, and we are all weavers working together hand-to-hand, heart-to-heart, using a common thread.

May our service today unite us in the spirit of peace.

In The World:

* Consider how you will join the force of charitable service at home or in the community today.

* You can check out <u>serve.gov</u> or <u>911day.org</u> to find volunteer opportunities.

* Share your service on social media using #911Day.

In The Heart:

* I radiate the peace and love I feel within to all of humanity.

The Beautiful Gift of Today

Believe. Cherish. Enjoy.

No matter what you've done or left undone, no matter who you've hurt or who hurt you, no matter how it might seem to be an exercise in pride and hubris—relentlessly love yourself. No excuses, no caveats, just love yourself the way that you are so loved by the divine in this very moment.

And then present yourself with a few gifts:

BELIEVE in yourself. Believe that you have everything you will ever need to live a peaceful and joyful life. Believe in your goodness and unlimited potential. Believe in your capacity to love and be loved. Believe in the compassionate care of an all-loving God. Believe in a benevolent universe and the army of angels that are sent to assist you. Believe in your strength, flexibility and the will to rise up under any circumstances.

Believe in the beautiful gift of today.

CHERISH yourself. Your tender self. Yes, you. Cherish your family and friends, your colleagues and clients. Cherish the birds and trees and animals and sky and the incredible beauty of nature. Cherish the chance to live out this day with choices and chances.

Cherish the beautiful gift of today.

ENJOY yourself. Enjoy the feeling of being an embodied, walking, breathing human on the planet. Enjoy the smiles and laughter that reflect delight and awe. Enjoy the music and rhythm, the paint and the pencils, the creative expression of life. Enjoy the food and the drink, the love and the warmth, the peace and the kindness.

Enjoy the beautiful gift of today.

In The World:

* You deserve to flood yourself with lovingkindness. Pay yourself a few compliments. Do something special for yourself today. Remind yourself that you are believed in, cherished and are here to enjoy life.

In The Heart:

* I believe in myself, in my goodness and in my light. I show myself how much I love myself, my life and the gift of today.

Simplicity

Simplicity is good for the soul.

Less can be so much more. Less stress, more peace. Less technology, more interaction. Less noise, more nature. Less worry, more joy. Less stuff, more space—in heart and home.

Simplifying our surroundings can bring a feeling of brightness and openness to not only the house but also to the soul. Our spaces reflect our state of being and when we set them up to be clear, clean, bright, open, meaningful and loving, we naturally align with the higher vibration. And vice versa. The more clarity we gain through meditation and prayer, the more drawn we are to have our homes reflect the beauty of our expanding souls.

Donating to community organizations that serve those in need is a thoughtful way to simplify while sharing our abundance with others. A little research will save their volunteers time and energy and get your reusables quickly and efficiently into the right hands.

Start today with one drawer, closet, tabletop or corner. Not only will you make space for more peace, but another soul will treasure your treasures.

In The World:

✴ Donate locally. Research the list of needs of each organization online, and separate your donations according to what they accept.

✴ Keep a bag for donations in an out-of-the-way place and add to it regularly. When it's full, wash and fold the clothes, stack them in a paper shopping bag and mark it "washed." Bring men's suits and outerwear on hangers. Avoid throwing unfolded clothes in leaf bags. These are gifts for souls.

✴ Most libraries accept used books of all kinds. Some police and fire stations take stuffed animals. Many counties collect used electronics once a month.

In The Heart:

✴ I take steps toward a simpler way of life. I divest easily of the possessions I don't need or use, taking great joy in sharing my abundance with others.

The Wisdom of Nature

A walk in nature walks the soul back home.

It was not the smoothest of mornings. Friends were sick and needed help. The inbox was overflowing. A brother needed to talk. Posts begged to be made. Writing beckoned. My desk was covered over in notes. What did I do? I walked out the front door with a smile of relief.

There's sage advice that says the busier we are, the longer we need to meditate. I agree and would add to that a nice, relaxing mid-day walk. The more we decide to do, the more conscious we need to be—about being.

Our highest wisdom comes when we open the floodgates of our inner voice. The art of allowing this opening doesn't happen in a flurry of activity, but in the oasis of calm and beauty. So when we want to do our best, most creative work or most insightful and patient parenting, it is essential to take regular pauses to check in with divine wisdom and make space for answers to provide for us exactly what we need at just the right time.

Nature sits in wait outside our door to provide the required space and beauty. Even a short walk with a keen eye for beauty and an open heart for joy can refresh our outlook and connect us with our soul's grace.

Make time as often as possible to duck out of the fast lane and walk the soul back home.

In The World:

✳ Take a walk today. Enjoy, appreciate and be in awe of the sights and sounds of nature. She is designed to plug us into our oneness with all things and with the universal wisdom of the soul.

In The Heart:

✳ In gratitude, I appreciate the glory of nature. I allow the miracles of her calm beauty to bring me to balance and to open my heart to my highest wisdom.

Grace Is Here

Grace is the gift of abundant blessings freely given.

Grace is here today. She's overflowing. Not only for the deserving, the perfect and the organized. But also for the humble, the weak and the messy. She brings abundant blessings. Grace is here today.

Grace is here today. There is nothing to fear. She will take the lead in uncertainty. She will rally strength in weary bones. She will raise you up on strong, soft wings when there is little hope. Grace is here today.

Grace is here today. Breathing the wind of guidance into your sails and bringing free fuel for your spirit. She is in your prayer of gratitude and your song of joy. She is in your cry of frustration and your tears of suffering. She is picking you up and laying you down. Grace is here today.

Grace is here today. All is well. She will quietly remind you of your worth. She will provide opportunity for your unique gifts to shine forth. She will quell shame and protect a vulnerable heart. She will remind you to love yourself fully, completely and always. Grace is here today.

Grace is here today. She is in your hands as you nurture. She is in your heart as you love. She is propelling you forward as you travel your path. She is in your mind planting seeds of divine wisdom. Grace is here today.

And tomorrow, she will be again.

In The World:

* Grace is a gift from God, freely given. There is an endless supply flowing right where you are. Just turn your eyes slightly in her direction and you will feel her flow. Step into her. Ask for her. Use her many blessings.

In The Heart:

* I stand with an open heart, ready to receive Grace as she walks with me through every moment of this day.

Small Things with Great Love

*Power can be quiet. Change the world daily with small acts of love,
support and kindness.*

We have power. Not the kind of power that needs victory over an enemy
but the kind of power that rises up in us every day as we go about our
work with love. It's everyday power. It never leaves and it never wanes.
We always have it and can always use it.

The most effective power is not loud and aggressive. Power can be quiet
and humble, especially when wielding the weapons of love, support and
kindness. Power is "the capacity or ability to direct or influence the
behavior of others or the course of events." That's just what we will do.

Today when we shower everyone who comes into our orb with love, we
will change the vibration of everything around us. A loving gesture for
your partner, a hug for a child, a compliment to a co-worker will actually
change the wavelength of the energy in the room. And the best part is that
they will rise toward your level of loving vibration. That is changing the
world.

You don't have to believe me. Scientists are now concurring with what
saints and mystics have known all along. That the more loving we are, the
more love we foster in our energy field. The kinder we are, the kinder
other people will tend to be. When we lift up someone, we not only lift
ourselves as George Washington Carver so beautifully said, but we lift
everyone else up too.

We have that power in the small things we do today. Let's use it well.

In The World:

✳   Be mindful to distribute as much lovingkindness in your world today
as possible. Monitor your thoughts as well; they are just as powerful
as your words and actions. And remember, this is not homework. It's
spirit work that will bring countless blessings to you and to all beings.

In The Heart:

✳   I am a walking, talking beam of endless light and love. I shine radiant
energy on everyone I see and think of today.

Relentless Optimism

Oh happy day.

At a recent wedding reception, the father of the bride stood with a great grin, raised his glass to his daughter and new son-in-law and said, "I hope you come to realize, as your mother and I did, that life is fun!"

Really? Fun? Wow. This is surprisingly great advice.

What if we lived in a world of relentless optimism? What if, for an entire day, we thought positive thoughts, holding in our hands a glass half-full? What if we had an eye for beauty and delight and looked on the tasks at hand with purpose and a sense of creativity and joy?

I do believe that the father of the bride had it right. Life is not only supposed to bring us lessons through pain but also lessons through fun. The kind of fun that comes from allowing joy to hold a prominent daily presence. Our joy is waiting to be set free from the suit and tie of seriousness, and to burst out in awe of the miraculous world we live in. She's playful and she's ready to dance.

There is nothing stopping us but us. Yes, we have worries and problems and grief. But we also have joy and love and awe—demanding equal time.

In The World:

* Decide to make today a day of relentless optimism. Start by planting a joyful intention for the day. In thought, word and actions, phrase everything in the positive. Find the light in all situations. Do small things that bring you joy.

* Allow your soul smile to become your outward smile. Smile often.

* Then let that joy seep into the way you interact with others. Let your joy translate into lightness, lovingkindness and play.

In The Heart:

* I follow a path of joy, seeking out experiences that bring me happiness. I allow my beautiful light to shine joyfully and raise the vibration of everything around me.

The Inner Oasis

The more we practice, the more natural it becomes.

Presence is bringing full awareness to the moment we are in, filtering out distractions and bringing our attention to the task at hand. The combined stresses of life fade to the background as we focus on being right here, doing whatever it is we are doing right now.

As we know, one way to improve our ability to come into the present moment is to calm the mind in meditation. Meditating has now become a morning and evening fact of life and the rewards are filtering into all aspects of life. Right? No worries. Any time is the perfect time to refresh or renew the practice.

Between our regular meditations, when we are "in the world," we can use short meditations—for even one or two minutes—that are refreshing, calming, centering and good for our health and clarity. They open the window of communication to our higher wisdom, returning us to our spiritual perspective.

We want to bring ourselves to this calming connection as many times a day as possible. The more we practice, the more natural it becomes.

The following S.T.O.P. method is adapted from a lecture by Deepak Chopra on mindfulness. Enjoy the beauty of your inner oasis.

In The World:

S.T.O.P. Method - When you want to return to your spiritual center:

✳ Stop what you're doing.

✳ Take three deep breaths and smile everywhere in your body.

✳ Observe what is happening in your body and mind.

✳ Proceed with lovingkindness, joy, compassion and love.

In The Heart:

✳ Any time of day, I use my breath to calm my body and enter the oasis of spirit.

The Light Enters You

Be the love that reminds someone that we belong to each other.

Yesterday, as I unloaded my items on the belt at the grocery store, I noticed the cashier adjusting her head scarf over fuzzy wisps of hair. I don't know much about chemo hair, but instead of ignoring what I had seen, I softly said, "Growing back?" She said, "Yes, finally. But I don't have eyebrows or lashes yet." It opened the door to a conversation that lasted the duration of my checkout, during which I was honored to hear about her courageous journey through cancer. In that small exchange I could feel that something meaningful had happened for both of us.

My post office is a small place where people talk about their lives as they buy stamps and mail packages. From my regular Etsy mailings, I learned that Tina's beloved friend was suffering from a serious illness. After the grocery run, I stopped by the post office to mail my usual packages, and asked Tina about her friend. She reached a hand over the counter and told me things were not so good. We held hands, and I told her I would be praying for her and her friend.

Moments of grace spontaneously erupt; waterfalls pour into a split second. One minute we are in the safe zone of greetings and weather, and the next, a window opens to something deeper, giving us the chance to connect on another level.

Perhaps our common experience of pain cracks our outer shells, and we recognize each other on the inside. "The wound is the place where the light enters you," Rumi reminds us. A crack in the armor gives us an opening to be the love that reminds someone that they are not alone.

In The World:

* Be awake as you interface with the world today. Notice, listen, look outside yourself. Be a force of love in gentle ways. Sometimes even a smile can turn around a dark day in someone's heart.

In The Heart:

* Today I am an instrument of love, connected to all beings. I am awake to my heart of compassion. I am the love that reminds someone that we belong to each other.

Absence as Presence

Hear the angels sing.

When I was a teenager, my mother gave me a book that would change my life: Raymond Moody's *Life After Life.* Dr. Moody was a pioneer of the study of near-death experiences (NDEs), and his personal interviews with people who had clinically died, spent time in the afterlife, then were revived, were groundbreaking. Today there are many books detailing personal experience of life after death and several websites of doctors who are currently studying it where we can read countless stories of NDEs from all over the world.

The hallmarks of almost every story bring comfort to the bereaved and peace to anyone who fears the moment of death. This is real—and really beautiful.

Having the context of a beautiful afterlife didn't take away the pain of the loss of my daughter, but it laid the foundation of a deeper peace. I celebrate her presence daily, knowing that beyond her physical absence she is here, she supports my life, she loves me beyond words and I will see her again.

The main concepts from Dr. Moody's book are the same ones that are told over and over again in the NDEs of people of all races and religions. I list below those that have meant the most to me over the years.

As we go out into the world with our joy and our pain, may we be a little more at peace, lifted by the knowing that we never lose our beloveds and that our love is without end. Listen—and hear the angels sing.

In The World: What we know from near-death experiences:

* After death there is a light of unconditional love (God) that is so bright, so pervasive, so beautiful that we want to stay forever. We have no pain and no sadness.

* Our consciousness remains intact and we have an almost immediate understanding of events in our lives and the impact of our lives on others.

* We are not alone. We are greeted by loved ones who have gone before us and angels or guides who assist us in the transition.

In The Heart:

* I am an eternal being living in the light of unconditional love.

SEPTEMBER 21

Building a Prayer

Be wise. Be strong. Be kind. Be you.

Decades ago, a prayer that would organically come to my heart every day was the simple: *May I be wiser and kinder.* That mantra was useful to me in the small moments of my busy life, encouraging the growth of wisdom and compassion.

Years later, the prayer would change along with the understanding that in order to practice wisdom and kindness, I needed a lot of strength and courage. The growth of spiritual knowledge, although the most natural thing for the soul, doesn't come so naturally amidst the noise of the world. Like any other educational process, it requires devotion, dedication, persistence, focus, strength, tenacity and *tapas* (burning desire) to stay the course.

And the prayer became: *May I be wiser and kinder and stronger.* I chanted this within for years while swimming, walking or running.

They say that all roads lead home, and this is surely true of spiritual paths. Everything we learn is processed through our hearts, so how we think of ourselves becomes vitally important. Being honest about who we are, authentic about how we express ourselves and sure about how completely loved we are by the divine become the most important building blocks of all. Self-compassion and self-realization are the bricks upon which we transform.

So in all things we must be ourselves. There is no wrong way when it is the authentic way. If we find joy in it, if we find love in it, if we believe in it, if we are passionate about it, we have found our road sign. We cannot take a wrong turn using the GPS of the heart. So the prayer became:

Be wise. Be strong. Be kind. Be you.

In The World:

✳ We can reinforce our lessons on the journey by coming up with short prayers to steer our learning. Yours might include: *Be open. Be peaceful. Be grateful. Be joyful. Be calm.* Come up with your personal version for today's path. Record it in your spiritual journal and allow it to become a daily mantra.

In The Heart:

✳ I am a unique and beautiful soul embarking on the journey of today with authenticity, joy and divine guidance.

In Perfect Time

*Autumn leaves are reminding me to release and just let go,
and open space with ease and grace for miracles to grow.*

The gentle onset of a new season can bring about a welcome change. When we open our hearts and surrender to transformation, we flow through the seasons of life with grace. The change of seasons in nature offers the chance to reflect on the change of seasons within us. May we open to new experiences that will bring inner growth as we release who we are in this moment, for what we might become. Have faith that everything happens in her perfect time.

There is a time for everything,
and a season for every activity under the heavens:
a time to be born and a time to die,
a time to plant and a time to uproot,
a time to kill and a time to heal,
a time to tear down and a time to build,
a time to weep and a time to laugh,
a time to mourn and a time to dance,
a time to scatter stones and a time to gather them,
a time to embrace and a time to refrain from embracing,
a time to search and a time to give up,
a time to keep and a time to throw away,
a time to tear and a time to mend,
a time to be silent and a time to speak,
a time to love and a time to hate,
a time for war and a time for peace.
Ecclesiastes 3:1-8 (NIV)

In The World:

✳ Contemplate the season of life you are in now and what season is approaching for you. Bless the outgoing season, thanking her for insights and lessons learned. Welcome in the new season, making space for blessings and small miracles to grow.

In The Heart:

✳ May I patiently release the past season of my life and open my heart to a new beginning. Bless this new day with limitless possibilities.

The Joy of Milkweed

There is nothing too small for gratitude.

My friends Paul and Cheryl teach songwriting to elementary school children. This year, Paul Reisler's organization, Kid Pan Alley, got a grant to partner up with the National Park Service. This is how it works: A class takes a field trip to the park and with the guidance of a park ranger, they wander through fields and along rustic paths looking for native plants and creatures. Then they use their common experience as a muse for writing a song together under Paul and Cheryl's musical direction. Creativity at its finest.

Yesterday the bus went up the mountain in the early morning in time to catch the dew on the morning grass. The children were given their instructions to look closely, to walk slowly, to feel with all their senses. Someone spotted a milkweed and was fascinated by its seed pod. Others gathered around in excited interest, noticing its pattern, colors and strength. Some sat down in the tall grass to study the miracle of caterpillars, butterflies and goldenrod.

This is soul food for a kid who lives in an apartment; an amazing expedition even for a kid who is a master at video games; a spirit of wonder for a kid who was never encouraged to look at nature this closely. Cheryl summed it up beautifully when she wrote, "Life will gift you with wonderful experiences when you are present to receive them." Oh, the joy of milkweed.

When we take pause to really look at the beauty that surrounds us with a heart of wonder, gratitude rises in abundance for the humble, the simple and the small. When we live in awe of the unfathomable miracle of our lives, there is nothing too small for gratitude.

In The World:

* Walk through this day with a grateful heart, mindful of small gifts of wonder.

* Voice a whisper of *thank you* from the heart for even the smallest blessing.

In The Heart:

* My heart is open with awareness of all of the gifts that surround me now. The more grateful I am, the more beauty I see.

Blue Love

Love is the greatest gift we can give.

When we close our eyes, each of us enters a personal oasis. With a few breaths to still our thoughts, we find that our oasis is calm, wise and serene, always at the ready to send out and receive an endless store of divine love.

Entering the calm of the soul, we know that although our experience is completely unique, it is connected to the soul of all beings that have ever existed or will ever exist. As part of our shared fabric, what we feel, what we imagine and what we create transforms everything around us.

One way to impact the energy within our homes, our communities and on our planet today is to send out a wave of love on the breath. Small meditations can make a big difference in our own mind, body and soul. And when we change ourselves, we change our world too.

Love is the greatest gift we can give.

In The World:

∗ Take a comfortable seat, feet on the floor or crossed-legged, spine straight and face relaxed.

∗ On the inhale, imagine a wave of peaceful blue love pouring into your heart, filling the infinite space within and magnifying unconditional acceptance and love.

∗ On the exhale, see the wave of blue love moving from your heart and filling your home, your community and wrapping the earth in peace.

∗ Spend a few minutes inhaling and exhaling the wave of blue love, magnifying your beautiful energy and sending it to all beings and to the earth.

In The Heart:

∗ I am filled with an endless supply of love and I freely share it with all beings.

Puppy Downshifting

Rest is not an option; it is a necessity.

My inner goddess is strongly relating to a passed out puppy. She is worn out from the daily dance. Running around, retrieving things, sitting, staying and loving people can be exhausting. I hear my wise inner voice ordering me to rest. And what do I do? I keep on going so I can complete just one more thing. And then one more thing.

And what does a puppy do? She collapses into the soft shag rug for a deep, rejuvenating nap.

You would think that after all the reading and writing I do about the essential value of self-care and the spiritual anchor of self-love that I would be a master at taking naps and resting when my eyes, wrists, body and soul are weary. No, my "off" button seems to be busted, but I have promised myself to do better with this.

Rest is not a reward that comes at the end of a long day of doing small things with great love. Rest is not an added bonus, a cherry on top or something we do if we have time after everyone else is served and happy.

Rest is not an option—it is a necessity. When we release, relax and wind down, clarity and calm rise up. We cannot give from an empty well. When we are replenished and energized, all else flows with greater ease and grace.

Puppies rest without guilt and so can we. I don't know about you, but this goddess is taking a nap today.

In The World:

✳ When your wise inner self sends the message that it's time to rest, stop and listen. Set a timer and close your eyes. Invite deep rejuvenation into every cell. See yourself surrounded by light and peace. Ask that you awaken refreshed, alert, calm and ready to focus.

In The Heart:

✳ I rest when I am tired and feel deep peace surrounding me. My body fills with light and energy and I rise refreshed, clear and calm.

❧

Grief 101: Comfort That Comforts

My love is with you.

During our lifetimes, most of us will have occasion to console someone who has suffered the loss of a child, and we want to do it in a way that is most compassionate. No one teaches us what to say, so we flounder in the uncomfortable void and frequently, despite our best intentions, we utter phrases that end up being hurtful. The information here is usually confined to grief groups, but I knew you would want to know. Next time you have the opportunity to comfort someone, your love will be truly felt and heard.

In The World: These phrases can be unintentionally hurtful:

❋ *Things happen for a reason.* We don't know what that reason might be right now and in the moment, it's hard to fathom that unbearable suffering would be inflicted on anyone for any reason.

❋ *You are young. You can have more children.* But we don't know that. And even if I had a whole crop of live children, I would never have that one. Children are irreplaceable.

❋ *It's God's will.* This can feel like a harsh judgment being handed down to the bereaved parents. No matter how spiritual or religious the person is, it's best not to get in God's shoes right now.

❋ *I know how you feel—my grandmother just died.* The loss of a child is very different from other losses. Resist sharing your own story.

❋ *At least...* It's not a good time to remind the bereaved of a silver lining.

❋ *Call me if you need something.* Simply drop off a comforting gift.

These phrases might bring comfort:

❋ *I'm so sorry for your loss. My love is with you.*

❋ *I've been thinking about you and your family. I'm here for you.*

❋ *I will always remember your beautiful Simon.* (Use the child's name.)

❋ *You are in my heart, my thoughts and my prayers.*

In The Heart:

❋ I am open to learning how to be a more loving and compassionate person in the world.

Grief 201: What We Need to Know

I cannot lose you. You live in my heart.

I know you're tempted to skip this page but hang in there if you can. Take a moment and clear your mind of death discomfort. Deep breath. This won't be painful, I promise.

So many of us slip through life avoiding conversations about death and grief like the plague. So why not stop, turn around and look her in the eye? Death will happen to us, but before that, it will happen all around us. People we love will die, and we find ourselves completely unprepared to face grief. When you know a little about it ahead of time you won't feel like you've completely lost your mind when it's your turn. It's just another sacred part of life.

In The World:

* Grief demands our attention. It is important work that requires soul space. Learn about it.

* There's no timetable. It's a personal journey and you walk at your own pace. There are no wrong ways to grieve.

* Grief is not a linear process; it ebbs and flows, possibly for the rest of your life. Stay with the feelings as they arise. Let them flow through you without judgment.

* Tell your story to a compassionate listener. Connect with others who have had a similar loss. Speaking your truth puts your experience into words and weaves the loss into your life going forward.

* Accept the help of loving people who offer it. They want to do something for you, and you need the support. Ask for what you need.

* Working with your hands—knitting, gardening, coloring—can be soothing. Writing letters and journaling can be comforting. Exercise can be helpful. Extra sleep can be necessary.

* You are the guardian of your grief. Be incredibly kind to yourself. Set limits where you need them. Do only what you feel up to doing. Go back to work part-time to ease your way in.

In The Heart:

* I allow the feelings of every stage of my life to move through me with compassion and without judgment. I am at peace where I am today.

Mending with Kindness

Kind words are a gift of healing. —Tiny Guru

When my mother spoke this phrase to me—*kind words are a gift of healing*—I was moved by the idea that the kind words were a gift *and* had the power to heal. I could see the words surrounded in light and knitting together a hole in the heart where self-esteem should be or being the salve that finally prompts the mending of a wound that would not heal.

Our words wield power, especially the beautiful, kind ones. We lose nothing by spreading them liberally throughout our day, and as these loving beams of light come through us to others, we find ourselves in the path of that gift of healing too.

Look for the possibilities, the chances, the openings, the opportunities, the small words, the humble moments—to be kind. Make a habit of formulating words of kindness and allow them to replace other thought habits.

Instead of negative words that might open wounds in ourselves and others, let's contribute to the healing of ourselves and of our world. We mend and we knit with one kind word at a time.

In The World:

* Ask: *How can I be kind today?* Imagine what kind words would lift your spirits and gift them to others. Keep it simple and real.

* If you know someone is in a challenging situation, offer words of encouragement.

* Consider volunteering for a group of people who are going through a life experience that you have been through. Kind words from someone who has walked the road ahead of them can be especially helpful and healing.

In The Heart:

* Kind words flow from me naturally to those who need them most.

Calling All Archangels

Angels, be with me now.

Today is the feast of Michaelmas, also known as Feast of the Archangels, celebrated in some traditions as a day to recognize Archangels Michael, Gabriel, Uriel and Raphael. There are many more archangels as well, all of whom are healers and protectors in the higher realm of angels.

The prayers below can be used at any time of need. Remember to request assistance in alignment with the highest good of all and to be open to creative solutions. The archangels are extensions of divine love, sent by God, here for our assistance. We are not praying *to* them as much as *through* them.

In The World:

∗ Dear Archangel Michael (Who Is as God), Leader of Angels: Please defend, protect and guide me as I face each decision of this day. Cleanse me of darkness and negativity, and keep me safe from harm. Lift the walls of doubt, fear and worries, filling me with strength, peace and divine wisdom. Remind me of my worthiness as a spiritual being and of my soul's constant connection with God.

∗ Dear Archangel Gabriel (Strength of God): Please open my heart to messages of spiritual insight. Help me to clearly express my truth with kindness and love, and to creatively use this day in alignment with my divine purpose. Assist me in overcoming fear, and fill me with strength, love and grace. Guide me through changes in my life.

∗ Dear Archangel Uriel (Fire of God): Please light the fires of illumination, and facilitate any necessary transformation and rebirth in me. Assist me in realizing my goals and aspirations, imparting ideas and insights that light my way. Guide me in unlimited possibilities, so I might be used by divine will for the highest good of all.

∗ Dear Archangel Raphael (Healer of God): Please bring to me the divine light of complete healing—physically, mentally and emotionally—restoring me to my spiritual wholeness. Help me to activate my own healing and creative energies. Shine healing grace on all humans, plants and animals, and to our beautiful planet earth.

In The Heart:

∗ Angels are present with me, assisting me in becoming my highest self and supporting me in every decision of the day.

Inspiration from the Inspired

It is in doing what inspires you that you become an inspiration for others.

In 1873, American lawyer and Presbyterian church elder, Horatio Spafford, was detained from a family holiday in England. He sent his wife and daughters ahead, and the Ville du Havre was struck by another vessel and sank; 226 people, including his four daughters, died that day. Crossing the ocean alone to meet his wife, he wrote the beloved hymn of hope, "It Is Well with My Soul."

In 1905, Canadian-American writer Civilla Martin and her husband were visiting the Doolittles. Mrs. Doolittle had been bedridden for twenty years, and her husband had disabilities which confined him to a wheelchair. Yet, they brought inspiration to all who knew them. "What was their secret?" the Martins asked. Mrs. Doolittle replied, "His eye is on the sparrow, and I know He watches me." Her simple testament of faith inspired Ms. Martin to write the hymn, "His Eye Is on the Sparrow."

In 1994, during the Rwandan genocide, Immaculate Ilibagiza spent 91 days hiding silently with seven other women in a tiny bathroom in her pastor's house. She walked in a joyous student of 115 pounds and left at 65 pounds, alone, nearly all of her family murdered. During that time, she taught herself English with only a Bible and a dictionary, and prayed unceasingly. Once freed, she forgave those who killed her family and got a job at the United Nations, where she continues her work for peace, faith and forgiveness.

In 2012, at age 24, Aimee Copeland was zip-lining when she fell into a river, gashing her leg. She contracted a rare form of flesh-eating bacteria that ultimately claimed both of her hands and feet. She says that her accident led her clearly to her purpose—inspiring others with severe disabilities. She shares her enthusiastic love of life, her powerful strength of spirit and her faith in overcoming challenges through the Aimee Copeland Foundation and a constant stream of motivational speeches.

In The World:

∗ Today, we celebrate life. When we focus on what inspires us and share our enthusiasm for life, we are an inspiration for everyone around us.

In The Heart:

∗ With a heart of gratitude, I love and celebrate my life, despite my challenges.

October
Be present.
Let the day flow with grace.
Expect joy. Be positive.
Serve with compassion.
Speak only kindness.
Impart only love.
Never forget you're not alone.
Give thanks for everything.
See goodness in others. mary davis

EVERY DAY SPIRIT

October Blessings

Be present. Be here. Today, we can guide our thoughts back to the present moment with gentle focus and live fully right where we are.

Let the day flow with grace. Grace flows through us easily when we are in tune with the subtle voice of intuition. Open and listen for guidance.

Expect joy. Be positive. Imagine a fulfilling day unfolding, in which we accomplish much and experience joy in the process. Welcome the light.

Serve with compassion. Acts of service when performed with love lend immeasurable light to our day. Be watchful for ways to serve.

Speak only kindness. Speak only kind words. Think only kind thoughts. Be kind to yourself and to those who cross your path or your mind.

Impart only love. Send out all thoughts and words on the wings of love so that we may love one another, love ourselves, love the unlovable.

Never forget you're not alone. Let's remind ourselves often today that we are always supported, guided and unconditionally loved as we are.

Give thanks for everything. Gratitude will shift the perspective of the day from one of lack to one of abundance. Give constant thanks.

See goodness in others. Each of us has a soul that is made of beauty and love. Assume the best in others so they may rise to their highest light.

Love Is Who We Are

Hold a candle. Share a smile. Lift a spirit. Spread the light.

I have long held on to the belief that we live in a benevolent universe where the power of good far outweighs the power of evil. In the relentlessly positive world that I envision, there is always an available beam of light shining out from the depths of even the weariest soul, to illuminate the darkness. Mean-spiritedness withers in the face of kindness; hate and racism fold in the presence of love and truth. But the continuing affront to the heart by acts of terror on the innocent and undefended has even my beam flickering in the wind of change.

Our shared cry of despair is in the air. We grieve for anguished families and friends, for Las Vegas, for our world, for our shattered hearts. We shed a new river of tears, and carry deep sadness in the face of the unimaginable horror now being endured by our fellow souls. We grieve again for Orlando and Newtown, and all of the dear ones lost to violence and their beloveds who live on. But a beacon of light calls us home.

Unspeakable acts of violence beg us to make decisions about what kind of energy we bring to the world. And ultimately, we have to choose where our focus continues to go. Do we make a conscious decision to bless the world and raise it up with our love, or do we feed the darkness with fear? If we choose love, our every thought, word and action must reflect our choice in every moment.

We begin the process of healing right where we are. We use our presence, our song, our calm, our joy and our tenderest kindness today to brighten dark corners. We use a voice of compassion, a heart of unconditional love, a prayer of passion and an act of benevolence to lift the vibration. We use peaceful action under the guidance of our deepest wisdom.

Love, peace and prayer are not the stuff of spiritual lightweights but the greatest, most powerful weapons in the universe. Our united message of love can become a massive beacon of divine light. We are together now for just this reason. Let's light the way, shoulder to shoulder, heart to heart, lantern to lantern. We can rise to this. Love is who we are.

In The World:

✳   Today, be the embodiment of love in thought, word and action.

In The Heart:

✳   I am an instrument of peace and share the highest vibration of love.

The Garden Tribe

Friends are flowers in the garden of the heart.

Like a perennial garden, our old friends follow us through the seasons of our lives. They know our secrets, they know our families, they know our stories. They easily bridge the time and miles, supporting us during transitions and losses, diagnoses and dilemmas. These friends ground our lives with perspective; they see the whole picture through the lens of unconditional love.

Our new friends, like annual blooms, beam into our lives as blessings, providing daily comfort and joy. These friends walk us through moves, marriage and divorce; they companion us through grad school or when we go back to school; they are the like minds from yoga, work, the neighborhood, church, or volunteering. These friends bless our lives for a season and lift us up by sharing our day-by-day burdens and celebrations with understanding and grace.

Each friend is a flower in the garden of the heart, making our hearts home to exquisite beauty. Each flower is unique and irreplaceable. Each season unlike any other, enduring time, bridging miles, rejoicing in common experience. Each friend a treasure, entering our lives at the perfect time and place.

Thank you, dear ones, for making life infinitely more colorful and beautiful.

In The World:

* If you are feeling alone or in need of counsel today, call on a friend. They will be honored to hear from you.

* If you regret the lapse of a friendship, it's never too late to reach out. If it doesn't rekindle, know that some of the most beautiful flowers are annuals. Perhaps they have already graced your life in the way they were meant to.

* If you haven't found your people yet, they are out there. Your tribe awaits you. Open your heart to planting the seed of a new friendship. It will come.

In The Heart:

* I am eternally grateful for the soul companionship of my friends. I bless them, old and new, for the infinite beauty they bring to my life.

Surprise and Color

Be in the moment and notice what is.

I just sat down to write and the shy paint horse Little Joe came right up to the fence, his white and brown patches brightly beaming in the pouring rain. My favorite cardinal flew in front of the window and sits on the eve of the cabin, tail fluttering right over my head. They are messing with my plan to extoll the virtues of an ordinary rainy day, throwing in a splash of surprise and color.

Now a blue jay has arrived and is perched on a high branch for perspective, while a tiny yellow guy is leaping and flipping from branch to branch, a goldfinch version of break dancing. I'm laughing and wondering if it's a cosmic joke or just nature's way of reminding me that a lot happens when I really look.

But that's all we need to do, right? Just be in the moment and notice what is. When we don't project our mood onto this brand new, shining day, we are open to surprises and delights. We respond as we are led to, open wide and listening, loving all the way. We will know what to do moment by moment.

The only difference between an amazing day, an average day and a disaster day is the way we think of it right in this moment. And clearly, we can't assume what we might find in this moment, or the next, or the next. We arrive with an open mind and accept what is with gratitude. And usually, it's pretty amazing.

In The World:

* Wipe the slate clean. Assume only that this day will be a work of art and will unfold exactly as it is meant to.

* Offer up a note of gratitude for whatever perfection is about to transpire.

* Ask for guidance to keep you in the moment, to keep your heart light, to keep you blessed, safe and open.

In The Heart:

* Thank you for this most amazing day. I am blessed with whatever unfolds in my life today and accept it with an open heart.

The Highest Goal

Life is fragile. There is nothing more precious than love.

One of my hospice patients has lost almost everything. When she first received the devastating diagnosis of a rare degenerative disease, Claire was retired and living a joyful life in Florida, where she tended a garden of orchids and sat by the ocean with her feet in the sand, reading for hours daily. She treated herself to a set and style once a week, along with a mani and pedi. She had a radiant smile and an infectious laugh and beneath that, she was strong-willed, brutally honest and fiercely independent.

First she lost motor control in her right foot and gave up driving. So went the salon, shopping and reading at the beach. Her son moved her up North to assisted living so he could see her daily and supervise her care. In that move, she lost her home, her dear friends and her independence.

When I met her she was in a wheelchair, unable to walk for any distance. I watched as week after week she endured new losses. Her left arm, then her right, thus her ability to talk on her phone, change the TV channel, feed herself. A few months ago, she stopped speaking. I know. It's a lot to fathom.

And still, Claire's room is alive. Caregivers spend their breaks watching TV with her, painting her nails, doing her hair, doling out sips of water and bits of chocolate. They call her Mama Claire. On the outside, it seems as if Mama Claire has lost everything, but she has not lost her ability to love and be loved.

Psychiatrist Viktor Frankl, in riveting reflections on his experience in a Nazi concentration camp concludes that, "Love is the ultimate and the highest goal to which Man can aspire." He goes on to say that when our only achievement is in enduring our suffering honorably, we can still find fulfillment through love. When all else is lost, love remains. We always have the power of love.

In The World:

* Imagine being Claire and how the power of love would manifest in your life. Know that if you were faced with an unthinkable challenge, you would rise to it with a strength you never knew you had.

In The Heart:

* I believe in the enduring and transformative power of my love.

Love at Work

May I approach all work in the spirit of joy and creativity.

Sometimes our work life gets the smallest portion of ourselves. Not in the amount of time we spend there, but in the amount of love and energy we bring to it. It's not that we intend to withhold our greatness at work, but we tend to look upon it as separate. There's work life and there's home life. There's The Me that goes to work and The Me at home.

When we lift up to a higher perspective, our work and our personal lives are one and the same. It can help to think of work as a chance to make an offering of our talents to serve a greater purpose; to arrive as our best selves, powered by unlimited stores of love, putting joy and creativity into every task. Tension and resistance dissolve as we relax into the flow of creation and the energy of accomplishment. *Use me,* might be the prayer.

Beloved Indian guru Paramahansa Yogananda speaks to the integration of our personal, spiritual and professional lives in his book, *Metaphysical Meditations*: "I will do everything with deep attention: my work at home, in the office, in the world—all duties great and small will be performed well. On the throne of silent thoughts the God of peace is directing my actions today."

When we bring to work the awareness of our connection with infinite guidance, nothing is too challenging. When we make a special offering of our work, nothing is ever boring. When we work for a higher purpose, our work life and our home life unite as a ministry, anchored in love.

In The World:

✳ Treat your work today as an important ministry. Bring special attention to each conversation and to every task. Spread positivity, peace and joy as you go.

In The Heart:

✳ I approach all work with a sense of purpose and in the spirit of joy and creativity. I make an offering of the results of my work to something greater than myself.

Meditation for Calm

I am filled with serenity and calm in mind, body and soul.

Most of us feel the effects of stress, sometimes first thing in the morning. So before we go any further, let's get off to a beautiful start by practicing this calming meditation with exhales longer than the inhales. Breathe as you read:

Inhale peace. Exhale stress, 2, 3. Inhale calm. Exhale worry, 2, 3.

Bring your attention to the breath. We can use it to calm the nerves, focus the mind and center the soul. Let's do this again:

Inhale peace. Exhale stress, 2, 3. Inhale calm. Exhale worry, 2, 3.

Great. Next we will reel in our thoughts. This gets a little tricky because they have a mind of their own. So you have to hijack your thoughts from your mind and give them a new assignment. All they have to do is think these phrases on the breath for a moment. Thanks, Mind. Breathe as you read:

Inhale peace. Exhale stress, 2, 3. Inhale calm. Exhale worry, 2, 3.

That's better. Back to borrowing your thoughts from your mind—you can do this anytime but your thoughts are not going to stop playing around on their own. You have to give the orders and tell them it is time for a rest. Write yourself a note, set your phone alarm or do it on your lunch break. When the time comes:

Inhale peace. Exhale stress, 2, 3. Inhale calm. Exhale worry, 2, 3.

Now sit for just a moment with eyes closed and a quiet heart.

In The World:

* The big happy benefit here is that when you calm down, you connect more with the real you. When you're not in a spin, you are more authentic, you can feel your intuition, you can shoot off a focused prayer, you can look outside yourself and be present to the blessings. It's a humble practice with lofty goals.

In The Heart:

* I am filled with serenity and calm today in mind, body and soul. I use my breath to remain relaxed, healthy, focused and connected to spirit.

OCTOBER 8

This Glorious Day

Write through me this unwritten chapter of my life.

The special prayer, This Glorious Day, was penned during one of the most difficult times in my life, and I have said it every morning since. You can freely substitute any name for the higher power that you are comfortable with. I imagine the essence of Christ Consciousness to be of the tenderest of love and the wisdom of God.

Jesus Christ, come into my heart
and create with me this glorious day.
Walk through me
so I will know where to go.
Speak through me
so my words may be of kindness and peace.
Pray through me
so I may know how to assist.
Praise God through me
so I may know how to serve.
Think through me
so my ideas lead me
to what You would have me do.
Be joyous through me
so I may celebrate the beauty of all creation.
Parent through me
so I may be respectful and helpful.
Be a friend through me
so I may love and be loved in return.
Work through me
so I may do my work in the consciousness of God.
Write through me
this unwritten chapter of my life.
Jesus Christ, come into my heart
and create with me this glorious day. Amen

In The World:

✳ Say the prayer slowly, imagining each scene as it plays out. Write it in your journal if you'd like to add it to your morning practice.

In The Heart:

✳ I invite divine grace to act through me to create this glorious day.

In the Arms of Angels

You can never go wrong with purple.

Aunt Sissy grew wings today. She took on a lightness that she never knew in her earthly life, nor I expect, ever thought she'd know. Sissy didn't expect anything for herself. She was taught from a young age that she would not amount to much and mostly she believed that.

But not when it came to her painting. During her best years, she painted with wild abandon, decorating furniture, walls, ceilings and canvases with a whimsical fairyland of flowers, trees, streams and wings. One weekend, she came to the house and painted vines interlaced around a gallery of family photos on the hall wall. Another weekend she painted flowers on Maya's dressers. She adorned shelves with angels and trees, and trays with fields and fences. She was generous, free and joyful with her paints.

She taught every child and grandchild that came to her tiny house to paint too. She let them make messes and was the first to laugh at accidents and spills. They could use any colors they wanted, and she would always advise, finger toward the heavens, "You can never go wrong with purple!" She told them that everything they painted was a masterpiece and that they were important and oh, so loved.

You'd never know that Sissy suffered from severe depression most of her life. You'd never know that when the paintbrush was not in her hand, she was in bed watching movies through the dark, sleepless nights. She lived the very difficult existence of not recognizing her irreplaceable beauty, light and power.

All that changed today. She grew wings just like the ones she painted countless times, and she's lighter than air now. All the dark has lifted and she rests in the light of unconditional love. She understands what she came here for, and her radiant, magnificent spirit is in the arms of angels.

In The World:

* Remember today that there is no scale on the planet grand enough to measure the importance of your life in the world. Celebrate your magnificence.

In The Heart:

* There is only one love like mine. My talents are unique and valuable. My life is an irreplaceable gift to the world.

Love over Fear

I choose faith over anxiety, hope over worry, love over fear.

These simple words can serve us in two ways: as an affirmation and as a practice. When fears arise, affirmations can move us gently toward the light, even as we face the darkness. They make us mindful of our thoughts and of our choice to direct them with faith and hope. Choosing to do this, over and over again, is the practice. When worries settle in, we always have the choice to look at them through the eyes of love.

When we make an offering of our challenges with a brave, patient and open heart, we surrender to the highest possible outcome. With affirmations and the practice of faith, hope and love, we can turn this day into something beautiful.

Today I choose faith and when I do, my anxiety dissolves and my focus becomes the right outcome for the highest good of all. I believe that all things are possible, and I trust that incredible blessings walk the path right beside impossible pain. I know that I will live through this, thrive through this, become new through this. Today I choose faith.

Today I choose hope and when I do, my worries retreat and my focus becomes a better outcome, one beyond my ability to see. I imagine a future where my concerns are solved with the ever-present support of spirit. I surrender my need to control and I offer my problems, great and small, to divine guidance, knowing I am heard. Today I choose hope.

Today I choose love and when I do, my fears fade and my focus becomes seeing all things through the eyes of love. Every decision I make today comes from a heart of love. Every thought I think today is sent out on the wings of love. I have nothing to fear. I am an eternal being and by the power of love, all things can be solved. Today I choose love.

In The World:

∗ Today when you recognize the signs of doubt and fear, stop and recite this calming prayer from Julian of Norwich: *All shall be well, and all shall be well, and all manner of thing shall be well.*

∗ Send light and imagine the highest outcome for all concerned. Then let it go and open your heart to the possibility of perfect solutions.

In The Heart:

∗ In every thought and action today, I have a choice. I choose faith over anxiety, hope over worry and love over fear.

꙳ ꙳

Give Kindness Wings

Kindness shared goes on infinitely like seeds of love on wings of flight.

The small, everyday act of kindness didn't end with the act of kindness. It went right into the department store and on to the cashier. From there it spread to her customers for the remainder of her shift.

It went into homes and travelled by conversations in kitchens and by texts through phones. It also travelled in traditional ways, by car and train, by bus and plane, where it flew over mountains.

From there it rained into lakes and rivers, where it flowed around turns and trees until it reached an ocean of souls.

Your kindness was heard by welcoming ears, felt by weary hands, tasted by hungry souls and it warmed needing hearts. From the hearts and souls, it went on infinitely like seeds of love on wings of flight.

It all got started when you carried the bag for the elderly man or held the door for the mother with the double stroller. It was all set in motion when you complimented a stranger or wrote a thoughtful note to someone in the season of grief.

It never stopped. You sowed the seeds of love and they took off on wings of flight. You gave kindness wings.

In The World:

✳ We will never know how our simple acts of kindness have been paid forward from heart to heart. Be generous with compliments, smiles and encouragement.

✳ Be on the lookout for opportunities to be helpful, expecting nothing in return.

✳ Be kind in your thoughts about yourself and all other beings.

In The Heart:

✳ Genuine kindness flows with ease from my heart to all who cross my path today.

View from a Boat

With practice, we become more tranquil until we are an exact replica of the divine love that surrounds us.

In the land of dirt roads and one lane bridges, my kayak and I got lost this morning finding a new lake; but the end result was stunning. Nestled between mountains was the stillest body of water I had ever been on, and so clear that you could see all the way to the bottom from the middle of the lake. The surface was a perfectly smooth mirror, capturing the exact reflection of the fall trees that were towering red and gold above it.

This beautiful image of a still lake can be used to illustrate the mind in meditation with the image of the colorful trees as divine love. When our thoughts are active, there are ripples on the surface of the lake of our mind. It remains deep and it has the potential to reflect the trees clearly, but as long as the ripples are on the surface, our reflection is out of focus. Divine love is always present, but we don't provide a crystal clear reflection of it like the mountain lake I was on today.

When we calm our thoughts in meditation, the surface of our lake becomes clearer. With practice, we become more tranquil until we are an exact replica of the divine love that surrounds us. It's an amazing process and one that we can all experience.

In his journal from Walden Pond in the 1840s, Henry David Thoreau echoes the same excitement about meditation, how "we become like a still lake of purest crystal and without an effort our depths are revealed to ourselves. Such clarity!" Yes, such clarity. And such peace and love. "To be calm, to be serene! There is the calmness of the lake when there is not a breath of wind...So it is with us." So it is with us. We are that.

In The World:

✳ With newfound enthusiasm, recommit to your meditation practice for at least five or ten minutes twice a day. Move up to fifteen minutes if you feel ready or add longer sessions on the weekends.

✳ In addition to countless spiritual benefits, you will experience decreased anxiety and negative emotions as well as increased memory and joy. You will be more focused, healthier, calmer and more joyful.

In The Heart:

✳ Beneath my thoughts, I am a crystal clear reflection of divine love.

Center of Gravity

I take steps to restore equilibrium in my life.

It's easy to get thrown off kilter and lose our center of gravity when we have too much work and too little play; too much stress and too little calm; too many screens and too little nature; too much world and too little silence. If this sounds familiar, consider taking a seriously lighthearted look at balance.

I am not the poster child for this topic. Ahem. I'm the queen of overworking, blowing past lunch time, scratching out mile long to-do lists that no human could ever accomplish. For the sake of a little illustration here, that is *not* balance. However, I do recognize the perils of my over-enthusiasm and when I notice I've lost my center of gravity by working too many straight hours, I implement practices that distribute my time more evenly. One small step at a time toward equilibrium. And it works no matter how far afield I've strayed.

It only takes a mindful moment to remember to eat (good idea!), to take a deep breath, to connect with spirit, to ask for assistance from our guides or to walk outside. We can say *thank you*, we can talk to our angels, we can organize a bit of time to feed the soul, we can set phone reminders.

And we can do it all in the spirit of fun and enjoy the process of reeling in our adventurous minds and schedules before we flame out. No self-blame. It's all in a day's work.

Balance is "the stability produced by an even distribution of weight." No problem. We know when we are tipping to one side. And we know how to come home to the powerful, magnificent center of ourselves again and again.

In The World:

✳   Be aware of areas of your life that are out of balance. Show self-compassion when considering how to cut back. Revive spiritual practices that are grounding for you: walking in nature, meditation, gratitude practice. You will know exactly what you need.

In The Heart:

✳   I am centered, balanced, joyful and calm. I take steps to restore equilibrium to my life.

OCTOBER 14

Peaceful Joyful Thankful

Believe in yourself and in the power of your dreams.

I'm going to get through this. No matter what today holds, I'm ready. I am peaceful. I am joyful. I am thankful.

I've got three positive thoughts to get the day going on a high note. It's all I need. I am peaceful. I am joyful. I am thankful.

No opinion of me matters except my own. I love myself unconditionally. I am peaceful. I am joyful. I am thankful.

I have dreams. I have goals. I'm not giving up on them and will hold them in my heart until they come true. I am peaceful. I am joyful. I am thankful.

I am lighthearted. I love my life, and I use each day as an opportunity to make the world a better place. I am peaceful. I am joyful. I am thankful.

I am strong, courageous and steady. I am confident in my abilities, and the right plans unfold for me with ease and grace. I am peaceful. I am joyful. I am thankful.

I matter. What I do today matters. I'm an integral part of the workings of the world. My energy is needed. I am peaceful. I am joyful. I am thankful.

I am guided by spirit. I am never alone. Unlimited support is available to me in every decision of this day. I will ask for assistance. I am peaceful. I am joyful. I am thankful.

In The World:

* Any positive affirmations you choose for today will steer you in the direction of a better outcome—even if you're not quite there yet. Believing in yourself and in the power of your dreams is the first step.

* Add some new affirmation to your spiritual journal to use on days when your energy needs a boost.

In The Heart:

* I have complete faith in myself and in the benevolence of the universe. I open my heart today to all of the blessings that will come my way.

Faith and the Fawn

In all things the spirit remains calm, steady, wise, strong and whole.

The squirrels are collecting and burying nuts; the horses are circling the field in the rain. The leaves are beginning the long slow process of changing hue; the wind is gently sweeping away the ones that have volunteered to fly first. All is well out my window on this fall afternoon as if nature was born of faith.

And all is well with the spirit too. Even in dramatic changes and challenges, the spirit remains calm and steady. Even in confusion and indecision, the spirit remains strong and sure. Even in depression and defeat, the spirit remains wise and well. Even in our most profound brokenness and exhaustion, the spirit remains whole.

The other day as I stood on the split rail fence visiting the horses, I saw two tiny fawns grazing on the other side of the field, sharing the space with their muscular friends, looking up at me with happy curiosity. Every few minutes they would jump straight up, bump sides in a mid-air high-five, then frolic a bit and go back to grazing. The joyful little guys bravely migrated closer and closer to me, daring each other to go first.

I stepped slowly off the fence, offered them love, and started walking slowly up to the cabin. When I got to the door, I turned to see them right behind me with ears up, trusting, wondering, waiting. They were too young to be afraid.

They were born of faith, believing in a benevolent world.

And so can we be—open, patient, vulnerable—trusting that all is well with the soul. We have learned fear, but we were born of faith. And to faith we can return.

In The World:

✳ Remember today that the spirit is always complete and unbroken. Have faith that all is well and that this season of the heart is unfolding as it should.

In The Heart:

✳ I have nothing to fear because I am an eternal spirit, and through all experiences my essence remains calm, steady, wise, strong, and whole.

Namaste

The divine light within me honors the divine light within you.

Although I miss being in the community of a yoga class, in my soul my mat is right there in line with the group. Since being diagnosed with osteoporosis, I found it more comfortable to practice at home, where I could modify poses and tailor the practice to suit my needs. But wherever we practice from, we share moments of common expansion, creativity, compassion, grace, wisdom and joy. We are together in the yoga class of the heart.

I have discovered something in the last few years that has breathed a lot of life into my yoga practice. It gives me a great fullness, *purna*, and contentment. It raises me up with a lightness of being. And it's perfectly simple.

I give it away.

Not every pose. Not every day. But when someone is on my mind, I offer them a breath. When a situation is troubling me, I offer it a pose. When the concerns of my heart or the needs of a friend join me on my mat, I surrender and bring them into the fold.

Yoga is the union of mind, body and soul. The word means to join, or to unite. The practice is one of movement on the breath. We are bringing all aspects of ourselves together in one moment using the breath as a tool of calm and focus.

What a beautiful opportunity to be in union with others also, directing some powerful love to where it most needs to go while easing the anxiety of what might be troubling us. Unity within ourselves. Unity outside ourselves.

More on this practice tomorrow.

In The World:

✳ Today, choose part of one activity to offer up to something or someone other than yourself. It could be your commute into work, folding laundry or your morning walk. *I offer this breath to...* Then send a few loving breaths to your intention.

In The Heart:

✳ *Namaste.* The divine light within me honors the divine light within you.

Namaste - Part 2

The whole universe is in my heart.

Before we begin any yoga practice, we take a moment to get centered and to set an intention. Seated on the mat, I imagine my heart as the center of my being. Right there in the middle of my chest, right here in the body of little me, is a spark of divinity. So instead of divinity being outside myself where we might converse during the day as friends, the whole universe is now in my heart. There is a brilliant, golden light, pulsating with overflowing love and joy. I am the sun. No, *everything* is the sun. I sit and center until I'm feeling this brilliant sun clearly.

After some warming stretches I stand for Sun Salutations, *Surya Namaskar*, which is the part of the practice we can use as an example of the offering. I describe the poses in English for clarity:

I *inhale* with arms sweeping up, and envision my breath touching the glorious illumination in my heart center. *Exhaling* to Forward Bend, I see this gift of light going to my friend, my first intention. *Inhale* to Lunge, touch divine love. I hold the light in my heart as I step back to Plank. *Exhale* to Low Plank, light to my friend. *Inhale* to Cobra, touch divine love within. *Exhale* to Downward Facing Dog, light to my friend...

And so I continue with the Sun Salutation, slowly, evenly, breathing into the sun in my heart and out to my intention. Each breath is taken deliberately, with complete focus, handling them as precious guests, not wanting to cheat a single one with a wandering mind. Compassion begins to draw me in, tie me to the breath, to all love, to service, to the joy of the unending circle of giving and receiving love.

Sometimes I write down a list of names, but more often a name crosses my mind and I flow with whatever images I have of those in need. On some days I offer one pose; on others it's a series of Sun Salutations. Sometimes a whole practice is for one person or situation, or for the world. It need not be planned. The right intention always arises and directs us to where it is most needed. More thoughts on yoga tomorrow.

In The World:

✳ Give the beautiful gift of your loving energy to someone else on your mat or on your walk today.

In The Heart:

✳ I freely share my endless compassion and love with all other beings.

~V~

Namaste - Part 3

We are one with all things.

On the surface it may seem that yoga is just a series of poses, however yoga postures *(asanas)* are but one of many branches of yoga leading toward enlightenment. Yoga is much deeper than the poses alone. It can be an opening to a world so vast that we might spend a lifetime exploring but one sandy beach of this mighty ocean. No matter how far we get in our journey toward enlightenment, the truth remains:

We are one with all things. We are one with the infinite. And it's all love.

It's easy to let that basic precept fade in a world that sweeps us ever more fiercely toward self-interest and self-defense. But every day we can choose to meditate on the infinite, to practice mindfulness, to approach stillness so that we might discover our true nature during this lifetime—that we are made of one divine love. And the source is infinite. The well will never run dry—there is always enough to share with those in need of love and healing. Yoga on the mat can become yoga in the world.

All of the practices we use on our spiritual journey join to softly lift the veil that covers who we really are. When the curtain is moved aside, the beautiful light shining forth is your unique ray of divine sun. And that light is always at the ready to be shared in the form of a loving thought with another precious being. The well of compassion runs deep.

Share the love. Shine the light. And may we have the deepest compassion for each other as we walk this path together. Namaste and blessings.

In The World:

∗ You are a ray of divine love with the power to lift and to heal from afar. Practice using the breath to guide your soul's energy toward a specific intention. Begin in small ways with a few breaths. Expand the practice to other contemplative activities such as walking, praying, yoga, or simply as a meditation.

In The Heart:

∗ I use the power of my love and light to share beautiful energy. In the process of sharing it, I recognize my oneness with all beings—great and small.

Gratitude in the Dumps

I am blessed. I am content. I am grateful.

Oh no. The dogwoods that were stripped bare by the hungry caterpillars think it's spring and are trying to grow new leaves. A black bear climbed the red bud tree to steal bird seed and broke the beautiful branch. Meanwhile, inside the house, Adam called me, confused and slurring. The leaves, the branch and my heart are broken. And so opened the floodgates of brokenness.

Once there was momentum, all kinds of troubles ensued. I found myself suddenly in the company of tragedy and challenges, worst case scenarios and fear. Which can be a healthy thing to do sometimes—to sit with the pain for so long that we are in it, one with it. It tells a story. It teaches and enlightens. It releases tears. It sets the compass to a new North.

Then there are times like this one when I really don't want to do all that. I choose to be done worrying for today. I've examined the pain and I know it well. I've listened and learned and changed. I've offered my prayers, lit the candles, sent my light, taken the steps, imagined the best and have faith that spirit hears me. I want to feel better in this moment. *Now*, please.

And I find that gratitude is my way through. As I keep my eyes on the horses, the trees and the birds, I see beauty. As I keep my heart on abundance while cooking my meal, I feel blessed. As I focus on my work, I'm totally content. As I consider my health, my friends, my family, my music—I am grateful. So grateful.

And this gratitude does not depend on the leaves, the branch or my friend's health. It's something I make inside myself.

In The World:

* In the moments of today that beg for relief from troubles, turn your sights in the direction of beauty and abundance; reminders of the many gifts that render us infinitely blessed.

In The Heart:

* I look around me now and focus on the many ways that I am fortunate. I am blessed. I am content. I am grateful.

~V~

Forgiveness Manifesto

I release the past and let it go out to the sea of my soul,
to blend with my waves and become part of my strength.

I want to be free and present in the only moment in which I can live my life. This one.

I resolve to stop reviewing past mistakes and missteps made by myself and others.

I decide to release the anger I hold that is directed at those who have hurt me.

I choose to trust in the goodness of the human heart while being aware of my vulnerabilities.

I believe that the world is benevolent and conspires to assist me in the manifestation of my highest good.

I honor myself and know I am worthy of love and joy.

I unchain myself from thoughts which bind me to any hint of darkness.

I open my heart to that which is loving and light and leads me to the fulfillment of my purpose.

I declare that I forgive all past actions and request that any residual pain be reflected away from the light of my sun.

I release the past and let it go out to the sea of my soul, to blend with my waves and become part of my strength.

I am whole. I am worthy.

I am light. I am free.

In The World:

✳ Forgiveness is freedom. Copy this out or write your own Forgiveness Manifesto in your journal in which you declare your intention to forgive yourself and others. The written word is a powerful mobilizer of our future goals and dreams. Be free.

In The Heart:

✳ I forgive all past actions and request that any residual pain be deflected away from the light of my sun.

❧

A Worry Break

*May I let go of all I can't control and open my heart to receive
the blessings of this moment.*

We all know this—that we have the power to release what we can't
control. But we can use a little reminding every now and then when we
forget the beauty of our lives minus the weight of the world on our
shoulders.

There is precious little that we have control over; most especially not the
way other people act or what they believe to be true. We don't control
the world or the actions of anyone in it, save ourselves. Our work today
is to be present, to create with love and joy, to take care of each other and
to respond from a place of peace.

The habit of control gets sticky when we allow things that are outside our
jurisdiction to take up residence in our minds for long periods of time.
Our anxiety is often rooted in other people's lives and in decisions that
they alone can make. We can't fix them. Meanwhile, our precious present
moment is hijacked by worry, and the things we can't control end up
controlling us. Not the outcome we are looking for.

Whenever we choose to, we can take a break from the negative cycle and
release what we can't control. Simply set the burden down if a solution is
not being crafted right now. If we are not actively working on it, we put
it aside.

Then turn inward and notice that there is a new space in the heart. We
breathe deeper. We become present to the moment we are in and notice
that there is beauty right where we stand.

Within each of us is a well of peace that never leaves. When we open our
hand and let go of the weight of the world, we open our heart to receive
the blessings of this moment. And see that the peace we seek was right
here all along.

In The World:

﹡　Just for today, take a worry break. Practice allowing your anxiety or
fear to take a reprieve, and focus your love on the activity of the
present moment.

In The Heart:

﹡　Today may I let go of all I can't control and open my heart to receive
the blessings of this moment.

A Higher Vibration

Surround yourself with those who reflect the beauty in you.

Ever wonder why some people feel great to be around and others, not so much? We all have an energy field that is in constant interaction with those around us, and their energy field is interacting with ours. The energy of those who are around us matters to the well-being of our spirit.

Whenever possible, be around honest people who encourage you, mirror your goodness and see the best in you. Your highest self shines through in the presence of people who reflect your best qualities and bring those out in you. These are souls who see the beauty in you even when you can't see it.

We don't always choose who we get to be around. Members of our own families or people we work with might not be so good at reflecting the beauty in us. With some conscious tools, we can make the most of our energy spent in the company of lower vibrations. It's good practice and gives us a chance to make a positive difference in our surroundings.

Always remember that the energy we project to people—and the energy they project to us—makes a difference. The strength of the vibrations we give and receive today can change our world.

In The World:

* Whenever possible, surround yourself with those who reflect the beauty in you.

* Expect the best of people. Imagine them as they should be so they might rise to your expectations.

* Imagine yourself enveloped in white light and ask for protection when spending time with people whose energy feels low or dark.

* The Law of Vibration says that everything is made of energy, and energy always flows in the direction of the higher vibration. Keep vibrating high and raise the vibration of those around you.

In The Heart:

* My highest and most beautiful energy is what I give to this day. I gravitate to people who bring out my best self.

━◦❖◦━

Molding Love into Things for God

God needs us so He may create through our hands.
We need God so we may create through His love.

Today we get to make something brand new. It doesn't really matter what—we could make a birthday cake or make a deal or make someone smile with our kindness. Every single thing that we create today wasn't there before. Not the cake, not the deal, not the smile, not the energy we put into this day. We are the creative tools of the divine, molding love into new things.

I often wonder if that might be what this whole experience on earth is for—molding love into things for God.

Brother Lawrence was a seventeenth century Carmelite lay brother in Paris, known for the practice of finding God's presence in even the smallest task. He performed menial jobs in the monastery for decades, cooking and repairing sandals, keeping God in his thoughts at all times. For him, even the smallest action put him to use as a channel for God's love. When he was doing it for God, every lowly task he was given took on great value. People would seek out the wisdom of this humble brother because he exuded such an abiding peace.

If we were assigned a duty from an ambassador or queen, we would pay special attention to the smallest details, bringing excellence and our best selves to the task at hand. The work would be considered the highest honor.

Let's be used like that today. Let's be an implement, an instrument of incredible love. Let's be present and attentive as the hands of the divine, creating with tools of humility in the field of thanksgiving—molding love into things for God.

In The World:

✳ Consider being a present and attentive channel of divine love today. In every small thing you make, create something beautiful for God.

In The Heart:

✳ Use me today. I am a willing instrument of love and peace.

~✢~

A Soft and Peaceful Blessing

*Today may peace settle into your heart, may joy measure your success
and may thanks rise with each step.*

Today may peace settle into your heart.

May it soften the sharp edges of concern and loosen the tension around
your seams. May this peace take up residence, quiet at first, hidden below
the fray but faithfully there. Today you are aware of her presence. It
releases your shoulders and lets your guard down. It tells you it's okay to
relax—that it's safe here. *You can put your burden down*, it says. May peace
settle into your heart.

Today may joy measure your success.

May it measure a small success, like enjoying a quiet moment for yourself,
and a big success, like being kind to yourself in your thoughts for a whole
day. May joy transform your experience, just for today, even in the face
of small disasters, and allow you to laugh at the absurdity of life in those
moments. May your happiness color this day with awe for the amazing
beauty that surrounds you. May joy measure your success.

Today may thanks rise with each step.

Everywhere you look, may you see another blessing, with every footfall
leading to another precious gift. May it bubble up and over the top—this
feeling of being grateful for this and grateful for that. May it add up to a
critical mass like a mountain of thanksgiving for the gift of your life. May
thanks rise with each step.

In The World:

∗   Introduce a soft and peaceful blessing into your heart. No matter what
    the day brings, you will walk on the foundation of calm, joy and
    gratitude. Allow this special day to bless you back.

In The Heart:

∗   I walk through this day with peace in my heart, with joy as the
    measure of my accomplishments and with gratitude rising with each
    step.

Deer Independence

You have more strength than you know, more calm than you believe, more power than you imagine, more courage than you dream.

A family of seven deer has been living in the woods nearby and visiting the field, grazing alongside the horses for a few weeks now. The stars of nature's show are the two spotted fawns, gleeful and adorable. Whenever I see them from my writing window, my love leaps out of my heart and down the field.

Last week in the dark of night, I was awakened by a chilling, unfamiliar howl. It was joined by a chorus of what might be a pack of eastern coyotes—the coyote-wolf hybrid that have been seen around these farms. The next morning the deer were not on the field. For a full week there was no sign of them.

Then one rainy morning, one of the babies walked slowly across the field alone. After grazing, he curled up, unprotected in the pouring rain and lay there for hours. I imagined the worst and wanted to save him.

Yesterday, *both* little deer, now losing their spots, wandered slowly past my writing window. Oh joy! The rest of the family joined them later after the young ones had exercised their independence. Like creatures great and small, they were learning the power of using their own instincts, strength and courage. The young deer on the field in the rain last week wasn't lost, only venturing out to discover the world on his own.

To grow spiritually is a little like leaving home. We treasure the field of spiritual wisdom that informs and inspires us daily, but we must also trust the wisdom of our own voice and venture out independently sometimes. We need to sit in a field of rain, open and alone, and let tears wash us clean. We need to face challenges and joys by listening to the voice within and having faith in that constant presence. We have all the power we need to find heaven on earth. And to find our way back home.

In The World:

* Just for today, put down the books and practices. Listen with focused attention to your inner wisdom. That *is* the practice. Have faith and follow your divine lead.

In The Heart:

* I have more light than I know, more guidance than I believe, more love than I imagine, more beauty than I dream.

The Joy of Simple Things

May the joy of simple things color the canvas of your soul.

Sometimes joy shows up like the muted colors of dawn—soft, slow, gentle, serene. This is not the usual celebratory way we think of joy but it's joy even so. This calm bliss can rise in us like the sun, awakening our souls to the awareness of our incredible good fortune. We are alive.

An opening in the heart is all that is required. Even a crack, really, is enough. This awe can bubble up through this tiniest of openings at the sight of something beautiful like a sunset, a bird or a flower. It comes without asking; it comes without calling.

It's built in, this sense of appreciation for living. Like grace, we don't have to earn it, chase it down, or be extra well-behaved. It creeps into our awareness and showers us with gentle joy unbidden.

Appreciation and joy are inseparable partners. If you have one, you have the other. Sources of joy, like sources of gratitude, are countless. Be present. Be open. Breathe it in deeply. Be in awe. Savor the moments.

These are your paintbrushes. Notice and honor the simple things, and you will have lifted the brush to the canvas and painted her with joy.

In The World:

✳ Take a look around and bring to mind something that brings you joy. Count the simple and the small. Whisper a thank you for the coffee, for the sunrise, for the bird song.

✳ Bring this soft focus of joy with you on your daily round. Notice small blessings in new ways. Whisper thanks as you go.

✳ Notice how those around you become drawn to you and to your soul painting. Your joy is contagious.

In The Heart:

✳ I notice and appreciate the simple things and small moments that surround me each day and bring me joy.

Speak Love

Love comes with a feeling that always heals, always empowers, always lifts, always endures and can always build a bridge.

A friend of mine, who had been estranged from her sister and brother-in-law, was nervous about attending a wedding where she would be seeing them for the first time in years. Hurtful things had been said but the pain had mostly faded with time. She knew it was an opportunity to build a bridge.

Afterward she told me that although they seemed to have little in common with one another, she was overcome with love at the sight of them. She realized that she didn't have to talk about anything in particular, she only needed to speak in a loving way and that the *feeling of love* was silently spoken. They laughed, danced and built a bridge.

Last Friday after roller coaster months of sobriety highs and drunken lows, Adam called me, smashed. He was light-hearted, funny and child-like. I somehow had the grace to resist my urge to launch into a scolding lecture. Something told me to just be love. So I laughed with him; I let him tell some rambling stories; I encouraged him; and I'm sure he doesn't even remember making the call. But I know he received the *feeling of love* and that was all that needed to be silently spoken.

Love has many languages. They all hold the same power because love speaks volumes all by itself. When words seem inadequate, when you've done your best explaining and you're just not getting through, remember that love comes with a feeling that always heals, always empowers, always lifts, always endures. And can always build a bridge.

In The World:

* Sometimes people just need to be loved. Even when they have made mistakes. Even when they have been mean. Even when they get a tattoo that you don't love. Sometimes we just need to speak love.

In The Heart:

* Today I release my instinct to judge, and in its place I offer a gift wrapped in the language of love.

Light Always Wins

We are one with the light of each other. We are one with the light of God.

When the earth turns away from the sun, we don't fear that the light has been extinguished. We know the sun is there; we just can't see it. In the same way we can trust that the light of the soul cannot be extinguished. It's always there, always brilliant and always connected to the light of God and all other beings. We always have the potential to be light-workers.

Together we are travelers on the road to awakening. Every day, we discover ways of connecting with and giving rise to our eternal soul. As we progress, we begin to see that we are much bigger than we thought we were, recognizing our divinity as an integral part of our being.

This recognition of the soul self *is* the awakening. We see that we have the light of the divine within us. It's always there, even when our smaller selves are hard at work keeping the dark of night in place.

We are waking up to this knowledge together. We know that we are eternal beings in finite human form. We know that we are made of the light and that this light is a common aspect of all beings. We know we are one with the light of each other. We know we are one with the light of God.

Darkness is the absence of light, so the real work is to relentlessly shine the light of our love in all the dark places where it is needed. Elkhart Tolle says it this way: "You cannot fight against the ego and win, just as you cannot fight against darkness. The light of consciousness is all that is necessary. You are that light." So shine on and shine brightly.

As we walk together in this global awakening, we will tip the scales toward a lasting good by the light of our spirit. We will stand strong in the light of love. Darkness doesn't stand a chance.

In The World:

* Recognize yourself as the light-worker that you are. Use your presence, your joy, your calm and your love today to brighten dark corners.

In The Heart:

* I am a brilliant being of light. When I remember my eternal nature, I am able to turn darkness into light.

꧖

The Path of Others

*May I respect the path of others and refrain from thinking
that my way is the only right way.*

Sometimes we feel really confident about the way we are living and the choices we are making in our lives. And with the very best of intentions, it seems like a good idea to weigh in on other people's lives on topics like diet, exercise, housekeeping, parenting, politics or religion. It seems like we know what's best for our family, friends and even strangers. We have great ideas of how we would propose to fix things if we were them.

And we try it out to find our efforts are met with anger or resistance, and it doesn't turn out the way we planned. Oops.

The only life we really get to make choices for is our own. With regard to the choices of others, it helps to consider that maybe what we see as a misstep will be the gift of grace that propels them to their own right path. Maybe the challenge they face is necessary for their growth. Maybe they are just not ready or able to release the habit, anger, fear or grief just yet.

It doesn't mean we have to stay in the presence of dark, angry energy but we do need to respect the individual journey of all souls and refrain from judgment. We can trust that all is in divine order and remember that what everyone *does* need is support and encouragement, compassion and prayer, grace and a hot meal.

In The World:

∗ Always reserve the right to refrain from discussions on politics and religion with people you don't know well—and family for that matter.

∗ Offer support and be thoughtful about suggestions.

∗ Remember the power of prayer when it's hard to know how to assist.

In The Heart:

∗ I respect the path of others and refrain from thinking that my way is the only right way. I honor all beings and withhold my judgment.

Step into the River

The river of amazing grace flows by us at all times.
We need only to step into the water.

The river of grace is always right here beside us. Steady and strong, she is endlessly flowing, ready to offer her gifts anytime, anywhere. To allow her divine blessings to work through us, we need only to acknowledge her presence, open our arms and open our hearts. And we need to step in. Every request for grace is a baptism of sorts, a holy moment when we wash away our merely human skin and accept our need for a higher power.

After the Speak Love talk with Adam, I was once again completely devastated and at a loss for how to help. I asked for the grace to lay it in God's hands. I wrote, *God, thank you for bringing Adam to complete health and healing*, and I put it in the God Box. I prayed Rosaries for him, imagining him only as his happy, healthy self, surrounded by white light. And I let it go.

Today my intuition nudged me to call him, and I knew immediately when he answered that he was sober. Without waiting for me to speak, he launched into an enthusiastic (en Theos: in God) plan for his wellness. It was all the same stuff I had heard before. But this time *he was the one who asked for the grace*. He wanted to be in the river. This was his idea. He said it perfectly: "I realize that I can't do this without my higher power."

Grace. He asked for grace.

It seems counterintuitive, but it is in the moment of surrender that we are granted the power of spiritual assistance. We usually discover this when we are completely beaten down, desperate, knees on the cold, hard tile. But it doesn't have to be this way. The river of grace is always right here beside us waiting for us to step in.

In The World:

✳ Set down your armor. Give up your will to do it alone. Let go of control. Accept the army of angels that is here for you. Step into the river of grace.

In The Heart:

✳ I open myself completely to receive the abundant gift of grace in every moment of this beautiful day.

Liminal Time

We can trust that great love is knocking on our front door.

Many of the ghostly traditions we will take part in tonight were passed down to us from the Feast of Samhain, a Celtic New Year's festival that marked the end of the abundant harvest season and the beginning of the cold dark of winter. This very night was considered *liminal time*, when the veil between the earthly realms and spirit realms was very thin, allowing fairies, witches and demons to roam freely. Food and drink were set out to appease the spirits.

Liminal time, derived from the Latin word for "threshold," is a time of transition, an in-between space where one thing has ended and another has not yet started. The dawn of the day is an example; when it is no longer night, but not fully daylight. It is a place of suspending doubt, having faith that the light is on the way.

The most exciting of all thresholds is the one between heaven and earth. It is the space we access every time we pray, every time we invite divine assistance into our day, every time we rejoice in the beauty of nature. It is in liminal time where great saints and sages, healers and mystics, Jesus and Buddha walked with one foot in the spiritual world and the other here on earth.

Even though we can't see it, the benevolent power of spirit is always present, always available, always assisting us from just beyond the veil. We can trust that great love is knocking on our front door—on All Hallows' Eve—and beyond.

In The World:

✳ After the candy is put away, the kids are in bed, the party is over, the TV is off, take a breath—a quiet breath—and use this night of liminal time to say hello to the divine ones who guide you. Ask all the hallowed ones for the power of spirit to guide your every step here on earth for the highest good of all.

In The Heart:

✳ Powerful sources of good work through me from heavenly realms, assisting my journey on earth.

November
Be present.
Let the day flow with grace.
Expect joy. Be positive.
Serve with compassion.
Speak only kindness.
Impart only love.
Never forget you're not alone.
Give thanks for everything.
See goodness in others. mary davis

EveryDaySpirit

November Blessings

Be present. Be here. Today, we can guide our thoughts back to the present moment with gentle focus and live fully right where we are.

Let the day flow with grace. Grace flows through us easily when we are in tune with the subtle voice of intuition. Open and listen for guidance.

Expect joy. Be positive. Imagine a fulfilling day unfolding, in which we accomplish much and experience joy in the process. Welcome the light.

Serve with compassion. Acts of service when performed with love lend immeasurable light to our day. Be watchful for ways to serve.

Speak only kindness. Speak only kind words. Think only kind thoughts. Be kind to yourself and to those who cross your path or your mind.

Impart only love. Send out all thoughts and words on the wings of love so that we may love one another, love ourselves, love the unlovable.

Never forget you're not alone. Let's remind ourselves often today that we are always supported, guided and unconditionally loved as we are.

Give thanks for everything. Gratitude will shift the perspective of the day from one of lack to one of abundance. Give constant thanks.

See goodness in others. Each of us has a soul that is made of beauty and love. Assume the best in others so they may rise to their highest light.

Your Life Has Changed Mine

You are always and forever in my heart.

The impact of a single life is immeasurable. No matter how short their time on earth, a soul is a soul, coming here for a reason, with a mission and a purpose. Every person who has touched our lives and passed on before us changes us in countless ways. Their lives have been gifts to ours and their essence lives on through our love.

The highest honor we can give someone is to recognize the importance of their time on earth and to offer gratitude for the indelible mark they made on our hearts. Ceremonies—even small, informal ones—help us to connect with their memory after death. We can set aside time on their birthday or day of passing. We can visit a gravesite, prepare a special cake, light a candle, create a memory book, write a letter or simply take time to feel how we were touched and changed by their presence.

In The World: *Thank you for your life. You have changed me forever.*

* Thank you to our parents, who gave us life, who loved us the best they knew how and taught us the lessons we needed most;

* Thank you to our children, gone too soon, who broke our hearts by their absence, only to transform us into something new, richer and deeper for having shared the beauty of their love;

* Thank you to our spouses, the one who walked with us, the one who left first, the soul mates who live in our hearts;

* Thank you to our friends, who were companions on the road of life, who supported us through the joys and sorrows;

* Thank you to our ancestors, who braved the challenges of their lives so they might pass on a better way of life for us;

* Thank you to the brave men and women who gave their lives willingly in protection of our beliefs and freedoms;

* Thank you to our teachers, guides and mentors who expanded us and enlightened us with their wisdom.

In The Heart:

* Today I radiate blessings of thanksgiving to all of the souls who have left this world before me. Thank you for changing me with your life.

Drive-By Love

Lift up someone else and you will lift yourself.

I don't know many people in my little country town, but I know that Sharron is everyone's right-hand person. She cares for countless horses and maintains their stalls. She feeds dogs and cats when their owners are away. She takes care of the llamas and the sheep behind the inn. She takes care of her large family. And she takes care of me.

Yesterday, I set out on a walk at dusk; my tired, achy body and soul moving slowly under the weight of Sissy's memorial service over the weekend. Sharron's pickup truck slowed to a stop when she saw me and I leaned in, relaxed by her easy presence. From under her baseball cap, her brown eyes inspected my face. There was no hiding.

"Just got back from my aunt's memorial service, Sharron. I'm spent." She reached out and held the hand that rested on her window. "I'm so sorry about your aunt," she said with such love that tears welled in my eyes. She told me about Margaret's funeral last weekend, how her kids spoke about their mother. She told me I needed to be careful walking, there were wolves spotted at the next farm. Rummaging around on the seat, she pulled out a whistle and tucked it into my palm. In five minutes, in the middle of the road, Sharron had taken care of my body and soul.

When I got back to my driveway, I stood still in the dark by the road and just listened. Under the half moon, the birds sang their goodnights from tree to tree; the horses quietly enjoyed a hay dinner; the frogs emerged around the pond; and I took my first deep breath in days. The world had righted itself. Love had cracked open my heart and diluted the dark with her light. In the presence of simple, drive-by love, gravity released me into the welcoming arms of an unspoken, "I'm here with you in this moment."

This, I thought, *is the feeling of being lifted up by love.*

In The World:

* Today, in simple ways, be the love that lifts up someone else. Be lifted too, knowing that your love has changed another for the better.

In The Heart:

* From my deep well of love, I share freely with others, lifting them up through small acts of kindness and compassion.

❧

Rebirth and Renewal

Forgive yourself and let it go.

I was once my own worst enemy, berating myself for things I'd done or left undone, said or left unsaid. Perfectionism run amok. I would hold on to my sadness and shame, as if they were life preservers in the ocean of mistakes. If you join me in being a harsh self-critic, or if you have made a life altering mistake that is difficult to forgive yourself for, remember this:

Holding yourself hostage for actions of the past does not serve you. It won't right any wrongs, even any scores or facilitate any new growth. It dims the light of self-love, self-esteem and confidence. Negative self-talk is not humility, but a destructive force that hides the radiance of your organic beauty.

Self-forgiveness is merely an acceptance of our imperfection and an invitation to once again align with divine love. It's a process and a practice that brings rebirth, redirection and renewal. It's a chance to recognize our innate goodness and begin again. When we forgive ourselves and release regrets, we find the freedom to go forward and live the lessons we have learned, pursuing our passions with newfound wisdom and an open heart.

So practice a little love directed at you. We all make mistakes and we are doing the best we can. Forgive yourself. Release it. Breathe deeply. Begin anew.

In The World:

* Be aware of negative self-talk. Notice the harmful dialogue and stop. Stop now.

* Speak to yourself on a soul level. Use affirmation or repeat the following: *I forgive myself and I have learned from this. I have received the lessons. I release it now. I am a new person going forward.*

* Soul-to-soul forgiveness is helpful when there is another person involved who has died or is not present. Have the conversation with them. Tell them what you are regretful about. Thank them for the lessons. Then release.

In The Heart:

* I release regrets and forgive myself for past mistakes. I honor lessons learned and the person I have become through my experiences.

Ask Your Doctor If It's Right for You

Peace and love to everyone.

Oh what a beautiful day to share with each other a salve that immediately makes everything feel a little better. It's a prescription medicine that you can give under the radar, without anyone knowing, without appointments and medical insurance. It is a drug from the spirit for the spirit. Today we give out free Peace and Love to everyone who passes by the office of our heart.

In The World: Prescription Insert for Peace and Love:

✱ Clinical Description: Peace and Love are organic compounds found in the spirit of every individual. In cases where they are completely covered up by the daily grind, a few doses will wake up the latent Peace and Love within the patient.

✱ Indications and Usage: This prescription is indicated at all times, and especially on days of low vibration. It is particularly effective against negativity and hopelessness, complaint and feelings of lack. Administering Peace and Love in conjunction with one another compounds their effectiveness.

✱ Side Effects: Reactions may include but are not limited to: increase in gratitude, spontaneous singing, being kind to others for no apparent reason, joy as evidenced by smiling, laughing, dancing and a general amount of lightening up, as well as a notable increase in vibration. There are no contraindications.

✱ Dosage and Administration: The administering clinician first takes a few moments to acknowledge her own overflowing stores of Peace and Love. She imagines the remedy in her heart center, and radiating out from her heart to a radius of about ten feet from the body. She can see the energy as being blue, green or white, although pink and gold work nicely also. Administration is automatic, however simple thoughts like—*Peace to you Claire* and *Love to you Annie. Peace to you Susan* and *Love to you, Alice*—may increase strength and effectiveness. The patient will receive the perfect dose that is needed. Repeat as often as necessary.

✱ Ask your doctor if it is right for you.

In The Heart:

✱ I am one with divine love and have unlimited stores of light to share. I change the world today by sharing Peace and Love with everyone.

Book of Thanksgiving

I'm seeing the good and the gift of each breath.
All is well with my soul, feeling thankful and blessed.

When Maya was two, we started a Thanksgiving tradition. A few days prior to the holiday, we'd make a blank book from construction paper, a hole punch and some yarn. On the front it said, "I am thankful for..." and on the back we wrote the year. Then, surrounded by crayons, colored pencils or markers, depending on her age, she took her time over the following hours or days to write and illustrate one thing on each page.

The book was spontaneous, imperfect, messy and honest. Without prompting, the early books included God—drawn with white crayon in a tiny fist making a tight circle of light—mom and dad, milk, juice, her blanket, her favorite stuffed animal, the cat. As she grew, the books included friends, extended family, music, the moon, the sky. Simple things. Everyday things. The things that surrounded her all the time.

In the fall of each year, as we gather supplies for the current year's book, we laid out past books on the dining room table as a colorful and hilarious reminder of small, special things—the gifts and blessings that graced each year. They are a treasure.

Thanksgiving is a day of gathering with loved ones, centered around a bountiful meal. It's also a chance to remember the sweet, small things that bring meaning and joy to our lives every day of the year. Come home to your heart for the holiday, making an offering of your gratitude.

In The World:

* Make your own list in your journal or on the back cover of a recycled greeting card. Keep it going in the days leading up to Thanksgiving, adding to it along the way. Open to the idea that gratitude can extend to the intangibles of faith, hope, grace, love, compassion and peace.

* Help kids (yours, your nieces and nephews, kids at a shelter, kids down the street, your students) to make a Thanksgiving book. Cut special paper in halves or quarters. Punch holes every inch at the top or along one side. Thread ribbon or yarn through the holes, adding beads or charms as you go. Get out your crayons and play.

In The Heart:

* I open my heart and offer gratitude for each small joy. All is well with my soul, feeling thankful and blessed.

Waging Peace on Our Health

My mind is calm. My body is healthy. My spirit is joyful.

One afternoon, after a particularly stressful conversation on the phone, my mother had an outbreak of a strange illness. Her lips swelled painfully, her mouth became severely dry, eating caused a stinging sensation and swallowing was difficult. These symptoms came and went relentlessly for six months, during which time she lost weight and almost all interest in food.

She reluctantly saw five specialists, each doctor finding nothing and sending her on to the next. When she returned full circle to the first doctor, he shook his head and said he had no answers for her. "Well, that's okay," my mother replied. "I've decided I'm not going to have it anymore." Just like that. And the symptoms have been in remission for months.

What we believe about our health has a powerful effect on our immune system. If our approach to a diagnosis, a treatment plan, or a diet is driven by fear, we miss out on the benefits of our loving inner wisdom. It's always a good time to make positive affirmations about our health. Make use of the toolbox within.

In The World:

* *My mind is calm.* Our bodies are constantly communicating with us. Take the time to be still and ask your body what you need to know. Ask what course of treatment is right for you. Ask what changes your illness is leading you toward. Listen. You will know what resonates with you.

* *My body is healthy.* We should spend at least as much time thinking of our bodies in perfect wellness as we do focusing on discomfort. Thank your body for its service, its health, its strength, its energy. The placebo effect works because what we believe to be true impacts our healing. Believe in your wellness.

* *My spirit is joyful.* Instead of waging war on illness, we can wage peace and treat ourselves with loving care. Do something that brings you joy every day. Laughter has been known to improve outcomes with no adverse side effects.

In The Heart:

* My mind is calm. My body is healthy. My spirit is joyful.

Beacons That Light the Way

Blessings abound.

Beautiful gifts of insight come to us from those who walk the spiritual road before us—saints, gurus, prophets, sages, our spiritual heroes, mentors and teachers. Even a single thought or word from an enlightened master can spark an understanding within us, illuminating our path. There are men and women of all faiths, who have spent their lives in pursuit of a personal experience of God, and their stories are like beacons that light the way for our own spiritual progress.

On the first of the month, Christians worldwide celebrated All Saints' Day, honoring the holy teachers who shared their journey to divine love. St. Francis de Sales says that we can "unite our hearts to these celestial spirits and blessed souls" and learn from them like "the young nightingale learns to sing from the older ones."

May their simple and encouraging words remind us that not only saints and sages, but all of us, are on the spiritual adventure of finding the holy in the small and the sacred in the everyday. Small things. Great love.

Go forth and set the world on fire. —St. Ignatius of Loyola

Pray, hope and don't worry. —St. Padre Pio

Just do small things with great love. —St. Teresa of Calcutta

Be who you are and be that well. —St. Francis de Sales

God lives also among the pots and pans. —St. Teresa of Avila

For love is the beauty of the soul. —St. Augustine of Hippo

Be who you were created to be and you will set the world on fire. —St. Catherine of Sienna

In The World:

＊ Consider reading some biographies of great teachers in your faith tradition. Incorporate into your heart the teachings that resonate with you and your personal journey.

In The Heart:

＊ I remember and honor the great teachers who came before me as beacons to light my way and deepen my understanding.

The Value of Virtues

We can disagree and still be kind.

In the arena of politics, the gloves have come off, and hearing grown people who call themselves leaders argue so meanly and so publicly has been jarring. I have no TV, radio or cell reception at home, but the few hours a week when I am in town with the company of my car radio are a true test of my sanity and faith in humanity.

We were taught respect, right? Along with sportsmanship and integrity— Little League and all? We were told that you could express your opinion without beating up on the other person as a human being. We didn't call people names, especially not into microphones. Not often, anyway.

The coming holidays will bring us together with beloved family and friends with varying points of view in tow. Even differing philosophies and religions agree that good moral standards are inherent to the development of our common humanity. Here's a small recap of a few virtues that might come in handy when we respectfully agree to disagree.

In The World:

* Courtesy: being polite and giving people the feeling that they are valued and respected.

* Honesty: expressing our unique point of view truthfully and sincerely. Anger and cruelty don't usually help us express honesty.

* Kindness: showing that we care about the other person. It aims to assist and uplift, and to avoid hurting the other unnecessarily.

* Respect: treating others with dignity and honor. When we respect others, they often rise and treat us in a dignified manner in return.

* Tolerance: accepting differences and understanding that our way is not the only right way. It is refraining from judging someone based on their appearance or beliefs.

* Integrity: having moral principles and a compass by which we steer our beliefs. It means if someone dehumanizes another on our page or in our presence, we speak up and kindly tell them the house rules.

In The Heart:

* Today, I am kind to all people, even those whose opinions differ from mine. It is possible to be honest and authentic while being kind.

Love Stayed Standing

*We are here together at the same place and time only to learn
to love each other better.*

It's a most glorious day outside. A brilliant sky holds a warm fall sun and a soft wind has the bright gold leaves dancing their way to the ground. The field takes on a radiant glow and countless birds, large and small drift by with no particular destination. It's pure peace outside my window. And pure torture in my heart.

Crashing again, this time harder and longer than ever, Adam timed his drinking binge with a Sunday visit from three of his kids and their significant others. The resulting mess set off dominoes of pain, one by one knocking down the newly built and fragile blocks of hope, trust, forgiveness and faith.

I asked the questions within: *Are there times when grace is not enough? Are there problems that we cannot solve through prayer? What happens when we pray our hearts out, ask angels endlessly, implore the God of all things, imagine, lift, cajole, support—and the boulder insists on rolling back down the mountain?*

Olga assured me that all the prayers were heard, which raised me up to a new perspective. Perhaps the scenario could have been worse. And just maybe, his plight in this life is a gift for all those around him—an opportunity to practice compassion, to love beyond boundaries, to dig deeper into the understanding of unbearable pain, to respect the path of others, to surrender to that which we alone cannot fix.

Olga also suggested that I call him for the sole reason of telling him I love him. Which I just did. And in that small moment, our love radiated through the mountain, the boulder, the dominoes and us. Love stayed standing.

In The World:

* In impossible things, in unbearable pain, in unfixable situations, have faith, stay hopeful, and above all, show love.

In The Heart:

* My life intersects with all other lives so I might learn the lessons of unconditional love.

Trust in the Abyss

Everything is in divine order.

Most of us don't like the feeling of not knowing where we are going. We like to have a plan that gets us to the goal by the quickest route. Living in the space between chapters of life is everyone's worst nightmare, prompting us to scramble out as soon as possible. It tests the limits of our faith and our ability to trust in providence.

When I was writing songs, I used to treasure being in the space I call *the abyss*. Being in the abyss means you have creative permission to *not* know where a song is going when you first start to write. It is trusting that if the first idea is allowed to come forth, the next, better idea, will present itself. If you judge too early, you miss the keeper line. Floating in the abyss sends out an invitation with no limits; whatever comes through you is equally welcomed and considered. Nothing is ruled out during this most valuable part of the creative process.

We all experience these times of in-between, where waiting for direction can be torture. Maybe we've outgrown our job, but a new possibility has not presented itself yet. We feel stuck in the abyss, not sure what will unfold for us next. We may be emerging from the end of a marriage, but new life has not yet begun. We feel unsure, every day in unchartered territory. Hey, wait! I know that story.

All of life is creation, and being in the abyss can be fertile ground. It is a time of listening and being open to every lead. It is a time of dreaming and of giving yourself permission to welcome whatever flows through without judgment. It's a time to have faith that divine order lives even in the places where there seems to be no order at all.

It's a time of trusting that something beautiful is being created.

In The World:

✳ Send out an invitation to all of your guards and guides to light your path with clear direction and perfect timing. Listen. Relax. Have faith.

In The Heart:

✳ I give myself permission to trust what I cannot see.

Fearless and Full of Love

I let my worries go so I can open to the good that surrounds me now.

The things we worry about are the things that we fear *might* happen. I'm not a big worry person, but for the sake of research, I took a scrap of paper just now and wrote down what I was worried about. I got eight things in about thirty seconds. So much for not being a worry person. Hmm. I don't want to admit to that. I don't want to live my life *afraid*.

I want to be fearless. I want to be courageous and unshakable. I want to face this day with the joy of believing in myself—having faith that with this brush of love I will paint a most beautiful day. A masterpiece. Which is impossible to do if I'm afraid of all kinds of disastrous things happening.

I propose we transform our worries from a list of things we are afraid might happen to a list of things that we want to happen—changing worst case scenarios into ideal end results.

So when the worries arise, instead of being swept away down the slippery slope of doom, we think *Our holiday travel will flow with ease and grace,* or *Send extra angels to Louis and Ryan.* When the familiar dark cloud settles in, we say *Bless me to finish this project on time,* or *Send loving light to Lu, Deb and Angelina.* If we can apply this to both thoughts and words, the worry list becomes obsolete.

We have talked a lot about choosing love over fear. Perhaps the best definition of fearless is to be filled with love. That's it. I don't want to live this day afraid; I want to live this day fearless and filled with love.

In The World:

* Experiment today with transforming your worry list. Be mindful and diligent in converting what you are afraid will happen into what you want to happen. My one-woman research shows incredible results.

In The Heart:

* Today I transform my fears into ideal end results. I let my worries go so I can open my eyes to the good that surrounds me now.

It Is Good

Simply loving your life today is the most beautiful thing you can do.

Today we go easy; we start where we are. This day, as it is, is enough. *We* are enough. Today, we allow our possessions to be enough, our homes to be enough, our jobs to be enough, our families to be enough, our friends to be enough.

We embrace the beautiful gift of this moment in time.

And we simply love it. We love our lives, right where we are, right now. We become whole in our brokenness. We become whole in our gratitude. We become whole in our acceptance of what is.

Today is the unique place where our life journey has taken us. We breathe and give thanks for the breath of life. Look around and give thanks for every single blessing. The whole mess that love and loss has made. Just love it completely.

Today, the most spiritual thing we can do is to love our life fully. We find joy without asking for more. We give deep thanks with no qualifications. We open our hearts, raise up our hands, shake our heads and wonder how the heck we got so lucky.

We relax from striving and racing. We become whole in our smallness. We become whole in our pain. We become whole in our vastness. We become whole in our awe. We become whole with the Creator of all things.

Today, we step back and think, *Yes, it is good. This life of mine is so good.*

In The World:

* Just for today, rest in the acceptance of what is. Don't judge it or analyze it. Rest where you are in your heart. Allow gratitude to pour freely from your soul. Decide to love your life today. Just as it is. Especially as it is.

In The Heart:

* I focus on the incredible abundance and beauty that surrounds me now. Today I celebrate, with God and the angels, the gift of my life.

The Sparrow and the Envelope

Life is fragile. Love is eternal.

I witnessed a death this morning and I am still shaken. Everything started out fine. As I sat at the window to write, a woodpecker flew straight to the roof over my head and peeked down to say hi to me. I laughed out loud. The Carolina wrens were being pretend roosters on the now bare red bud trees, singing out for dawn. A ruby cardinal hopped down the path, and a flock of sparrows flew in to join the bird party.

It was during the sparrow commotion that I heard the sickening thud of my little friend flying into the window. I looked up in time to see where he landed, wings out and beautiful, in a thick pile of leaves. I waited for him to move. I prayed that he was not scared or in pain. I admired the miracle of his feathers and the enthusiastic wings that carried him on his flight home.

Oh life, how fragile we are. One minute we are partying with friends; the next, silent in a pile of leaves, soul in the next world. Which is why I am going to finish My Envelope today.

A few years back, I read an article about making end-of-life preparations that would ease the paperwork burden on loved ones. I downloaded a handy form where I filled out information, noting where important documents could be found. I also downloaded a medical directive, which sits blank in My Envelope. I plan to include a few recordings from my songwriter days and a note for my daughter. Not a big time capsule, but a gift of making the paperwork of death a little lighter for those who are not enjoying the benefits of a stress-free afterlife.

Now, I'm off to a bird funeral. The program includes a few verses of Amazing Grace and a eulogy thanking this sweet bird for being an inspirational friend.

In The World:

✳ Take a moment to start Your Envelope. My list came from *Decide. Create. Share.* and is called "Valuable Documents at Your Fingertips." Also find a simple medical directive form for your state. Fill it all out, add something personal and fun, then tell someone where Your Envelope is.

In The Heart:

✳ I am brave, wise and compassionate in all ways.

❧

Sparrow Turned Phoenix

Look on the bright side.

He rose from the dead! The little sparrow—he's alive! After writing the solemn piece honoring his airborne death, I dutifully donned my gardening gloves and rubber boots, and wrestled the shovel from the back of the porch closet. I rounded the corner just in time to see him hop out of his leafy tomb and compose himself on the walkway. He stretched out one wing, then the other. After a few hops, he flew to a low branch on the red bud tree, wondering where the bird party had gone.

No need for Amazing Grace. He had plenty of that.

Not many of us will get to witness a resurrection but most of us will find, over and over again, that our worst fears never materialize. Life has a beautiful way of continuing to give us mornings and second chances. Just when we think the story is over, we get surprise endings and miracles. There are all kinds of ways that we survive the dropping of the other shoe. Like the little sparrow, we dust ourselves off and carry on.

A variety of cultures look to the sparrow's larger, mythological cousin for a hopeful symbol of new beginnings. The phoenix goes down in flames, only to rise out of the ashes reborn, spreading giant wings of renewal and transformation. To the sparrow, that might be a dramatic analogy, but to us, it's yet another in a long line of comforting stories throughout the history of mankind that say we are not easily deterred. We have incredible stores of strength. We get back up. As Maya Angelou says, "Still, like air, I rise."

No one has ever hurt their eyes by looking on the bright side.

In The World:

✳ When we don't know how the next chapter will end, we can look toward the clouds or we can look on the bright side. We can place our bets on the dead sparrow or keep an eye open for the risen one. We can be defeated or have inimitable faith and a happy knowing that today, anything is possible.

In The Heart:

✳ With a spirit of courage and strength, I have faith in the perpetual possibility of positive outcomes.

Tabula Rasa

*May today be the dawn of a shining new beginning. I release the past and
open to receive blessings beyond my wildest dreams.*

Welcome to a new day, a clean slate, an open book. It features a sunrise
that has never existed before, marking the dawn of a shining new
beginning. Today is a *tabula rasa* made just for you. It is a pure gift.

Today is not merely a continuation of yesterday, but a chance to be just a
little bit more: more patient, more compassionate, more joyful, more
mindful, more forgiving. We can accomplish this incremental growth by
taking a few moments each evening to give thanks, to review the day and
to release regrets.

St. Ignatius of Loyola, a sixteenth-century Spanish priest and founder of
the Jesuit order, published a volume called *The Spiritual Exercises*, which
holds one of his most beloved prayers—The Daily Examen. In this five-
part prayer, we look over our day with an eye for its blessings and how
they have changed us.

We can use a version of The Examen or your gratitude journal to end the
day with a mindful offering of gratitude and a request for tomorrow's
grace. This way we make each day a blank slate upon which to write our
unique story in the best and most beautiful way. May your today be
blessed beyond your wildest dreams.

In The World:

This version of The Daily Examen is inspired by Fr. James Martin and
Anne Kerning:

* Presence - Allow yourself to be in the presence of God and ask for
  assistance with the prayer.

* Gratitude - Think of what in the day you are especially thankful for.

* Review - Review the day, being mindful of where you felt God's
  presence most. Recall feelings of loving and being loved.

* Regret - Notice what you regret and ask for forgiveness.

* Grace - Ask for a portion of grace for tomorrow.

In The Heart:

* May today be the dawn of a shining new beginning. I release the past
  and open to receive blessings beyond my wildest dreams.

❧

You Can't Take It with You

I live in the heart of all I have truly loved.

Soon after the sparrow died and rose from the dead, I got to work on My Envelope. I updated the form, listing where important documents could be found and dutifully filled in my medical directive. There were some squeamish moments in there—imagining my loved ones making decisions for me as I lie there surrounded by angels. Yikes. This is the ultimate reality check. But we forge on, Spiritual Warriors! We can get through this and it's a gift. Really it is.

After the forms were completed, I moved on to the fun part. I whittled my collection of recordings from my songwriter days down to just a few CDs, and made some new covers for them. In the envelope they went, followed by a little happy dance celebrating the completion of the packet.

Then a thought stopped me in mid-booty shake. Why would I wait until I'm dead to give Maya the songs from my career that I am most proud of? That seemed to be strange timing.

So I busted back into the envelope, took the CDs out, and sealed it back up. I wrapped them in tissue and gave them to Maya next time she came home from college. That felt better! A few days later, she called me to say she had been driving around with my CDs and really loved having them. She had questions about the songs and about that time in my life. By sharing a piece of what I loved, we opened up a new conversation between us. She's learning more about my heart and soul—*before* the angels come to escort me home.

In The World:

✳ Think about what you love that you might share with your beloveds while you are still here. It might be your favorite recipe, picture or gardening tip. Maybe a painting or favorite quote or prayer. Could be a pair of earrings, rosary beads, mala beads, your class ring. Half the fun is thinking about what you have loved that will live on. The other joy is sharing a piece of you.

In The Heart:

✳ I am an eternal being who lives on forever through the people and things I have loved in my life.

Autumn Horse Therapy

Release and make room for new growth.

I've been spinning since I got to Hunter's Road. Literally. Out on the horse field or down the middle of the street, I spin down the hill like a whirling dervish, arms out to the sides, laughing. Breathless and stumbling, I then raise my arms to the sky, welcoming guidance, delighted to be completely alone in nature, watching, listening, following her lead of growing and releasing.

Yesterday, after a spinning episode, Shadow and Brother Time were nearby grazing and we struck up a conversation. We looked around and agreed that nature was putting on quite a show, with the whole field reflecting a brilliant glow of golden leaves. Spaced throughout were breathtaking splashes of neon orange and ruby red.

I mentioned to the horses that the trees were raining leaves that were spinning through the air. Sort of like me. With the slightest breeze, they would release what they had nurtured; faithfully filling the sky with floating investments in the future. Sort of like me.

"Hey, you guys," I said quietly to my friends, "Do you know that I'm releasing my old life? Leaf by leaf I'm letting go, making room for new growth." They nodded with understanding. Horses make the best therapists.

"Let's bless the leaves, then bless the space," I suggested. "We can bless the ending that will create the emptiness that holds the new adventure." *Good idea,* was their sweet, silent reply. Then Shadow, Time and I stood still in the golden world of constant motion, with blessings spinning and falling, trees swaying and releasing, encouraged by the wind to rain down leaves.

In The World:

✳ Think about what you might release to make room for new growth. Acknowledge your transition from one season of life to the next.

✳ Journal about what you are releasing and what you are inviting in. See if any of these items should to be added to your Gratitude in Advance practice.

In The Heart:

✳ I freely open and release all that is fulfilled and completed. I create a beautiful space for future blessings.

The Eyes of Gratitude

Through the eyes of gratitude, everything is a miracle.

When in need of ways to lift the spirits, we need look no further than the practice of gratitude. Every time we whisper a prayer of thanks, we immediately transform the feeling of the moment from lack to abundance. The simple act of noticing the blessing shifts the energy from mundane to miraculous.

Waking up to another day of life is a magnificent gift. So we can start right there with a gentle and heartfelt, *Thank you for this beautiful day.*

Within this precious day will come countless gratitude opportunities—moments that might ordinarily fly by without much attention; moments that offer choices and chances; small moments in which we can notice the blessings. *That tree is such a beautiful color of gold.* Simply notice. *I love that painting she made me.* Just feel it.

After we notice, we can acknowledge the gift by following up with a short offering of appreciation—*thank you*—and we begin to shift. This humble act of expressing gratitude opens our hearts to the abundance that lies within us and around us all the time. When we nurture this awareness, looking for beauty and miracles, we find beauty and miracles. The more we give thanks, the more blessings we see and the more abundance we feel.

Notice the gift and say *thanks* from right where you are and watch how gratitude chases away the mindset of lack and makes sweet miracles of small moments. This vast perceptual change manifests through something as simple as seeing the world with a different set of eyes. The grateful eyes of the soul.

In The World:

* Use your notebook to start or recharge your Gratitude Practice, writing three or more things you are grateful for every morning or evening.

* Use a kitchen counter note or calendar alerts to remind you to stop and be thankful for the gift of this moment.

In The Heart:

* Today I notice all of the small blessings that surround me. I am grateful for the countless gifts of beauty and love. I love this day.

~v~

A Little Soul Care

Take care of the soul that takes care of others.

Thanksgiving is just around the corner, and we're already as crispy as a deep fried bird. This can't be good. The gratitude in the air can be sucked out of the room by lists that are worthy of a three ring binder. Our morning practices are shortened in the time crunch, and our souls are in need of some serious tuning up. I think it's time for tea.

There will be no shortage of demands on our resources, so there's no time like the present to implement a little soul care to reconnect, tune in and calm down. This is when we ask for assistance in getting through the sticky note jungle of tasks. Yes, this is where we get the clarity and support to get through the day with joy, ease and grace. We should not have to function without our biggest source of support.

So when we get flustered and cranky, let's stop, drop and roll over to the nearest teapot. Let the world spin without us for a few moments. It's totally possible to get through incredibly busy, stressful days while feeling a center of calm balance. It is our natural state of grace. We can totally do this. We just need to put on our own oxygen mask first.

In The World:

* Whatever happens, don't skip your morning spiritual practice, which will start the day in the grounding presence of your divine support team and center you for all of your tasks going forward. During the day:

* Take a tea break with some deep calming breaths as you retool your plan.

* Take a short stretch break on your yoga mat or a quick walk in nature.

* Use prayer, affirmations or a mantra as you cook and clean.

* Play music that lifts your spirits.

In The Heart:

* I care for myself as well as I care for others. I treat myself with love, patience and respect, knowing that soul care is not selfish, but essential.

NOVEMBER 21

You Are Not Forgotten

For the grieving, a kind friend. For the discouraged, grace and ease.
For those in need, help and hope. For the troubled, a moment of peace.

Facing the holidays is especially hard for those who have less and the many who have suffered a loss or endured a tragedy. You are not forgotten and you are not alone.

If you are grieving, we acknowledge your loss and will remember your loved one in our hearts. We understand that a holiday table is an especially painful reminder of those who are missing. Make space for your feelings, allowing them to move through your open heart. Let your family and friends be of help.

If you are lonely, sad, sick, discouraged, in financial need or other trouble, we remember you today. May our prayers rise to meet you and to lift you up to a moment of peace. May you continue to hope, in the face of all darkness, that the light will shine again. You are not forgotten and you are not alone.

In The World:

* Be gentle with yourself, and be the guardian of your time and your tenderness at the holidays. Do only what resonates with your heart.

* Don't keep things locked inside. Talk to a friend about your feelings. Find a way to honor your special circumstances this holiday season by lighting a candle, journaling, or sharing a story or picture online.

* Accept help from others—or be of help to others in need. There are countless ways to lift each other up at the holidays and beyond.

* If you have a friend in need, ask if they might want to join you for a holiday dinner. Consider a special way you can honor their story.

In The Heart:

* I honor my unique circumstances at the holidays, acknowledging my loss in ways that make me feel most comfortable.

Gratitude Now

Gratitude is my beacon and my hope. Gratitude is my wind and my wings.
Gratitude is my prayer and my song. Gratitude is my joy and remembering.

Thanksgiving. We woke up today and we gather here together. Let's give thanks for another day of living and loving.

My wish for you is that you have so many things to be grateful for that you can't get your heart around it all. However, if this is not your finest hour, that's okay too. Being thankful isn't all about what's going right. It's about finding the light in what has happened and what's happening right now. The reverberation of gratitude expressed *now* becomes a gift for the future. Like an affirmation, it changes our trajectory and we find ourselves in a new story—one that transcends darkness.

Gratitude now becomes a light, a beacon of hope. It shines into the darkness, and illuminates the next step and the next. It brings the dawn to the dark night, takes some fear out of the fire. It's a lantern, a candle, a ray of sunshine that shows us the rewards of faith.

Gratitude now becomes a vehicle, our wind and our wings. It provides momentum when our lives have stalled. It lifts us up so we can catch the draft and sail effortlessly for a few miles. It's a jump start, an angel wing, a breath that gets us from here to there.

Gratitude now becomes an offering, our prayer and our song. It speaks of promise and sings with notes that harmonize our souls. It connects us with our highest selves and with the flow of grace. It's a familiar melody, a whisper, a prayer from the heart.

Gratitude now becomes soul food, our joy and confidence in our connection with spirit. It feeds us with laughter and reminds us of our strength. It nourishes us when we are starving for good. It's sweet contentment, a soul smile and a reminder to give thanks—yet again.

In The World:

* We gather here together on Thanksgiving to make an offering of gratitude. Let your heart be light—and full. Be content. Allow gratitude to fill your spaces with hope for a beautiful today and a brighter tomorrow.

In The Heart:

* Today I give thanks for my life, for the chance to love and for the wealth of gifts—all things great and small—that surround me now.

~V~

Lighting up Black Friday

Be kind to anyone who crosses your path or crosses your mind today.

Oh Black Friday, are you really a thing? Do we have to lose half our tribe to shopping on a family weekend? The day after the turkey, I want to stay in my sweats and glean wisdom from the matriarchs in the kitchen while heating up leftovers. I want to read the paper and catch up with my journal under a cozy quilt. I want to play with the kids and take a long walk with the cousins. Oh Black Friday, tell me it has all been a bad dream and that you will place the day after Thanksgiving back into the warm, welcoming arms of relaxation.

I know, it's not going to happen. And who am I to judge the glory of Black Friday when I'm really not much of a shopper...at all. For many, I'm sure there is a lot of fun and the chance for a nice dose of holiday spirit in the Black Friday shopping tradition. And a little kindness can make it even brighter.

If you find yourself out there amongst the other gold rushers in the name of incredible deals, you might take this golden opportunity to exercise some holiday cheer by way of kindness. As this is the official start of the holiday shopping season, it stands to reason that the spirit of the holidays should be present: kindness, love, compassion, generosity, joy, peace. These are the hallmarks of this magical time. And they can bring big light into Black Friday.

In The World:

∗ Consider ways to brighten the experience with kindness. You can chat with others while waiting in line; share your unused Macy's coupons; offer a kind word to the mom with the crying baby; compliment what someone is wearing; let someone go ahead of you in a line.

∗ In your mind, you can excuse the people who jostle you; refuse to let anyone else's behavior jar you from your calm kindness; bless people who seem to need blessing as they cross your path.

In The Heart:

∗ I radiate kind, calm and compassionate energy, especially in times when those around me are anxious.

No One Can Shine like You Do

Today I focus on love.

My niece Mary was a track star from a young age. She won countless long distance titles and was being scouted by elite colleges as a sophomore in high school. But low bone mass led to a string of stress fractures, and eventually on a sad spring day of her junior year, after yet another crushing MRI, she knew she had to take a break from running. Mary grieved as any of us would when we lose what we are passionate about.

Then one morning she woke with a thought. "Today is a special day. I will never have today again." She didn't want to miss any more time being angry and disappointed. She was ready to face the day with a new kind of energy—one that focused on what she had instead of what she lost. Her circumstances had not changed. She did.

We have within us the courage to face life's challenges. We have a choice about what kind of energy we carry with us. We can focus on love or focus on lack; we can embody a positive attitude or perpetuate a negative one; we can become a beacon of light or remain in the void. Sounds simplistic and it really is. We bring our energy with us wherever we go and we decide what it's going to be.

If you are in fresh grief or a deeply challenging time in your life, you need to be with that. You will know when the time is right to take small steps toward trusting life. It doesn't have to be now. Just know that your perception of today depends on where your heart lies.

When it is time to shine the light of your love, it will be an amazingly beautiful addition to the light of the world—and to your own life. We need you here, beaming beside us, raising vibrations. No one can shine like you do.

In The World:

✳ Be aware today of what kind of energy you are bringing with you. Make a conscious choice to be who you want to be going forward.

In The Heart:

✳ I cannot control the world, but I can control my response to life's events. I choose love. I choose compassion. I choose gratitude. I choose peace.

❧

Like a Who Down in Whoville

*May you be inspired by giving, changed by love, filled with peace
and touched by miracles.*

It was Thanksgiving, and I was in high school when my mother made the proposition to the family. Actually, it was more like a decree. She said that since two of my brothers were in college and two of us in high school— and it was challenging to know what everyone wanted for Christmas—we were not going to give Christmas gifts within the family anymore. Instead, we would make a priority of spending time together at the holidays, and we would give special status to birthdays. It was a radical idea for the time, and in her gentle little speech, Tiny Guru stealthily stripped Christmas down to the bare wood of a manger.

I remember feeling like it was daring, trusting that Christmas would be wonderful even without gifts, sort of like every Who down in Whoville when they realized Santa was not coming. I told a few friends and they expressed their deepest sympathy, but secretly, my heart grew three sizes that year. "It came without ribbons. It came without tags. It came without packages, boxes or bags...What if Christmas, he thought, doesn't come from a store. What if Christmas, perhaps, means a little bit more." Dr. Seuss and Tiny Guru had us thinking.

We kept up our tradition, and even now I buy few gifts at Christmas, usually somewhat small and somehow meaningful. I like giving angels, ornaments and small framed prints of quotes that the recipient might like. I don't spend a lot of time or money. And if I'm not inspired or am feeling rushed, I make up for it later and the right gift idea usually comes sweetly and easily.

A gift is only the symbol of the love. It is the mirror of the light. It is the reflection of the brilliance. We are all just as whole and beautiful without them. So worry not about giving the perfect gift. That has already been given.

In The World:

✳ Don't sweat the gifts unnecessarily. Write a loving letter and wrap it up. Donate to a charity you know the person supports. Plan a lunch instead of a gift exchange. Each gift is only a placeholder for love.

In The Heart:

✳ I am inspired by giving, changed by love, filled with peace and touched by miracles.

I Am the Ocean

When we reach our limit, healing asks us for gentleness in loss,
patience with tears, kindness with the heart and hope for tomorrow.

Next week I will enjoy a sojourn in Florida and close on my house by the sea. In preparation, I traversed the long empty road to the house of my marriage with the goal of going over some finances and picking up a few pieces of furniture. Seemed simple enough.

We did well with our tender hour of untangling our lives, but when we finished our casual meeting there was still an ocean of feelings left unsaid. The years we shared in that house floated in the air just above the kitchen table. They were in the counters, in the walls, in the pictures. *I need to let go again*, I thought. Our kindness to each other reminded me of our sweet and loving early years together. *I need to let go again.* Then came yet another unexpected wave of longing; yet another love letter of the soul to let go of. The beloved crazy cat.

Living with Ollie was like living with a beautiful, wild tiger. He spent most of his life prowling outside, rarely sitting on a lap, and he had a very limited ability to accept love. But I learned how to love him mightily anyway, and he became my silent companion when I lived there alone. He is in past tense because he is dying. And seeing him for the last time undid me. It is too much to ask to let go of him too.

I thought I had handled the mountains of letting go and still there is more. Maybe there will always be more. Maybe I am the ocean. I crash down in a broken wave on the shore of what was my life and wash away every grounded footprint in my path. I am the ebb and flow of constant change. I am letting go, then I am receding back into wholeness. I am flowing forth with the moon of newness and rebirth and I am ebbing into healing, quiet, relative stasis. I am erasing every footprint; I am creating new ones with each step.

In The World:

* The constant growing and releasing during big life changes can seem unending. Be patient with yourself in the ebb and flow of transition and transformation. Breathe deeply and feel it all without grasping.

In The Heart:

* I am strong and whole. Through the constant change in my life, I remember that all I have loved still lives within my heart.

Your Old Self

Love yourself. See the good. Be calm. Find joy. Give thanks.

In the process of moving, sometimes we discover remnants of our old lives and pieces of our old selves that have been relegated to the past and all but forgotten. Just as we look upon our future selves with love, imagining that the best will unfold, we can look upon our past selves with love, not to dwell or lament, but to honor and offer gratitude.

When I went to the old house the other day, I carted out boxes of tapes from my music career. There were lots of studio recordings, but also live tapes, which can be a tad scary to listen to. Feeling brave last night, I took a random tape of myself and dear friend, sax player Al Williams, at our decade-long house gig at a local restaurant. I braced myself for what might be disappointment. I was expecting "her," the old me, to be pretty rough, because I remember mostly her flaws.

But something very different happened. I listened with new ears. I wasn't critical or horrified. I marveled at our confidence and our unique sound. I could hear the hours of practice that went into the set and was amazed by the soul in some long-forgotten songs. We were having fun and playing our hearts out. I called Al and we listened together through the phone, laughing about those times, those songs, about living the dream.

And I saw in that moment, that in order to love ourselves here and now, we have to love the person we once were, the person who learned the lessons, who was in the trenches, who made mistakes, who survived the pain to get to this point. We need to love her too.

In The World:

* Take a moment to thank the many versions of you that learned the lessons that brought you to this moment. Look upon her with compassion and unconditional love. Forgive her. Accept her. Invite her to be part of you. Honor her for paving the way to who you have become.

In The Heart:

* I am here in this moment because of every experience I have had along the way. I look with compassion on my journey from there to here.

All We Need Is Less

Simplify the holidays.

Sometimes all we need is less. Especially now. To be grateful for less.

If you're having a hard time remembering that this season of the year is filled with holidays that celebrate gratitude, light, love, rebirth, transformation, peace and joy, perhaps we can turn that around a bit, my friend.

We can reclaim this sacred time for ourselves and those we love by doing a little planning, ahead of time. We can create some precious space for what feeds the soul and open the heart to the spirit of the holiday that we're celebrating. We can then weed out what is depleting our time and energy, distracting us from what is most meaningful. Simplify and feel richer for it.

In The World:

Here are a few ways we might simplify the holidays and make more room for joy, downtime and togetherness:

∗   Refine the gift list, shopping and buying for fewer people.

∗   Email friends ahead of time and suggest not exchanging gifts. Plan an ornament exchange or a lunch instead.

∗   Aim to be finished shopping by mid-December with serenity intact.

∗   Bring out only the decorations that truly bring you joy.

∗   Think about the most meaningful way to send cards. Or not. Begin with enough time to send them, or hit send, with thoughts of love.

∗   Think about what might nourish the soul that you'd like more time for—music, reading, quiet contemplation, family, friends, unscheduled downtime, traditional services, volunteering. Make time for the meaningful.

In The Heart:

∗   This year, I connect more deeply with the meaning of the holidays. I have time for what is joyful, loving, peaceful and light-filled.

~ ❦ ~

Advent Waits

Listening. Waiting. Patience. They are all acts of love.

It's quiet. The leaves have finished falling except a few that have held on the longest. I am in solidarity with them. I have waited a long time to move on with my life. In a few days, I close on my house. Then back to Hunters Road for a few more precious weeks of preparation before I make my move.

Often in life we find ourselves in wait; not there yet, but in a place of mystery, expectation and hope. It's not altogether comfortable to be in the space that precedes the main event. It requires patience while we watch and listen for signs. The fact is that most times when we are waiting, we are wishing the waiting was over and the next chapter would ensue already.

But waiting is not idle time, or merely a void between meaningful places. Waiting has sacred purpose. Even our souls love preparation. The holy repose. The quiet that fills us and grows us; readying us for higher consciousness and deeper understanding.

When I was a child, we always had an Advent wreath in the house this time of year. Four Sundays before Christmas, the first candle was lit, carols sung, prayers whispered. The next Sunday two. On the Sunday when all four candles were lit, Christmas was days away. It was an exciting natural calendar marking patience before the celebration.

Our bodies and minds might be shopping, but our souls naturally want to wait. In this Season of Lights, we are preparing a place in our hearts into which rebirth takes place. Let's listen. And be patient. And wait. Let's open and receive, preparing the way—for the greatest love.

In The World:

✳ Be still for a moment now. Allow yourself to thoughtfully examine what makes this time personal and special for you. You can enlist the help of a higher being to help you to find more depth in the holiday season. Make space to contemplate your sacred traditions. They will add meaning to every gift, every party, every song.

In The Heart:

✳ I make space and prepare my heart for the brightest light.

Rest, Dear One, Rest

Simply to be is to do something very important.

When we step away at the height of busyness in a non-stop day, often we are gifted with the clarity, focus and flow to get back in the game and accomplish twice as much, in half the time, with more quality. In a society that values doing, it's good to remember that simply *to be* IS doing something. Something very important.

I know. It's a time of year when life just doesn't allow us to slow down much. A mere fifteen minutes with a cup of tea while the kids are coloring can shift things. A power nap can leave us refreshed and clear. Taking something off the list for today to make breathing room helps enormously. Writing in a time out to rest, however short, has benefits that will reverberate for the rest of the day.

My friend Jen is a nurse practitioner, mom of three and runs a popular inspirational page. She wrote today that she was shutting down the page for however long it took to "feed her soul." Maria, who teaches yoga non-stop and is the mom of hungry teenagers, always makes time in her busiest days for Yoga Nidra. When Lyndy burns out from her caretaker job, she takes a hot bath with an inspirational book. You can find Olga on a long walk in nature when she needs an oasis from her work as a teacher of yoga, meditation and Reiki. In the wise words of self-care leader Eleanor Brownn, "You can't serve from an empty vessel." Amen, my friend.

The actual *doing* that results from this kind of *being* comes in many forms. Below are just a few benefits to encourage you to move *being* up on your list today. It's the most productive thing you can do. Rest, dear one, rest.

In The World:

* During rest time, resistance falls away, so when we resume our tasks, our intuitive wisdom is readily available and solutions more visible. Rest serves our overall health, allowing our bodies to recover from stress. Downtime also brings renewed energy and vitality to mind, body and soul. Last but not least, a holy pause gives us the chance to ask our Spiritual A-Team for a little assistance.

In The Heart:

* I listen to the cues of my mind, body and soul and rest when I am tired. I am precious and worthy of tender loving care.

Image text:
December
Be present.
Let the day flow with grace.
Expect joy. Be positive.
Serve with compassion.
Speak only kindness.
Impart only love.
Never forget you're not alone.
Give thanks for everything.
See goodness in others. mary davis
EveryDaySpirit.net

December Blessings

Be present. Be here. Today, we can guide our thoughts back to the present moment with gentle focus and live fully right where we are.

Let the day flow with grace. Grace flows through us easily when we are in tune with the subtle voice of intuition. Open and listen for guidance.

Expect joy. Be positive. Imagine a fulfilling day unfolding, in which we accomplish much and experience joy in the process. Welcome the light.

Serve with compassion. Acts of service when performed with love lend immeasurable light to our day. Be watchful for ways to serve.

Speak only kindness. Speak only kind words. Think only kind thoughts. Be kind to yourself and to those who cross your path or your mind.

Impart only love. Send out all thoughts and words on the wings of love so that we may love one another, love ourselves, love the unlovable.

Never forget you're not alone. Let's remind ourselves often today that we are always supported, guided and unconditionally loved as we are.

Give thanks for everything. Gratitude will shift the perspective of the day from one of lack to one of abundance. Give constant thanks.

See goodness in others. Each of us has a soul that is made of beauty and love. Assume the best in others so they may rise to their highest light.

❧

Army of Angels

Angels go where we go. Ask for help and keep asking.

I finished packing the car in the pre-dawn pouring rain, covering my computer and printer with towels and tucking them into the only available space in the car—behind the seat. The back of my SUV was stuffed like a jigsaw puzzle with bankers boxes topped off by my heavy and precious green kayak. I had only slivers of visibility out any given window, so my plan was to drive from Virginia to Florida in the right lane. Yes, things were a little iffy from the start.

Buoyed by the vision of closing on my new home, I was undaunted as I drove over the mountains in a blinding storm. I took my time, my tea was hot and I enjoyed the relief of knowing that the hard work of this transition was behind me. That's when I hit a dense wall of fog. I couldn't see five feet in front of me for a long half hour in southern Virginia. Then there was the hour plus of dead stopped traffic in North Carolina for some poor soul's vehicle fire.

As my enthusiasm was starting to wane, traffic began to move and the sun peeked out of some small spots of bright blue sky. Woohoo! Smooth sailing ahead. And just then, a car with two young girls pulled up next to me on the highway, pointing to the back of my car and mouthing the words, "Flat tire!"

Angels. I need angels, I thought. I remembered reading Doreen Virtue's words: "Powerful angels are protecting you, your loved ones and our planet right this very minute. You are safe." I took a deep breath. An exit ramp appeared almost immediately, and I slowly made my way to the stop sign. There was nothing to the right. Nothing to the left. Scrubby wheat-colored bushes filled fields as far as I could see. I wasn't even sure what state I was in. I kept my mind silent and open to direction. And the answers came. (Stay tuned. To be continued tomorrow!)

In The World:

❋   In every decision we make today, let's consult with our inner voice. We have access to all the guidance we will need. Ask and remain open.

In The Heart:

❋   I embody more courage, more peace, more strength and more divine support than I will ever realize. I am growing into my spiritual energy.

Army of Angels - Part 2

I always know the way when I listen with a quiet and open heart.

I knew answers would be forthcoming and I needed to be still. But I was painfully aware of my vulnerability. I resisted getting out of the car to look at the flat tire so as not to call attention to my aloneness—a small woman, traveling solo with a car packed to the gills, in the middle of nowhere—literally.

I started out slowly to the right and *immediately got the hit to make a U-turn.* It felt like a strong urge. Almost a voice but not quite. I listened and reversed course, rolling down the empty two-lane road until I spotted an old gas station sprouting up in the distance like a mirage. Pickup trucks dotted the dusty parking lot; men outside laughed and chatted. I pulled off the road on the far side of the station, wanting to stay under the radar until I knew what to do.

With an open mind I turned over the options. I have roadside assistance, but the spare was buried under everything I owned plus a kayak; and the spare was not going to get me to Florida. Then *I got the strong feeling that my first step was to find out where on earth I was.* With a deep breath, I strode confidently into the old shop and asked the man behind the counter for the address. As he wrote, he looked up with kind eyes and said, "Are you alright?"

I replied steadily, "Do you have a mechanic here?" "No," he said, "but see that dirt road across the street? You'll find a mechanic down there." *It felt right.* I slowly bumped and prayed my way to the only building on that tiny road—the open bays of an auto repair shop. A cheerful mechanic wiped off his hands and took a look at my packed, limping car, shaking his head. "I'm so sorry. We don't do tires." But I *knew* there was a reason I was there. (Story ends tomorrow!)

In The World:

* Let's ask for guidance today and listen with an open mind for answers in the form of intuition, a kind stranger, a strong feeling, a song, a sign.

* If you get the *feeling* you should do something, follow your instincts.

In The Heart:

* I have access to universal wisdom through my intuition. I always know the way when I listen with a quiet and open heart.

Army of Angels - Part 3

Angels guide me to perfect solutions with ease and grace.

The happy mechanic went on to advise me not to wait for roadside assistance as it was getting late in the day. "How about I put air in the tire and that will get you to the Goodyear place about two miles away." His directions included turning left at Mary's Diner, which felt like a very good sign indeed.

A few minutes later, I turned into a tiny Goodyear shop at the edge of a small South Carolina town. A young man behind the counter looked up as I entered, and asked how I was. Like my other two angel messengers, he exuded compassion. It was just enough to melt my composure, and I dissolved into tears as I explained that I got a flat tire driving from Virginia to Florida. In my mind, I finished that sentence with *to start my life over after my marriage ended.* I was suddenly exhausted and could barely breathe.

"Give me your keys," he said. He started out the back door. "Don't you want me to tell you which car is mine?" I asked. "I'll find it," he said as the screen slammed. Alone in the shop, I paced in circles as tears streamed down my face. These were more than flat tire tears. These were years-of-tired tears.

About ten minutes passed when I had a stomach-churning realization. My car held everything of material value to me—all of my computers, my phone, my kayak—and I had just given my keys to a stranger. I ran out the front door to where I had left my car and it was gone. I re-entered the shop just as the young man was coming in the back door. He set my keys down on the counter and said, "You're all set. That will be twelve dollars."

I'm sure the people back at Mary's Diner heard me scream. The amazing army of angels had me back on the Interstate in thirty minutes...flat.

In The World:

* When things go sideways today, suspend judgment and trust that an easy resolution is in sight. Believe it. Enlist the help of angels. Ask and listen. Receive and follow your intuition.

In The Heart:

* My angels lead me to perfect solutions with ease and grace.

Choices at the Crossroads

I trust my inner voice.

By looking at the moments in the previous story where spirit interceded, we can see how it's possible to be transported from one helpful circumstance to the next when we ask for assistance and listen to the inner voice. The choices made at each crossroad can apply to almost any situation we might find ourselves in.

Listen to the call of spirit in your life to assist others. What if the young girls in the car on the Interstate didn't tell me I had a flat? I hadn't heard the rumble yet. I may have passed the exit that held all of the solutions for me at that moment. Something compelled them to flag me down. Spirit works within us for the highest good of others too.

Trust and act on your instincts. They are always right. As I turned right at the bottom of the exit ramp, I had the feeling I was going in the wrong direction. I immediately turned around. If I had not, I would have missed all the angels who helped me. I may have missed the closing on my house. Rumi's wisdom reminds us, "There is a voice that doesn't use words. Listen."

Sometimes messages from spirit don't make perfect sense. Follow them anyway. As I sat outside the gas station deciding what to do, I could have checked Google Maps on my phone to see where I was. That never occurred to me. The clear message was to *go inside and ask where you are.* If I didn't go in, I would not have been led to the happy mechanic.

Trust your gut feelings. They, too, are signposts. I didn't have to trust the happy mechanic's plan. But as soon as he mentioned Mary's Diner in his directions, I got a zing and an overwhelming sense that all was well.

In The World:

✳ Today, in a moment of uncertainty, silently ask spirit to lead. The request can be directed to God, angels, spirit—whatever or whoever is your higher power. Then gently listen for direction. Let it be easy. Trust and act on it.

In The Heart:

✳ I thank my mind for its wonderful work, then ask it to take its marching orders from the inner voice of my soul.

Sanderling Gurus

Find the beauty in imperfect imbalance.

I am centered. I am balanced. I am calm. But it's the holidays, so no, not really. I have the nagging feeling that I should be these things at all times, which sort of adds to the imbalance. Maybe wanting to be centered all the time is not a realistic ideal. Do ya think? And perhaps imbalance has some perks.

I went to run things by my favorite little beach birds. Sanderlings are hilarious, bulbous little guys, teetering on stick legs upon which they sprint, leaning forward at lightning speed—like the Usain Bolt of the Sand Olympics. They have amazing instincts and timing, chasing the surf out as it ebbs, wildly poking around for a fresh meal, and racing back toward shore as the tide flows in, so as not to be washed out to sea. Down and back they run.

Then I saw that one of them had only one stick leg, hopping in rhythm alongside his friends. He was perfectly balanced, even when standing still—a little ball atop a stick, calm and steady. Oh no! There was *another* with only one leg! What happened here? Shark appetizers? A mysterious rash of Sanderling amputations? Then, a miracle. They untucked their other little legs!

I came to learn that, like other long-legged birds, they stand on one leg *on purpose* to save energy and retain heat. They get so comfortable on one leg that they don't bother to untuck the other one for a while. They practice balancing in challenging circumstances. What wise little Sanderling gurus.

So instead of wishing our imbalance away, maybe we need some time here on one leg, getting used to it. We can approach it as practice for retaining strength, facing challenges and increasing our joy in *all* circumstances. Then when we put our other leg down and come back to full speed, we will know the depth of our soul's energy, and how truly blessed we were all along.

In The World:

* Be with your imperfect imbalance today. Find the beauty in it. Let the day flow with grace as it is, instead of as you wish it would be.

In The Heart:

* I am centered. I am balanced. I am calm. And if not, that's okay too.

Saint Francis Returns

Love is the best gift of all.

Of all the kind souls on the planet, some are of the angelic, exceedingly thoughtful variety. They are those people who remember unique things about who we are and what we love. They are those who have a special knack for giving meaningful gifts that we treasure.

Dick and Helen are two such people. After years of spending their winters in Florida, they decided it was time to sell their second home and stay put in their native New Hampshire. I was the fortunate one who bought their home, just down the street from where my parents lived for decades. In fact, they knew each other back in the day, before Dad died and Mom moved inland to assisted living.

On the back patio of my parents' house lived a beautiful Saint Francis statue that was my nature-loving mother's pride and joy. He holds a cross and has a peaceful bird on his shoulder. Mom painted him a light chalk blue distressed with white, giving him a heavenly glow. She washed and blessed him often, and I'm sure he blessed her right back. When she moved, she gave the heavy, holy, cement mystic to her neighbor Ray as she no longer had a yard to admire him in.

Remembering this, the week before closing, Dick and Helen visited Ray, and they made a beautiful plan to relocate Saint Francis to what would be my new patio. When I arrived for the walk-through with my mother so she could visit with her old friends again, there was Francis, beaming his familiar love at us from the patio. Mom and I could barely breathe through our tears. Our hearts overflowed with gratitude and the honor of witnessing such thoughtfulness.

Love transforms little things into big things.

In The World:

*   In this time of gift giving, we might consider what someone really values and finds meaningful; gifts of the heart, of the spirit, of love, of joy; gifts that reflect who we are and what we love. It may be something you already own.

In The Heart:

*   Each day I become a kinder, more thoughtful, more mindful version of myself.

When Things Are Too Good

I am blessed. I am content. I am grateful.

I am a walking, breathing *Thank You*. All of the small treasures of beauty and light that surround me elicit overflowing gratitude—every warm sunrise morning; each breath of salt air and glimpse of the ocean. Yet still, I am just a little "off." I'm not sure how to handle so much joy and alignment. Can things be *too* good? After years of struggle and challenge, and countless affirmations that all is well, I don't seem to know how to act when all is...actually well.

Maybe I need some joy therapy. Happy practice. What is wrong with me that I can't feel the big, dancing *Woohoo!?* I just bought the little house of my dreams, and it's about a hundred steps from the ocean. The previous owners left me countless beautiful things in a most thoughtful way. I have family close by and it is the perfect place to begin my new life. Don't get me wrong—it's not that I'm not happy and exceedingly grateful. It's that I know there is another level of the *acceptance of abundance* that I have not allowed into my soul yet.

The other day I heard the wise and wonderful author Wes Moore say in an interview with Oprah: "You are not here because of someone else's benevolence. You are here because this is where you belong." He went on to talk about "Imposter Syndrome" and how so many of us have trouble believing in our value, wisdom and worth. Perhaps that's it. Somewhere deep down, I feel unworthy. So I ask for the grace to offer deep gratitude while learning to accept abundance. I ask for the grace not only to believe in miracles, but also to receive them.

In The World:

❋   Ask for the grace to open and fully receive, believing that divine mind puts no limits on abundance. The limits are all in your mind. Release them.

❋   Ask for the grace to accept yourself, faults and all, as a person worthy of great joy, beauty, fulfillment and dreams come true.

In The Heart:

❋   Even when I am unable to reciprocate, I receive graciously. When a friend or God gives me a gift, I know my gratitude and joy are enough.

DECEMBER 9

A New Standard

Wishing you a day filled with peace, love and joy.

Most of us gain weight at the holidays because so much is on our shoulders. We are expected to be psychics as we shop online for the perfect gifts for our beloveds, sight unseen. We are expected to clean and decorate the house, host the family in addition to their pets and cook for the troops while looking our brightest in an Ugly Sweater. We are expected to be the communications director, sifting through barrels of extra emails, texts and social media posts, wishing well to friends, extended family in other countries and everyone we ever went to school with—in addition to our real jobs.

Yes, despite our best poinsettia hairbands, we might be stretched a little thin.

So I suggest we revise our standards and allow the messages of the season—peace, love and joy—to serve as our guide. Similar to the Marie Kondo method, where an item is salvaged or pitched based on the joy it brings, let us consider each extra activity on our list and ask the question, "Can I do this while still retaining my peace (composure and calm), love (goodwill toward all people and pets), and joy (a good mood)?" If the answer is *no*, we have options. When we revise our standards, we actually lift our spirits.

In The World:

* Make shopping easy on yourself: a gift card, something that you have or can make easily, a lunch in January, a donation, a loving letter, school supplies for a shelter instead. Start your list early next year, picking up meaningful small gifts along the way. Suggest ending or replacing the gift exchange.

* Remember you don't have to cook and bake everything. There are lots of pre-made options that will leave your peace, love and joy intact.

* Don't feel pressured to reply to every electronic card that comes in. Put them in a folder and read them at your leisure. They are a gift, not homework.

In The Heart:

* I respect myself enough to allow peace, love and joy to be the measure of my activities this week. I protect my right to make room for the joys of the spirit and the peace to hear the voice of my soul.

DECEMBER 10

Loving Messengers

Spirit speaks in ways that only the heart can hear.

I returned from my Florida adventure yesterday and took off for the post office this morning to pick up my mail. Deep in thought as I drove down Hunters Road on my way home, a brilliant red cardinal sailed across the street, nearly grazing my windshield. Oh joy! One small bird on one little road, and I knew that heaven and earth had merged for a moment. I laughed and sang out a hearty *Thank you!*, knowing I was on the right track with what I was pondering at that moment. My cardinal always appears at the crossroads.

For many years, cardinal sightings have been spirit messengers for me. They have appeared as signs of hope, grace, faith, joy and confirmation of a particular direction or validation of a thought. Their unmistakable color and unique song catch our attention even in the most turbulent, distracted moments, and they bring us gifts of love from the spirit realm in all seasons.

The day my mom turned sixty, a cardinal visited her home and tapped on the window for the entire day. Since then, he has visited regularly at auspicious times and she sees her "Angel Bird" as a spiritual gift. A friend of mine had a cardinal turn up the evening her friend died, and she had the distinct feeling it was a sign from her friend that she was safe and sound on The Other Side.

There are countless stories of cardinals or butterflies showing up in prominent places soon after a death or when one is thinking of a loved one who has passed on. It's the feeling of *knowing* that makes these events especially significant, as the inner voice of intuition is our litmus test of truth. We know when something holds meaning.

Spirit speaks to us through an open heart, loud and clear, and sometimes in a beautiful shade of red.

In The World:

* Allow the comfort of spirit messengers into your soul. Nature, in communion with spirit, speaks in ways that only the heart can hear.

In The Heart:

* I am open to receive comfort and joy through the beauty of nature. What catches my eye may be a loving message for me.

A Gift from Spirit

Pure, unconditional love and kindness are always healing, always helpful, always welcomed. When in doubt, just be kind.

Yes, spirit is always speaking to us with messages that guide our way. These messages arrive through "Angel Birds" and friends, through moments of silence and through our very thoughts. And *just* as I wrote these words a cardinal flew into the tree closest to the window, singing an enthusiastic song of agreement!

In the days since Adam's last drinking adventure, I have been considering a completely different tactic: to back off my phone calls nudging him toward meetings, sponsors and steps, and just offer lovingkindness and silent prayer. I have been torn, and it has been taking up space in my heart. I don't want to give up on him in any way, but I have the nagging feeling that my constant pressure is hurting his already open wounds.

This morning, as I sat at my writing desk distracted by deer, a frog chorus, a bigger-than-usual snake and some Carolina wrens and their mini-mes, I was clearly prompted by spirit to open a drawer in my desk that I hadn't cleaned out in years. My eyes went to a tiny gem, *The Pocket Pema Chodron*, and I opened it randomly to a little story about one of her meditation students, Dan. He had been doing well with his drug and alcohol problem until a recent binge that had Chodron quite upset. *Well isn't this a timely story,* I marveled.

"You should never have expectations for other people. Just be kind to them," her teacher Trungpa Rinpoche told her. He said she should help Dan in small ways and bring happiness into his life by any means possible. He reminded her that setting goals for others is asking them to live up to our own ideals. Instead, we should just be kind.

That was *exactly* the spirit message I needed.

In The World:

✳ Pure, unconditional love and kindness are always healing, always helpful, always welcomed. When in doubt, just be kind.

In The Heart:

✳ Today I notice when I am confusing my goals with the goals of others. I support my loved ones with kindness, right where they are.

The Soul Voice

We are one with all wisdom and love.

The flat tire story is still in my heart, now a week later. It's a roadside example of what we all have access to—guidance from something greater than ourselves. A Course in Miracles puts it sweetly: "Let me remember I am one with God...for God is our Companion as we walk the world a little while." Or drive as the case may be.

We can live in this space of connection and clairvoyance. We are made for this. And to that end, here is an attempt to find worthy words with which to reel in these lessons to serve as a reminder when we next forget.

In The World:

* The soul voice that speaks through our intuition is available to all of us. We are each made of the same particles with a consciousness that can tune in to the frequency of universal wisdom and divine love.

* The use of this internal GPS is dependent on our ability to quiet the chatter of the mind. Once we turn down the static—and we *can*—positive messages for the highest good of all are more easily intuited.

* This connection with source is what we are always seeking: All love, all joy, all wisdom. Being one with God is not a grandiose idea or one reserved for the holiest of holy people. It's ours to experience now.

* We don't have to try hard to tune in; it's like an underground spring that bubbles up when we *let go* of the many details we feel compelled to hold and the countless things we want to control. It's like suspended animation, an exhale in which we trust the unknown and *allow* the guidance to come.

* In the space of listening, everything is holy. Our awareness is heightened, and every person, creature and thing plays a vital role. We see ordinary things in a new light. We stand taller, strengthened by newfound insight. Contentment creeps in. We feel more generous. When the soul voice leads, an elegant harmony ensues.

In The Heart:

* I am always connected to the source of all wisdom and all love. I listen and allow guidance to lead me. My mind, body and soul are in harmony.

Mindfulness and the Send Button

Anger is multiplied in the presence of anger.
Anger is divided in the presence of love.

I almost hit Send last night on an angry letter, but in the nick of time I was jolted out of my self-righteous coma. Thank you, Facebook Angel.

A few times a day, I check my daily posts on four social media sites to see what's going on and answer comments. I'm sure you know that when Facebook decides it's time for a change, things on your page can go sideways. Business pages have extra boxes that seem to change just when you've gotten your page the way you want it. On their behalf, I am grateful to Facebook every single day for the forum and for the precious community of souls that I love so deeply. But as business people, it's uncomfortable when someone else changes what our community sees first.

Last night I opened my page to find, front and center, images from over two years ago. I had ads running and wanted new visitors to my page to see current material. I tried to get rid of the dinosaur posts but they wouldn't budge. So, I searched the problem, and there were pages of rages from businesses with the same issue. I read many of them and it got my anger column all stirred up. We talk here about kindness being contagious. Well, methinks anger is too.

Someone posted a direct link to give Facebook feedback on the matter, so I hammered out a scathing letter with lines like, "On what planet would a business want to be introduced with two-year-old photos?" As I read it through to edit my zingers, I thought, *What am I doing? There's a person who is going to read this. There's a soul on the other end who is going to get my blast of dark energy. Is this who I want to be?*

So, I added, "Dear Beautiful Facebook Friends: I really appreciate your hard work, but..." and that changed the whole tone. I signed off, "With love and light to you tonight." And no lie, ten minutes later, my page was fixed.

In The World:

* In all you write today, be aware of the way it might feel to be on the receiving end. Be peaceful. Especially in the line of customer service, be patient and compassionate to those who are trying to assist you.

In The Heart:

* I reflect peace and kindness in person and in the cyber universe.

~✦~

The Playbook of Saint Nick

May your holidays be filled with the spirit of joy, the wisdom of sight,
the heart of love and the soul of light.

Saint Nick was a bit more fiery than jolly. Born in the year 270 to wealthy, devout parents who both died when Nicholas was young, he was raised by his uncle and became a monk and later a beloved bishop in what is now Turkey.

It is said that from the time his parents died, he was devoted to giving away his wealth to the poor. There are stories of him as an anonymous benefactor, throwing bags of gold into windows under cover of darkness. These bags sometimes landed in shoes and stockings left by the hearth to dry. He became associated with gift-giving but was also known to assist sailors at sea, protect children who were in danger, and was a vocal defender of his faith, paying the price with long years of imprisonment. So many miracles are attributed to him that he was called, "Nicholas the Wonderworker." Saint Nick was love in action.

Bringing some wonder and miracles into our gift-giving might be just what we need to fire up our holiday spirit. This fierce, compassionate, opinionated monk created his own playbook of living and giving. And this year, we can too.

In The World:

* We can fill the holidays with *the spirit of joy* by putting as much emphasis on enjoying our families and friends as we do on shopping.

* We can fill the holidays with *the wisdom of sight* by making space and time for personal contemplation of the meaning of the season in our hearts.

* We can fill the holidays with *the heart of love* by being miracle-workers of thoughtfulness, giving within our means and passing on to our kids by example some creative and loving alternatives to traditional gifts.

* We can fill the holidays with *the soul of light* by channeling Saint Nick through our generosity toward those in real need at the holidays.

In The Heart:

* I create space in my life for contemplation and define for myself what form of giving resonates with joy in my heart.

Into the Hands of God

Be the strength, Lord, in my struggle. Be the dawn in my dark.
Be the calm in my chaos. Be the haven for my heart.

We need not carry our burdens alone for another day. Stop now and rest for a moment. Breathe deeply and exhale fully. Then put your pride aside and surrender everything to your higher power. Surrender your mind, surrender your fears and surrender your darkness—to the divine. Today is a new day and you are not in it alone.

Surrender comes first. It is a humble act that brings us power far greater than our own. We step aside and let the divine take the lead, and on this alternate path, we become a channel through which unlimited clarity and wisdom can flow. We align with divine mind and become fertile ground for breakthroughs, miracles and infinite possibility.

We don't surrender once, or twice, but over and over again. Any time we feel ourselves sinking under the weight of the world, we let go and let God. In every struggle, we ask for strength. In every dark night of the soul, we ask for the dawn. In every situation where chaos overwhelms the heart, we ask for calm. In every storm, we ask to be moored in a safe haven. It is through surrender that the comfort appears and the answers are made clear.

When we surrender our burdens into the hands of God, we are no longer alone, but lifted by a force of love far more powerful than our pain. We are always heard and always answered with grace.

In The World:

＊ Today, tear down the veil of separation and make an offering of your situation. Allow limited thinking to be replaced with calm, hope and light.

＊ Each time fear returns, surrender with a gentle prayer, having faith that a perfect plan is manifesting miracles for you in its perfect time. *Be the strength, Lord, in my struggle. Be the dawn in my dark. Be the calm in my chaos. Be the haven for my heart.*

In The Heart:

＊ I surrender my burdens into the hands of my higher power and make an offering of every part of my life.

~❧~

Be Amazed

Every moment is a sacred moment.

Every day we bear witness to the sacred as it spins by in the guise of a plain old everyday moment. It's in the sweet sun ray that warms the skin. It's in the softly falling snow that blankets the earth in silence. It's in the full moon that shows her face at sunset as we carpool home. It's in the paint chip colors of flowers and birds.

Maybe the sacred is a little harder to locate in overwhelming stacks of paperwork on the desk, in car repairs, in dental work. The sacred can be impossible to find in the pain of a child, the death of a spouse or a terminal diagnosis.

But there is love in the fabric of all things outside in the world and inside the universe of the heart. To locate the coordinates of divinity, the only tool we need is awareness. And maybe to gently remember that each moment bears the gift of life and of the chance to love. This small moment, this precious day will not come again. We have never seen a day like this before.

If we turn our gaze ever so slightly and view our day as saturated in sacred sights and sounds, then this moment right here, right now, where we are, broken and messy, is a holy moment.

Maybe we could just listen and be held. Maybe we could stop and be present to small chances and offerings, knowing that something greater is between the lines, beneath our wings, over our heads, at our backs. Right where we are, on this beautiful, amazing day, every moment is sacred.

In The World:

✳   Allow yourself to be amazed today. In the best and worst possible moments, be aware, be in awe, be grateful and be transformed.

In The Heart:

✳   I am thankful for this precious moment and for the chance to love. I seek and find the holy in the small and the sacred in all things.

Beautiful Small Things

Notice something beautiful. Appreciate the gift. Give thanks.

It's almost sunset and I sit weary in pajama pants and my coziest sweatshirt at the little table outside. The sky is a dark, ultramarine blue and the sun has already caught the edges of the clouds, painting them orange and gold. The birds are starting their evening conversations—more relaxed, melodic versions of their morning songs. The tree frogs are revving up and the pond frogs are croaking. A half-moon spies down on me from a perfect vantage point directly overhead.

The horses were on the field just moments ago, and I was excited for a visit to sort through the events of the day, but they have moved on. I need them now.

I circled this very table, round and round on the altar of this morning's sunrise, offering thanks. With my move coming soon, my gratitude for this place of sweet energy is overflowing. I drink in the sights and sounds with great love and thirst. I take pictures with my heart. I marvel at the gift. I am in awe of the inhabitants of this plot that I borrow.

But between sunrise and sunset swirled decades of memories as I made my last trip to the old house, carrying out, among the pictures and CDs, the box that holds my wedding dress and the container that once held Angela's ashes.

Now, as darkness descends on the field and on this day, as the nighttime creatures stir and their daytime friends rest, I stop and notice the beautiful small things. The beautiful small things that bring my heart home to this moment. The beautiful small things that resurrect my pain and lingering sadness. The beautiful small things that heal me, that bless me, that embrace me.

The beautiful small things that remind me of the gifts.

In The World:

* When our energy is fragmented, the sights and sounds of small, beautiful things can ground us and bring us back to joy, peace and gratitude.

In The Heart:

* I notice beauty. I appreciate the gift. I humbly give thanks.

꧂

Tangled Lights and All

Enjoy the small moments. Do one thing at a time with love.

My father was very nearsighted, so when he took off his glasses to don his yearly Santa suit, he couldn't see a thing. My mother, holding back laughter, would lead him from the laundry room, where the pillows were stuffed in and the white beard was attached, to the front door, where he would ring the bell like any polite visitor. Even though we had a fireplace in our California home, Santa always surprised us, appearing at the front door about an hour after my dad left for the hardware store. Sad how Dad always missed Santa.

After gently holding each of us on his giant knee and asking us if we had been good, he would give us our gifts. Santa then left out the front door with my mother stealthily guiding him to the homes of some lucky neighbor kids. Flanders Road lore has it that one year, blind as he was, Santa waved and joyfully called out, "Ho, Ho, Ho and a Merry Christmas!" to a mailbox.

I asked Mom about this many years later, and she said they had so much fun doing that each year. We were four children spanning six years, so there was about a decade of Santa visits until the last no longer believed. Ten years of laughing their hearts out on Christmas Eve.

The holiday season is a chance to bring new magic to old traditions. Each time we sit to untangle the lights, unwrap the ornaments or decorate the mantle, may we be present to the traditions and memories we are making in our hearts now. Each time we hear the songs, bake the cookies, and light the special candles, may we be present to the love upon which the holiday was born. May we be mindful of the joy that lives right where we are—tangled lights and all.

In The World:

✳ Slow down, even if the world is speeding up. Be present, even if the world is distracted. Let your heart be light. Enjoy the moments. Do one thing at a time, with love.

In The Heart:

✳ I enjoy the small moments of this season and celebrate love in every small way that it enters my life today.

Be Still and Know

Allow stillness to enter your bones and unfurl your soul.

Take a breath and remember. Inhale. Exhale and soften. Know that you are in the flow of grace and that all is well. Know that you have access to all of the wisdom you will ever need and that this moment of stillness is a precious gift. It is our greatest investment in today.

Here are just a few of the many reasons why we find power in the pause:

It encourages a sense of calm and well-being;

It allows us to make more considered decisions;

It activates the soul's wisdom from which we are guided;

It reminds us of our expansive nature;

It lowers our blood pressure;

It calms the chatter of the mind;

It opens the heart to the inner voice;

It heightens our intuition and clairvoyance;

It allows us to release our worries and fears;

It reveals the beauty and serenity that reside within;

It provides clarity from which to imagine the highest possible outcomes.

In The World:

✳ Our contemplative practice offers countless gifts any time of year. Meditation and prayer soothe the soul and transform us through daily practice. The rewards reach across all aspects of our being. Take a breath today and remember. Allow stillness to enter your bones and unfurl your soul. Be still and know.

In The Heart:

✳ I have a calm center from which all wisdom arises.

Lessons Learned from Loss

You live in my heart. You walk on my road.
You breathe of my air. You dance in my soul.

Today is her birthday. My daughter Angela would be 20 years old today. She was quietly stillborn except for the sound of Kathleen Battle's sacred collection, *Grace.* I am sometimes asked by newly bereaved parents what the view is like from here and what follows are my ever-evolving lessons. Every walk with grief is unique. Take only what resonates in your heart.

In The World:

✳ *There was the me before loss and the me after loss.* Nothing from my previous life seemed remotely familiar in my new reality. I cracked into a million pieces and was completely disoriented. It was impossible to return to who I was. A new me was assembled.

✳ *I lost the illusion that I had any idea what my life would look like tomorrow, or next week, or next month.* When something happens so traumatically, so tragically, so suddenly, it blows away the false belief that we have control over anything in our lives. We don't. Those who know loss are in on this secret, and it makes us live more in the present. I still don't hang my hat on any future plans.

✳ *I am now intimately connected to everyone who has suffered any kind of loss.* The details vary but the bond remains. I know the crushing pain in the chest that makes it hard to breathe; the burn behind the eyes, the constant lump in the throat. When her heart stopped, I was an instant member of the club of compassion for all loss. I treasure the honor of being one with suffering.

✳ *My life is a deeper ocean.* Small inconveniences are inconsequential. I don't spend time on small worries or small talk. I have little patience for negativity and a greater appreciation of the precious nature of life.

✳ *As far down as I had slipped under the weight of pain, I can now tolerate more joy on the other end of the spectrum.* Pain is more painful, yet beauty is more beautiful, joy more joyful.

✳ *I love her as much as ever, and her memory is comforting.* She continues to change me. I look forward to her birthday as a sacred holiday. When I cry tears for her today, they are tears of indescribable beauty.

In The Heart:

✳ You are always and forever in my heart.

Lightness of Being

Let your heart be light.

Today in the Northern Hemisphere we celebrate the winter solstice, which marks the onset of winter and the darkest day of the year. From this place of darkness, we hold on to hope for the light and warmth to come. We face the possibilities of birth and rebirth, of blessings and miracles. We have faith that from this cold yet fertile ground will grow new life from seed to bloom.

The winter holidays of many faith traditions begin in the dark and use light as an important symbol of hope. Hanukkah is the eight-day Jewish Festival of Lights, celebrating the miracle of one day's sacred oil lighting a lamp for a full eight days. The miracle is symbolized by the nine candles of the menorah candelabra, which are lit on successive nights until all are aglow on the last evening. Christians celebrate the birth of Jesus in the 45-day season of Advent and Christmas with wreaths, trees and Nativity scenes illuminated by candles, lights and stars. A special candlelight service is held on Christmas Eve to welcome "The Light of the World." In the seven-day African-American celebration of Kwanzaa, light is used to symbolize seven principles, with one candle illuminating one principle each night until all candles are lit.

These and other winter holidays fall at a time of relative darkness in the bleak mid-winter. They begin in the dark and are illuminated one candle, one light and one star at a time. They symbolize a gradual awakening of hope, faith and possibilities. They are the beginning, the birth, the rebirth of the flame.

The harsh brightness of the commercial holidays is, in many ways, the antithesis of these celebrations. This time of year is all about gentle faith in miracles. Stay with the light of your heart and remember that now is the time to begin again in hope. Now is the time to begin again in peace. Now is the time to begin again in joy. Tomorrow, there will be more light. And the next day, more light. And grace pours in with the light.

In The World:

＊ Celebrate the return of light today by burning a candle to represent light in the darkness and the illumination of your awakening.

In The Heart:

＊ My heart sings in the darkness with hope in the dawn of a new and beautiful tomorrow.

~🙟~

Saying Goodbye

It is written on my heart.

Leaving is hard. Endings are difficult. Moving is disorienting. Changes descend upon us—big changes in addition to the small ones that are pelting us all the time—sometimes catching us unawares. It is the nature of life.

Last night, I ran an errand in my tiny adopted town: the town that welcomed me when I finally made the break from my old life, the town of 185 isolated, nature-loving souls at the foot of the mountains. Snow had just begun to fall on happy garland-covered street lamps, and the Christmas lights danced on familiar trees and historic buildings. The church bells rang as I stood still in the post office parking lot. I looked hard at the scene that I would not see many times again. I wrote it on my heart. *Stay within*, I whispered. *I don't want to lose you.*

I did the same thing when my daughter died. I took a picture in my mind and I wrote it on my heart. I knew I could never forget those moments holding her because they were written within. Over the years, the ink dissolves a little and becomes part of our cells, our blood, our energy. It doesn't go away. It becomes one with us.

We will all live through a series of leavings. Spirit takes us on a scavenger hunt toward our purpose, yet away from people, places and things that we love and that have altered us. Ultimately these people, places and things accompany us from their new outpost inside. Everywhere we've been, everyone we've loved—it is all still here, written on our hearts.

In The World:

＊ Remember today that you have lost nothing in all of the leavings of your life. You grow fuller and stronger because of where you have been and who you have loved. You have agreed to these lessons and will meet again.

In The Heart:

＊ I now honor the loving memories that I have moved on from in my life. I bless them, I thank them and I carry them with me always.

꧂

The First Christmas

*We have within us a North Star that always leads back
to peace, love and joy.*

Once my family was invited to a nativity party hosted by some dear friends who have travelled the world, collecting nativity scenes along the way. They had set them up on tables throughout the house, with tiny lights twinkling around them like stars. Some were bright and celebratory, some muted and gentle. They were crafted from a variety of materials from wood, to ceramic, to banana leaves. Some were huge, taking up most of a table, and some were tiny, with figures no more than an inch high. And they all had one thing in common.

They all expressed great abundance in the backdrop of lack. There was great joy, yet an absence of most of the things we associate with fun. There was radiant peace, in the midst of what we usually think of as turmoil—exposure to the elements, no clean beds or running water. There was great love in the presence of displacement and division. Each nativity showed wealth in the setting of extreme poverty.

It's no wonder that we sometimes have trouble feeling the spirit of the season. The level of gratitude and humility in the first Christmas story is unimaginable. Today we expect, we demand, we desire, we climb, and when we fall short, we consider ourselves lacking. We are disconnected; our outward idea of abundance is not reflective of the riches within.

Having material abundance of any magnitude is not wrong. It is when we substitute it for inner peace that we feel empty. What we have is not *who we are*. We are unchangeable; a reflection of the divine child in the nativity scene. We are already rich. We have within us a North Star that always leads back to peace, love, joy and abundant blessings. When we lead from there, we *are* the spirit of the season.

In The World:

✳   Take a few moments to contemplate the simplicity of the original story and to connect with how you want to receive the season of lights in your heart.

In The Heart:

✳   I am an unchangeable expression of divine love, rich with blessings, abundant with peace, filled with light.

Silent Night, Holy Night

All is calm. All is bright.

Christmas was fast approaching, and Father Joseph Mohr had a problem. As pastor of Saint Nicholas Church, he was responsible for presenting an inspirational program for his congregation at the Christmas Eve service. Music played an essential role in the Mass, and the organ at the church was broken and would not be fixed in time.

Fr. Mohr remembered he had written a poem several years earlier about the night when the angels announced the birth of Christ. He took his poem to the local teacher and church organist, Franz Gruber, and asked if he would write a melody on guitar that could be sung at the Christmas Eve service.

On December 24, 1818, in the tiny town of Oberndorf outside of Salzburg in what is now Austria, the new composition, "Silent Night," was sung for the very first time. The people of Oberndorf adored *"Stille Nacht, Heilige Nacht,"* and it spread to several other Alpine communities. It was soon adopted by two well-known musical families (think Von Trapp Family in "The Sound of Music") and the song spread through all of Europe, where to this day it is often reserved for December 24th only, in a simple, candlelit moment at the end of the Christmas Eve service.

"Silent Night" has since been translated into hundreds of languages and dialects, and is one of our most beloved Christmas carols. Would this sweetly inspired song have come to light if the organ had not been broken? Out of what seemed like a problem, or at least a significant inconvenience for Fr. Mohr, came great beauty, and a Christmas gift to the world.

In The World:

✳ Today, may we approach our challenges as possibilities. May we approach our problems as opportunities. May we be open to receiving answers in creative ways.

In The Heart:

✳ I open to the possibility that my problems are gifts to grow me into my potential and to add richness to my experience of life and love.

Comfort and Joy

Rejoice!

May today bring us simple things in simple packages. Easy-to-use things. Things we can tuck into our hearts and don't require instructions or batteries. Simple things like love and peace, like comfort and joy.

It's a simple day really. One that is filled with innocence, humility and lack of pretense. *Isn't there anyone who knows what Christmas is all about?* wails Charlie Brown in my favorite holiday movie scene. *Sure, Charlie Brown, I can tell you what Christmas is all about,* says Linus quietly and calmly. He's got this.

He drags his blanket to the stage and asks for light. (Which is a good idea for us today—asking for light.) Then with the lisp of a child and the simplicity of just another day hanging with his friends, he recites Luke:

And there were in the same country shepherds abiding in the field, keeping watch over their flock by night. And, lo, the angel of the Lord came upon them, and the glory of the Lord shone round about them: and they were sore afraid. And the angel said unto them, Fear not: for, behold, I bring you tidings of great joy, which shall be to all people. For unto you is born this day in the city of David a Saviour, which is Christ the Lord. And this shall be a sign unto you; Ye shall find the babe wrapped in swaddling clothes, lying in a manger. And suddenly there was with the angel a multitude of the heavenly host praising God, and saying, Glory to God in the highest, and on earth peace, good will toward men.

That's what Christmas is all about, Charlie Brown.

May today bring us simple things in simple packages. May the holiday you celebrate bring meaning and peace within. May the love of Christmas expand in your heart today, tomorrow and each day of the year. May there be peace on earth, goodwill toward all.

In The World:

✳ Breathe in the love. Imagine arms wide, face toward the sky, feeling peace and gratitude. Relax your mind, bask in your spiritual practice and perhaps even listen for the angels. You have the greatest love— right here, right now. Allow it to enter your soul.

In The Heart:

✳ My heart is open and I receive the simple yet radiant moments of Christmas.

❦

The Greatest Love

Inhale gratitude. Exhale love.

For the joy, relief, exhaustion and love of yesterday: *inhale gratitude, exhale love.*

For faith and grace to magnify in our hearts and raise us even higher in the coming year: *inhale gratitude, exhale love.*

For the baking and cleaning, for the songs and the smell of evergreen, for candles and cardinals: *inhale gratitude, exhale love.*

For meals celebrated, family and friends united, miles traveled, moments shared: *inhale gratitude, exhale love.*

For gifts given and received, for the light in our hearts that they represent, for the joy they bring: *inhale gratitude, exhale love.*

For vacation days, a moment of silence, a change of scenery, an insight: *inhale gratitude, exhale love.*

For the absence of a loved one, who is so very present in the room: *inhale gratitude, exhale love.*

For sacred traditions and ceremonies that ground us to ourselves, our families, our community: *inhale gratitude, exhale love.*

For the expansion of our hearts into a higher and lighter consciousness of love: *inhale gratitude, exhale love.*

In The World:

✳ Steal a moment for the silence of the heart, to just be and embody the gifts of the season.

In The Heart:

✳ In profound gratitude, I open to receive the greatest love I have ever been able to hold. I share my love in everything I do today.

❦

Grocery Store Inspiration

Peace on earth, goodwill to all.

We know now that starting the day off on a high note provides momentum for the rest of the day. What if we did that on a larger scale, starting the year off on a high note, providing momentum for the year ahead?

In the checkout line of Trader Joe's yesterday, I asked my cashier how her holidays were. "I am *so* glad it's over!" she announced with a big smile. The relief was palpable. Then she added something interesting. "What really saved Christmas for me was going to a midnight service on Christmas Eve. It was the only time I felt happy and peaceful. Just singing the carols with others, and the candles...nothing earth-shaking really...but it was just what I needed."

A simple connection with spirit and with others, a quiet moment, candlelight, songs of love and peace—that's what rose to the top. It seems like these are things we'd want to keep after the holidays are over. So, I ventured a little further since I had a pretty full shopping cart.

"Maybe instead of those feelings being over after the holidays, we should skim off the parts we really like and use them to jump start the New Year. This way we get to keep the extra dose of love and peace."

"I like that idea!" she said. "Me too," chimed in the woman behind me. We laughed, I took my receipt, and when I got out into the parking lot, I was sure I felt the extra love and peace of the holidays, now behind us, catapulting me into the New Year with joyous momentum on wings of grocery store inspiration.

In The World:

* Contemplate what was the best of your holiday season; in busyness or in loneliness, through connections or through isolation, think about what made its way through to your soul.

* Take a moment to hold that in your heart. Write it in your journal, and allow it to gift you with peace and positive energy for the coming year.

In The Heart:

* Every time I feel peace, my peace is shared in the world.

DECEMBER 28

A State of the Heart

Today may joy bless you. May hope inspire you. May love heal you.
May light guide you.

I wake at dawn, wrap in a blanket and head out to soak in the last sights and sounds rising up from this sleepy, hallowed ground. Today is my last day on Hunters Road.

I nestle in at the little table, and everyone shows up for the going-away party. The woodpecker provides percussion while the breakdancing goldfinch flips around on the closest tree. Male and female cardinals dart by in flashes of crimson. Throaty croaks come from the pond as the rooster, who has it right this morning, acts as emcee, announcing the new precious day over and over again.

The tiniest hummingbird floats past and after a few attempts, turns off her motor and sits still on a low branch. She reminds me of myself.

Chickadees, wrens, sparrows, crows, hawks—they all pass through with a wave. The horses walk single file up to the field to graze, my beloved Shadow leading the parade. I hear cows in a distant field and think of Abraham and my first months here. *Will I ever feel this way again?*

Come to think of it, I didn't feel this way when I got here. I was distracted by the endless decisions of moving away from my home and my marriage. But like the little hummingbird, after a few attempts I turned off my motor here on Hunters Road and I perched on a branch. I stayed still.

And then I started to see beauty everywhere in the tiniest of things, and a great love rose up. The more I loved, the more love flowed out of everything.

Maybe Hunters Road is not a place, but a state of the heart. Maybe Hunters Road is where gratitude heals things, where grace finds us and where hope rises like the sun.

In The World:

✳ For a moment, be still and take delight in the tiniest of things. Allow a great love to rise up and wordlessly expand in a heart of gratitude. Take a breath of new grace, new light.

In The Heart:

✳ Right here, right now, my healing and my hope begin.

DECEMBER 29

Ceremonies

May the New Year bless you.

Acknowledging transitions with spiritual ceremonies can transform our very souls and magnify the powers of healing and gratitude. They mark the intersection of where we've been and where we are going, creating a clear sense of before and after. Ceremonies can highlight the blessings of lessons learned, or mark a new beginning. New Year's Eve gives us a chance to do both.

A few years ago, when Maya and I were visiting family over New Year's Eve, we found ourselves in a hotel room after an early dinner with a few hours to go before we welcomed in the new year. We went out on the beach and gathered handfuls of shells. Then we made lists: On one side, we listed the events and feelings of the past year that we were ready to be free of, and on the other side, we listed the events and virtues we wished to call into our hearts for the year to come. With felt markers, we tattooed each shell with something from our list, making piles of keepers and of those we were ready to release.

With pocketsful of shells and stars as our witness, we carried out a little ceremony on the beach. One by one, we took each shell from the release pile, and privately imagined it, thanked it for the lessons learned, blessed it, and threw it into the surf. The freedom was exhilarating. We repeated the ceremony last year, and the shells lined up on my window sill reflect my keeper visions back to me daily.

This year, my niece Hanna was visiting the mountain cabin and we did a variation on the theme. We wrote our messages on smooth stones, hiked up a mountain, and threw them off. Sacred space was once again made for the blessing of new beginnings.

In The World:

* Create your own version of the ceremony, and release the difficult blessings of the past year to create space for a joyful year of your highest dreams.

* Record the list of blessings to keep and release in your journal for contemplation next year as you create your lists anew.

In The Heart:

* I release the year that is now complete and open to unlimited blessings of the year to come.

The Daily Masterpiece

Be honest. Be kind. Be brave. Believe.
Lead with your heart and follow your dreams.

On my last night on Hunters Road, I had a dream. It was a beautiful day, and I was driving up the winding mountain road that heads west. From a simultaneous aerial view, I could see the whole country, sea to shining sea, laid out on the other side of the mountain in her magnificent beauty. A masterpiece of infinite possibilities lay ahead.

I started driving as I always do—on switchbacks that snaked steeply through dense forest. Then I realized something new. *I could create the road as I went along.*

With no warning, there would be a fork leading in another direction. A wordless conversation ensued. *Right or left? Turn or don't turn? Shall we make a brand new road where there is not one?*

I was clairvoyantly discussing every decision with a powerful and compassionate force. We were painting the masterpiece together and it was a work in progress. The whole scene seemed to be a tiny thumbnail of co-creation with the divine.

The most awesome thing of all was: There were no mistakes. There was no judgment and no stress. The entire journey up the mountain, with a palate of unlimited choices, was for the fun of it—and for the joy of painting with a master.

What if every day we are being given the chance to co-create a masterpiece with our God—a constant conversation, a give and take, a friendly companionship that lifts all limitations and raises us to a higher version of ourselves?

We choose. Remember, there are no mistakes here. But hey, it seems like a worthy experiment to see what works better for us—to create alone—or to enter the dream and paint with a master.

In The World:

✳ Make today an experiment with co-creation. Bring a divine loving force into every minute, every hour, every decision great and small.

In The Heart:

✳ I invite the infinite wisdom of divine love to create the masterpiece of this day with me. With every brushstroke, I paint with a master.

We Fly

*My bird, one day you'll fly from this place. I hope you'll take with you this
song; I hope you'll sing it with your grace. Oh my blackbird, sing.*
—*Maya Davis*

Here we are, sitting on the edge of the split rail fence on Hunters Road,
ready for flight. We are traveling light, empty of the weight of that which
no longer serves our highest good. We look forward in faith, knowing that
when we listen to the heart, we know exactly where to go. We have
learned that everything we need for sacred travel, we have within.

We have all of the wisdom we need to navigate the journey.

We have all of the light necessary to illuminate our way.

We have cultivated stillness and assembled the tools of calm.

We have established a friendly relationship with God.

We welcome divine guidance in the small moments of each day.

We have patience to hold space for the darkness.

We have listened and learned from the songs of nature.

We have joy that gently rises from within.

We have gratitude that liberates limitless abundance.

We have the eyes to see beauty in small things.

We surrender to the flow of grace and to the power of love.

We have practiced making an offering of our day.

We look outside ourselves with kindness, love and compassion.

Yes, today we are ready for the beauty and the light. So with outstretched
wings and eyes to the sky, we open to grace...and we fly.

In The World:

✳   Receive in your heart this blessing for the precious year before you.

In The Heart:

✳   Bless this year with love and light. Bless this year with faith and sight.
Bless this year with grace and ease. Bless this year with joy and peace.

Mary Davis is a wisdom seeker, spiritual teacher, visionary, graphic artist and mystic entrepreneur. Her wallpaper app, Every Day Spirit Lock Screens, brings a little love, beauty and inspiration to phones around the world. Mary received her BSN from Georgetown University's School of Nursing, after which she spent many fun years as a musician, songwriter, producer, piano teacher and yoga instructor. She completed her Compassionate Bereavement Counseling certification in 2017 and plans to work with parents who have lost children and in hospice care. She has a house by the sea and lives a contemplative life in harmony with nature.

Every Day Spirit

Let's stay connected: www.everydayspirit.net

Join the Facebook community: www.facebook.com/everydayspirit1

Get the mobile app: *Every Day Spirit Lock Screens.* Available in the App Store and Google Play.

If you enjoy the book and the app, and have a moment to write a positive review, it would be so appreciated. Reviews are the single most powerful way to reach others. Thank you from the heart.

Special Books

Blankemeier, Lorraine. *Gift of Time: A Sacred Journal.* Indian River, FL: Rich River Publishing Company, 2016.

> *This is my mother's book of conversations with her beloved guides. It's a deeply spiritual and lovingly honest journey of her personal spirituality.*

Cacciatore, Joanne. *Bearing the Unbearable: Love, Loss, and the Heartbreaking Path of Grief.* Somerville, MA: Wisdom Publications, 2017.

> *A stunningly beautiful and comforting book on grief and loss that should be required reading for all of us. I received my Compassionate Bereavement Certification with Dr. Cacciatore. She's a beautiful and powerful spirit, and this book is saturated with amazing grace.*

Rasmussen, Olga R. *Meditation Pure and Simple.* Washington, DC: Meditation Pure and Simple Publishing, 2014.

> *This offering is from my friend Olga, who is a wise and experienced meditator. Short, simple and compassionate, it is my favorite book for beginning meditators. There is also an online meditation course at: meditationsimple.com*

Infant Loss and Grief

Cacciatore, Joanne. *Bearing the Unbearable: Love, Loss, and the Heartbreaking Path of Grief*. Somerville, MA: Wisdom Publications, 2017.

D'Arcy, Paula. *When Your Friend Is Grieving: Building a Bridge of Love*. Wheaton, IL: Harold Shaw Publishers, 1990.

Gillette, Andy. (2015, February 27). *Six Tips for Talking with Parents Who Have Lost a Child to Miscarriage, Stillbirth or Infant Death*. Still Standing Magazine. *StillStandingMag.com*.

McCracken, Elizabeth. *An Exact Replica of a Figment of My Imagination: A Memoir*. New York: Little, Brown and Company, 2008.

Three Minus One: Parents' Stories of Love and Loss. Ed. Sean Hanish and Brooke Warner. Berkeley, CA: She Writes Press, 2014.

Virtue, Doreen, & Van Praagh, James. *How to Heal a Grieving Heart*. Carlsbad, CA: Hay House, 2013.

Other Resources

National Suicide Prevention Lifeline - 1-800-273-8255. suicidepreventionlifeline.org

>   *It's good to have this close at hand if need be.*

Kris Carr at KrisCarr.com.

>   *Kris is my go-to for delicious recipes for health and healing.*

Dr. Helen Powell-Stoddart at DrHelenPS.com.

>   *Dr. Helen is a friend and experienced doctor who shares wholesome recipes and healing wisdom.*

Maria Hamburger at mariahamburger.com.

>   *Maria is a friend, a wise teacher and an expert in Yoga for Multiple Sclerosis and Yoga for Musicians. This site is new and growing.*

Steve Wolf at awasepublishing.com.

>   *Steve is a talented friend with the most beautiful Yoga Nidra CDs and the voice of an angel. You will adore the grace of his meditations.*

Bibliography

A Charlie Brown Christmas. Screenplay by Charles Schultz. Dir. Bill Melendez. CBS. 1965.

A Course in Miracles. Tiburon, CA: Foundation for Inner Peace, 1975.

Angelou, Maya. *Rainbow in the Cloud: The Wisdom and Spirit of Maya Angelou*. New York: Random House, 2014.

Angelou, Maya. *I Know Why the Caged Bird Sings*. New York: Random House, 2009.

Angelou, Maya. *The Collected Autobiographies of Maya Angelou*. New York: Modern Library, 2004.

Angelou, Maya. *Maya Angelou: Poems: Just Give Me a Cool Drink of Water 'fore I Diiie, Oh Pray My Wings Are Gonna Fit Me Well, And Still I Rise*. New York: Bantam Books, 1981.

Ban Breathnach, Sarah. *Simple Abundance: A Daybook of Comfort and Joy*. New York: Warner Books, 1995.

Bowen, Connie. *I Believe in Me: A Book of Affirmations*. Unity Village, MO: Unity Books, 2005.

Brownn, Eleanor. *Mile 9*. New York: Bookmark Publications, 2009.

Borysenko, Joan. *Pocketful of Miracles: Prayers, Meditations, and Affirmations to Nurture Your Spirit Every Day of the Year*. New York: Warner Books, 1994.

Brennon, Barbara A. *Hands of Light: A Guide to Healing Through the Human Energy Field*. New York: Bantam Books, 1987.

Bryant, Edwin F. *The Yoga-Sutras of Patanjali: A New Edition, Translation, and Commentary*. Berkeley: North Point Press, 2015

Burnham, Sophy. *A Book of Angels*. New York: Ballantine, 1990.

Byrne, Lorna. *Angels in my Hair: The True Story of a Modern-Day Irish Mystic*. New York: Three Rivers Press, 2011

Byrne, Lorna. *Love From Heaven: Practicing Compassion for Yourself and Others*. New York: Atria, 2014.

Byrne, Lorna. *Stairways to Heaven*. London: Coronet, 2010.

Campbell, Joseph. *The Power of Myth*. New York: Anchor Books, 1991.

Carr, Kris. *Crazy Sexy Juice: 100+ Simple Juice, Smoothie & Elixir Recipes to Super-Charge Your Health.* Carlsbad, CA: Hay House, 2016.

Chodron, Pema. *Always Maintain a Joyful Mind: And Other Lojong Teachings on Awakening Compassion and Fearlessness.* Boston: Shambhala Publications, 2007

Chodron, Pema. *Start Where You Are: A Guide to Compassionate Living.* Boston: Shambhala Classics, 2001

Chodron, Pema. *The Pocket Pema Chodron.* Boston: Shambhala Publications, 2008.

Clark, Glenn. *The Man Who Talks With Flowers: The Intimate Life Story of Dr. George Washington Carver.* Redford, VA: Wilder Publishing, 2011.

Copeland, Aimee. <u>aimeecopelandfoundation.org</u>. Aimee Copeland Foundation.

DeVries, Marja. *The Whole Elephant Revealed: Insights into the Existence and Operation of Universal Laws and the Golden Ratio.* Winchester, UK: Axis Mundi Books, 2012.

Dillard, Annie. *Pilgrim at Tinker Creek.* New York: Harper & Row, 1974.

Dooley, Mike. *Life on Earth: Understanding Who We Are, How We Got Here, and What May Lie Ahead.* Carlsbad, CA: Hay House, 2016

Doty, James R. *Into the Magic Shop: A Neurosurgeon's Quest to Discover the Mysteries of the Brain and the Secrets of the Heart.* New York: Avery Publishers, 2016.

Dyer, Wayne. *The Forever Wisdom of Wayne Dyer.* PBS Documentary. Carlsbad, CA: Hay House, 2016

Easwaran, Eknath. *Your Life Is Your Message: Finding Harmony with Yourself, Others & the Earth.* Tamales, CA: Nilgiri Press, 1992.

Frankl, Viktor E. *Man's Search for Meaning: An Introduction to Logotherapy.* New York: Simon and Schuster, 1959.

Gandhi, Mohandas K. Ed. Thomas Merton. *Gandhi on Non-Violence: A Selection from the Writings of Mahatma Gandhi.* New York: New Directions Publishing, 1965.

Gawande, Atul. *Being Mortal: Medicine and What Matters in the End.* New York: Metropolitan Books, 2014.

Gibran, Kahlil. "On Friendship." *The Prophet.* New York: Alfred A. Knopf Publisher, 1923.

Hanh, Thich Nhat. *Living Buddha, Living Christ.* New York: Riverhead Books, 1995.

Hanh, Thich Nhat. *Peace is Every Step: The Path of Mindfulness in Everyday Life.* New York: Bantam Books, 1991.

Hanh, Thich Nhat. *The Miracle of Mindfulness: A Manual on Meditation.* Boston: Beacon Press, 1987.

Herz-Sommer, Alice. *The Lady in Number 6: Music Saved My Life.* Documentary. Malcolm Clarke, 2013.

Hicks, Esther and Jerry. "The Abraham-Hicks Placemat Process." *Ask and It Is Given.* Carlsbad, CA: Hay House, 2004.

Hoff, Benjamin. *The Tao of Pooh.* New York: Penguin Books, 1982.

The Holy Bible: New Revised Standard Version. New York: Oxford University Press, 2010.

Ilibagiza, Immaculate. *Left To Tell: Discovering God Amidst the Rwandan Holocaust.* Carlsbad, CA: Hay House, 2014

Iyengar, B. K. S. *Light on Pranayama: The Yogic Art of Breathing.* New York: Crossroad Publishing Company, 1999.

Iyengar, B. K. S. *Light on Yoga.* New York: Schocken Books, 1966.

Judith, Anodea. *Eastern Body Western Mind: Psychology and the Chakra System as a Path to the Self.* Berkeley: Celestial Arts Publishing, 1996.

Jung, Carl G. *Carl Jung: The Wisdom of the Dream.* BBC Documentary, 1998.

Kabat-Zinn, Jon. *Wherever You Go, There You Are: Mindfulness Meditation In Everyday Life.* New York: Hyperion, 1994.

King, Martin L. "The Drum Major Instinct." *A Knock at Midnight: Inspiration from the Great Sermons of Reverend Martin Luther King, Jr.* 1968. Ed. Claiborne Carson and Peter Holloran. New York: Warner Books, 1998.

Kondo, Marie. *The Life-Changing Magic of Tidying Up: The Japanese Art of Decluttering and Organizing.* Emeryville: Ten Speed Press, 2014.

Lamott, Anne. *Bird by Bird: Some Instructions on Writing and Life.* New York: Pantheon Books, 1994.

Lawrence, Brother. *Practicing the Presence of God.* Wheaton, Illinois: Harold Shaw, 1991.

Lindbergh, Anne Morrow. *Gift from the Sea.* New York: Pantheon Books, 1955.

Maclean, Dorothy. *To Hear the Angels Sing: An Odyssey of Co-Creation with the Devic Kingdom.* New York: Lindisfarne Press, 1990.

Martin, James. *Jesus: A Pilgrimage.* New York: HarperCollins, 2014.

Martin, James, & Kerning, Anne. *The Daily Examen Card,* CardsByAnne.com.

McNamara, P. *You Really Need to be Tracking Your Dreams.* Web blog post. *Dream Catcher.* Psychology Today. 1 August, 2017.

Meera, Mother. *Answers Part 1.* Germany: Meerama Publications, 2004.

Merton, Thomas. *Contemplative Prayer.* New York: Penguin Random House, 1971.

Merton, Thomas. *Thoughts in Solitude.* New York: Farrar, Straus and Giroux, 1999.

Mirriam-Webster Dictionary. mirriam-webster.com

Moody, Raymond. *Life After Life.* New York: Bantam Books, 1975.

Moore, Wes. *The Work: My Search for a Life That Matters.* New York: Random House, 2015

Moorjani, Anita. *Dying to Be Me: My Journey from Cancer, to Near Death, to True Healing.* Carlsbad, CA: Hay House, 2014.

Myss, Caroline. *Anatomy of the Spirit: The Seven Stages of Power and Healing.* New York: Three Rivers Press, 1996.

Nichols, Wallace J. *Blue Mind: The Surprising Science That Shows How Being Near, In, On, or Under Water Can Make You Happier, Healthier, More Connected and Better At What You Do.* New York: Little Brown and Company, 2014.

Norris, Gunilla. *Being Home: Discovering the Spiritual in the Everyday.* New York: Bell Tower, 1991.

Norris, Gunilla. *Inviting Silence: Universal Principles of Meditation.* New York: BlueBridge, 2004.

Oliver, Mary. "Storage." *Felicity.* New York: Penguin Press, 2016.

Pradervand, Pierre. *The Gentle Art of Blessing: A Simple Practice That Will Transform You and Your World.* New York: Atria Paperback, 2009.

Rilke, Ranier Maria. *Letters to a Young Poet.* Ed. Stephen Mitchell. New York: Random House, 1984.

Rinpoche, Sogyal. *The Tibetan Book of Living and Dying.* San Francisco: Harper San Francisco, 1992.

Rosenberg, Marshall B. *Non-Violent Communication: A Language of Life.* Encinitas, CA: PuddleDancer Press, 2015.

Rumi. *A Year With Rumi: Daily Readings.* Ed. Coleman Barks. New York: HarperOne, 2006.

Rumi. *The Love Poems of Rumi.* Ed. Deepak Chopra. New York: Harmony Books, 2008.

Saint Francis de Sales. *Introduction to the Devout Life.* New York: Cosimo Classics, 2010.

Saint Francis de Sales. *Set Your Heart Free.* Notre Dame, IN: Ave Maria Press, 2008.

Seuss, Dr. *How the Grinch Stole Christmas.* New York: Random House, 1957.

Silver, Tosha. *Outrageous Openness: Letting the Divine Take the Lead.* New York: Atria Books, 2014.

Taylor, Barbara Brown. *Learning to Walk in the Dark.* New York: HarperOne, 2014.

Taylor, Barbara Brown. *An Altar in the World.* New York: HarperOne, 2009.

Taylor, Terry Lynn. *Messengers of Light: The Angels' Guide to Spiritual Growth.* Tiburon, CA: H. J. Kramer Inc., 1990.

Thoreau, Henry D. *Henry David Thoreau: A Writer's Journal.* Ed. Carl Bode. New York: Dover Publications, 1960.

Thoreau, Henry D. *Walden.* Boston: Beacon Press, 2004.

Tolle, Eckhart. *The Power of Now: A Guide to Spiritual Enlightenment.* Novato, CA: New World Library, 1999.

Tolle, Eckhart. *Stillness Speaks.* Novato, CA: New World Library, 2003.

Virtue, Doreen. *The Essential Doreen Virtue Collection.* Carlsbad, CA: Hay House, 2013.

Williamson, Marianne. *A Year of Miracles: Daily Devotions and Reflections.* New York: HarperOne, 1964.

Yogananda, Paramahansa. *Metaphysical Meditations.* Los Angeles: Self-Realization Fellowship, 1946.

Yogananda, Paramahansa. *Spiritual Diary: An Inspirational Thought for Each Day of the Year.* Los Angeles: Self-Realization Fellowship, 1964.

Yogananda, Paramahansa. *Where There Is Light.* Los Angeles: Self-Realization Fellowship, 1964.

Young, Sarah. *Jesus Calling: Enjoying Peace in His Presence.* Nashville: Thomas Nelson, 2015.

Spiritual Practices

Prayers and Blessings

Angels, be with me. Watch over me and guard my every step. Guide me through the endless details of this day. Let's walk together. Amen

Divine Grace, I step into your flow and know that I will receive the perfect guidance. Thank you for assisting me in each decision of this day.

Bless me with a calm center in the storms of my life.

Archangel Michael, defend me, protect me and guide me. Fill me with strength, peace and wisdom.

Archangel Raphael, heal me in mind, body and soul. Fill me with clarity, creativity and health.

Archangel Uriel, light the fires of illumination. Fill me with the energy of transformation and rebirth.

Archangel Gabriel, help me to overcome fear. Communicate messages of clear guidance. Fill me with strength of spirit, love and grace.

Archangel Metatron, shine your light, dazzling like the sun, in my darkest corners. Fill me with a clear connection with the divine.

God, I know there is a beautiful plan for today and that you will help it unfold with ease and grace. Thank you for showing me the way.

Bless my mind with calm and sight. Bless my heart with love and light. Bless my day with grace and ease. Bless my world with hope and peace.

I am thankful for the divine plan that is in action for _____. Her health and healing are happening now and all of her needs are being met for the highest good of all.

Thank you for putting a perfect plan in motion to relax my mind, body and soul. Assist me in using my inner tools to find deep peace. I trust that a beautiful plan is unfolding in my life today and that I have nothing to fear. Thank you for helping me return to my natural state of calm.

~⅄⅊~

Dear Guardian Angel, Help me to honor my limits and listen for signs of burn-out. Help me to slow down before I wear thin. Remind me to enjoy relaxation. Help me to trust that if I can't get through my list today, you will help me accomplish things easily and in their perfect time. Help me to know that this journey is meant to be fun and that joy is a spiritual practice. Remind me to take myself lightly. Help me to always lead from spirit, nourishing my soul so I may be able to share with others from a place of abundance. Help me to wake up every morning knowing that I am supported and guided, and that when I listen, I will always know the way.

~⅄⅊~

Thank you for pointing me to the best ways to use my energy right now. Show me what to do next, and help me to accomplish everything with ease and grace in its perfect time.

~⅄⅊~

Thank you for this precious day. May I use it well. May I have a keen eye for joy and beauty, and the delights of small things. May I spread love and kindness generously, laugh easily, and feel the ever-present peace of your light with every breath and with every step. Amen

~⅄⅊~

Mary, Queen of Angels, send an army of your angels to those in need today. Big and small, please send them all for the highest good. Thank you my dear Mary. Amen

~⅄⅊~

May I be blessed with wisdom, patience and strength, and with all the gifts I need to flow through this amazing day with ease and grace.

~⅄⅊~

Bless me to be the hands of Your work, the steps of Your path and the rays of Your sun.

~⅄⅊~

Be the strength, Lord, in my struggle. Be the dawn in my dark. Be the calm in my chaos. Be the haven for my heart.

Jesus Christ, come into my heart

and create with me this glorious day.

Walk through me

so I will know where to go.

Speak through me

so my words may be of kindness and peace.

Pray through me

so I may know how to assist.

Praise God through me

so I may know how to serve.

Think through me

so my ideas lead me to what You would have me do.

Be joyous through me

so I may celebrate the beauty of all creation.

Parent through me

so I may be respectful and helpful.

Be a friend through me

so I may love and be loved in return.

Work through me

so I may do my work in the consciousness of God.

Write through me

this unwritten chapter of my life.

Jesus Christ, come into my heart

and create with me this glorious day. Amen

Bless my eyes
to see goodness.
Bless my words
to speak kindness.
Bless my heart
to feel compassion.
Bless my soul
to radiate love.